AUSTRALIA

TOP SIGHTS, AUTHENTIC EXPERIENCES

THIS EDITION WRITTEN AND RESEARCHED BY

Hugh McNaughtan,
Kate Armstrong, Brett Atkinson, Carolyn Bain, Celeste Brash,
Peter Dragicevich, Anthony Ham, Paul Harding, Alan Murphy,
Miriam Raphael, Charles Rawlings-Way, Benedict Walker,
Steve Waters, Meg Worby

Lonely Planet's
Ultimate Australia Itinerary

BRIAN LAWRENCE/GETTY IMAGES ©

This is Lonely Planet's ultimate Australia itinerary, which ensures you'll see the best of everything the country has to offer.

For other recommended paths to travel, check out our itineraries section (p18). For inspiration on themed travel, see If You Like... (p24).

Week 1

Sydney to the Whitsundays

Australia's biggest and best-known metropolis, **Sydney** (p35) is the obvious place to start your Aussie odyssey. You could easily spend weeks here, but you can find your feet and get a feel for the place in three days. Next head north for a beach experience.

✈ **1hr 15min**

Arrive in the high-class hippie haven of **Byron Bay** (p99) for a couple of days of sun and surf, then continue your coastal journey.

🚗 **2hr** to Brisbane then
✈ **1hr 45min** to Hamilton Island

The magical **Whitsundays** (p129) are further north (drive, or fly from Brisbane to Hamilton Island, a starting point for trips to the Whitsundays). Boats exploring the Unesco-protected **Great Barrier Reef** (p111) also leave from Hamilton.

✈ **1hr 10min** to Cairns then
🚗 **2hr 20min** to the Daintree

PAPUA
NEW GUINEA

Torres Strait

Thursday
Island   Cape York

SOUTH PACIFIC OCEAN

NATIONAL
p231

Gulf of
Carpentaria

Cape York
Peninsula

THE DAINTREE p141

Port Douglas

Cairns

Coral Sea

Townsville

**THE WHITSUNDAYS
p129**

Airlie Beach

Mackay

**GREAT BARRIER
REEF p111**

Mt Isa

QUEENSLAND

Rockhampton

Simpson
Desert

Bundaberg   Fraser
Island

Lake Eyre
North

Noosa

Lake Eyre
South

⊙**BRISBANE**

H
LIA

BYRON BAY p99

Coffs Harbour

Tamworth

Port Augusta

**Broken
Hill**

NEW
SOUTH
WALES

Port Macquarie   Lord Howe
Island
(NSW)

yre
insula

Mildura

Newcastle

Adelaide

⊙**SYDNEY p35**

roo
and

Albury

☆**CANBERRA p85**

ACT

▲Mt Kosciuszko

VICTORIA

Ballarat

MELBOURNE p153

Geelong

King
Island

Bass Strait

Flinders
Island

Tasman Sea

Launceston

TASMANIA

HOBART p193

Welcome to Australia

Australia's cultural and geographic identity has been forged by 4.5 million years of isolation. The country's harsh, beautiful landscape has a resilience that rubs off on the people.

No matter which Australian city you're wheeling into, you'll never go wanting for an offbeat theatre production, a rockin' live band, lofty art-gallery opening, movie launch or music festival mosh. This was once a country where 'cultural cringe' held sway – the notion that anything locally produced simply wasn't up to scratch. But these days the tables have turned. Aboriginal arts – particularly painting and dance – seem immune to such fluctuations and remain timelessly captivating.

Most Australians live along the coast, and most of these folks live in cities. It follows that cities here are a lot of fun. Sydney is a glamorous collusion of beaches, boutiques and bars. Melbourne is all arts, alleyways and Australian Rules football. Canberra transcends political agendas. The chilly southern sandstone city of Hobart offers the warmest of welcomes. Many city dwellers love to escape the big smoke for the big skies of the red centre, the tropical forests of the far north, or the pounding surf of an unspoilt beach.

Australia plates up a multicultural fusion of European techniques and fresh Pacific-rim ingredients. Of course, beer in hand, you'll still find beef, lamb and chicken at Aussie barbecues. Don't drink beer? Australian wines are world-beaters: punchy Barossa Valley shiraz, Hunter Valley semillon and cool-climate Tasmanian sauvignon blanc. Tasmania produces outstanding whisky too. Need a caffeine hit? You'll find cafes everywhere, as Australians take their coffee seriously.

escape the big smoke for the big skies of the red centre

Uluru (Ayers Rock; p218)
FEARGUS COONEY / GETTY IMAGES ©

INDONESIA

Savu Sea

Timor Sea

Arafura

Melville Island

Bathurst Island

Darwin

Jabiru

Arnhem

Joseph Bonaparte Gulf

Katherine

INDIAN OCEAN

Cape Leveque

The Kimberley

Broome

Port Hedland

Karratha

The Pilbara

North West Cape

Exmouth

Gibson Desert

NORTHERN TERRITORY

Alice Spri

Little Sandy Desert

Yulara

Shark Bay

WESTERN AUSTRALIA

Great Victoria Desert

SOU AUSTRA

Geraldton

Kalgoorlie-Boulder

Nullarbor Plain

Perth

Great Australian Bight

Bunbury

Esperance

Pe

Port Lincol

Albany

Kang Is

SOUTHERN OCEAN

N

0   500 km
0   250 miles

From left: Sydney Opera House (p38); Maguk Gorge, Kakadu National Park (p234); Melbourne (p153)

Week 2

The Daintree to Kakadu National Park

Things get more rugged as you head north to the **Daintree Rainforest** (p141), deep in subtropical Far North Queensland. Then return to Cairns and fly directly to the red heart of the continent.

🚗 **2hr 20min** to Cairns then
✈ **2hr 45min** to Uluru

Catch a sunrise or sunset at **Uluru-Kata Tjuta National Park** (p215), with its unearthly rock formations and ancient Aboriginal culture, then journey north.

✈ **3hr 30min** to Darwin via Alice Springs then
🚗 **3hr**

Take a tour to immerse yourself in the untouched wetlands and gorges of **Kakadu National Park** (p231), then head to the best of the west.

🚗 **3hr** to Darwin then ✈ **3hr 45 min** to Perth (direct from Darwin) 🚗 **30min**

Staying Longer

Fremantle to Canberra

To extend your trip, head to **Fremantle** (p249) in Western Australia. A short drive from Perth, it's a good place to soak up some coastal history.

🚗 **3hr**

Head even further south to experience the bucolic wine 'n' surf country of **Margaret River** (p261), then it's back to Perth for a flight east.

🚗 **3hr** then ✈ **3hr 30min**

Stay a few nights in **Melbourne**, Australia's cultural and sporting capital, before catching a flight south to Tasmania.

✈ **1hr 15min**

Explore the Georgian harbourside and the Museum of Old and New Art (MONA) in **Hobart** (p193) before returning north to the nation's capital.

✈ **3hr**

Find political intrigue and great art in **Canberra** (p85), then it's a short flight back to Sydney.

Best of Australia
Contents

Plan Your Trip
Australia's Top 12

RICHARD I'ANSON / GETTY IMAGES ©

Sydney

To much of the world, Sydney (p35) is Australia: a happy, sun-washed place with great beaches, broad accents and delectable food. But Australia's oldest, boldest city is much more than a national cliché. Spread out around the deepest (and, some would say, the most beautiful) natural harbour in the world is a buzzing concentration of great art, shopping, culture and major events. And then, there are its indelible icons: the instantly recognisable Sydney Opera House and Sydney Harbour Bridge. Sydney Opera House (p38)

1

2

Canberra

Though Canberra (p85) is only a century old, Australia's purpose-built capital has always been preoccupied with history. So it's not surprising that the major drawcard here is a portfolio of lavishly endowed museums and galleries focused on interpreting the national narrative. Institutions such as the National Gallery of Australia, National Museum of Australia, National Portrait Gallery and Australian War Memorial offer visitors a fascinating insight into the country's history and culture – both ancient and modern.

National Museum of Australia (p88)

3

Byron Bay

Up there with kangaroos and Akubra hats, big-hearted Byron Bay (just Byron to its mates; p99) is one of the enduring icons of Australian culture. Families on school holidays, surfers and sun-seekers from across the globe gather by the foreshore at sunset, drawn to this spot on the world map by fabulous restaurants, a chilled pace of life and an astonishing range of activities on offer. But mostly they're here because this is one of the most beautiful stretches of coast in the country.

JEFF HUNTER / GETTY IMAGES ©

Great Barrier Reef

Unesco World Heritage listed? Check. Oprah Winfrey endorsed?
Check. The Great Barrier Reef (p111) is as fragile as it is beautiful.
Stretching more than 2000km along the Queensland coastline,
it's a complex ecosystem populated with dazzling coral, languid
sea turtles, gliding rays, timid reef sharks and tropical fish of
every colour and size. Whether you dive down to it, snorkel over
it or explore it via scenic flight or glass-bottomed boat, this vivid
undersea kingdom and its coral-fringed islands is unforgettable.

PETER HENDRIE / GETTY IMAGES ©

The Whitsundays

You can hop around a whole stack of tropical islands in this seafaring life and never find anywhere with the sheer beauty of the Whitsundays (p129). Travellers of all monetary persuasions launch yachts from party-town Airlie Beach or from sprawling Hamilton Island and drift between these lush green isles in a slow search for paradise (you'll probably find it in more than one place). Don't miss Whitehaven Beach – one of Australia's best. Wish you were here?

Whitehaven Beach (p153)

5

RICHARD I'ANSON / GETTY IMAGES ©

The Daintree

Everyone in Australia knows its name, but the Daintree (p141) still suffers from an identity crisis: is it a village? Is it a national park? A river? A World Heritage area? It's actually all four, but mostly it's a rainforest – an amazing, remote tropical wilderness with incredible biodiversity and more precious jungle-meets-sea beaches than you have lazy afternoons to spare. Get back to nature with a canopy walk, a crocodile-spotting cruise or a 4WD trip, then amble south to the pristine beaches of sophisticated Port Douglas. Mossman Gorge

6

GRANT DIXON / GETTY IMAGES ©

Melbourne

Why the queue? Oh, that's just the line to get into the latest hot 'no bookings' restaurant in Melbourne (p153). The next best restaurant/chef/cafe/barista/food truck may be the talk of the town, but there are things locals would never change: the leafy parks and gardens in the inner-city suburbs; the crowded trams that whisk the creative northerners south to sea-breezy St Kilda; and the allegiances that living in such a sports-mad city brings.

Flinders Street Station (p164)

7

Hobart

Hobart (p193) is Australia's second-oldest city, and perhaps its prettiest. Cut off from the rest of the continent in its island fastness, it's developed a gentle, idiosyncratic culture that's been boosted of late by flourishing food and arts scenes. MONA is the emblem of the latter – an innovative, world-class institution described by its owner as a 'subversive adult Disneyland'. But the antique parts of this content little city endure: Salamanca Place, the Battery and many other sights evoke the far-off colonial days when it was Australia's second city.
Salamanca Market (p199)

ALL OUR PRODUCE IS GROWN ORGANICALLY BY US ON OUR FARM

BEETROOT $4.50

KALE $3.50

CHOI $3.50

SILVER BEET $3.5

ENDIVE

RADISH

WATERMELON

FRENCH B.FAST

SPRING ONION $3.50

PARSLEY $3

JODIE GRIGGS / CONTRIBUTOR / GETTY IMAGES ©

9

Uluru-Kata Tjuta National Park

No matter how many times you've seen it on postcards, nothing prepares you for the burnished grandeur of Uluru (Ayers Rock) as it first appears on the outback horizon. With its remote desert location, deep cultural significance and dazzling natural beauty, Uluru is a pilgrimage well worth the many hundreds of kilometres it takes to get there. But Uluru-Kata Tjuta National Park (p215) offers much more: along with the equally captivating Kata Tjuta (the Olgas), there are mystical walks, sublime sunsets and ancient desert cultures to encounter. Kata Tjuta (the Olgas; p222)

BETHUNE CARMICHAEL / GETTY IMAGES ©

Kakadu National Park

Kakadu (p231) is literally another world. This staggering array of Aboriginal art (and living Aboriginal culture), lush wetlands, ancient gorges and abundant wildlife is spread across nearly 20,000 sq km of Australia's Top End. It's a place that many Australians have never been to, yet one that holds a central place in the country's mythology. Visitors – whether they choose to simply dip in with a day's guided tour or take the plunge on a longer camping trek – find it hard to shake this land that time forgot. Twin Falls (p237)

10

ORIEN HARVEY / GETTY IMAGES ©

Fremantle

Fremantle (p249) – Western Australia's major port, 22km south of Perth – is a raffish, artsy harbour town, defined by a classic cache of Victorian architecture. It's an isolated place – closer to Singapore than Sydney – but, like any port, the world washes in on the tide and washes out again, leaving the locals buzzing with global zeitgeist. Expect craft-beer breweries, live-music rooms, hipster bars, late-night coffee joints, Indian Ocean seafood shacks, buskers, beaches, markets, and students on the run from the books. Little Creatures (p258)

JANELLELUGGE / GETTY IMAGES ©

Margaret River Region

The decadent joy of drifting from winery to winery along eucalypt-shaded country roads is just one of the delights of Western Australia's southwest (p261). There are caves to explore, historic towns to visit and spring wildflowers to ogle. Surfers bob around in the world-class breaks near Margaret River, but it's not unusual to find yourself on a white-sand beach where the only footprints are your own. In late winter and early spring, cast an eye offshore to spot whales migrating along the 'Humpback Highway'.

Plan Your Trip
Five-Day Itinerary

RICHARD I'ANSON / GETTY IMAGES ©

Beach Breaks & Top Tipples

Margaret River and Fremantle are renowned for wineries and a blissful beachside lifestyle. Five days spent in this delightful corner of Western Australia are enough to get your fill of sun, surf and some of the country's best sustenance.

❶ Fremantle (p249)

Book your first two nights' accommodation in **Freo**, where this itinerary starts. Although you can get around Freo by public transport, you'll need a hire car to explore Margaret River with maximum flexibility. By train, Freo is 30 minutes ($4.50) from Perth.

Start your first day at **Fremantle Prison**, a stern limestone pile built by convicts that offers wonderful permanent exhibitions as well as tours through its rock-hewn tunnels. Lunch at the convivial **Bread in Common** will fortify you for a fascinating **Indigenous Heritage Tour**, leaving from Cliff St on the harbour and introducing you to the world of the Noongar and Wadjuk peoples, traditional owners of the land.

Day two starts off at the **Maritime Museum**, before surveying the top-notch produce of the late-Victorian **Fremantle Markets** (Friday to Sunday), also the

From left: The Sail & Anchor (p258), Fremantle; Canal Rocks (p266), Margaret River

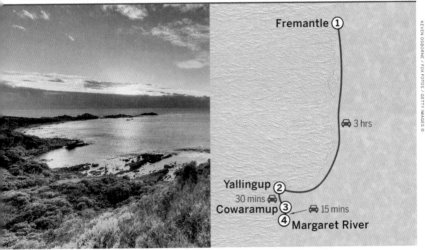

Fremantle ①

🚗 3 hrs

Yallingup ②
30 mins 🚗
Cowaramup ③ 🚗 15 mins
④ Margaret River

KEVIN OSBORNE / FOX FOTOS / GETTY IMAGES ©

venue for lunch. Then it's off to Victoria Quay, where **Oceanic Cruises** will whisk you away for a spot of whale-watching (September to December). **Little Creatures** brewery is the ideal spot to get your land legs back, over a pale ale and pizza.

🔾 Fremantle to Yallingup
🚗 3 hrs

❷ Yallingup (p266)

On day three, collect your hire car and head south to **Yallingup**. Head for the eerie limestone chambers of **Ngilgi Cave**, then spend an afternoon exploring the stunning white-sand beaches to build up an appetite for dinner at the delightful gallery-restaurant **Studio Bistro**.

🔾 Yallingup to Cowaramup
🚗 30 mins

❸ Cowaramup (p268)

After a mid-morning lesson on day four with **Yallingup Surf School**, it's on to **Cowaramup** and the many-medalled **Vasse Felix** for wine tasting and lunch.

🔾 Cowaramup to Margaret River township
🚗 15 mins

❹ Margaret River (p270)

From Cowaramup, proceed to the township of **Margaret River** for dinner at **Miki's Open Kitchen**.

On your last morning, arrange to be collected by **Margies Big Day Out** for a final bash at the region's food and wine. Then, if you're keen on cramming in one more sight before travelling back to Perth, there's always raptor-spotting at **Eagles Heritage** wildlife park, a few minutes' drive south of town.

Plan Your Trip
Ten-Day Itinerary

TANYA ANN PHOTOGRAPHY / GETTY IMAGES ©

Island Times & Rainforest Retreats

Tropical and subtropical Queensland form a vast playground of dense rainforests, uninhabited islands, perfect beaches and, of course, the world's largest coral reef. In 10 days, you can have your fill of all these wonders, yet never feel especially rushed.

❶ Agnes Water & Town of 1770 (p122)

Distances here are significant; this itinerary includes two long road trips but flights are also possible. Start your tour in the delightful twin towns of **Agnes Water & Town of 1770**, five hours' drive north of Brisbane. Explore the laid-back streets, grab lunch at **Getaway Garden Café**, then spend the afternoon kayaking with **1770 Liquid Adventures**. Day two is all about the reef. **Lady Musgrave Cruises** leaves from 1770, spending five hours on Lady Musgrave Island and skimming over the coral in a semisubmersible.

➡ Agnes Water & Town of 1770 to Hamilton Island
🚗 **9 hrs** then ⚓ **1½ hrs**

From left: Whitehaven Beach (p135), the Whitsundays; green turtle, Great Barrier Reef (p111)

④ Port Douglas
1 hr 🚗 ③ Cairns

🚗 7½ hrs

Airlie
Beach

1½ hrs ⛴ ② Hamilton
Island

🚗 9 hrs

Agnes Water/Town of 1770 ①

JEFF HUNTER / GETTY IMAGES ©

② Hamilton Island & the Whitsundays (p129)

Day three is a road trip – it's more than 700km to Shute Harbour plus just over an hour by ferry to **Hamilton Island**, the major jumping-off point in the Whitsundays and a good place to base yourself. The next morning, head to the marina to take your pre-booked place on the superfast **Camira** catamaran as it loops around **Whitsunday Island**, stopping at the unparalleled Whitehaven and Chalkies Beaches for frolics, snorkelling and lunch.

On day five explore **Long Island**: get acquainted with the local rock wallabies, and luxuriate in the classic Whitsunday landscape. Then on day six **Cruise Whitsundays** can ferry you to **Airlie Beach**, the area's major mainland centre, to pick up a cruise to the southern reef. Stay in Airlie overnight, getting plenty of sleep for the drive tomorrow.

🔾 Airlie Beach to Cairns
🚗 7½ hrs

③ Cairns (p124)

Day seven heralds the 620km drive to **Cairns** – you'll want to just relax when you get there, so a dip in the swimming lagoon and dinner at **Tokyo Dumpling** will be the answer. The next day it's either diving or snorkelling in the inner reef gardens, or on the outer reef.

🔾 Cairns to Port Douglas
🚗 1 hr

④ Port Douglas (p148)

Head north on day nine to **Port Douglas**, your base for the next two days. Spend the first getting to know this tropical haven, lazing on **Four Mile Beach** and perhaps enjoying some fine dining and theatre at **Flames of the Forest**. On your last morning, let **Tony's Tropical Tours** collect you for a day of river cruising, four-wheel driving and walking through the most gorgeous sections of the Unesco-protected **Daintree Rainforest**.

Plan Your Trip
Two-Week Itinerary

Urban Adventures

This triumvirate of cities, including Australia's oldest, largest and most diverse, can easily occupy two weeks of your time. Each has wonderful dining, culture and sights to divert you, yet all bring something highly distinctive to the table.

❶ Sydney (p35)

Day one finds you in **Sydney**, Australia's biggest, boldest and most famous metropolis. Spend your first day exploring the Quay and the city's two greatest icons, the **Harbour Bridge** and **Opera House**. Then, there's the **Rocks**, dripping with the tangible history of the city's colonial past.

The following day, hop on a ferry to **Taronga Zoo**, then zip on to **Manly** for a dip, a feed and a sundowner. On day three, turn your back on the water, walk uphill, and explore the wealth of museums, parks and historical buildings central Sydney has to offer.

Begin day four marvelling (and eating) at the **Sydney Fish Market**, a lazy 30-minute stroll from the Quay. On your way back, stop by **Darling Harbour** for retail therapy, **Aquarium** adventures and a bite to eat. Take the bus the next morning to world-

From left: BridgeClimb (p41), Sydney Harbour Bridge; *AMARNA* by James Turrell, MONA (p196), Hobart

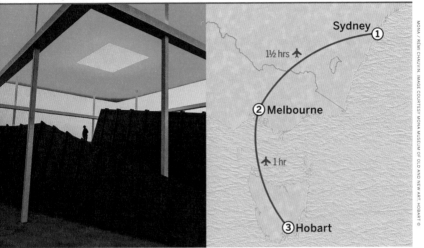

famous **Bondi** for a swim and some celeb-spotting, then walk to **Coogee** after lunch.

For your final day in Sydney, head to the city's fashionable heart, taking a bus to **Surry Hills** and **Darlinghurst** to lose yourself among the boutiques and bistros.

○ Sydney to Melbourne
✈ 1½ hrs

❷ Melbourne (p153)

Fly to **Melbourne** on day seven. Spend the day north of the city centre, exploring the **Royal Exhibition Building** and **Melbourne Museum**, then diving into the bohemian suburbs of **Carlton**, **Fitzroy** and **Collingwood**.

The next morning, take an iconic tram ride in central Melbourne then experience the city's laneways, **Federation Square**, **Chinatown**, the **State Library** and endless shopping.

After an improving morning at the **National Gallery** on day nine, another tram takes you to **St Kilda**, the beach, and a vibrant set of bars and restaurants. The next day, explore **Birrarung Marr** and the **Botanic Gardens**, before catching an afternoon AFL match at the **MCG**. Finish the day with insane views and extraordinary modern Australian food at **Vue de Monde**.

○ Melbourne to Hobart
✈ 1 hr

❸ Hobart (p193)

On day eleven catch a flight south to Hobart, then explore the city's quay, **Mawson's Huts Replica Museum**, **Battery Point** and **Salamanca Place**.

The wonderful **MONA**, a little way out of town, is a worthy destination for your final day.

Plan Your Trip
If You Like...

JULIET COOMBE / GETTY IMAGES ©

Beaches

Bondi Beach Join Sydney-siders to carve up the surf or just laze around and people-watch. (p46)

Whitehaven Beach Powdery white sand and crystal-clear waters, in the Whitsundays. (p135)

Four Mile Beach Four miles of stunning, palm-fringed sand in Port Douglas. (p148)

Heron Island At the southern end of the Great Barrier Reef, a superb, isolated cay where the coral runs right up to the beach. (p121)

Lady Elliot Island Ringed by the Great Barrier Reef, this remote Queensland island is the place to play castaway. (p120)

Wilderness

Litchfield National Park Highly rated Northern Territory national park, great for bushwalking, camping and swimming. (p245)

Wilson Island Part of a national park in the Southern Reef Islands off the coast of Queensland. Camp here for stunning beaches and wildlife encounters. (p121)

Sydney Harbour National Park For an inner-city nature experience, stroll around this protected bushland, minutes from the metropolis. (p43)

Alice Springs Desert Park Central Australian wildlife and bushland open-air exhibits, with interpretation from park rangers. (p225)

Fine Dining

Attica Melbourne playground of one of Australia's most creative chefs, Ben Shewry. (p182)

Rockpool Sydney's temple of modern Australian gastronomy. (p71)

Vue de Monde Other-worldly Melbourne fine diner mixing classic French with mod Australian. (p179)

Quay Stunning Sydney views plus adventurous cuisine; on the World's Best Restaurants list. (p70)

Sage Dining Room Subtle French plays on local ingredients, in Canberra's Gorman House Arts Centre. (p95)

The Source Located in the heart of MONA, Hobart's outstanding modern art hub. (p197)

From left: Hot-air ballooning over the Yarra Valley (p185); The Ian Potter Centre: NGV Australia (p156)

ESCHCOLLECTION / GETTY IMAGES ©

Pubs & Live Music

Knopwood's Retreat Cosy Hobart watering hole with an open fire. (p211)

Sail & Anchor Fremantle craft-beer pub sporting the tag line, 'In fermentation, there is truth'. (p258)

Basement Sydney venue hosting international and local musicians. (p78)

Lord Nelson Brewery Hotel Atmospheric sandstone pub in Sydney's Circular Quay. (p75)

Esplanade Hotel Melbourne institution in St Kilda, with live music nightly. (p187)

Corner Hotel Popular Melbourne venue for local and international bands. (p187)

Republic Bar & Café Hobart's number-one live-music pub. (p212)

Art Galleries

National Gallery of Australia Canberra home to 7500-plus works by Aboriginal and Torres Strait Islander artists. (p88)

MONA Australia's most thematically challenging art museum, located in Hobart. (p196)

NGV International Melbourne home to wonderful travelling exhibitions. (p166)

Museum of Contemporary Art One of the country's best galleries; on Sydney's Circular Quay. (p54)

National Portrait Gallery Stunning Canberra collection of the faces of Australia. (p89)

Araluen Arts Centre The heart of the thriving Alice Springs arts scene. (p226)

Indigenous Culture & History

Kakadu National Park Extraordinary rock-art galleries in the Northern Territory. (p231)

Koorie Heritage Trust Southeastern Aboriginal culture; tours and traditional art. (p164)

Uluru-Kata Tjuta Cultural Centre Understand Aboriginal laws and customs. (p219)

Wardan Aboriginal Centre Introduces visitors to the Aboriginal culture of Yallingup, Western Australia. (p266)

Fremantle Indigenous Heritage Tours Covers the history of the Noongar and Wadjuk people. (p255)

Plan Your Trip
Month By Month

KRZYSZTOF DYDYNSKI / GETTY IMAGES ©

January

January yawns into action as Australia recovers from its Christmas hangover, but then everyone realises: 'Hey, this is summer!' The festival season kicks in with sun-stroked outdoor music festivals; Melbourne hosts the Australian Open tennis.

✱ Sydney Festival

Sprawling over three summer weeks, this fab affiliation of music, dance, talks, theatre and visual arts – much of it free and family-focused – is an artistic behemoth (www.sydneyfestival.org.au).

✱ MONA FOMA

In Hobart, MONA FOMA (MOFO; www.mofo.net.au) is MONA's Festival of Music & Art. Under the auspices of Brian Ritchie, the bass player from the Violent Femmes, it's as edgy and progressive as the museum itself.

✱ Australia Day

Australia's 'birthday' (www.australia-day.com) falls on 26 January, the date when the First Fleet landed in 1788. Australians celebrate with picnics, barbecues and fireworks. In less mood to celebrate are the Indigenous Australians, who refer to it as Invasion Day or Survival Day.

February

February is usually Australia's warmest month: hot and sticky up north as the wet season continues, but divine in Tasmania and Victoria.

✱ White Night

White Night (www.whitenightmelbourne.com.au) is an annual all-night cultural event held in Melbourne. The city is illuminated in colourful projections, forming a backdrop to art, music, film, food and fashion.

March

March is harvest time in Australia's vineyards and can be just as hot as January and February, despite its autumnal status. Melbourne's streets jam up with the Formula One Grand Prix.

From left: White Night projection, Melbourne; ski season, Thredbo (p299)

GRAHAM MONRO / GM PHOTOGRAPHICS / GETTY IMAGES ©

♣ Sydney Gay & Lesbian Mardi Gras

A month-long arts festival (www.mardigras.
org.au) culminating in a flamboyant parade
along Sydney's Oxford St on the first Saturday in March attracts 300,000 spectators.

♣ Sydney Royal Easter Show

Ostensibly an agricultural show, this wonderful Sydney tradition (www.eastershow.com.
au) is a two-week fiesta of carnival rides,
kiddie-centric show bags and sugary horrors.

April

Melbourne is atmospheric as European
trees turn golden then maroon. Up north the
rain is abating and the desert temperatures
are becoming manageable. Easter means
pricey accommodation everywhere.

☆ Byron Bay Bluesfest

Every Easter, Byron Bay on the NSW north
coast swells to breaking point with rock,
folk and blues fans, here for a five-day extravaganza of rootsy tunes (www.bluesfest.
com.au). The line-up is invariably awesome.

May

The dry season begins in the Northern
Territory, northern Western Australia and
Far North Queensland: relief from humidity.
A great time to visit Uluru (Ayers Rock),
before the tour buses arrive in droves.

June

Winter begins: snow falls across the
Southern Alps ski resorts and football
season fills grandstands across the country.
Peak season in the tropical north: waterfalls
and outback tracks are accessible
(accommodation prices less so).

⛷ Ski Season

When winter blows in (June to August),
snow bunnies and powder hounds dust off
their skis and snowboards and make for
the mountains (www.ski.com.au).

July

Pubs with open fires, cosy coffee shops
and empty beaches down south; packed
markets, tours and accommodation up

north. Bring warm clothes for anywhere south of Alice Springs. Don't miss 'MIFF'.

☆ Melbourne International Film Festival

Right up there with Toronto and Cannes, MIFF (www.miff.com.au) has been running since 1952 and has grown into a wildly popular event; tickets sell like piping-hot chestnuts in the inner city.

♣ Festival of Voices

Sing to keep the winter chills at bay during this quirky festival (www.festivalofvoices. com), featuring performances, workshops, cabaret and choirs at venues around Hobart.

August

August is when southerners, sick of winter's grey-sky drear, head to Queensland for some sun. Last chance to head to the tropical Top End and outback before things get too hot and wet.

♣ Cairns Festival

Running for three weeks from late August to early September, this massive art-and-culture fest (www.cairns.qld.gov.au/festival) brings a stellar program of music, theatre, dance, comedy, film, Indigenous art and public exhibitions.

September

Spring heralds a rampant bloom of wildflowers across outback WA and SA. Flower festivals happen in places such as Canberra and Toowoomba. Football finishes and the spring horse-racing carnival begins.

♣ Floriade

Celebrating Canberra's spectacular spring flowers from September to October, Floriade (www.floriadeaustralia.com) is one for the garden lovers. Entry is free.

☆ Australian Rules Grand Final

The pinnacle of the Australian Football League (AFL; www.afl.com.au) season is this high-flying spectacle in Melbourne, watched (on TV) by millions of impassioned Aussies.

October

The weather avoids extremes everywhere: a good time to go camping or to hang out at some vineyards (it's a dirty job, but someone's gotta do it...).

☆ Jazz in the Vines

The Hunter Valley's proximity to the Sydney jazz scene ensures a top line-up at Tyrrell's Vineyard (www.jazzinthevines.com.au).

November

Northern beaches may close due to 'stingers' – jellyfish in the shallow waters off north Queensland, the NT and WA. Outdoor events ramp up; the surf life-saving season flexes its muscles on beaches everywhere.

☆ Melbourne Cup

On the first Tuesday in November, Australia's (if not the world's) premier horse race chews up the turf in Melbourne (www.melbournecup.com). The country does actually pause to watch the 'race that stops a nation'.

♟ Margaret River Gourmet Escape

Western Australia's contribution to the national circuit of fine food-and-wine fests (www.gourmetescape.com.au).

⊙ Sculpture by the Sea

In mid-November, the clifftop trail from Bondi Beach to Tamarama in Sydney transforms into an exquisite sculpture garden (www.sculpturebythesea.com).

December

School's out! Holidays begin a week before Christmas. Cities are packed with shoppers and the weather is desirably hot. Up north, monsoon season is under way: afternoon thunderstorms bring pelting rain.

⚓ Sydney to Hobart Yacht Race

The world's most arduous open-ocean yacht race is the 628-nautical-mile Sydney to Hobart (www.rolexsydneyhobart.com) departing Sydney Harbour on Boxing Day. The winners sail into Hobart around December 29...four days at sea is a good excuse for a party!

Plan Your Trip
Get Inspired

RICHARD I'ANSON / GETTY IMAGES ©

Read

The Narrow Road to the Deep North (Richard Flanagan; 2014) From Hobart to the Thai-Burma Death Railway. Man Booker Prize winner.

Montebello (Robert Drewe; 2012) British nuclear tests in Western Australia: part memoir, part exposé.

Oscar & Lucinda (Peter Carey; 1988) How to relocate a glass church.

Voss (Patrick White; 1957) Contrasts the outback with Sydney colonial life.

The Secret River (Kate Grenville; 2005) Convict life in the 19th century.

Watch

Gallipoli (director Peter Weir; 1981) Nationhood in the crucible of WWI.

Lantana (director Ray Lawrence; 2001) A moving meditation on love, truth and grief.

Australia (director Baz Luhrmann; 2008) Over-the-top period romance in northern Australia.

Ten Canoes (directors Rolf de Heer and Peter Djigirr; 2006) Entirely in Aboriginal language.

The Hunter (director Daniel Nettheim; 2011) Grumpy Willem Dafoe goes hunting for the last Tasmanian tiger.

Listen

Back in Black (AC/DC; 1980) Essential rock; key track 'Back in Black'.

The Rubens (The Rubens; 2012) Croony and catchy; key track 'Lay it Down'.

Internationalist (Powderfinger; 1998) Brisbane's best; key track 'Passenger'.

Circus Animals (Cold Chisel; 1982) Cold Chisel's peak; key track 'Bow River'.

Diorama (Silverchair; 2002) Post-grunge splendour; key track 'The Greatest View'.

Plan Your Trip
Family Travel

RICHARD I'ANSON / GETTY IMAGES ©

Don't underestimate the vast distances in Australia: the open road may be just the tonic for stressed-out parents, but it's probably not numero uno on the kids' hit-list. Australia's cities, however, abound with attractions designed for bright young minds and bodies of boundless energy.

Need to Know

Changing facilities In most towns and shopping malls

Cots Usually available in midrange and top-end accommodation

Health High first-world standards

High chairs Widely available in restaurants and cafes

Kids' menus Widely available in less-formal restaurants and cafes

Nappies (diapers) Widely available

Strollers Even on public transport you'll get a helping hand

Transport All public transport caters for young passengers

Practicalities

Lonely Planet's *Travel with Children* contains a wealth of useful information, hints and tips.

Most shopping centres and all cities and major towns have public baby change facilities; ask the local tourist office or city council for details. It is your legal right to publicly breastfeed anywhere in Australia.

Top-end hotels and many (but not all) midrange hotels cater for children. B&Bs, however, often market themselves as sanctuaries from all things child related. Many cafes, pubs and restaurants have dedicated kids' menus or will provide small serves from the main menu.

If you want to leave Junior behind for a few hours, many of Australia's licensed childcare agencies offer casual care. Check under 'Baby Sitters' and 'Child Care

MITCH REARDON / GETTY IMAGES ©

Centres' in the *Yellow Pages*, or contact the local council for listings.

Child and family concessions often apply to accommodation, tours, admission fees and transport, with discounts as high as 50% off the adult rate. However, the definition of 'child' varies from under 12 to under 18 years. Accommodation concessions generally apply to children under 12 years sharing the same room as adults. On the major airlines, infants travel free provided they don't occupy a seat – child fares usually apply between the ages of two and 11 years.

Australia has high-standard medical services and facilities: items such as baby formula and disposable nappies are widely available. Major hire-car companies supply baby capsules and booster seats, charging around $18 for up to three days' use, with an additional daily fee for longer periods.

Sights & Activities

There's no shortage of active, interesting or amusing things for children to focus on

The Best for Kids

Sydney Sea Life Aquarium (p59)

AFL footy at the Melbourne Cricket Ground (p160)

Territory Wildlife Park (p240)

Sydney Harbour ferries (p42)

Salamanca Market (p199)

Taronga Zoo (p63)

in Australia. Museums, zoos, aquariums, science centres and pioneer villages have historical, natural or interactive exhibits to get kids involved. And of course, outdoor destinations are always a winner. This guide has hot tips for keeping kids occupied in Sydney, Melbourne and Hobart...and when in doubt, take them to the beach!

Plan Your Trip
Need to Know

When to Go

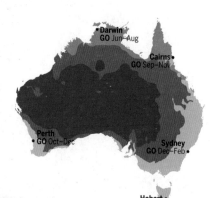

Desert, dry climate
Dry climate
Tropical climate, wet/dry seasons
Warm to hot summers, mild winters

Darwin GO Jun–Aug
Cairns GO Sep–Nov
Perth GO Oct–Dec
Sydney GO Dec–Feb
Hobart GO Jan–Mar

High Season (Dec–Feb)

○ Summertime: local holidays, busy beaches and cricket.

○ Prices jump 25% for big-city accommodation.

○ Outdoor rock concerts, film screenings and food festivals abound.

Shoulder (Mar–May & Sep–Nov)

○ Warm sun, clear skies, shorter queues.

○ Easter (late March or early April) is busy with Aussie families on the loose.

○ Autumn leaves are atmospheric in Victoria and Tassie.

Low Season (Jun–Aug)

○ Cool rainy days down south; mild days and sunny skies up north.

○ Low tourist numbers; attractions open shorter hours.

○ Head for the desert, the tropical north or the snow.

Currency
Australian dollars ($)

Language
English

Visas
All visitors to Australia need a visa, except New Zealanders. Apply online for an ETA or eVisitor visa.

Money
ATMs widely available. Credit cards accepted in most hotels and restaurants.

Mobile Phones
European phones will work on Australia's network, but most American and Japanese phones will not. Use global roaming or a local SIM card and prepaid account.

Time
Australia has three main time zones: Australian Eastern, Central and Western Standard Time. Sydney is on AEST, which is GMT/UTC plus 10 hours.

Daily Costs

Budget Less than $100

o Dorm bed: $25–35

o Double room in a hostel: from $80

o Simple pizza or pasta meal: $10–15

o Short public-transport bus or tram ride: $4

Midrange $100–280

o Double room in a midrange hotel/ motel: $100–200

o Breakfast or lunch in a cafe: $20–40

o Short taxi ride: $25

o Car hire per day: from $35

Top end More than $280

o Double room in a top-end hotel: from $200

o Three-course meal in a high-end restaurant: from $80

o Nightclub cover charge: $10–20

o Domestic flight Sydney to Melbourne: from $100

Websites

Exchange Rates (www.xe.com) Current exchange rates.

Lonely Planet (www.lonely planet.com/australia) Destination information, hotel bookings, traveller forum and more.

Tourism Australia (www.australia.com) Main government tourism site with visitor info.

Bureau of Meteorology (www.bom.gov. au) Nationwide weather forecasts.

The Australian (www.theaustralian.com. au) National broadsheet newspaper online.

Parks Australia (www.environ ment.gov.au/parks) Info on national parks and reserves.

Coastalwatch (www.coastal watch.com) Surf reports and surf-cams.

Opening Hours

Opening hours vary from state to state, but use the following as a general guide.

Banks 9.30am to 4pm Monday to Thursday, until 5pm Friday.

Bars 4pm until late

Cafes 7am to 5pm

Pubs 11am to midnight

Restaurants noon to 2.30pm, 6pm to 9pm

Shops 9am to 5pm Monday to Friday, until noon or 5pm Saturday

Supermarkets 7am to 8pm; some 24 hours.

Arriving in Australia

Sydney Airport (p80) Airport Link trains run to the city centre every 10 minutes from around 5am to 1am (20 minutes). Pre-booked shuttle buses service city hotels. A taxi into the city costs $45 to $55 (30 minutes).

Melbourne Airport (p188) SkyBus services (24-hour) run to the city (25 minutes), leaving every 10 to 30 minutes. A taxi into the city costs around $65 (25 minutes).

Getting Around

Australia is the sixth-largest country in the world: how you get from A to B requires some thought.

Car Travel at your own tempo, explore remote areas and visit regions with no public transport. Hire cars in major towns; drive on the left.

Plane Fast-track your holiday with affordable, frequent, fast flights between major centres. Carbon offset your flights if you're feeling guilty.

Bus Reliable, frequent long-haul services around the country. Not always cheaper than flying.

Train Slow, expensive and infrequent...but the scenery is great!

For more, see the **Survival Guide** (p300)

TOMMY CLARKE / GETTY IMAGES ©

SYDNEY

Sydney

Sydney is the capital that every other Australian city loves to hate – but what that really means is that they all want to be just like it: sun-kissed, sophisticated and self-confident. Built around one of the world's most beautiful natural harbours – with its maze of lazy bays and sandstone headlands – Sydney hosts three of Australia's major icons: the Sydney Harbour Bridge, Sydney Opera House and Bondi Beach.

But the attractions don't stop there... This spectacular city also houses magnificent museums and restaurants, a vivacious performing-arts scene and yet more sublime beaches. As the sun goes down, hip bars and clubs light up as Sydneysiders wage war against sleep... So wake up! Sydney is as good as it gets.

❶ In This Section

♣ What's On

Sydney Festival (www.sydneyfestival.org.au; ⊙ Jan) Sydney's premier arts and culture festival showcases three weeks of music, theatre and visual art.

Sydney Gay & Lesbian Mardi Gras (www.mardigras.org.au) A two-week festival culminating in the world-famous parade and party on the first Saturday in March.

New Year's Eve (www.sydneynewyearseve.com; ⊙ 31 Dec) The biggest party of the year, with flamboyant firework displays on the harbour.

CBCK-CHRISTINE / GETTY IMAGES ©

PETE SEAWARD / LONELY PLANET ©

Discover more
www.lonelyplanet.
com/sydney

ANDREW WATSON / GETTY IMAGES ©

Balmoral

Balmoral Beach

Balmoral
Beach

Sydney
Harbour
National Park

Mosman

Sydney
Harbour
National Park

Camp
Cove

Watsons Bay

Taronga Zoo

Taylors
Bay

Nielsen Park
(Sydney Harbour
National Park)

Vaucluse

Sydney Harbour
(Port Jackson)

**SYDNEY
HARBOUR**

Shark
Island

SE

Clarke
Island

Point
Piper

Rose Bay

eth

Darling
Point

*Double
Bay*

*Bushcutters
Bay*

Double
Bay

Rose Bay

Edgecliff

Bellevue Hill

ddington

Bondi
Beach

Woollahra

BONDI BEACH

Bondi
Park

Centennial
Park

Bondi
Junction

Bondi

*Bondi
Bay*

Central Sydney Map (p56)
Kings Cross, Darlinghurst & Woolloomooloo Map (p62)

0 — 2 km
0 — 1 mile

Clockwise from top left: wombat; Mod Oz cuisine; dining on Sydney's Circular Quay; Ménage A'trois, performer in the Imperial Hotel Drag Show; Bondi to Coogee coastal path

BOOK YOUR ACOMMODATION ONLINE
www.lonelyplanet.com /hotels

CATHERINE SUTHERLAND / LONELY PLANET ©

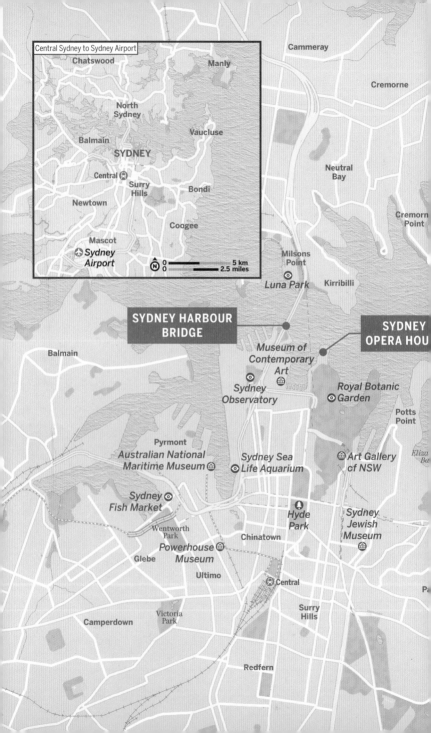

Central Sydney to Sydney Airport

Chatswood

Manly

North
Sydney

Vaucluse

Balmain

SYDNEY

Central ◎

Surry
Hills

Bondi

Newtown

Coogee

Mascot

✈ Sydney
Airport

N 0
0

5 km
2.5 miles

Cammeray

Cremorne

Neutral
Bay

Cremorn
Point

Milsons
Point

Luna Park ◎

Kirribilli

Balmain

**SYDNEY HARBOUR
BRIDGE**

Museum of
Contemporary
Art

**SYDNEY
OPERA HOU**

Sydney ◎
Observatory

🏛

Royal Botanic
◎ Garden

Potts
Point

Pyrmont

Australian National
Maritime Museum 🏛

Sydney Sea
◎ Life Aquarium

Eliza
Bay

🏛 Art Gallery
cf NSW

Sydney ◎
Fish Market

Wentworth
Park

Chinatown

Hyde
Park

Sydney
Jewish
Museum
🏛

Powerhouse 🏛
Museum

Glebe

Ultimo

Central
🚉

Camperdown

Victoria
Park

Surry
Hills

Pa

Redfern

Planning Ahead

☑ **When to Go**
The peak season is from Christmas until the end of January, which coincides with summer school holidays and the hot weather. Spring (September to November) is dry and warm.

ⓘ **Arriving in Sydney**
Taxis from the airport to the city cost up to $55 and depart from the front of the terminals. Airport shuttles head to city hotels for around $15. Trains depart from beneath the terminal but charge a whopping $18 for the short journey into the city.

Country and interstate trains arrive in Haymarket, in the heart of the city. Follow the signs downstairs to connect to local services or head to Railway Sq for buses.

➡ Sydney in Two Days

Start with our **Rocks and Circular Quay walking tour** (p52), then follow the harbourside walkway to the **Art Gallery of NSW** (p55). Catch an evening show at the **Sydney Opera House** (p78).

Next day, climb the **Harbour Bridge** (p41), soak up the scene at **Bondi** (p46), take the clifftop walk to **Coogee** (p50), then hoof it back to Bondi for dinner at **Icebergs** (p75).

➡ Sydney in Four Days

Jump on a ferry on day three and chug across the harbour to **Manly** (p63) for a surf lesson, then stroll through **Sydney Harbour National Park** (p43). That night, head to stylin' **Surry Hills** (p72) for dinner and drinks. On day four, dig into Sydney's convict heritage at the **Hyde Park Barracks Museum** (p55), then spend the afternoon **shopping** (p68) for designer originals.

From left: Emu at Taronga Zoo (p63); Martin Place (p57) performance; Dining out (p70); Shopping in Paddington
ADRIANA ASSEMANY / GETTY IMAGES ©; ANDREW WATSON/GETTY IMAGES ©; OLIVER STREWE / GETTY IMAGES; © LONELY PLANET/ GETTY IMAGES ©

NIGEL PAVITT / JOHN WARBURTON-LEE PHOTOGRAPHY LTD / GETTY IMAGES ©

Sydney Opera House

Gazing upon the Sydney Opera House with virgin eyes is a sure way to send a tingle down your spine. Gloriously curvaceous and pointy, the Opera House perches dramatically at the tip of Bennelong Point.

Great For...

☑ Don't Miss

The Opera House during the Vivid Festival (www.vividsydney.com), when the 'sails' are spectacularly lit up, and top-drawer musicians perform.

Design & Construction

Danish architect Jørn Utzon's competition-winning 1956 design is Australia's most recognisable visual image. It's said to have been inspired by billowing sails, palm fronds and Mayan temples, and has been poetically likened to nuns in a rugby scrum and the sexual congress of turtles. The seemingly solid expanse of white is actually composed of tiles – 1,056,000 self-cleaning cream-coloured Swedish tiles, to be exact.

The Opera House's construction was itself truly operatic. The predicted four-year construction started in 1959. After a tumultuous clash of egos, delays, politicking, death and cost blow-outs, Utzon quit in disgust in 1966 and it finally opened in 1973. Utzon and his son Jan were commissioned for renovations in 2004, but Utzon died in 2008 having never seen his finished masterpiece in the flesh.

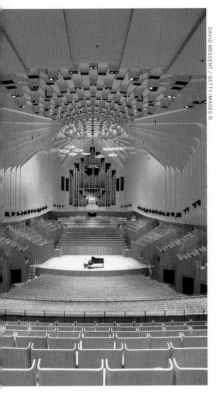

DAVID MESSENT / GETTY IMAGES ©

❶ Need to Know

Map p56; ☏02-9250 7250; www.sydneyopera-house.com; Bennelong Point; tours adult/child $37/20; ⊘tours 9am-5pm; 🚇Circular Quay

✕ Take a Break

Take in postcard-perfect views and taste exquisitely crafted cuisine at Quay (p70).

★ Top Tip

Most events (over 450 of them annually!) sell out quickly, but partial-view tickets are often available on short notice.

Tours

The interiors don't live up to the promise of the dazzling exterior, but if you're curious, one-hour guided tours depart throughout the day. You can book ahead for tours in various languages, including Auslan sign language, and Access Tours can be arranged.

Not all tours can visit all theatres because of rehearsals, but you're more likely to see everything if you go early. A highlight is the **Utzon Room**, the only part of the Opera House to have an interior designed by the great man himself. The extended two-hour early-morning backstage tour ($165, departs 7am) includes the Green Room, stars' dressing rooms, stage and orchestra pit.

Performances

Inside, dance, concerts, opera and theatre are staged in the **Concert Hall**, **Joan**

Sutherland Theatre, **Drama Theatre** and **Playhouse**, while more intimate and left-of-centre shows inhabit the **Studio**. The acoustics in the Concert Hall are superb. Companies regularly performing here include the following:

Australian Ballet (☏1300 369 741; www.australianballet.com.au; tickets $39-289)

Australian Chamber Orchestra (☏02-8274 3888; www.aco.com.au; tickets $46-127)

Bangarra Dance Theatre (Map p56; ☏02-9251 5333; www.bangarra.com.au; Pier 4/5, 15 Hickson Rd; tickets $30-93; 🚇Wynyard)

Opera Australia (☏02-9318 8200; www.opera.org.au; Sydney Opera House; tickets $49-199; 🚇Circular Quay)

Sydney Symphony Orchestra (☏02-8215 4600; www.sydneysymphony.com)

Sydney Theatre Company (Map p56; ☏02-9250 1777; www.sydneytheatre.com.au)

The free monthly What's On brochure lists upcoming events, including Kids at the House – a pint-sized entertainment program.

SENG CHYE TEO / GETTY IMAGES ©

Sydney Harbour Bridge

Sydney's second-most-loved construction inhabits the intersection of practicality and great beauty. The views it provides are magnificent, whether you're walking over it or joining a BridgeClimb expedition up and over its central rainbow of steel.

Great For...

☑ Don't Miss

The 9km Bridge Run, part of the Sydney Running Festival (www.sydneyrunning festival.com.au), which sees thousands thunder across the 'coathanger'.

The Structure

At 134m high, 1149m long, 49m wide and 52,800 tonnes, the Sydney Harbour Bridge is the largest and heaviest (but not the longest) steel arch in the world. It links the Rocks with North Sydney, crossing the harbour at one of its narrowest points.

The two halves of chief engineer JJC Bradfield's mighty arch were built outwards from each shore. In 1930, after seven years of merciless toil by 1400 workers, the two arches were only centimetres apart when 100km/h winds set them swaying. The coathanger hung tough, the arch was bolted together and the bridge finally opened to the public two years later.

The bridge is the centrepiece of Sydney's major celebrations, particularly the New Year's Eve fireworks. In 2007, when it

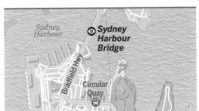

❶ Need to Know

The 1km walk across the bridge is free and takes about 20 minutes.

✕ Take a Break

Call into the **Harbour View Hotel** (Map p56; 📞02-9252 4111; www.harbourview.com. au; 18 Lower Fort St; ⏱11am-midnight Mon-Sat, to 10pm Sun; 📶; 🚉Circular Quay) for a post-bridge beverage.

★ Top Tip

The centrepiece of the city's biggest celebrations, the bridge is at its best on New Year's Eve when it erupts in pyrotechnics.

reached its 75th birthday, 250,000 people celebrated by walking across the great span.

Crossing the Bridge

The best way to experience the bridge is on foot – don't expect much of a view when crossing by train or car (driving south there's a toll). Staircases access the bridge from both shores; a footpath runs along its eastern side.

BridgeClimb

Once only painters and daredevils scaled the Harbour Bridge – now anyone can do it. Make your way through the **BridgeClimb** (Map p56; 📞02-8274 7777; www.bridgeclimb. com; 3 Cumberland St; adult $218-348, child $148-228; 🚉Circular Quay) departure lounge and the extensive training session, don your headset, an umbilical safety cord and

a dandy grey jumpsuit, and up you go. If you're afraid of heights, the scariest part is crossing over the mesh catwalk under the bridge; on the curved span the track is wide enough that you never see straight down.

Tours last 2¼ to 3½ hours – a preclimb comfort stop is a smart idea. A 90-minute sampler is available but it only goes halfway and never reaches the summit. The priciest climbs are at dawn and sunset.

Pylon Lookout

The bridge's hefty pylons may look as though they're shouldering all the weight, but they're largely decorative – right down to their granite facing. There are awesome views from the top of the **Pylon Lookout** (Map p56; www.pylonlookout.com.au; adult/child $13/6.50; ⏱10am-5pm; 🚉Circular Quay), atop the southeast pylon, 200 steps above the bridge's footpath. Inside the pylon there are exhibits about the bridge's construction, in-cluding an eight-minute film which screens every 15 minutes.

PETER PHIPP / GETTY IMAGES ©

Sydney Harbour

Stretching 20km inland from the South Pacific Ocean to the mouth of the Parramatta River, this magnificent natural harbour (the deepest in the world) is the city's shimmering soul and the focus of most visitors' stays.

Great For...

☑ Don't Miss

The spectacular Boxing Day opening to the Sydney to Hobart yacht race.

Orientation

Forming the gateway to the harbour from the ocean are North Head and South Head. The former fishing village of Watsons Bay nestles on South Head's harbour side, and the city's favourite day-trip destination, Manly, occupies a promontory straddling harbour and ocean near North Head.

The focal point of the inner harbour and the city's major transport hub is Circular Quay, home to the Sydney Opera House and the recently renovated Museum of Contemporary Art (MCA).

Exploring the Harbour

If you can, try to base yourself somewhere on, or at least near, the harbour.

So much of what makes the city unique clusters around its shores, and exploring

Sydney
Harbour

Circular
Quay

ℹ Need to Know

All ferries stop at Circular Quay.
Purchase an Opal or MyFerry ticket; for
details, visit www.transport.nsw.gov.au/
customers/ferries/sydney-ferries.

✕ Take a Break

Cafe Sydney (Map p56; ☏02-9251 8683;
www.cafesydney.com; Level 5, Customs
House, 31 Alfred St; mains $38-39; ⊘noon-
11pm Mon-Fri, 5-11pm Sat, noon-3.30pm Sun;
☒Circular Quay) offers harbour views, an
outdoor terrace and plenty of seafood.

★ Top Tip

Middle Harbour is a quieter section,
ideal for mucking about in a kayak.

this visually arresting area from the water
is one of Sydney's great joys. There's no
need to shell out on a pricey cruise when
you can see exactly the same sights from
a ferry. Board a ferry to Watsons Bay
and then sweeten the deal with the river
service to Parramatta. You'll cover far
more distance than the average cruise
and all for a maximum of $15 on an Opal
transport card.

What's Nearby?

Sydney Harbour
National Park   National Park

Sydney Harbour National Park protects
large swaths of bushland around the
harbour shoreline, plus several harbour
islands.

   In among the greenery you'll find walking tracks, **scenic lookouts**, Aboriginal

carvings, beaches and a handful of historic
sites. The park incorporates **South Head**
(Cliff St; ⊘5am-10pm; ☒Watsons Bay) and
Nielsen Park (Shark Beach; Vaucluse Rd;
☒325) on the south side of the harbour, but
most of the park is on the North Shore –
including Bradleys Head, Middle Head,
Dobroyd Head and **North Head** (p64).
(www.nationalparks.nsw.gov.au)

OpenAir Cinema   Cinema

Right on the harbour, the outdoor
three-storey screen here comes with
surround sound, sunsets, skyline and
swanky food and wine. Most tickets are
purchased in advance, but a limited
number of tickets go on sale at the door
each night at 6.30pm; check the website
for details. (www.stgeorgeopenair.com.au;
Mrs Macquaries Rd; tickets $37; ⊘Jan & Feb;
☒Circular Quay)

Sydney Harbour

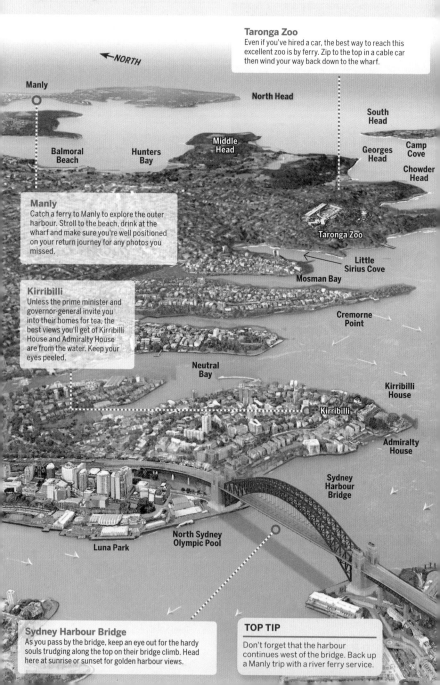

Taronga Zoo
Even if you've hired a car, the best way to reach this excellent zoo is by ferry. Zip to the top in a cable car then wind your way back down to the wharf.

←NORTH

Manly

North Head

South Head

Georges Head

Camp Cove

Chowder Head

Balmoral Beach

Hunters Bay

Middle Head

Manly
Catch a ferry to Manly to explore the outer harbour. Stroll to the beach, drink at the wharf and make sure you're well positioned on your return journey for any photos you missed.

Taronga Zoo

Little Sirius Cove

Mosman Bay

Kirribilli
Unless the prime minister and governor-general invite you into their homes for tea, the best views you'll get of Kirribilli House and Admiralty House are from the water. Keep your eyes peeled.

Cremorne Point

Neutral Bay

Kirribilli House

Kirribilli

Admiralty House

Sydney Harbour Bridge

North Sydney Olympic Pool

Luna Park

Sydney Harbour Bridge
As you pass by the bridge, keep an eye out for the hardy souls trudging along the top on their bridge climb. Head here at sunrise or sunset for golden harbour views.

TOP TIP
Don't forget that the harbour continues west of the bridge. Back up a Manly trip with a river ferry service.

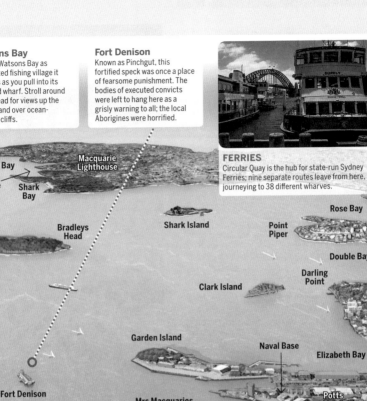

Watsons Bay
Imagine Watsons Bay as the isolated fishing village it once was as you pull into its sheltered wharf. Stroll around South Head for views up the harbour and over ocean-battered cliffs.

Fort Denison
Known as Pinchgut, this fortified speck was once a place of fearsome punishment. The bodies of executed convicts were left to hang here as a grisly warning to all; the local Aborigines were horrified.

CHERYL FORBES/GETTY IMAGES ©

FERRIES
Circular Quay is the hub for state-run Sydney Ferries; nine separate routes leave from here, journeying to 38 different wharves.

Watsons Bay

Macquarie Lighthouse

Vaucluse Bay   **Shark Bay**

Bradleys Head

Shark Island

Rose Bay

Point Piper

Double Bay

Darling Point

Clark Island

Garden Island

Naval Base

Elizabeth Bay

Fort Denison

Mrs Macquaries Point

Potts Point

Woolloomooloo Finger Wharf

Government House

Farm Cove

Royal Botanic Garden

Sydney Opera House

Circular Quay

The Rocks

Sydney Opera House
You can clamber all over it and walk around it, but nothing beats the perspective you get as your ferry glides past the Opera House's dazzling sails. Have your camera at the ready.

Circular Quay
Circular Quay has been at the centre of Sydney life since the First Fleet dropped anchor here in 1788. Book your ferry ticket, check the indicator boards for the correct pier and get onboard.

Bondi Beach

Definitively Sydney, Bondi is one of the world's great beaches: ocean and land collide, the Pacific arrives in great foaming swells and all people are equal, as democratic as sand. It is the closest ocean beach to the city centre (8km away), has consistently good (though crowded) waves, and is great for a rough-and-tumble swim.

Great For...

ⓘ Need to Know

Campbell Pde: 🚌 380

Bondi Icebergs Swimming Club (p49)

OLIVER STREWE / GETTY IMAGES ©

★ **Top Tip**

The red-and-yellow flags indicate the sections of beach patrolled by surf lifesavers. Always swim between the flags.

Surfers carve up sandbar breaks at either end of the beach. Two surf clubs – Bondi and North Bondi – patrol the beach between sets of red-and-yellow flags, positioned to avoid the worst rips and holes. Thousands of unfortunates have to be rescued from the surf each year (enough to make a TV show about it), so don't become a statistic – swim between the flags. If the sea's angry or you have small children in tow, try the saltwater sea baths at either end of the beach.

North Bondi is a great place to learn to surf, and well-established surf school **Let's Go Surfing** (📞02-9365 1800; www.letsgosurfing.com.au; 128 Ramsgate Ave; board & wetsuit hire 1hr/2hr/day/week $25/30/50/150; ⏲9am-5pm; 🚌380) offers lessons catering to practically everyone. There are classes for grommets aged seven to 16 (1½ hours,

$49) and adults (two hours, $99; women-only classes available), or you can book a private tutor (1½ hours, $175). There's a second shop in Bondi Pavilion.

Prefer wheels to fins? There's a **skate ramp** (Queen Elizabeth Dr; 🚌380) at the beach's southern end. If posing in your budgie smugglers (Speedos) isn't having enough impact, there's an outdoor **workout area** (Queen Elizabeth Dr; 🚌380) near the North Bondi Surf Club. Coincidentally (or perhaps not), this is the part of the beach where the gay guys hang out.

Bondi Pavilion has changing rooms, lockers, cafes and a gelato shop.

What's Nearby?

Bondi Pavilion   Building
Built in the Mediterranean Georgian Revival style in 1929, 'The Pav' is more a cultural

Bondi Beach

centre than a changing shed, although it does have changing rooms, showers and lockers. There's a free art gallery upstairs, a theatre out the back and various cafes and a bar lining the ocean frontage, including the extremely popular Bucket List (www.thebucketlistbondi.com). (www.waverley.nsw.gov.au; Queen Elizabeth Dr; ⏰9am-5pm; 🚌380)

Bronte Beach   Beach
A winning family-oriented beach hemmed in by sandstone cliffs and a grassy park, Bronte lays claims to the title of the oldest surf lifesaving club in the world (1903). Contrary to popular belief, the beach is named after Lord Nelson, who doubled as

> ★ **Top Tip**
> At the beach's northern end is a grassy spot with coin-operated barbecues.

MANFRED GOTTSCHALK / GETTY IMAGES ©

the Duke of Bronte (a place in Sicily), and not the famous literary sorority. There's a kiosk and a changing room attached to the surf club, and covered picnic tables near the public barbecues. (Bronte Rd; 🚌378)

Aboriginal Rock Engravings   Archaeological Site
On the clifftop fairways of Bondi Golf & Diggers Club, a short walk north from Bondi Beach, lies a flat patch of rock carved by the Eora Aboriginal people (look for it about 20m southeast of the enormous chimney, and watch out for flying golf balls). Some of the images are hard to distinguish, though you should be able to make out marine life and the figure of a man. The carvings were regrooved in the 1960s to help preserve them. (5 Military Rd; 🚌380)

Bondi Icebergs Swimming Club   Swimming
Sydney's most famous pool commands the best view in Bondi and has a cute little cafe. (📞02-9130 4804; www.icebergs.com.au; 1 Notts Ave; adult/child $6/4; ⏰6.30am-6.30pm Fri-Wed; 🚌380)

Bondi Markets   Market
On Sundays, when the kids are at the beach, their school fills up with Bondi characters rummaging through tie-dyed secondhand clothes, original fashion, books, beads, earrings, aromatherapy oils, candles, old records and more. There's a farmers market here on Saturdays. (www.bondimarkets.com.au; Bondi Beach Public School, Campbell Pde; ⏰9am-1pm Sat, 10am-4pm Sun; 🚌380-382)

> ✗ **Take a Break**
> Ice-cream vendors strut the sand in summer. Note that alcohol is banned on the beach.
>
> ☑ **Don't Miss**
> Bondi Markets: bringing clothes, crafts, jewellery and more to the beachfront every Sunday.

Walking Tour: Bondi to Coogee

Arguably Sydney's best walk, this coastal path shouldn't be missed. On a warm day, plan to cool off at any of the beaches en route. There's little shade on this track, so make sure you slap on the sunscreen before setting out.

Distance: 6km
Duration: 3 hours

✗ Take a Break

The best lunch option is Bronte's Three Blue Ducks (p74); cut through the reserve right before Waverley Cemetery and head up Macpherson St.

Start Bondi Beach, 🚌 380

❶ Bondi Beach

Starting at Bondi Beach, take the stairs up the south end to Notts Ave, passing above the glistening Bondi Icebergs pool complex. Step onto the clifftop trail at the end of Notts Ave. Walking south, the blustery sandstone cliffs and grinding Pacific Ocean couldn't be more spectacular (watch for dolphins, whales and surfers).

❷ Tamarama Beach

Small but perfectly formed, Tamarama Beach has a deep reach of sand, totally disproportionate to its width.

❸ Bronte Beach

Descend from the clifftops onto Bronte Beach and take a dip, lay out a picnic under the Norfolk Island pines or head to a cafe

for a snack and a caffeine hit. After your break, pick up the path at the other end of the beach.

❹ Waverley Cemetery

Some famous Australians are among the subterranean denizens of the amazing cliff-edge Waverley Cemetery. On a clear day this is a prime vantage point for whale watchers.

❺ Clovelly Beach

Pass the locals enjoying a beer or a game of lawn bowls at the Clovelly Bowling Club, then breeze along past the cockatoos and

Coogee Beach

OLIVER STREWE / GETTY IMAGES ©

canoodling lovers in Burrows Park to sheltered Clovelly Beach, a fave with families.

6 Gordons Bay

Follow the footpath up through the car park, along Cliffbrook Pde, then down the steps to the upturned dinghies lining Gordons Bay, one of Sydney's best shore dive spots.

7 Dolphin Point

This grassy tract at Coogee Beach's northern end has superb ocean views and the Giles Baths ocean pool. A sobering shrine commemorates the 2002 Bali bombings. Coogee was hit hard by the tragedy, with 20 of the 89 Australians killed coming from hereabouts. Six members of the Coogee Dolphins rugby league team died in the blast.

8 Coogee Beach

The trail then lands you smack-bang onto glorious Coogee Beach. Swagger up to the rooftop of the Coogee Pavilion and toast your efforts with a cold beverage.

Finish Coogee Beach, 🚌 372-373

Walking Tour: A Rock-Quay Road

Soak up the atmosphere of the Rocks on this stroll through Sydney's historic centre. There are lots of shops, cafe and photo opportunities in this area, so take your time and your camera.

Distance: 3.5km
Duration: 2 hours

✕ Take a Break
Wet your whistle with a refreshing ale at the iconic Lord Nelson Brewery Hotel (p75).

Campbell's Storehouses

Start Cadman's Cottage, Circular Quay

❶ Cadman's Cottage

Sydney's oldest house was built on a now-buried beach for Government Coxswain John Cadman in 1816. Head north along Circular Quay West past the Overseas Passenger Terminal.

For a killer harbour view, head up to the level-four observation deck in the turret on the northern end.

❷ Campbell's Storehouses

Further along the quay, these storehouses were built in 1839 by Scottish merchant Robert Campbell to house his stash of tea, alcohol, sugar and fabric. Such buildings were common around Circular Quay into the early 20th century, but most have been demolished since.

❸ Dawes Point

Follow Hickson Rd past the Park Hyatt and into the small park at the end of Dawes Point for perfect Opera House views.

As you pass under the Harbour Bridge, keep an eye out for Luna Park on the opposite shore.

Walk past Walsh Bay's gentrified Edwardian wharves and then cross the road and cut up the stairs (marked 'public stairs to Windmill St').

❹ Arthur Payne's House

Continue up Ferry Lane to see the foundations of the house of Arthur Payne, first victim of the 1900 bubonic plague outbreak.

At the corner of Windmill St is the Hero of Waterloo, a contender for the title of Australia's oldest pub.

❺ Argyle Cut

Turn right on Lower Fort St and head to Argyle Pl, then hook left into Argyle St and

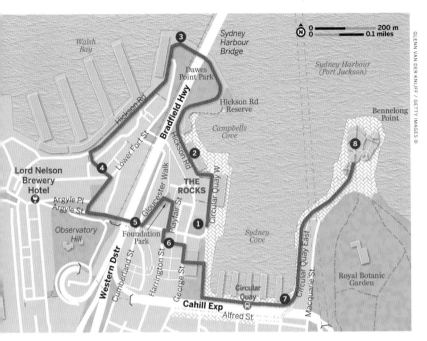

stroll through the Argyle Cut. Convict labourers excavated this canyonlike section of road clear through the sandstone ridge that gave the Rocks its name. The work began in 1843 with hand tools, and was completed (with the aid of dynamite) in 1867.

❻ Suez Canal

Just past the Cut take the stairs to the left and head along Gloucester Walk to Foundation Park.

Take the stairs down through the park, duck around the building at the bottom and exit onto Playfair St. Cross Argyle St into Harrington St then turn left into Suez Canal. One of few remaining such lanes, it tapers as it goes downhill until it's less than a metre wide (hence the name, which is also a pun on the word 'sewers'). Constructed in the 1840s, it was notorious as a lurking point for members of the 19th-century Rocks Push street gang.

❼ Sydney Writers Walk

Turn right into George St and cut through the Museum of Contemporary Art. Exit onto Circular Quay and follow the waterline to the Sydney Writers Walk. These metal discs, set into the Circular Quay promenade, hold ruminations from prominent Australian writers and the odd literary visitor such as Mark Twain, Germaine Greer, Peter Carey, Umberto Eco and Clive James.

❽ Sydney Opera House

Continue along Circular Quay East. The heaven-sent sails of the Sydney Opera House are directly in front of you, adjacent to an unmissable perspective of the Sydney Harbour Bridge off to the left.

Finish Sydney Opera House, 🚇Circular Quay

◎ SIGHTS

◎ Circular Quay & the Rocks

The site of Australia's first European settlement has evolved unrecognisably from the days when its residents sloshed through open sewers and squalid alleyways.

The Rocks remained a commercial and maritime hub until shipping services moved from Circular Quay in the late 1800s.

It wasn't until the 1970s that the Rocks' cultural and architectural heritage was recognised. The ensuring tourist-driven redevelopment saved many old buildings, but has turned the area east of the bridge highway into a tourist trap where kitsch cafes and shops hocking stuffed koalas and ersatz didgeridoos reign supreme. Nevertheless, it's a fascinating place to explore on foot.

Royal Botanic Garden   Gardens

These expansive gardens are the city's favourite picnic destination, jogging route and snuggling spot. Bordering Farm Cove, east of the Opera House, the gardens were established in 1816 and feature plant life from Australia and around the world. They include the site of the colony's first paltry vegetable patch, but their history goes back much further than that; long before the convicts arrived, this was an initiation ground for the Gadigal people. (Map p56; ☏02-9231 8111; www.rbgsyd.nsw.gov.au; Mrs Macquaries Rd; ◷7am-8pm Oct-Feb, to 5.30pm Mar-Sep; ⛴Circular Quay) 🅿 FREE

Museum of Contemporary Art   Gallery

One of the country's best and most challenging galleries, the MCA is a showcase for Australian and international contemporary art. Aboriginal art features prominently. The fab Gotham City–style art deco building bears the wounds of a redevelopment that has grafted on additional gallery space and a rooftop cafe/sculpture terrace – and ruined the George St facade in the process. (Map p56; ☏02-9245 2400; www.mca.com.au; 140 George St; ◷10am-5pm Fri-Wed, to 9pm Thu; ⛴Circular Quay) FREE

Rocks Discovery Museum   Museum

Divided into four chronological displays – Warrane (pre-1788), Colony (1788–1820), Port (1820–1900) and Transformations

Royal Botanic Garden

GLENN BEANLAND / GETTY IMAGES ©

(1900 to the present) – this excellent museum digs deep into the Rocks' history and leads you on an artefact-rich tour. Sensitive attention is given to the Rocks' original inhabitants, the Gadigal people. (Map p56; 02-9240 8680; www.rocksdiscoverymuseum. com; Kendall Lane; 10am-5pm; Circular Quay) FREE

Sydney Observatory Observatory
Built in the 1850s, Sydney's copper-domed, Italianate observatory squats atop pretty Observatory Hill, overlooking the harbour. Inside is a collection of vintage apparatus, including Australia's oldest working telescope (1874). Also on offer are audiovisual displays, including Aboriginal sky stories and a virtual-reality **3D Theatre** (adult/child $10/8; 2.30pm & 3.30pm daily, plus 11am & noon Sat & Sun). Bookings are essential for night-time **stargazing sessions** (adult/child $18/12). (Map p56; 02-9921 3485; www.sydneyobservatory.com.au; 1003 Upper Fort St; 10am-5pm; Circular Quay) FREE

◉ City Centre
Art Gallery of NSW Gallery
With its classical Greek frontage and modern rear, this much-loved institution plays a prominent and gregarious role in Sydney society. Blockbuster international exhibitions arrive regularly and there's an outstanding permanent collection of Australian art, including a substantial Indigenous section. The gallery also plays host to lectures, concerts, screenings, celebrity talks and children's activities. A range of free guided tours is offered on different themes and in various languages; enquire at the desk or check the website. (Map p62; 1800 679 278; www.artgallery.nsw.gov.au; Art Gallery Rd; 10am-5pm Thu-Tue, to 10pm Wed; ; St James) FREE

Macquarie Street Area
A swath of splendid sandstone colonial buildings graces this street, defining the central city's eastern edge. Many of these buildings were commissioned by Lachlan Macquarie, the first NSW governor with a vision of Sydney beyond its convict origins. He enlisted convict architect Francis

Best Places to Cool Off
Bondi Beach (p46) Plunge into the waves at Sydney's famous beach.

Camp Cove (p64) Sheltered, family-friendly Sydney Harbour beach.

Hyde Park (p57) Sydney's lungs: a formal park with avenues of trees and swathes of lawn.

North Shore beaches (p63) Sandy string of unpretentious surf beachs from Manly to Palm Beach.

Above: Egg exhibit, Sculpture by the Sea (p28)
OLIVER STREWE / GETTY IMAGES ©

Greenway to help realise his plans, and together they set a gold standard for architectural excellence that the city has, alas, never since managed to replicate. (Map p56; Martin Place)

Hyde Park Barracks Museum Museum
Convict architect Francis Greenway designed this squarish, decorously Georgian structure (1819) as convict quarters. Between 1819 and 1848, 50,000 men and boys did time here, most of whom had been sentenced by British courts to transportation to Australia for property crime. It later became an immigration depot, a women's asylum and a law court. These days it's a fascinating (if not entirely cheerful) museum, focusing on the barracks' history and the archaeological efforts that helped reveal it. (Map p56; 02-8239 2311; www.sydneylivingmuseums.com.au; Queens Sq, Macquarie St; adult/child $10/5; 10am-5pm; St James)

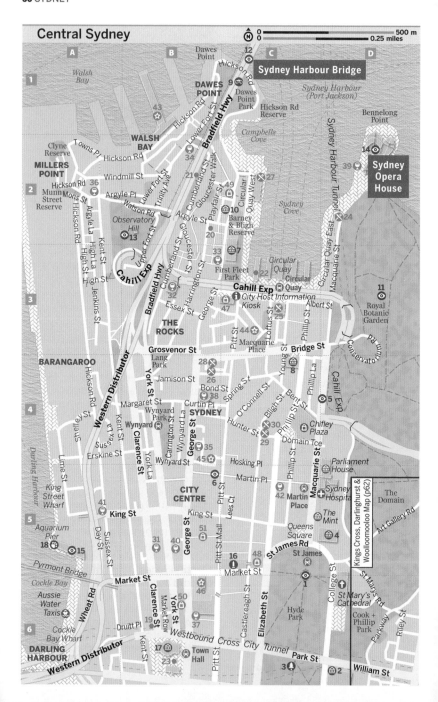

Central Sydney

N

0   500 m
0   0.25 miles

Walsh Bay

Dawes Point

12

Sydney Harbour Bridge

Sydney Harbour (Port Jackson)

Bennelong Point

DAWES POINT 9

Dawes Point Park

Hickson Rd Reserve

Campbells Cove

14

Sydney Harbour Tunnel

39

Sydney Opera House

43

WALSH BAY

Clyne Reserve

Towns Pl

Hickson Rd

34

MILLERS POINT

Windmill St

Hickson Rd 36

Munn Street Reserve

Mons St

Argyle Pl

Watson Rd

Lower Fort St

Trinity Ave

21

Cumberland St

Gloucester Walk

Playfair St

49

Circular Quay West

27

Sydney Cove

High St

Kent St

Argyle La

Observatory Hill

13

Upper Fort St

Gloucester St

Argyle St

10

Barney & Bligh Reserve

20

High La

Jenkins St

High St

Cahill Exp

Bradfield Hwy

Cumberland St

Harrington St

33

7

First Fleet Park

22

Circular Quay

Circular Quay

Macquarie St

Circular Quay East

11

Royal Botanic Garden

Conservato

Cahill Exp

32

Essex St

George St

47

i City Host Information Kiosk

25

Albert St

Phillip St

THE ROCKS

44

Macquarie Place

Loftus St

Pitt St

Bridge St

Grosvenor St

BARANGAROO

Hickson Rd

Western Distributor

York St

Lang Park

Jamison St

28

26

Bond St

38

Spring St

O'Connell St

Bligh St

Bent St

Phillip La

Young St

8

5

Cahill Exp

Margaret St

Shelley St

Kent St

Clarence St

Sussex St

Erskine St

Wynyard Park

Wynyard

Curtin Pl

SYDNEY

George St

Carrington St

Wynyard La

Wynyard St

Hunter St

30

Phillip St

29

Domain Tce

Chifley Plaza

35

45

Hosking Pl

Macquarie St

Parliament House

6

Martin Pl

CITY CENTRE

King Street Wharf

41

King St

King St

Pitt St

Lees Ct

King St

42 **Martin Place**

Sydney Hospital

The Mint

4

Parliament House

Darling Harbour

Aquarium Pier

18

15

Pyrmont Bridge

Cockle Bay

Day St

Sussex St

George St

31

40

51

Pitt St Mall

Queens Square

The Domain

Art Gallery Rd

Kings Cross, Darlinghurst & Woolloomooloo Map (p62)

16

48

St James Rd

St James

1

Market St

Market St

Aussie Water Taxis

Clarence St

Wheat Rd

Market St

46

50

York St

Market Row

19

Castlereagh St

Elizabeth St

Hyde Park

St Mary's Cathedral

Cook + Phillip Park

College St

St Marys Rd

Cockle Bay Wharf

Druitt Pl

37

Westbound Cross City Tunnel

Park St

DARLING HARBOUR

Kent St

17

23

Town Hall

Pitt St

3

2

Riley St

Western Distributor

William St

Central Sydney

Hyde Park   Park

Formal but much-loved Hyde Park has manicured gardens and a tree-formed tunnel running down its spine which looks particularly pretty at night, illuminated by fairy lights. The park's northern end is crowned by the richly symbolic art deco **Archibald Memorial Fountain** (Map p56) featuring Greek mythological figures, while at the other end is the **Anzac Memorial**. (Map p56; Elizabeth St; 🚇St James & Museum)

Museum of Sydney   Museum

Built on the site of Sydney's first (and infamously pungent) Government House, the MoS is a fragmented, story-telling museum, which uses state-of-the-art installations to explore the city's people,

places, cultures and evolution. The history of the indigenous Eora people is highlighted – touching on the millennia of continuous occupation of this place. Be sure to open some of the many stainless-steel and glass drawers (they close themselves). (Map p56; MoS; 🖉02-9251 5988; www. sydneylivingmuseums.com.au; cnr Phillip & Bridge Sts; adult/child $10/5; ⏰9.30am-5pm; 🐾; 🚇Circular Quay)

Martin Place   Square

Studded with imposing edifices, long, lean Martin Place was closed to traffic in 1971, forming a terraced pedestrian mall complete with fountains and areas for public gatherings. It's the closest thing to a main civic square that Sydney has. In

2014 the Lindt cafe at 53 Martin Pl was the site of a 16-hour siege, ending in the death of two hostages and the gunman. At the time of writing, a permanent memorial to the victims was being planned. (Map p56; R Martin Place)

Sydney Tower Eye   Tower
The 309m-tall Sydney Tower (built 1970–81) offers unbeatable 360-degree views from the observation level 250m up – and even better ones for the daredevils braving the Skywalk on its roof. The visit starts with the 4D Experience: a short 3D film giving you a bird's-eye view (a parakeet's to be exact) of city, surf, harbour and what lies beneath the water, accompanied by mist sprays and bubbles. It's actually pretty darn cool. (Map p56; ✆ 1800 258 693; www.sydneytowereye.com.au; 100 Market St; adult/child $27/16, Skywalk $70/49; ⊙ 9am-9.30pm; R St James)

> *an intimidating array of sharks and rays passes overhead*

Sydney Sea Life Aquarium

Sydney Town Hall   Historic Building
Mansard roofs, sandstone turrets, wrought-iron trimmings and some over-the-top balustrades: the French Second Empire wedding-cake exterior of the Town Hall (built 1868–89) is something to behold. Unless there's something on, you can explore the halls off the main entrance. The wood-lined concert hall has a humongous pipe organ with nearly 9000 pipes, once the largest in the world. It's used regularly for recitals, some of which are free. (Map p56; www.sydneytownhall.com.au; 483 George St; ⊙ 8am-6pm Mon-Fri; R Town Hall)

Chinatown   Area
With a discordant soundtrack of blaring Canto pop, Dixon St is the heart and soul of Chinatown: a narrow, shady pedestrian mall with a string of restaurants and their urgently attendant spruikers. The ornate *paifang* (dragon gates) at either end are topped with fake bamboo tiles, golden Chinese calligraphy (with English translations), ornamental lions to keep evil spirits at bay and a fair amount of pigeon poo. (www. sydney-chinatown.info; R Town Hall)

ANDREW WATSON / GETTY IMAGES ©

Darling Harbour & Pyrmont

Dotted between the flyovers and fountains of Sydney's purpose-built tourist hub (opened for the bicentennial in 1988) are some of the city's highest-profile paid attractions. In Pyrmont, on the harbour's western shore, the Star casino complex has had an expensive do-over, yet it remains like such establishments the world over: big and soulless beneath a thin veneer of glamour.

If you're after a slice of real Sydney life you won't find it here, but it's still worth an hour's walkabout.

Darling Harbour and Pyrmont are serviced by ferry and light rail.

Sydney Sea Life Aquarium   Aquarium

As well as regular wall-mounted tanks and ground-level enclosures, this impressive complex has two large pools that you can walk through, safely enclosed in Perspex tunnels, as an intimidating array of sharks and rays passes overhead. Other highlights include clownfish (howdy Nemo), platypuses, moon jellyfish (in a disco-lit tube), sea dragons and the swoon-worthy finale: the two-million-litre Great Barrier Reef tank. (Map p56; ☏02-8251 7800; www.sydneyaquarium.com.au; Aquarium Pier; adult/child $40/28; ☺9.30am-8pm; ⓡTown Hall) ⌨

Wild Life Sydney Zoo   Zoo

Complementing its sister and neighbour, Sea Life, this large complex houses an impressive collection of Australian native reptiles, butterflies, spiders, snakes and mammals (including kangaroos and koalas). The nocturnal section is particularly good, bringing out the extrovert in the quolls, potoroos, echidnas and possums. As interesting as Wild Life is, it's not a patch on Taronga Zoo. Still, it's worth considering as part of a combo with Sea Life, or if you're short on time. Tickets are cheaper online. (Map p56; ☏02-9333 9245; www.wildlifesydney.com.au; Aquarium Pier; adult/child $40/28; ☺9.30am-7pm; ⓡTown Hall)

👪 Sydney for Children

Most kids love the **Sydney Sea Life Aquarium**, **Wild Life Sydney Zoo** and **Australian National Maritime Museum** (p60) at Darling Harbour, and the **Powerhouse Museum** (p60) in neighbouring Ultimo. Also worth investigating are the 'Tours for Tots' and 'Gallery Kids Sunday Performance' at the **Art Gallery of NSW** (p55) – details are on the gallery's website.

Elsewhere, **Taronga Zoo** (p63) and **Luna Park** (p63) are sure to please.

Organised kids' activities ramp up during school holidays (December and January, April, July and September); check these online resources for listings:

- www.sydneyforkids.com.au
- www.au.timeout.com/sydney/kids
- www.childmags.com.au

Above: Taronga Zoo
JULIET COOMBE / GETTY IMAGES ©

Chinese Garden of Friendship   Gardens

Built according to Taoist principles, the Chinese Garden of Friendship is usually an oasis of tranquillity – although construction noise from Darling Harbour's redevelopment can intrude from time to time. Designed by architects from Guangzhou (Sydney's sister city) for Australia's bicentenary in 1988, the garden interweaves pavilions, waterfalls, lakes, paths and lush plant life. (☏02-9240 8888; www.chinesegarden.com.au; Harbour St; adult/child $6/3; ☺9.30am-5pm; ⓡTown Hall)

Art Gallery of NSW (p55)

Australian National Maritime Museum
Museum

Beneath an Utzon-like roof (a low-rent Opera House?), the Maritime Museum sails through Australia's inextricable relationship with the sea. Exhibitions range from Indigenous canoes to surf culture, to the navy. Entry includes free tours and there are kids' activities on Sundays. The 'big ticket' (adult/child $27/16) includes entry to the vessels moored outside, including the submarine HMAS *Onslow*, the destroyer HMAS *Vampire* and an 1874 square-rigger, the *James Craig*, which periodically offers **sailing trips** (02-9298 3888; www.shf.org.au; Wharf 7, Pyrmont; adult/child $150/50; Pyrmont Bay). Normally a replica of Cook's *Endeavour* also drops anchor. (02-9298 3777; www.anmm.gov.au; 2 Murray St; adult/child $7/3.50; 9.30am-5pm; Pyrmont Bay)

Powerhouse Museum
Museum

A short walk from Darling Harbour, this science and design museum whirs away inside the former power station for Sydney's defunct, original tram network. High-voltage interactive demonstrations wow school groups with the low-down on how lightning strikes, magnets grab and engines growl. It's a huge hit with kids but equally popular with adults, touching on subjects such as fashion and furniture design. (02-9217 0111; www.powerhousemuseum.com; 500 Harris St; adult/child $15/8; 9.30am-5pm; ; Paddy's Markets)

Sydney Fish Market
Market

This piscatorial precinct on Blackwattle Bay shifts over 15 million kilograms of seafood annually, and has retail outlets, restaurants, a sushi bar, an oyster bar and a highly regarded cooking school. Chefs, locals and overfed seagulls haggle over mud crabs, Balmain bugs, lobsters and slabs of salmon at the daily fish auction, which kicks off at 5.30am weekdays. Check it out on a behind-the-scenes tour (adult/child $30/10). (02-9004 1108; www.sydneyfishmarket.com.au; Bank St; 7am-4pm; Fish Market)

ANDREW WATSON / GETTY IMAGES ©

⊙ Surry Hills & Darlinghurst

Surry Hills, Sydney's hippest suburb, is liberally scattered with corner pubs, fantastic eateries and quirky cafes and bars. Neighbouring Darlinghurst is synonymous with Sydney's vibrant and visible LGBTI community. The shabby lower end of Oxford St is home to most of the city's gay venues.

Australian Museum   Museum
This natural-history museum, established just 40 years after the First Fleet dropped anchor, is endeavouring to modernise. Dusty taxidermy has been interspersed with video projections and a terrarium with live snakes, while dinosaur skeletons cosy up to life-size re-creations. Yet it's the most old-fashioned sections that are arguably the best – the large crystal collection and the hall of skeletons. (Map p56; 🖉02-9320 6000; www.australianmuseum.net.au; 6 College St; adult/child $15/8; ⊙9.30am-5pm; 🗟; 🚇Museum)

Sydney Jewish Museum   Museum
Created largely as a Holocaust memorial, this museum examines Australian Jewish history, culture and tradition, from the time of the First Fleet (which included 16 known Jews), to the immediate aftermath of WWII (when Australia became home to the greatest number of Holocaust survivors per capita, after Israel), to the present day. Allow at least two hours to take it all in. Free 45-minute tours leave at noon on Monday, Wednesday, Friday and Sunday. (Map p62; 🖉02-9360 7999; www.sydneyjewishmuseum. com.au; 148 Darlinghurst Rd; adult/child $10/7; ⊙10am-4pm Sun-Thu, to 2pm Fri; 🚇Kings Cross)

⊙ Paddington & Woollahra

Paddington, aka 'Paddo', is an upmarket suburb of restored Victorian-era terrace houses, many with iron 'lace' detailing. The best time to explore Paddington's streets and laneways is on Saturday, when the Paddington Markets (p68) are held.

East of Paddington is the ritzy residential suburb of Woollahra. Just southeast, at the

 Kings Cross & Woolloomooloo

Crowned by a huge illuminated Coca-Cola sign, the 'Cross' has long been the haunt of Sydney's vice industry. Although once home to grand estates and stylish apartments, the suburb underwent a radical change in the 1930s, when wine-soaked intellectuals, artists and ne'er-do-wells rowdily claimed the streets. The neighbourhood's reputation was sealed during the Vietnam War, when American sailors based at nearby Garden Island flooded the Cross with a tide of drug-fuelled debauchery.

Although the streets retain an air of seedy hedonism, the area has recently undergone a cultural renaissance.

The suburb of Woolloomooloo, down **McElhone Stairs** (Map p62; Victoria St; 🚇Kings Cross) from the Cross, was once a slum full of drunks and sailors (and drunken sailors). Things are more genteel these days – the pubs are relaxed and **Woolloomooloo Wharf** is now home to a boutique hotel and a swath of upmarket restaurants. Outside the wharf is the famous **Harry's Cafe de Wheels** (Map p62; www.harryscafedewheels.com.au; Cowper Wharf Roadway; pies $5-7; ⊙8.30am-3am Mon-Sat, 9am-1am Sun; 🚇Kings Cross), where generations of Sydneysiders have stopped to sober up over a late-night 'Tiger' (beef pie served with mushy peas, mashed potato and gravy) on the way home from a big night out.

It's a 15-minute walk to the Cross from the city, or you could hop on a train. Buses 311 and 323–326 from the city also pass through here.

top end of Oxford St, is the 220-hectare **Centennial Park** (🖉02-9339 6699; www. centennialparklands.com.au; Oxford St; 🚇Bondi Junction), which has running, cycling, skating and horse-riding tracks, duck ponds, barbecue sites and sports pitches.

Kings Cross, Darlinghurst & Woolloomooloo

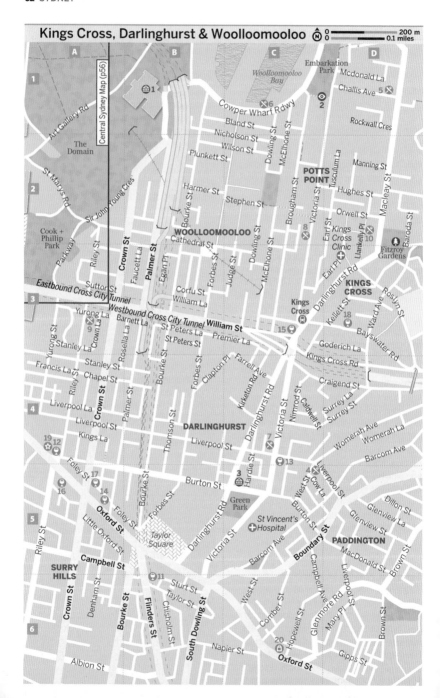

Kings Cross, Darlinghurst & Woolloomooloo

◎ North Shore

Just east of the Harbour Bridge is the stately suburb of Kirribilli, home to **Admiralty House** and **Kirribilli House**, the Sydney residences of the governor-general and prime minister respectively.

You can walk across the bridge to access Milsons Point, McMahons Point, Lavender Bay and Kirribilli, or take the short ferry ride from Circular Quay.

Luna Park   Amusement Park

A sinister chip-toothed clown face forms the entrance to this old-fashioned amusement park overlooking Sydney Harbour. It's one of several 1930s features, including the Coney Island funhouse, a pretty carousel and the nausea-inducing rotor. You can purchase a two-ride pass ($16), or buy a height-based unlimited-ride pass (from $30, cheaper if purchased online). Hours are extended during school and public holidays. (☎02-9922 6644; www.lunaparksydney.com; 1 Olympic Dr; ☺11am-10pm Fri & Sat, 2-6pm Sun, 11am-4pm Mon; ⛴Milsons Point) FREE

Taronga Zoo   Zoo

A 12-minute ferry ride from Circular Quay, Taronga Zoo has 75 hectares of bushy harbour hillside full of kangaroos, koalas and similarly hirsute Australians, and imported guests. The zoo's 4000 critters have million-dollar harbour views, but seem blissfully unaware of the privilege. Highlights include the nocturnal platypus

habitat, the Great Southern Oceans section and the Asian elephant display. Feedings and encounters happen throughout the day, while in summer, twilight concerts jazz things up. (☎02-9969 2777; www.taronga. org.au; Bradleys Head Rd; adult/child $46/23; ☺9.30am-5pm; ⛴Taronga Zoo) 🅿

Balmoral Beach   Beach

The beachy enclave of Balmoral faces off with Manly across Middle Harbour, and has some good restaurants and a beaut swimming beach. Split in two by an unfeasibly picturesque rocky outcrop, Balmoral attracts picnicking North Shore families. Swimmers migrate to the shark-netted southern end. (The Esplanade; 🚌245)

◎ Manly

Refreshingly relaxed Manly occupies a narrow isthmus between ocean and harbour beaches near North Head. It's the only place in Sydney where you can catch a harbour ferry to swim in the ocean.

Regular ferries travel between Circular Quay and Manly – it's one of Sydney's best-loved journeys.

Manly Beach   Beach

Sydney's second-most-famous beach stretches for nearly two golden kilometres, lined by Norfolk Island pines and scrappy midrise apartment blocks. The southern end of the beach, nearest the Corso, is known as South Steyne, with North Steyne

Spectator Sports

Sydneysiders are passionate about the National Rugby League (NRL; www.nrl.com); the season kicks off in March in suburban stadiums, with the grand final in early October.

Over the same period, hometown favourites the Sydney Swans and Greater Western Sydney Giants play in the Australian Football League (AFL; www.afl.com.au). The Swans play at the Sydney Cricket Ground (SCG) and the Giants at the Sydney Showground Stadium in Sydney's Olympic Park.

The cricket (www.cricket.com.au) season runs from October to March, with the SCG hosting interstate Sheffield Shield and sell-out international Test, Twenty20 and One Day International matches.

Above: AFL
ANTHONY PEARSE / AFL MEDIA / STRINGER / GETTY IMAGES ©

in the centre and Queenscliff at the northern end; each has its own surf lifesaving club. (🏊Manly)

Manly Sea Life Sanctuary   Aquarium
This ain't the place to come if you're on your way to Manly Beach for a surf. Underwater glass tubes enable you to become alarmingly intimate with 3m grey nurse sharks. Reckon they're not hungry? Shark Dive Xtreme (introductory/certified dives $280/205) enables you to enter their world. (📞1800 199 742; www.manlysealife-sanctuary.com.au; West Esplanade; adult/child $25/15; ⏰9.30am-5pm; 🏊Manly)

Manly Art Gallery & Museum   Museum
A short stroll from Manly Wharf, this passionately managed community gallery maintains a local focus, with exhibits of surfcraft, camp swimwear and beachy bits and pieces. There's also a ceramics gallery, and lots of old Manly photos to peer at. (www.manly.nsw.gov.au; West Esplanade; ⏰10am-5pm Tue-Sun; 🏊Manly) FREE

Manly Scenic Walkway   Outdoors
This epic walk has two major components: the 10km western stretch between Manly and Spit Bridge, and the 9.5km eastern loop around North Head. Either download a map or pick one up from the information centre near the wharf. (www.manly.nsw.gov.au; 🏊Manly)

Shelly Beach   Beach
This sheltered north-facing ocean cove is just a short 1km walk from the busy Manly beach strip. The tranquil waters are a protected haven for marine life, so it offers wonderful snorkelling. (🏊Manly)

North Head   National Park
About 3km south of Manly, spectacular, chunky North Head offers dramatic cliffs, lookouts and sweeping views of the ocean, the harbour and the city; hire a bike and go exploring. (North Head Scenic Dr; 🚌135)

🏃 ACTIVITIES

Sydney's best shore dives are at Gordons Bay, north of Coogee; Shark Point, Clovelly; and Ship Rock, Cronulla. Other destinations include North Bondi, Camp Cove and Bare Island. Popular boat-dive sites are Wedding Cake Island off Coogee, Sydney Heads, and off Royal National Park.

There's good snorkelling off Clovelly and Manly Beaches. **EcoTreasures** (📞0415 121 648; www.ecotreasures.com.au) 🏄, a company specialising in ecotourism, runs a popular Snorkel Walk & Talk tour in Manly.

Surf spots on the South Shore include Bondi, Tamarama, Coogee, Maroubra and Cronulla. The North Shore is home to a

Manly (p63)

dozen surf beaches between Manly and Palm Beach, including Curl Curl, Dee Why, Narrabeen, Mona Vale and Newport.

There are 100-plus public swimming pools in Sydney, and many beaches have protected rock pools. Harbour beaches offer sheltered and shark-netted swimming, but nothing beats Pacific Ocean waves.

Dive Centre Bondi — Diving

This Professional Association of Diving Instructors (PADI) centre offers learn-to-dive courses (three days $395), plus various boat and shore dives around Sydney. (☎02-9369 3855; www.divebondi.com.au; 198 Bondi Rd; ☉9am-6pm Mon-Fri, 7.30am-6pm Sat & Sun; 🚌380)

Dive Centre Manly — Diving

Offers snorkel safaris ($50), two-day learn-to-dive PADI courses (from $445), guided shore dives (one/two dives $95/125) and boat dives (two dives $175). (☎02-9977 4355; www.divesydney.com.au; 10 Belgrave St; ☉8.30am-6pm; 🚢Manly)

Champagne Sailing — Sailing

If you've got champagne tastes or ever fancied recreating Duran Duran's Rio video, charter a 10m catamaran and muster your 20 best friends to split the bill. (☎02-9948 1578; www.champagnesailing.com.au; 4hr charters $1200)

Sydney by Sail — Sailing

Departing daily from outside the Maritime Museum, Sydney by Sail offers cruises (three hours $165), private charters (with or without a skipper), romantic options for couples and internationally recognised learn-to-sail courses ($595). (☎02-9280 1110; www.sydneybysail.com; Festival Pontoon, Darling Harbour; 🚢Pyrmont Bay)

Manly Surf School — Surfing

Offers two-hour surf lessons year-round (adult/child $70/55), as well as private tuition. Also runs surf safaris up to the Northern Beaches, including two lessons, lunch, gear and city pick-ups ($120). (☎02-9932 7000; www.manlysurfschool.com; North Steyne Surf Club; 🚢Manly)

Andrew (Boy)
Charlton Pool Swimming

Sydney's best saltwater pool – smack
bang next to the harbour – is a magnet for
water-loving gays, straights, parents and
fashionistas. Serious lap swimmers rule
the pool, so maintain your lane. Wheelchair
accessible. (☑02-9358 6686; www.abcpool.
org; 1c Mrs Macquaries Rd; adult/child $6/4.50;
🕙6am-7pm Sep-Mar; 🚉Martin Place)

North Sydney
Olympic Pool Swimming

Next door to Luna Park is this art deco
Olympic-sized outdoor pool, plus a 25m
indoor pool, kids' splash zones, a gym
($18.50 with pool access), a crèche and a
cafe, all with unbelievable harbour views.
(☑02-9955 2309; www.northsydney.nsw.gov.
au; 4 Alfred St South; adult/child $7.10/3.50;
🕙5.30am-9pm Mon-Fri, 7am-7pm Sat & Sun;
🚉Milsons Point/Luna Park)

Wylie's Baths Swimming

On the rocky coast south of Coogee
Beach, this superb seawater pool (1907) is
targeted at swimmers more than splash-
abouts. After your swim, take a yoga class

($18), enjoy a massage, or have a coffee
at the kiosk, which has magnificent ocean
views. (☑02-9665 2838; www.wylies.com.au;
4b Neptune St; adult/child $4.80/1; 🕙7am-7pm
Oct-Mar, to 5pm Apr-Sep; 🚉372-374)

TOURS

Bike Buffs Bicycle Tour

Offers daily four-hour, two-wheeled tours
around the harbourside sights (including
jaunts over the Harbour Bridge), departing from Argyle Pl. Also hires bikes
($35/60/295 per half-day/day/week).
(☑0414 960 332; www.bikebuffs.com.au; adult/
child $95/70; 🚉Circular Quay)

BlueBananas Bicycle Tour

Take some of the puff out of a guided
cycling tour on an electric bike. Options
include the 1½-hour Bike the Bridge tour
($59) and the 2½-hour Sydney City Tour
($99). (Map p56; ☑02-9114 8488; www.blue
bananas.com.au; 281 Clarence St; 🚉Town Hall)

Bonza Bike Tours Bicycle Tour

These bike boffins run a 2½-hour Sydney
Highlights tour (adult/child $66/79) and a

MATT MUNRO / GETTY IMAGES ©

four-hour Sydney Classic tour ($119/99). Other tours tackle the Harbour Bridge and Manly. Also hires bikes ($15/35/50 per hour/half-day/day). (Map p56; 📞02-9247 8800; www.bonzabiketours.com; 30 Harrington St; 🚉Circular Quay)

Captain Cook Cruises Cruise
As well as ritzy lunch and dinner cruises, this crew offers the aquatic version of a hop-on, hop-off bus tour, stopping at Watsons Bay, Taronga Zoo, Garden Island, Circular Quay, Luna Park and Darling Harbour. (Map p56; 📞02-9206 1111; www.captaincook.com.au; Wharf 6, Circular Quay; 🚉Circular Quay)

Manly Ocean Adventures Boat Tour
Blast out to sea in a speedboat, following the coastline from Manly all the way to Bondi. From May to December they also offer whale-watching excursions. (📞1300 062 659; www.manlyoceanadventures.com.au; 1/40 East Esplanade; from $85; 🛥Manly)

Sydney Harbour Kayaks Kayaking
Rents kayaks (from $20 per hour) and stand-up paddleboards (from $25), and leads four-hour ecotours ($99) from near the Spit Bridge. (📞02-9960 4389; www.sydneyharbourkayaks.com.au; Smiths Boat Shed, 81 Parriwi Rd, Mosman; 🕙9am-5pm Mon-Fri, 7.30am-5pm Sat & Sun; 🚌173-180)

Natural Wanders Kayaking
Offers exhilarating morning tours around the Harbour Bridge, Lavender Bay, Balmain and Birchgrove. (📞0427 225 072; www.kayaksydney.com; Lavender Bay wharf; tours $65-150; 🚉Milsons Point)

I'm Free Walking Tour
Departing thrice daily from the square off George St between the Town Hall and St Andrew's Cathedral (no bookings taken – just show up), these highly rated three-hour tours are nominally free but are run by enthusiastic young guides for tips. The route takes in the Rocks, Circular Quay, Martin Place, Pitt St and Hyde Park.(Map p56; 📞0405 515 654; www.imfree.com.au; 483 George St; 🕙10.30am, 2.30pm & 6pm; 🚉Town Hall) FREE

Sydney Architecture Walks Walking Tour
These bright young archi-buffs run two 3½-hour cycling tours and five themed

★ Top Five Green Spaces
Centennial Park (p61)

Royal Botanic Garden (p54)

Hyde Park (p57)

Sydney Harbour National Park (p43)

Chinese Garden of Friendship (p59)

From left: Bondi Icebergs Swimming Club (p49); Sydney Opera House (p38) and the Sydney Harbour Bridge (p40); Balmoral Beach pier (p63)

BRETT DAVIES · PHOTOSIGHTFACES / GETTY IMAGES ©

SIMON WOOLLEY / GETTY IMAGES ©

Weekend Markets

Eveleigh Farmers' Market (www.eveleigh market.com.au; Carriageworks, 245 Wilson St; ☺8am-1pm Sat; ☒Redfern) Over 70 regular stallholders sell their goodies at Sydney's best farmers market, held in a heritage-listed railway workshop. Food and coffee stands do a brisk business; celebrity chef Kylie Kwong can often be spotted cooking up a storm.

Glebe Markets (www.glebemarkets.com. au; Glebe Public School, cnr Glebe Point Rd & Derby Pl; ☺10am-4pm Sat; ☒Glebe) The best of the west; Sydney's dreadlocked, shoeless, inner-city contingent beats a course to this crowded hippie-ish market.

Paddington Markets (www.paddington markets.com.au; 395 Oxford St; ☺10am-4pm Sat; ☒380) Originating in the 1970s, when they were drenched in the scent of patchouli oil, these markets are considerably more mainstream these days. They're still worth exploring for their new and vintage clothing, crafts and jewellery. Expect a crush.

Rozelle Markets (☎02-9818 5373; www. rozellemarkets.com.au; 663 Darling St; ☺9am-4pm Sat & Sun; ☒444-445) One of Sydney's best bargain-hunter markets, with very few tourists. Sift through antiques, collectibles, hippie jewellery, vintage clothes, plants, books and knick-knackery, with live folk music, palm readings and exotic food stalls as a backdrop.

Above: Rozelle Markets
RUDI VAN STARREX / GETTY IMAGES ©

two-hour walking tours (The City; Utzon and the Sydney Opera House; Harbourings; Art, Place and Landscape; and Modern Sydney). (☎0403 888 390; www.sydney architecture.org; adult/student walk $49/35, cycle incl bike $120/110)

🛍 SHOPPING

Opal Minded Jewellery
As good a place as any to stock up on that quintessential piece of Aussie bling. (Map p56; www.opalminded.com; 55 George St; ☺9am-6.30pm; ☒Circular Quay)

Australian Wine Centre Wine
This multilingual basement store is packed with quality Australian wine, beer and spirits. Smaller producers are well represented, along with a staggering range of prestigious Penfolds Grange wines. International shipping can be arranged. (Map p56; www.australianwinecentre.com; Goldfields House, 1 Alfred St; ☺10am-8pm Mon-Sat, to 6.30pm Sun; ☒Circular Quay)

Queen Victoria Building Shopping Centre
The magnificent Queen Victoria Building takes up a whole block and boasts nearly 200 shops on five levels. It's a High Victorian masterpiece – without doubt Sydney's most beautiful shopping centre. (Map p56; QVB; www.qvb.com.au; 455 George St; ☺11am-5pm Sun, 9am-6pm Mon-Wed, Fri & Sat, 9am-9pm Thu; ☒Town Hall)

Strand Arcade Shopping Centre
Constructed in 1891, the Strand rivals the QVB in the ornateness stakes. The three floors of designer fashions, Australiana and old-world coffee shops will make your short-cut through here considerably longer. (Map p56; www.strandarcade.com.au; 412 George St; ☺9am-5.30pm Mon-Wed & Fri, to 8pm Thu, 9am-4pm Sat, 11am-4pm Sun; ☒St James)

Westfield Sydney Mall
The city's most glamorous shopping mall is a bafflingly large complex gobbling up

Queen Victoria Building

Sydney Tower and a fair chunk of Pitt St Mall. The 5th-floor food court is excellent. (Map p56; www.westfield.com.au/sydney; 188 Pitt St Mall; ⊙9.30am-6.30pm Fri-Wed, to 9pm Thu; ℝSt James)

David Jones Department Store
DJs is Sydney's premier department store, occupying two enormous city buildings. The Castlereagh St store has women's and children's clothing; Market St has menswear, electrical goods and a high-brow food court. David Jones also takes up a sizeable chunk of Westfield Bondi Junction. (Map p56; www.davidjones.com.au; 86-108 Castlereagh St; ⊙9.30am-7pm Sat-Wed, to 9pm Thu & Fri; ℝSt James)

Paddy's Markets Market
Cavernous, 1000-stall Paddy's is the Sydney equivalent of Istanbul's Grand Bazaar, but swap the hookahs and carpets for mobile-phone covers, Eminem T-shirts and cheap sneakers. Pick up a VB singlet for Uncle Bruce or wander along the aisles in capitalist awe. (www.paddysmarkets.com.au; 9-13 Hay St; ⊙10am-6pm Wed-Sun; ℝCentral)

Market City Shopping Centre
This large shopping centre above Paddy's Markets includes a big food court, heaps of discount fashion outlet shops (cheap Converse anyone?), a supermarket and video-game parlours. (www.marketcity.com.au; 9-13 Hay St; ⊙10am-7pm; ℝCentral)

Capital L Fashion
This attractive boutique stocks women's clothing by up-and-coming Australian designers. Hip sales staff break from tradition and actually help you find and try on clothes. (Map p62; ☎02-9361 0111; www.capital-l.com; 100 Oxford St; ⊙10.30am-6pm; ℝKings Cross)

Poepke Fashion
One of Paddington's more interesting women's boutiques, stocking a curated range from Australian and international designers. (www.poepke.com; 47 William St; ⊙10am-6pm Mon-Sat, noon-5pm Sun; ☒380)

Opera Bar (p75)

> the Opera House on one
> side and the Harbour Bridge
> on the other

🍴 EATING

🍴 Circular Quay & the Rocks

Quay Modern Australian $$$
Quay is shamelessly guilty of breaking the rule that good views make for bad food. Chef Peter Gilmore never rests on his laurels, consistently delivering the exquisitely crafted, adventurous cuisine which has landed Quay on the prestigious World's Best Restaurants list. And the view? Like dining in a postcard. (Map p56; ☎02-9251 5600; www.quay.com.au; Level 3, Overseas Passenger Terminal; 3/4 courses $130/150; ⏱noon-2.30pm Tue-Fri, 6-10pm daily; ☒Circular Quay)

Momofuku Seiōbo Modern Australian $$$
The first restaurant outside the US opened by New York's gastronomic darling David Chang, Momofuku Seiōbo is a thorough destination diner. Bringing together the techniques, concepts and ideas of Japanese kaiseki (multi-course eating) and classical Western degustation, it's not one for the short of time, or funds. The two-hour degustation costs $185 (before wine) but is guaranteed to transport you to heaven. (www.momofuku.com/sydney/seiobo; The Star, 80 Pyrmont St; degustation, $185; ⏱noon-2pm Sat, 6.30-10pm Mon-Sat)

🍴 City Centre

Mamak Malaysian $
Get here early (from 5.30pm) if you want to score a table without queuing – this eat-and-run Malaysian joint is one of the most popular cheapies in the city. The satays are cooked over charcoal and are particularly delicious when accompanied by a flaky golden roti. (www.mamak.com.au; 15 Goulburn St; mains $6-17; ⏱11.30am-2.30pm & 5.30-10pm Mon-Thu, to 2am Fri & Sat; ☒Town Hall)

Mr Wong Chinese $$
Dumpling junkies shuffle down a dirty lane and into the bowels of an old warehouse for a taste of Mr Wong's deliciously addictive

Cantonese fare. There's a dark-edged glamour to the cavernous basement dining room. Despite seating 240, there are often queues out the door. (Map p56; 02-9240 3000; www.merivale.com.au/mrwong; 3 Bridge Lane; mains $25-38; noon-3pm & 5.30-11pm; Wynyard)

Din Tai Fung — Chinese $$
The noodles and buns are great, but it's the dumplings that made this Taiwanese chain famous, delivering an explosion of fabulously flavoursome broth as you bite into their delicate casings. Come early, come hungry, come prepared to share your table. It also has stalls in the Star and Westfield Sydney food courts. (www.dintaifung.com.au; Level 1, World Sq, 644 George St; dishes $11-19; 11.30am-2.30pm & 5.30-9pm; Museum)

Tetsuya's — French, Japanese $$$
Down a clandestine security driveway, this extraordinary restaurant is for those seeking a culinary journey rather than a simple stuffed belly. Settle in for 10-plus courses of French- and Japanese-inflected food from the creative genius of Japanese-born Tetsuya Wakuda. Book way ahead. (02-9267 2900; www.tetsuyas.com; 529 Kent St; degustation $220; noon-3pm Sat, 6-10pm Tue-Sat; Town Hall)

Inner West

Mary's — Burgers $
Not put off by the grungy aesthetics, the ear-splitting heavy metal or the fact that the building was previously a sexual health clinic and a Masonic temple? Then head up to the mezzanine of this dimly lit hipster bar for some of the best burgers and fried chicken in town. (6 Mary St; mains $14; 4pm-midnight Mon-Sat, noon-10pm Sun; Newtown)

Black Star Pastry — Bakery $
Wise folks follow the black star to pay homage to excellent coffee, a large selection of sweet things and a few very good savoury things (gourmet pies and the like). There are only a couple of tables; it's more a snack-and-run or picnic-in-the-park kind of place. (www.blackstarpastry.com.au; 277 Australia St; mains $7-10; 7am-5pm; Newtown)

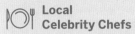

Local Celebrity Chefs

Bill Granger
Lifestyle chef and cookbook author whose food and style are thought by many to be quintessentially Sydney. Dine at his eponymous **bills** (Map p62; www.bills.com.au; 433 Liverpool St; mains $14-25; 7.30am-2.30pm; Kings Cross).

Luke Nguyen
Presents his own television programs (*Luke Nguyen's Vietnam, The Songs of Sapa, Luke Nguyen's Greater Mekong*), has written a number of cookbooks and plates up at **Red Lantern on Riley** (Map p62; 02-9698 4355; www.redlantern.com.au; 60 Riley St; mains $36-39; noon-3pm Thu & Fri, 6-10pm daily; Museum).

Matt Moran
Boasting **Aria** (Map p56; 02-9240 2255; www.ariarestaurant.com; 1 Macquarie St; lunch & pre-theatre mains $46, 2-/3-/4-course dinner $105/130/155; noon-2.30pm Mon-Fri, 5.30-11pm daily; Circular Quay), **Chiswick Restaurant** (p74) and **Opera Bar** (p75), Matt is known to millions of Australians through regular appearances on *MasterChef Australia*. His portrait hangs in the National Portrait Gallery in Canberra.

Neil Perry
The city's original rock-star chef (with ponytail to match) has a long list of cookbooks and TV appearances. He heads up **Rockpool Bar & Grill** (Map p56; 02-8078 1900; www.rockpool.com; 66 Hunter St; mains $26-115; noon-3pm Mon-Fri, 6-11pm Mon-Sat; Martin Place), **Rockpool** (Map p56; 02-9252 1888; www.rockpool.com; 11 Bridge St; lunch mains $35-55, 9-/10-course dinner $145/165; noon-3pm Mon-Fri, 6-11pm Mon-Sat, Circular Quay) and **Spice Temple** (Map p56; 02-8078 1888; www.rockpool.com; 10 Bligh St; dishes $14-45; noon-3pm Mon-Fri, 6-10.30pm Mon-Sat; Martin Place).

★ **Top Five Dining**

Quay (p70)

Tetsuya's (p71)

Mr Wong (p70)

Ester (below)

Bourke Street Bakery (below)

From left: Classic Australian meat pie; cheese tasting at the Rocks Markets; Archibald Fountain, Hyde Park (p57)

Ester   Modern Australian $$

Ester breaks the trend for hip new eateries by accepting bookings, but in other respects it exemplifies Sydney's contemporary dining scene: informal but not sloppy; innovative without being overly gimmicky; hip, but never try-hard. Influences straddle contin-ents and dishes are made to be shared. If humanly possible, make room for dessert. (☏02-8068 8279; www.ester-restaurant.com.au; 46 Meagher St; mains $26-36; ☺noon-5pm Sun, noon-3pm Fri, 6pm-late Tue-Sat; ☒Redfern)

🍴 Surry Hills & Darlinghurst

Messina   Ice Cream $

Join the queues of people who look like they never eat ice cream at the counter of Sydney's most popular gelato shop. Clearly even the beautiful people can't resist quirky flavours such as figs in Marsala and salted caramel. The attached dessert bar serves sundaes. (Map p62; www.gelatomessina.com; 241 Victoria St; 2 scoops $6; ☺noon-11pm; ☒Kings Cross)

Bourke Street Bakery   Bakery $

Queuing outside this teensy bakery is an essential Surry Hills experience. It sells a tempting selection of pastries, cakes, bread and sandwiches, along with sausage rolls which are near legendary in these parts. There are a few tables inside but on a fine day you're better off on the street. (www.bourkestreetbakery.com.au; 633 Bourke St; items $5-14; ☺8am-5pm; ☒Central)

Porteño   Argentine $$

Lamb and suckling pig are spit-roasted for eight hours before the doors even open at this acclaimed and extremely hip restaurant, devoted to the robust meatiness of Argentine cuisine. Arrive early to avoid a lengthy wait, although there's no hardship in hanging out upstairs at the very cool Gardel's Bar until a table comes free. (☏02-8399 1440; www.porteno.com.au; 358 Cleveland St; sharing plates $15-48; ☺6pm-midnight Tue-Sat; ☒Central)

Devon   Cafe $$

If it's boring old bacon and eggs you're after, look elsewhere. Devon shamelessly plunders the cuisines of 'multicultural

KIMBERLEY COOLE / GETTY IMAGES ©

Australia' to deliver an extremely creative menu, with plenty of twists on old favourites. There's even an 'Ogre's Happy Meal' (ox-tongue, apparently – we weren't tempted). (www.devoncafe.com.au; 76 Devonshire St; mains $14-21; ☺7am-4.30pm daily, 6-10pm Thu-Sat)

Devonshire   Modern European $$$

It's a long way from a two-Michelin-starred Mayfair restaurant to grungy old Devonshire St for chef Jeremy Bentley, although cuisinewise, perhaps not as far as you'd think. His food is simply extraordinary – complex, precisely presented and full of flavour. And while there's white linen on the tables, the atmosphere isn't the least bit starchy. (☎02-9698 9427; www.the devonshire.com.au; 204 Devonshire St; mains $37; ☺noon-2.30pm Fri, 6-10pm Tue-Sat; ⊠Central)

🍴 Kings Cross, Potts Point & Woolloomooloo

Room 10   Cafe $

If you're wearing a flat cap, sprouting a beard and obsessed by coffee, chances are you'll recognise this tiny room as your spiritual home in the Cross. The food's limited to sandwiches, salads and such – tasty and uncomplicated. (Map p62; 10 Llankelly Pl; mains $9-14; ☺7am-4pm; ⊠Kings Cross)

Ms G's   Asian $$

Offering a cheeky, irreverent take on Asian cooking (hence the name – geddit?), Ms G's is nothing if not an experience. It can be loud, frantic and painfully hip, but the adventurous combinations of pan-Asian and European flavours have certainly got Sydney talking. (Map p62; ☎02-9240 3000; www.merivale.com/msgs; 155 Victoria St; mains $25-38; ☺1-9pm Sun, noon-3pm Fri, 6-11pm Mon-Sat; ⊠Kings Cross)

Fratelli Paradiso   Italian $$

This underlit trattoria has them queuing at the door (especially on weekends). The intimate room showcases seasonal Italian dishes cooked with Mediterranean zing. Lots of busy black-clad waiters, lots of Italian chatter, lots of oversized sunglasses. No bookings. (Map p62; www.fratelliparadiso. com; 12-16 Challis Ave; breakfast $12-14, mains $22-31; ☺7am-11pm; ⊠Kings Cross)

⊗ Paddington & Woollahra

Vincent French $$

The glassed-in terrace of the Hughenden Hotel is the charmingly informal setting for this zippy bistro. The menu is excellent, revelling in classics such as cheesy soufflés, rich terrines, steak frites topped with butter, and fall-apart slow-roasted lamb shoulder. (☎02-8039 1500; www.vincent french.com.au; 14 Queen St; mains $26-36; ⊙noon-3pm Fri-Sun, 6-11pm Tue-Sun; ☐380)

Four in Hand Modern Australian $$$

You can't go far in Paddington without tripping over a beautiful old pub with amazing food. This is the best of them, famous for its slow-cooked and nose-to-tail meat dishes, although it also offers fabulously fresh seafood dishes and a delectable array of desserts. The bar menu (mains $19 to $29) is a more affordable option. (☎02-9362 1999; www.fourinhand.com.au; 105 Sutherland St; mains $34-42; ⊙noon-2.30pm & 6pm-late Tue-Sun; ☐Edgecliff)

Chiswick Restaurant Modern Australian $$$

There may be a celebrity at centre stage (TV regular Matt Moran) but the real star of this show is the pretty kitchen garden, which wraps around the dining room and dictates what's on the menu. Meat from the Moran family farm and local seafood feature prominently too. (☎02-8388 8633; www. chiswickrestaurant.com.au; 65 Ocean St; mains $31-38; ⊙noon-2.30pm & 6-10pm; ☐389)

Eastern Beaches

Three Blue Ducks Cafe $$

These ducks are a fair waddle from the water, but that doesn't stop queues forming outside the graffiti-covered walls for weekend breakfasts. The adventurous chefs have a strong commitment to using local, organic and fair-trade food whenever possible. (☎02-9389 0010; www.threeblueducks.com; 141-143 Macpherson St; breakfast $16-25, lunch $24-31, dinner $28-32; ⊙7am-2.30pm Sun-Tue, 7am-2.30pm & 6-11pm Wed-Sat; ☐378) ☑

Postcards at the Rocks Markets

ANDREW WATSON / GETTY IMAGES ©

A Tavola
Italian $$

Carrying on the tradition of its Darlinghurst sister, Bondi's A Tavola gathers around a big communal marble table where, before the doors open, the pasta-making action happens. Expect robust flavours, sexy waiters and delicious homemade pasta. (02-9130 1246; www.atavola.com.au; 75 Hall St; mains $22-38; noon-3pm Wed-Sun, 5.30-11pm daily)

Icebergs Dining Room
Italian $$$

Poised above the famous Icebergs swimming pool, Icebergs' views sweep across the Bondi Beach arc to the sea. Inside, bow-tied waiters deliver fresh, sustainably sourced seafood and steaks cooked with elan. To limit the hip-pocket impact, call in at lunchtime for a pasta and salad. (02-9365 9000; www.idrb.com; 1 Notts Ave; mains $40-48; noon-3pm & 6.30-11pm Tue-Sun; 380)

DRINKING & NIGHTLIFE

Circular Quay & the Rocks

Opera Bar
Bar

With the Opera House on one side and the Harbour Bridge on the other, this perfectly positioned terrace manages a very Sydney marriage of the laid-back and the sophisticated. A recent takeover by celebrity chef Matt Moran has shifted the food up a notch. There's live music or DJs most nights. (Map p56; www.operabar.com.au; lower concourse, Sydney Opera House; 11.30am-midnight Mon-Fri, 9am-midnight Sat & Sun; Circular Quay)

Lord Nelson Brewery Hotel
Pub, Brewery

Built in 1836 and converted into a pub in 1841, this atmospheric sandstone boozer is one of three claiming to be Sydney's oldest (all using slightly different criteria). The onsite brewery cooks up its own natural ales (try the Old Admiral). (Map p56; 02-9251 4044; 19 Kent St; 11am-11pm; Circular Quay)

Fortune of War
Pub

This 1828 drinking den retains much of its original charm and, by the looks of things, some of the original punters, too. There's

Swanky Downtown Bars

Ivy (Map p56; 02-9254 8100; www.merivale.com/ivy; Level 1, 330 George St; noon-late Mon-Fri, 6.30pm-late Sat; Wynyard) Hidden down a lane off George St, Ivy is a scarily fashionable complex of bars, restaurants, discreet lounges... even a swimming pool. It's also Sydney's most hyped venue; expect lengthy queues of suburban kids teetering on unfeasibly high heels, waiting to shed up to $40 on a Saturday for entry to Sydney's hottest club night, Pacha.

Marble Bar (Map p56; www.marblebarsydney.com.au; basement, 488 George St; 4pm-midnight Sun-Thu, to 2am Fri & Sat; Town Hall) Built for a staggering £32,000 in 1893 as part of the Adams Hotel on Pitt St, this ornate underground bar is one of the best places in town for putting on the ritz (even if this is the Hilton). Musos play anything from jazz to funk, Wednesday to Saturday.

O Bar (Map p56; www.obardining.com.au; Level 47, Australia Sq, 264 George St; 5pm-late; Wynyard) At around $20, the cocktails at this 47th-floor revolving bar aren't cheap, but they're still cheaper than admission to Sydney Tower – and it's considerably more glamorous. The views are truly wonderful.

Blu Bar on 36 (Map p56; www.shangri-la.com; Level 36, 176 Cumberland St; 5pm-midnight; Circular Quay) The drinks may be pricey, but it's well worth heading up to the top of the Shangri-La hotel for the views. The dress code is officially 'smart casual', but err on the side of smart if you can't handle rejection.

live music on Thursday, Friday and Saturday nights and on weekend afternoons. (Map p56; www.fortuneofwar.com.au; 137 George St; 9am-midnight Sun-Thu, to 3am Fri & Sat; Circular Quay)

City Centre

Baxter Inn   Bar

Yes, it really is down that dark lane and
through that unmarked door (it's easier to
find if there's a queue; otherwise look for
the bouncer lurking nearby). Whisky's the
main poison and the friendly bar staff really
know their stuff. (Map p56; www.thebaxterinn.
com; 152-156 Clarence St; ⊙4pm-1am Mon-Sat;
☒Town Hall)

Rook   Cocktail Bar

Seemingly designed for one-time grung-
sters turned stockbrokers, this covered
rooftop bar has an artfully dishevelled
look and serves a mean cocktail. It's not
cheap though. Is spending $50 on lobster
thermidor and then following it up with a
deep-fried Mars Bar the ultimate ironic
statement? (Map p56; www.therook.com.au;
Level 7, 56-58 York St; ⊙noon-midnight Mon-Fri,
4pm to midnight Sat; ☒St James)

Good God Small Club   Bar, Club

In a defunct underground taverna near
Chinatown, Good God's rear dancetaria
hosts everything from live indie bands
to Jamaican reggae, '50s soul, rockabilly
and tropical house music. Its success lies
in the focus on great music rather than
glamorous surrounds. (www.goodgod
goodgod.com; 55 Liverpool St; front bar free,
club varies; ⊙5-11pm Wed, to 1am Thu, to 3am
Fri & Sat; ☒Town Hall)

Slip Inn &
Chinese Laundry   Pub, Club

Slip in to this warren of moody rooms
on the edge of Darling Harbour and
bump hips with the kids. There are bars,
pool tables, a beer garden and Mexican
food, courtesy of El Loco. On Friday and
Saturday nights the bass cranks up at the
attached Chinese Laundry nightclub. (Map
p56; www.merivale.com.au/chineselaundry; 111
Sussex St; club $20-30; ⊙11am-late Mon-Fri,
4pm-late Sat; ☒Wynyard)

Spice Cellar   Bar, Club

Saunter down to this stylish underground
bunker for cocktails in the lounge bar. The
attached club has one of Sydney's hottest
little dance floors, which despite its size
attracts the occasional turntable legend to
its decks. (Map p56; www.thespicecellar.com.au;
58 Elizabeth St; ⊙bar 4pm-late Wed-Fri, 7pm-late
Sat, club 9pm-late Thu-Sun; ☒Martin Place)

Inner West

Earl's Juke Joint   Bar

The current it-bar of the minute, swinging Earl's serves craft beers and killer
cocktails to the Newtown hiperati. (407
King St; ⊙4pm-midnight Mon-Sat, to 10pm Sun;
☒Newtown)

Marlborough Hotel   Pub, Club

One of many great old art deco pubs in
Newtown, the Marly has a front sports bar
with live bands on weekends and a shady
beer garden. Head upstairs for soul food
and rockabilly bands at Miss Peaches, or
downstairs for all sorts of kooky happenings at the Tokyo Sing Song nightclub.
(☎02-9519 1222; www.marlboroughhotel.com.
au; 145 King St; ⊙10am-4am Mon-Sat, noon-
midnight Sun; ☒Macdonaldtown)

Surry Hills & Darlinghurst

Wild Rover   Bar

Look for the old sign on the window reading
'Gestetner's Surry Hills Shirt Warehouse'
and enter this supremely cool brick-lined
speakeasy, where a big range of craft
beer is served in chrome steins. Live
bands play upstairs a couple of nights a
week. (www.thewildrover.com.au; 75 Campbell
St; ⊙4pm-midnight Mon-Sat, to 10pm Sun;
☒Central)

Cliff Dive   Cocktail Bar

Head down the stairs and throw yourself
into a world of rough-hewn stone walls,
glowing tropical fish lanterns, Polynesian
knick-knacks and cocktails served in
tiki glasses. There are plenty of nooks to
hunker down in after you've worked up a
tropical sweat on the dance floor. (Map p62;
www.thecliffdive.com.au; basement, 16 Oxford Sq;
⊙6pm-3am Thu-Sat; ☒Museum)

Shady Pines Saloon   Bar

With no sign or street number on the door and entry via a shady back lane (look for the white door before Bikram Yoga on Foley St), this subterranean honky-tonk bar caters to the urban boho. Sip whisky and rye with the good ole hipster boys amid Western memorabilia and taxidermy. (Map p62; www.shadypinessaloon.com; Shop 4, 256 Crown St; ☺4pm-midnight; ⓡMuseum)

Hello Sailor   Cocktail Bar

Entered from lanelike Foley St, this 'seafood shack and cocktail bar' gets filled to the gills on the weekends. A diverse but hip crowd drops anchor until the wee hours, partying under maritime flags, navigation maps and sepia pictures of tall ships. (Map p62; www.hellosailor.com.au; 96 Oxford St; ☺5pm-3am Tue-Sun; 🛜; ⓡMuseum)

Green Park Hotel   Pub

The ever-rockin' Green Park has pool tables, rolled-arm leather couches, a beer garden with funky Dr Seuss–inspired lighting, and a huge tiled central bar teeming with travellers, gay guys and pierced locals.

(Map p62; www.greenparkhotel.com.au; 360 Victoria St; ☺11am-midnight Sun-Wed, to 2am Thu-Sat; ⓡKings Cross)

🚇 Kings Cross, Potts Point & Woolloomooloo

World Bar   Bar, Club

World Bar (a reformed bordello) is an unpretentious grungy club with three floors to lure in the backpackers and cheap drinks to loosen things up. DJs play indie, hip hop, power pop and house nightly. There are live bands on Fridays, but Wednesday (The Wall) and Saturday (Cakes) are the big nights. (Map p62; ☎02-9357 7700; www.theworldbar.com; 24 Bayswater Rd; ☺3pm-3am; ⓡKings Cross)

Kings Cross Hotel   Pub, Club

With five floors above ground and one below, this grand old pub is a hive of boozy entertainment which positively swarms on weekends. Head up to the roof bar for awesome city views, or drop by the 2nd-floor band room for a blast of live music. (Map p62; www.kingscrosshotel.com.au; 244-248 William St; ☺noon-1am Sun-Thu, to 3am Fri & Sat; ⓡKings Cross)

Chinese Garden of Friendship (p59)

RICHARD CUMMINS / GETTY IMAGES ©

Manly

Manly Wharf Hotel Pub
Harking back to 1950s design (bamboo and stone feature walls etc), this waterfront pub is perfect for sunny afternoon beers. Tuck away a few schooners after a hard day in the surf, then pour yourself onto the ferry. Sports games draw a crowd and DJs liven up Sunday afternoons. There's good pub food, too, with specials throughout the week. (www.manlywharfhotel. com.au; Manly Wharf; ⏱11.30am-midnight; 🚢Manly)

⊗ ENTERTAINMENT

Sydney
Opera House Performing Arts
The glamorous jewel at the heart of Australian performance, Sydney's famous Opera House has five main stages. Opera may have star billing, but theatre, comedy, music and dance are all performed here. (Map p56; 📞02-9250 7777; www.sydneyopera house.com; Bennelong Point; 🚆Circular Quay)

Moonlight Cinema Cinema
Take a picnic and join the bats under the stars in magnificent Centennial Park; enter via the Woollahra Gate on Oxford St. A mix of new-release blockbuster, art-house and classic films is screened. (www.moonlight. com.au; Belvedere Amphitheatre, cnr Loch & Broome Aves; adult/child $19/15; ⏱sunset Dec-Mar; 🚆Bondi Junction)

City Recital Hall Classical Music
Based on the classic configuration of the 19th-century European concert hall, this custom-built 1200-seat venue boasts near-perfect acoustics. Catch top-flight companies such as Musica Viva, the Australian Brandenburg Orchestra and the Australian Chamber Orchestra here. (Map p56; 📞02-8256 2222; www.cityrecitalhall. com; 2 Angel Pl; ⏱box office 9am-5pm Mon-Fri; 🚆Martin Place)

Basement Live Music
Once solely a jazz venue, the Basement now hosts international and local musicians working in many disciplines and

Gay & Lesbian Mardi Gras (p27)

MICHAEL TAYLOR / GETTY IMAGES ©

genres. Dinner-and-show tickets net you a table by the stage, guaranteeing a better view than the standing-only area by the bar. (Map p56; ☏ 02-9251 2797; www.the basement.com.au; 7 Macquarie Pl; admission $8-60; ⊠ Circular Quay)

Oxford Art Factory   Live Music
Indie kids party against an arty backdrop at this two-room multipurpose venue modelled on Andy Warhol's NYC creative base. There's a gallery, a bar and a performance space that often hosts international acts and DJs. Check the website for what's on. (Map p62; www.oxfordartfactory.com; 38-46 Oxford St; ⊠ Museum)

Sydney Theatre Company   Theatre
Established in 1978, the STC is Sydney theatre's top dog and has played an important part in the careers of many famous Australian actors (especially Cate Blanchett, who was co-artistic director from 2008 to 2013). Tours of the company's Wharf and Roslyn Packer theatres are held at 10.30am every Tuesday ($10). Performances are also staged at the Opera House. (Map p56; STC; ☏ 02-9250 1777; www. sydneytheatre.com.au; Pier 4/5, 15 Hickson Rd; ⊙ box office 9am-8.30pm Mon-Fri, 11am-8.30pm Sat, 2hr before show Sun; ⊠ Wynyard)

Belvoir   Theatre
In a quiet corner of Surry Hills, this intimate venue is the home of an often experimental and consistently excellent theatre company. Shows sometimes feature big stars. (☏ 02-9699 3444; www.belvoir.com.au; 25 Belvoir St; ⊠ Central)

Capitol Theatre   Theatre
Lavishly restored, this large city theatre is home to long-running musicals *(Wicked, Les Misérables, Matilda)* and the occasional ballet or big-name concert. (☏ 1300 558 878; www.capitoltheatre.com.au; 13 Campbell St; ⊠ Central)

State Theatre   Theatre
The beautiful 2000-seat State Theatre is a lavish, gilt-ridden, chandelier-dangling

⚥ LGBTI
♯♯ Sydney

Gay and lesbian culture forms a vocal and vital part of Sydney's social fabric. Oxford St, Darlinghurst, has long been the locus of the gay scene and every year on the first Saturday in March, tens of thousands of spectators line the street for the famous Sydney Gay & Lesbian Mardi Gras parade (www. mardigras.org.au).

Free gay media includes *SX* (www. gaynewsnetwork.com.au), the *Star Observer* (www.starobserver.com.au) and *Lesbians on the Loose* (www.lotl.com).

Most hotels, restaurants and bars in Darlinghurst, Surry Hills and Newtown are very gay-friendly. To party, check out the following:

Midnight Shift (Map p62; ☏ 02-9358 3848; www.themidnightshift.com.au; 85 Oxford St; admission free-$10; ⊙ 4pm-late Thu-Sun; ⊠ Museum) The grand dame of the Oxford St gay scene, known for its lavish drag productions.

Arq (Map p62; www.arqsydney.com.au; 16 Flinders St; ⊙ 9pm-5am Thu & Sun, 9pm-noon Fri & Sat; ⊠ Museum) This flash megaclub has a cocktail bar, a recovery room and two dance floors with high-energy house, drag shows and a hyperactive smoke machine.

Imperial Hotel (www.theimperialhotel. com.au; 35 Erskineville Rd; admission free-$15; ⊙ 3pm-midnight Sun-Thu, to 5am Fri & Sat; ⊠ Erskineville) The art deco Imperial is legendary as the setting for *The Adventures of Priscilla, Queen of the Desert*.

palace. It hosts the Sydney Film Festival, concerts, comedy, opera, musicals and the odd celebrity chef. (Map p56; ☏ 02-9373 6655; www.statetheatre.com.au; 49 Market St; ⊠ St James)

Online Resources

Destination NSW (www.sydney.com) Official visitor guide.

City of Sydney (www.cityofsydney.nsw. gov.au) Visitor information.

Sydney Morning Herald (www.smh. com.au) Daily newspaper

Lonely Planet (www.lonelyplanet.com/ sydney) Destination information.

Above: Flying fox, Royal Botanic Garden (p54)
EWEN CHARLTON / GETTY IMAGES ©

ℹ INFORMATION

MEDICAL SERVICES
Kings Cross Clinic (☏02-9358 3066; www. kingscrossclinic.com.au; 13 Springfield Ave; ⊙9am-6pm Mon-Fri, 10am-1pm Sat; ⋒Kings Cross) General and travel-related medical services.

St Vincent's Hospital (☏02-8382 1111; www. stvincents.com.au; 390 Victoria St; ⋒Kings Cross)

Sydney Hospital (☏02-9382 7111; www.seslhd. health.nsw.gov.au/SHSEH; 8 Macquarie St; ⋒Martin Place)

TOURIST INFORMATION
City Host Information Kiosk (www.cityof sydney.nsw.gov.au; cnr Pitt & Alfred Sts; ⊙9am-5pm; ⋒Circular Quay)

Hello Manly (☏02-9976 1430; www.hellomanly. com.au; Manly Wharf; ⊙9am-5pm; ⛴Manly) This helpful visitor centre, just outside the ferry wharf and alongside the bus interchange, has free pamphlets covering the Manly Scenic Walkway and other Manly attractions, plus loads of local bus information.

Sydney Visitor Centre (☏02-8273 0000; www.bestof.com.au; Palm Grove, behind IMAX; ⊙9.30am-5.30pm; ⋒Town Hall) Has a wide range of brochures, and staff can book accommodation, tours and attractions.

ℹ GETTING THERE & AWAY

AIR
Sydney Airport (☏02-9667 9111; www. sydneyairport.com.au; Airport Dr, Mascot) Has separate international (T1) and domestic (T2 and T3) terminals, 4km apart on either side of the runway.

BUS
Sydney Coach Terminal (☏02-9281 9366; www.sydneycoachterminal.com.au; Eddy Ave; ⊙6am-6pm; ⋒Central) All private interstate and regional bus travellers arrive at this terminal in front of Central Station.

TRAIN
NSW TrainLink (☏13 22 32; www.nswtrainlink. info) Runs services connecting Sydney with regional and interstate destinations. The major train hub is Central Station.

ℹ GETTING AROUND

TO/FROM THE AIRPORT
One of the easiest ways to get to and from the airport is with a shuttle company – most hotels and hostels will be able to organise this for you.

Airport Link (www.airportlink.com.au; adult/ child $18/14; ⊙4.30am-12.30am) is a strange service: it's a normal commuter train line, but you pay through the nose to use the airport stations (punters going to Wolli Creek, the next stop *beyond* the airport, pay $4). The trip from Central Station takes a mere 10 minutes or so.

Taxi fares from the airport are approximately $45 to $55 to the city centre, $55 to $65 to North Sydney and $90 to $100 to Manly.

PUBLIC TRANSPORT

Transport NSW (📞 131 500; www.transport nsw.info) Coordinates all of the state-run bus, ferry, train and light-rail services. You'll find a useful journey planner on its website.

BUS

Sydney Buses (📞 131 500; www.sydneybuses. info) Has an extensive network, operating from around 5am to midnight when less frequent NightRide services commence. You can buy a ticket from the driver on most services ($2.40 to $4.70) but you'll need an Opal card or prepaid paper ticket (available at newsagents) for prepay-only services.

FERRY

Most state-run ferries operate between 6am and midnight. The standard fare for most destinations is $6.20; boats to Manly cost $7.60.

Privately-owned **Manly Fast Ferry** (📞 02-9583 1199; www.manlyfastferry.com.au; adult/child $9/6) and **Sydney Fast Ferries** (📞 02-9818 6000; www.sydneyfastferries.com.au; adult/child $9.75/7.50; 📞) both have boats that blast from Circular Quay to Manly in 18 minutes.

LIGHT RAIL

Trams run between Central Station and Dulwich Hill, stopping in Chinatown, Darling Harbour, the Star casino and Glebe en route. Tickets cost $3.80 for a short journey and $4.80 for a longer one, and can be purchased from the conductor.

TRAIN

Sydney has a large suburban railway web with relatively frequent services, although there are no trains to the eastern or northern beaches. Trains run from around 5am to 1pm. A short inner-city one-way trip costs $4. Purchase your ticket in advance from an automated machine or a counter at the bigger stations.

CAR & MOTORCYCLE

Cars are good for day trips out of town and to some of the beaches, but driving one in the inner city is like having an anchor around your neck. Traffic is heavy and parking is both elusive and very expensive (expect upwards of $30 per day).

Integrated Tickets & Passes

Although you can still buy individual tickets for most services, a smart-card system called **Opal** (www.opal.com.au) also operates. The card can be obtained (for free) and loaded with credit at numerous newsagencies and convenience stores across Sydney.

When commencing a journey you'll need to touch the card to an electronic reader, which are located at the train station gates, near the doors of buses and light-rail carriages, and at the ferry wharves. You then need to touch a reader when you complete your journey so that the system can deduct the correct fare.

Advantages include cheaper single journeys, daily charges capped at $15 ($2.50 on Sundays) and free travel after taking any eight journeys in a week (it resets itself every Monday). You can use the Opal card at the airport stations, but none of the bonuses apply.

Paper-based **MyMulti** passes can be purchased at ferry and train ticket offices and many newsagencies and convenience stores, but you're much better off getting an Opal card instead. For instance, the MyMulti Day Pass costs $24 as opposed to the $15 Opal cap.

ROAD TOLLS

There are hefty tolls on most of Sydney's motorways and major links (including the Harbour Bridge, Harbour Tunnel, Eastern Distributor, Cross City Tunnel and Lane Cove Tunnel). For information about the system, go to www.sydneymotorways.com.

The tolling system is electronic, meaning that it's up to you to organise an electronic tag or visitors' pass through any of the following websites:

Roam (www.roam.com.au)

Roam Express (www.roamexpress.com.au)

E-Way (www.tollpay.com.au)

Service NSW (www.myrta.com)

Note that most car-hire companies now supply eTags.

TAXI

Metered taxis are easy to flag down in the central city and inner suburbs, except for at changeover times (3pm and 3am). Fares are regulated, so all companies charge the same. Flagfall is $3.50, with a $2.50 'night owl surcharge' after 10pm on a Friday and Saturday until 6am the following morning. The fare thereafter is $2.14 per kilometre, with an additional surcharge of 20% between 10pm and 6am nightly. There's also a $2.40 fee for bookings.

Legion Cabs (☎ 13 14 51; www.legioncabs.com.au)

Premier Cabs (☎ 13 10 17; www.premiercabs.com.au)

Taxis Combined (☎ 133 300; www.taxis combined.com.au)

WATER TAXI

Water taxis are a fast way to shunt around the harbour. Companies will quote on any pick-up point within the harbour and the river, including private jetties, islands and other boats.

Aussie Water Taxis (☎ 02-9211 7730; www.aussiewatertaxis.com; Cockle Bay Wharf) The smallest seats 16 passengers and can be rented per hour or point to point.

H2O Maxi Taxis (☎ 1300 420 829; www.h2owatertaxis.com.au) Smallest seats 21 people. Harbour Islands a speciality: Fort Denison/Cockatoo Island/Shark Island costs $110/125/150 for up to 10 people from Circular Quay. Has a handy quote calculator on its website.

Water Taxis Combined (☎ 02-9555 8888; www.watertaxis.com.au) Fares based on up to four passengers: Circular Quay to Watsons Bay $110; to Rose Bay $110; to Woolloomooloo $70. Also offers harbour cruise packages.

Yellow Water Taxis (☎ 02-9299 0199; www.yellowwatertaxis.com.au) Set price for up to four passengers, then $10 per person for additional people. Sample fares from King St Wharf: Circular Quay and Fort Denison $83; Taronga Zoo $95; Cockatoo Island and Shark Island $121; Watsons Bay $127.

Manly Beach (p63)

MANFRED GOTTSCHALK / GETTY IMAGES ©

Where to Stay

Sydney offers both a huge quantity and variety of accommodation, with solid options in every price range. Even so, the supply shrivels up under the summer sun, particularly around weekends and big events, so be sure to book ahead.

Neighbourhood	Atmosphere
Circular Quay & the Rocks	Big-ticket sights; vibrant nightlife; top hotels and restaurants. Tourist central, expensive, few affordable eateries.
Sydney Harbour	Everywhere is a pleasant ferry journey from town. Can be isolated; difficult to access nightlife.
City Centre & Haymarket	Good transport links; lots of sights, bars, eateries, hostels and hotels. Can be noisy and, in parts, ugly.
Darling Harbour & Pyrmont	Plenty to see and do; lively nightlife. Soulless; few affordable restaurants.
Glebe & Newtown	Bohemian; great coffee and shops; priced for locals. Few sights or hotels; getting to beaches requires effort.
Surry Hills & Darlinghurst	Sydney's hippest eating and drinking precinct; heart of LGBTI scene. Few actual sights; gritty in parts.
Bondi to Coogee	Sand, surf and sexy bods. No trains and a slow bus ride to the city.
Manly	Beautiful beaches; community feel. Not much to do if the weather's bad

YURY PROKOPENKO / GETTY IMAGES ©

Parliament House (p90)

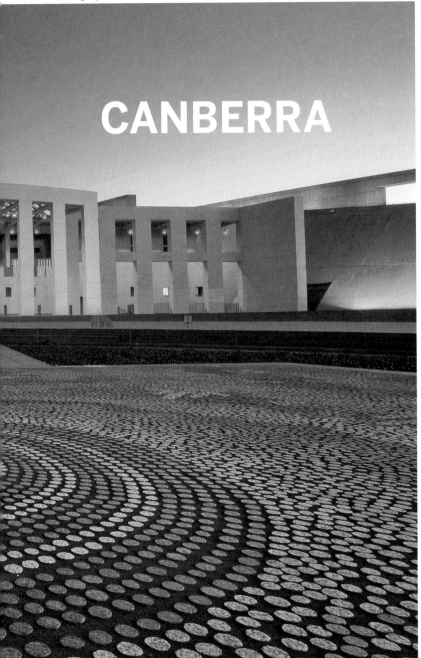

CANBERRA

Canberra

Designed by visionary American architect Walter Burley Griffin, who was assisted by his wife Marion Mahony Griffin, Canberra features expansive open spaces, aesthetics influenced by the 19th-century arts and crafts movement and a seamless alignment of built and natural elements.

It's a city that's dominated by politics, and the need to feed and entertain all those politicos and staffers; when Parliament isn't sitting, it can become strangely quiet. Unfortunately, Canberra is also totally geared towards the car – it's difficult to explore by public transport and almost impossible to do so on foot. You really need wheels (two or four) to do justice to the city's sprawling selection of sights, and the scenic hinterland, which also warrants exploration, is naturally even more remote.

❶ In This Section

From left: *Pear - version number 2* by George Baldessin, National Gallery of Australia (p88); tulips at Floriade
FROM LEFT: SIMON FOALE / GETTY IMAGES ©; TRAVEL INK / GETTY IMAGES ©

🎊 What's On

National Multicultural Festival (www.multiculturalfestival.com.au; ⏰Feb) Three days of art, culture and food.

Canberra Festival (www.events.act.gov.au; ⏰Mar) Canberra's birthday party.

National Folk Festival (www.folkfestival.asn.au; ⏰Easter) One of Australia's largest folk festivals.

Floriade (www.floriadeaustralia.com; ⏰Sep-Oct) Celebrating the city's spectacular spring flowers.

[Map of Canberra]

Bruce
Lyneham
Dickson   Hackett
Belconnen Way
O'Connor
Black
Mountain
Reserve
Turner   Ainslie
Northbourne Ave
William
Hovell Dr
Australian National
Botanic Gardens
National
Arboretum
Parkes Way
Australian
War Memorial
Fairbairn Ave
Majura Rd
National
Museum of
Australia
Parkes Way
Campbell
Lake
Burley
Griffin
Weston
Park
Royal
Canberra
Golf Course
National Gallery
of Australia
Morshead Dr
**Canberra
Airport**
Molonglo River
Yarralumla
Adelaide Ave
Parliament
House
Kingston
Pialligo Ave
Cotter Rd
Deakin
Manuka
Canberra
Monaro Hwy
Molonglo River
Fyshwick
Curtin
Yarra Glen
Griffith
Canberra Ave
Hughes
Red Hill

Canberra Map (p92)

➡ Arriving in Canberra

Australia's capital is well connected to the rest of the country by plane. It's less than an hour's flight from Sydney, and there are numerous flights a day. The airport is around 10 minutes' drive from the city centre.

The drive from Sydney is a little over three hours; or around five hours by bus.

From left: National Arboretum (p90); National Museum of Australia (p88)

FROM LEFT: KOKKAI NG / GETTY IMAGES ©; ANDREW WATSON / GETTY IMAGES ©

➡ Canberra in Two Days

Begin your day at the **National Gallery of Australia** (p88) or the **National Portrait Gallery** (p89). In the afternoon, attend Question Time at **Parliament House** (p90), then start your own debate over dinner at **Temporada** (p94). Next day, fill up on pastries at **Silo** (p95) then visit the **National Museum of Australia** (p88). Later, explore the **Australian National Botanic Gardens** (p91), and dine at **Ottoman** (p95) with the city's movers and shakers.

National Museum of Australia

ANDREW WATSON / GETTY IMAGES ©

National Museums & Galleries

You don't have to go far in Canberra to find a world-class museum or gallery. The city features some of Australia's best collections of art and artefacts, so it's worth putting at least one or two national institutions on your itinerary.

Great For...

☑ Don't Miss

Watch the National Museum's introductory film, shown in the small rotating Circa Theatre.

National Museum of Australia   Museum

Housed in an acclaimed postmodern building perched on Lake Burley Griffin, the National Museum is the country's foremost social history museum, exploring 50,000 years of Indigenous and modern Australian life. Exhibits focus on environmental change, Indigenous culture, national Australian icons and much more. The museum is on the route of the Canberra City Explorer (p93). (☎ 02-6208 5000; www.nma.gov.au; Lawson Cres, Acton Peninsula; admission to permanent collection free, guided tours adult/child/family $10/5/25; ⊗ 9am-5pm) FREE

National Gallery of Australia   Gallery

Includes an extraordinary Aboriginal Memorial from Central Arnhem Land created for Australia's 1988 bicentenary. The work

Australian War Memorial

EYEOFPAUL / GETTY IMAGES ©

ℹ **Need to Know**

Many of Canberra's museums and galleries are free, but be prepared to pay for temporary or special exhibitions.

✕ **Take a Break**

A picnic in Commonwealth Park, outside the National Museum on the lake shore, is a lovely way to spend a sunny lunchtime.

★ **Top Tip**

Plan to be at the War Memorial for closing time to hear the haunting Last Post played to honour the fallen.

of 43 artists, this 'forest of souls' presents 200 hollow log coffins (one for every year of European settlement) and is part of an excellent collection of Aboriginal and Torres Strait Islander art. Also exhibited is Australian art from the colonial to contemporary period, and Australia's finest collection of Asian art. Notable Pacific art and standout European and American works complete an impressive collection. (📞02-6240 6502; www.nga.gov.au; Parkes Pl, Parkes; admission costs for special exhibitions; 🕙10am-5pm) FREE

National Portrait Gallery   Gallery

This gallery tells the story of Australia through its faces – from wax cameos of Aboriginal tribespeople to colonial portraits of the nation's founding families and contemporary works such as Howard Arkley's Day-Glo portrait of musician Nick Cave. There is a good cafe for post-exhibition coffee. (📞02-6102 7000; www.portrait.gov.au; King Edward Tce, Parkes; 🕙10am-5pm) FREE

Australian War Memorial   Museum

Canberra's most rewarding museum experience includes halls dedicated to WWI, WWII and conflicts from 1945 to the present day. A spectacular aircraft hall segues to sound-and-light shows staged in the massive Anzac Hall. Most exciting are *Striking by Night,* recreating a WWII night operation over Berlin (staged on the hour), and *Over the Front: The Great War in the Air* (at a quarter past the hour). Entry to the museum is via a Commemorative Courtyard with a roll of honour of the nation's war dead. Free guided tours leave from the main entrance's Orientation Gallery regularly. Alternatively, purchase the Self-Guided Tour leaflet with map ($5). (📞02-6243 4211; www.awm.gov.au; Treloar Cres, Campbell; 🕙10am-5pm) FREE

Questacon   Museum

This kid-friendly science centre has educational and fun interactive exhibits. Explore the physics of sport, athletics and fun parks, cause tsunamis, and take shelter from cyclones and earthquakes. Exciting science shows, presentations and puppet shows are all included. (📞02-6270 2800; www.questacon.edu.au; King Edward Tce, Parkes; adult/child $20.50/15; 🕙9am-5pm)

◉ SIGHTS

Parliament House   Notable Building

Opened in 1988, Australia's national parliament building is dug into Capital Hill and has a grass-covered roof topped by an 81m-high flagpole. The rooftop lawns encompass 23 hectares of gardens and provide superb 360-degree views. Underneath incorporates 17 courtyards, an entrance foyer, the Great Hall, the House of Representatives, the Senate and seemingly endless corridors. Visit on a free guided tour (30 minutes on sitting days, 45 minutes on non-sitting days); these leave at 9.30am, 11am, 1pm, 2pm and 3.30pm.

Visitors can also self-navigate and watch parliamentary proceedings from the public galleries. Tickets for Question Time (2pm on sitting days) in the House of Representatives are free but must be booked through the Sergeant at Arms; tickets aren't required for the Senate chamber. See the website for a calendar of sitting days. (☏02-6277 5399; www.aph.gov.au; ☉from 9am Mon & Tue, from 8.30am Wed & Thu sitting days, 9am-5pm non-sitting days) FREE

National Arboretum   Gardens, Viewpoint

Located on land previously impacted by bush fires, Canberra's National Arboretum is an ever-developing showcase of trees from around the world. It is still early days for many of the plantings, but it is still worth visiting for the arboretum's spectacular visitor centre, and for the excellent views it offers over the city. Regular guided tours are informative, and there is a brilliant adventure playground for kids. Catch bus 81 (weekdays) or bus 981 (weekends) from the Civic bus interchange. (www.national arboretum.act.gov.au; Forest Dr, off Tuggeranong Parkway; ☉6am-8.30pm) FREE

Museum of Australian Democracy   Museum

The seat of government from 1927 to 1988, this building offers visitors a whiff of bygone parliamentary activity. It's most meaningful for those who have studied Australian history or closely followed political high jinks in Canberra, but still rewarding for other visitors. Displays cover Australian prime ministers, the roots of

Reconciliation Place

ANDREW WATSON / GETTY IMAGES ©

global and local democracy, and the history of local protest movements. You can also visit the old Senate and House of Representative chambers, the parliamentary library and the prime minister's office. (☎02-6270 8222; www.moadoph.gov.au; Old Parliament House, 18 King George Tce, Parkes; adult/concession/family $2/1/5; ⊙9am-5pm)

Aboriginal Tent Embassy — Historic Site

The lawn in front of Old Parliament House is home to the Aboriginal Tent Embassy – an important site in the struggle for equality and representation for Indigenous Australians.

Lake Burley Griffin — Landmark

The 35km shore of this lake is home to most of the city's cultural institutions. It was filled by damming the Molonglo River in 1963 with the 33m-high Scrivener Dam, and was named after American architect Walter Burley Griffin, who won an international competition with his wife – and fellow architect – to design Australia's new capital city in 1911. Highlights include the **National Carillon** and the **Captain Cook Memorial Water Jet** (⊙10am-noon & 2-4pm, plus 7-9pm daylight-saving months).

Reconciliation Place — Park

On the shore of Lake Burley Griffin, the artwork of Reconciliation Pl represents the nation's commitment to the cause of reconciliation between Indigenous and non-Indigenous Australians.

National Film & Sound Archive — Museum

Set in a delightful art deco building, this archive preserves Australian moving-picture and sound recordings. There are also temporary exhibitions, talks and film screenings in the Arc Cinema (adult/concession $10/8). (☎02-6248 2000; www.nfsa.gov.au; McCoy Circuit, Acton; ⊙9am-5pm Mon-Fri) FREE

Australian National Botanic Gardens — Gardens

On Black Mountain's lower slopes, these 90-hectare gardens showcase Australian floral diversity. Self-guided trails include the Joseph Banks Walk, and there's a 90-minute return trail from near the eucalypt lawn leading into the garden's higher areas before continuing into the Black Mountain Nature Park and on to the summit. The visitor centre is the departure point for **free guided walks**, departing at 11am and 2pm. On weekends, the **Flora Explorer Tour** (adult/child $6/3; ⊙10.30am & 1.30pm Sat & Sun) is negotiated by bus. (☎02-6250 9540; www.anbg.gov.au; Clunies Ross St, Acton; ⊙8.30am-5pm Feb-Dec, 8.30am-5pm Mon-Fri, to 8pm Sat & Sun Jan, visitor centre 9.30am-4.30pm) FREE

National Library of Australia — Library

This library has accumulated over six million items since being established in 1901. Don't miss the Treasures Gallery, where artefacts such as Captain Cook's *Endeavour* journal and Captain Bligh's list of mutineers are among the regularly refreshed display – free 40-minute tours are held at 10.30am daily and at 11.30am on Monday, Wednesday and Friday. (☎02-6262 1111; www.nla.gov.au; Parkes Pl, Parkes; ⊙Treasures Gallery 10am-5pm, reading room 10am-8pm Mon-Thu, 10am-5pm Fri & Sat, 1.30-5pm Sun) FREE

National Capital Exhibition — Museum

Learn about the Indigenous peoples of the Canberra area and see copies of exquisite Burley Griffin drawings of the city at this modest museum near Regatta Point. (☎02-6272 2902; www.nationalcapital.gov.au; Barrine Dr, Commonwealth Park; ⊙9am-5pm Mon-Fri, 10am-4pm Sat & Sun) FREE

ACTIVITIES

Canberra has an extensive network of dedicated cycle paths. The Canberra & Region Visitors Centre (p97) stocks the *Lake Burley Griffin Cycle Routes* brochure and the *Walking & Cycling Map* published by Pedal Power ACT (www.pedalpower.org.au).

Canberra

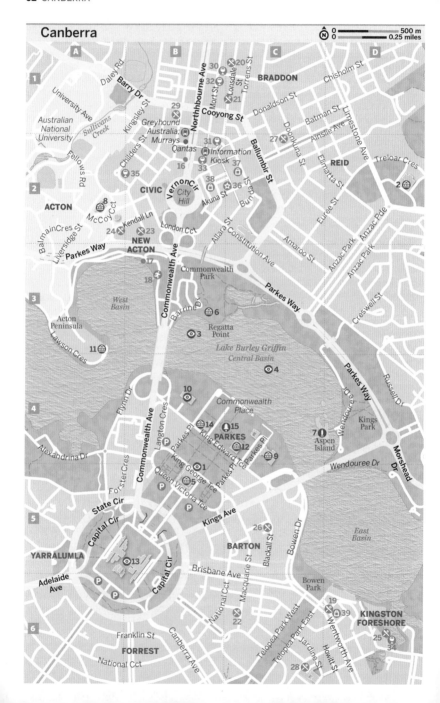

N 0 ———— 500 m
0 ———— 0.25 miles

BRADDON

Daley Rd
Barry Dr
University Ave
Australian National University
Sullivans Creek
Kingsley St
Childers St
Fellows Rd
Northbourne Ave
Cooyong St
Mort St
Lonsdale St
Torrens St
Chisholm St
Donaldson St
Batman St
Doonkuna St
Ainslie Ave
Limestone Ave
Treloar Cres

30
20
32
21
29
31
27

CIVIC
Greyhound Australia; Murrays
Qantas
16
Information Kiosk
33
37
38
36
35
VernonCir
City Hill
Akuna St
Ballumbir St
REID
Elmatta St
Euree St
Anzac Park
Anzac Pde
Anzac Park

ACTON
8
McCoy Cct
Kendall Ln
24
23
NEW ACTON
Parkes Way
BalmainCres
Liversidge St
Lawson Cres
London Cct
Allara St
Constitution Ave
Amaroo St
Parkes Way
Cresswell St
Russell Dr

17
18
Commonwealth Park

Acton Peninsula
West Basin
11
Barrine Dr
6
3
Regatta Point
Lake Burley Griffin
Central Basin
4

10
Commonwealth Place
Flynn Dr
Langton Cres
Commonwealth Ave
Parkes Pl
King Edward Tce
Parkes Pl
14
15
PARKES
12
9
7
Aspen Island
Kings Park
Wendouree Dr
Morshead Dr

1
5
King George Tce
Queen Victoria Tce
Kings Ave
State Cir
Capital Cir

YARRALUMLA
13
Adelaide Ave
Alexandrina Dr
Forster Cres

26
BARTON
Blackall St
Bowen Dr
East Basin
Capital Cir
Brisbane Ave
Macquarie St
Bowen Park
19
39
KINGSTON FORESHORE
25
34

FORREST
Franklin St
National Cct
Canberra Ave
National Cct
22
Telopea Park West
Telopea Park East
Jardine St
Howitt St
28
Wentworth Ave

Canberra

Real Fun   Boat & Bicycle Rental
Canoe, kayak and bike hire; also offers activity tours. (📞0410 547 838; www.realfun.com.au; kayak hire per 3 hours from $50)

Mr Spokes Bike Hire   Bicycle Rental
Near the Acton Park ferry terminal. (📞02-6257 1188; www.mrspokes.com.au; Barrine Dr, Acton; per hour/half day/full day $20/30/40; ⌚9am-5pm Wed-Sun, daily during school holidays)

🎫 TOURS

Balloon Aloft   Ballooning
Aerial views over Canberra – the ideal way to see the city's unique design. (📞02-6249 8660; www.canberraballoons.com.au; Kallaroo Rd, Pialligo; rides adult/child from $290/210)

Canberra City Explorer   Bus Tour
Handy hop-on, hop-off service with 13 stops. (📞02-9567 8400; www.canberracityexplorer.com.au; departs Melbourne Bldg,

Northbourne Ave; 24hr adult/child $35/20, 48hr $60/30; ⌚9am-6pm)

Lake Burley Griffin Cruises   Cruise
Informative lake cruises. (📞0419 418 846; www.lakecruises.com.au; adult/child $18/9; ⌚mid-Oct–mid-May)

🛍 SHOPPING

Canberra Centre   Mall
Canberra's premier shopping centre. Includes a multiscreen cinema. (📞02-6247 5611; www.canberracentre.com.au; Bunda St, Civic; ⌚9am-5.30pm Mon-Thu, 9am-9pm Fri, 9am-5pm Sat, 10am-4pm Sun)

Craft ACT   Homewares, Jewellery
Contemporary design store and exhibition space. (📞02-6262 9993; www.craftact.org.au; 1st fl, North Bldg, 180 London Circuit, Civic; ⌚10am-5pm Tue-Fri, noon-4pm Sat)

Old Bus Depot Markets Market

Arts, crafts, local artisan produce and regional wines. (📞02-6292 8391; www.obdm.com.au; 21 Wentworth Ave, Kingston; 🕑10am-4pm Sun)

National Library Bookshop Books

Exclusively Australian books. (📞02-6262 1424; http://bookshop.nla.gov.au; Parkes Pl, Parkes; 🕑9am-5pm)

EATING

Lonsdale Street Roasters Cafe $

In hip Braddon, this grungy-chic cafe serves up damn fine coffee. Just up the is a bigger branch (23 Lonsdale St; 🕑6am-4pm Mon-Wed, to 9.30pm Thu-Sat, 7am-7pm Sun) with a large terrace and a great menu of cafe favourites. (www.lonsdalestreetroasters.com; Shop 3, 7 Lonsdale St, Braddon; 🕑6.30am-4pm Mon-Fri, to 3pm Sat, 8am-2pm Sun)

Elk & Pea Mexican $

Say *hola* to another new opening along ever-evolving Lonsdale St. Mexican influences include spicy huevos rancheros eggs for brekkie, burgers and burritos for lunch, and Canberra's best tacos for dinner. Breakfast martinis and gazpacho Bloody Marys will give you a morning pick-me-up, and live music bubbles away from 3pm on Saturdays. (www.elkandpea.com.au; 21 Lonsdale St, Braddon; tacos $7.50, shared plates $15-20; 🕑8am-10pm Tue-Sun, to 3pm Mon)

Brodburger Burgers $

Brodburger started out as a lakeside caravan takeaway joint. Now in a permanent location, the flame-grilled burgers are as good as ever. Salmon, chicken and lamb ones all go well with Aussie beer or wine, but we can't go past the all-encompassing flavour-packed Brodeluxe. (📞02-6162 0793; www.brodburger.com.au; Glassworks Bldg, 11 Wentworth Ave, Kingston; burgers $13-20; 🕑11.30am-3pm & 5.30pm-late Tue-Sat, noon-4pm Sun)

Temporada Spanish $$

Spanish flavours dominate at our favourite new Canberra restaurant, and the chefs are keen to demonstrate their skill with wood-fired food. Oysters come out deliciously smokey, marinated lamb partners with grilled sausage and flatbread, and barbecued octopus is subtly refreshed with watermelon. Excellent cocktails, wines and Australian craft beers seal the deal. (www.temporada.com.au; 15 Moore St, Civic; small plates $8-15, large plates $20-36; 🕑noon-late Mon-Sat)

Močan & Green Grout Cafe $$

Often awash with morning sunshine, this New Acton cafe is one of Canberra's best places to start the day. Free-range-this and local-that feature on the concise seasonal menu, and an espresso and the baked Tripoli eggs will really kickstart your morning. Dinner is served from Tuesday to Saturday with small-plate highlights including Japanese-influenced soft-shell crab. (www.mocanandgreengrout.com; 1/19 Marcus Clarke St, New Acton; breakfast & lunch mains $9-16, dinner shared plates $16-25; 🕑7am-6pm Mon, to 9pm Tue-Sat, 8am-4pm Sun; 🛜)

Monster Kitchen & Bar Cafe $$

Concealed in the cool Hotel Hotel is one of Canberra's more versatile eateries. Hotel guests, New Acton trendies and politicians check their Twitter feeds over breakfast, before bar snacks and shared plates with a subtle Middle Eastern influence get everyone talking during lunch and dinner. At night it morphs into a bar (and a good place to overhear political gossip). (www.hotelhotel.com.au; Hotel Hotel, 25 Edinburgh Ave, New Acton; breakfast $11-24, bar snacks & shared plates $10-33; 🕑6.30am-1am)

Lanterne Rooms Malaysian $$

Serving expertly cooked Nyonya dishes in a colourful interior referencing Penang farmhouses from the colonial era, Lanterne Rooms is sophisticated and welcoming. (📞02-6249 6889; www.lanternerooms.chairmangroup.com.au; Shop 3, Blamey Pl, Campbell; lunch banquet $33.50, dinner mains $30-35; noon-2.30pm & 6-10.30pm Tue-Fri, 6-10.30pm Sat)

Silo Bakery   Bakery, Cafe $$

Sourdough bread, pastries and tarts are perfect breakfast temptations, and filled baguettes, rustic mains and cheese platters keep diners happy at lunch. Good coffee and wines by the glass complete the package. Book for lunch. (02-6260 6060; www.silobakery.com.au; 36 Giles St, Kingston; breakfast $9-22, lunch $20-22; 7am-4pm Tue-Sat)

Morks   Thai $$

Our favourite of the restaurants along the new Trevillian Quay development on the Kingston Foreshore, Morks offers a contemporary spin on Thai cuisine. Ask for a table outside, watch the punters shuffling to adjacent wholefood cafes, specialist coffee roasters and bustling bars, and enjoy the authentic Thai zip and zing of red duck curry or pork crackling with chilli jam. (02-6295 0112; www.morks.com.au; Trevillian Quay, Kingston Foreshore; mains $24-28; noon-2pm & 6-10pm Tue-Sat, noon-2pm Sun)

Sage Dining Room   French $$$

In the Gorman House Arts Centre, Sage is the home kitchen of French chef Clement Chauvin who once graced the kitchen at London's Claridges, and Maison Pic in France. Subtle French plays on local ingredients make for exquisite tastes. (02-6249 6050; www.sagerestaurant.net.au; Batman St, Braddon; 3-/5-course meals $75/95; noon-2pm & 5.30-10pm Tue-Sat)

Ottoman   Turkish $$$

This splendid Turkish restaurant in a sprawling villa is a favourite destination for Canberra's power brokers. Traditional dishes (meze, dolma, kebabs) are given a cunning mod Oz twist. Look forward to exemplary service and an expansive wine list. (02-6273 6111; www.ottomancuisine.com.au; cnr Broughton & Blackall Sts, Barton; mains $29-33, 7-course degustation menu $75; noon-2.30pm & 6-10pm Tue-Fri, 6-10pm Sat)

The 35km shore of this lake is home to most of the city's cultural institutions.

National Carillon and Lake Burley Griffin (p91)

Where to Stay

Canberra's accommodation is busiest during parliamentary sitting days. Hotels charge peak rates midweek, but drop rates at weekends. Peak rates also apply during the Floriade festival.

Try New Acton and Civic for boutique hotel options near nightlife venues, or Kingston for proximity to an established dining hub south of Lake Burley Griffin.

Above: Lake Burley Griffin (p91)
ANDREW WATSON / GETTY IMAGES ©

Malamay Chinese **$$$**
The spicy flavours of Sichuan cuisine entice at this restaurant. A glamorous interior fit-out channels Shanghai c 1930, and is a perfect setting for a leisurely set banquet or zesty mains, including lamb with cumin and chilli salt. (☎02-6162 1220; www.malamay.chairmangroup.com.au; Burbury Hotel, 1 Burbury Close, Barton; mains $33-38, lunch banquet $42, dinner banquet $65.50; ⊙noon-2.30pm & 6-10.30pm Tue-Fri, 6-10.30pm Sat)

DRINKING & NIGHTLIFE

BentSpoke Brewing Co Microbrewery
With 18 excellent beers and ciders on tap, BentSpoke is one of Australia's best craft brewers. Sit at the biking-themed bar or relax outside with a tasting tray of four beers ($16). Our favourite is the Barley Griffin Ale, subtly tinged with a spicy Belgian yeast. Good pub food too. (www.bentspokebrewing.com.au; 38 Mort St, Braddon; ⊙11am-midnight)

Rum Bar Bar
The city's biggest selection of rum combines with a cosmopolitan canal-front spot along the Trevillian Quay strip on the Kingston Foreshore. Cocktails, tapas and craft beer are additional drawcards, and other bars and pubs make the area a worthwhile after-dark or lazy afternoon destination. (www.facebook.com/therumbarcanberra; Trevillian Quay, Kingston Foreshore; ⊙5-10pm Tue, from 3pm Wed-Fri, from noon Sat & Sun)

Honky Tonks Bar
Canberra's compadres meet up here to eat tacos, drink margaritas and listen to eclectic sets from the DJ. It's loads of fun. (www.drinkhonkytonks.com.au; 17 Garema Pl, Civic; ⊙4pm-late Mon-Thu, 2pm-late Fri-Sun)

Knightsbridge Penthouse Cocktail Bar
Arty and gay-friendly, with good DJs, excellent cocktails and a mellow ambience. (☎02-6262 6221; www.knightsbridgepenthouse.com.au; 34 Mort St, Braddon; ⊙5pm-midnight Tue & Wed, 5pm-late Thu-Sat)

Wig & Pen Microbrewery
Long-standing Canberra brewpub now relocated on campus to the Australian National University's School of Music. Those lucky, lucky students… (www.facebook.com/wigandpen.canberra; 100 Childers St, Llewellyn Hall; ⊙11.30am-midnight Mon-Fri, 2pm-midnight Sat, 2-8pm Sun)

Phoenix Pub
The Phoenix is a staunch supporter of local music and has a laid-back and hip vibe. (☎02-6247 1606; www.lovethephoenix.com; 23 East Row, Civic; ⊙noon-1am Mon-Wed, to 3am Thu-Sat)

ENTERTAINMENT

Entertainment listings are in Thursday's *Canberra Times* and on the BMA website (www.bmamag.com). **Ticketek** (☎02-6219 6666; www.ticketek.com.au; Akuna St, Civic) sells tickets.

Palace Electric Cinema Cinema

Shows art-house and independent movies with cheaper Monday tickets. (02-6222 4900; www.palacecinemas.com.au/cinemas/electric; 2 Phillip Law St, NewActon Nishi)

 INFORMATION

Canberra & Region Visitors Centre (1300 554 114, 02-6205 0044; www.visitcanberra.com. au; 330 Northbourne Ave, Dickson; ◷9am-4pm) Around 3km north of Civic.

 GETTING THERE & AWAY

AIR

Qantas (www.qantas.com.au; Jolimont Centre, Northbourne Ave, Civic) and **Virgin Australia** (www.virginaustralia.com.au) flights connect **Canberra Airport** (www.canberraairport.com. au) with all Australian state capitals.

BUS

The interstate bus terminal is at the Jolimont Centre.

Greyhound Australia (1300 GREYHOUND; 1300 4739 46863; www.greyhound.com.au; ◷Jolimont Centre branch 6am-9.30pm) Frequent services to Sydney ($42, 3½ hours) and Melbourne ($91, nine hours).

Murrays (13 22 51; www.murrays.com. au; ◷Jolimont Centre branch 7am-7pm) Daily express services to Sydney ($42, 3½ hours).

CAR & MOTORCYCLE

The Hume Hwy connects Sydney and Melbourne, passing 50km north of Canberra. The Federal Hwy runs north to connect with the Hume near Goulburn, and the Barton Hwy (Rte 25) meets the Hume near Yass.

TRAIN

Kingston train station (Wentworth Ave) is the city's rail terminus. Book trains and connecting buses inside the station.

NSWTrainLink (13 22 32; www.nswtrain link.info) runs services to/from Sydney ($40, 4½ hours, two to three daily). For Melbourne, a NSWTrainLink coach to Cootamundra ($14, 2½ hours) links with the Sydney to Melbourne train service ($75, six hours). A daily **V/Line** (13 61 96; www.vline.com.au) Canberra Link service combines a train from Melbourne to Albury–Wodonga with a bus to Canberra ($55, 8½ hours).

 GETTING AROUND

TO/FROM THE AIRPORT

Canberra Airport is 8km southeast of the city. A taxi to the city centre costs around $50 to $55. **Airport Express** (1300 368 897; www. royalecoach.com.au; one way/return $12/20) runs between the airport and the city.

PUBLIC TRANSPORT

Canberra's public transport provider is the **ACT Internal Omnibus Network** (Action; 13 17 10; www.action.act.gov.au; adult/concession single trip $4.60/2.30, daily pass $8.80/4.40). The main bus interchange is along Alinga St, East Row and Mort St. See the **information kiosk** (East Row, Civic; ◷7.30am-5.30pm Mon-Fri) for route maps and timetables.

Purchase tickets from Action agents (including the visitors centre and newsagents), or on board from drivers.

TAXI

Cabxpress (02-6260 6011; www.cabxpress.com.au)

Canberra Elite Taxis (13 22 27; www.canberracabs.com.au)

MARK DAFFEY/GETTY IMAGES ©

BYRON BAY

Byron Bay

The reputation of this famous beach town precedes it to such an extent that first impressions may leave you wondering what all the fuss is about. The beaches are great, but what makes Byron special is the singular vibe of the town itself. It's here that coastal surf culture flows into the hippie tide washing down from the hinterland, creating one great alternative-lifestyle mash-up.

The town centre is low-rise and relaxed, and the locals are dedicated to preserving its essential small-town soul. Of course Byron does get crowded, and it also attracts its fair share of off-the-leash teens. Yet its unique atmosphere has a way of converting even the most cynical with its balmy days, endless beaches, reliable surf breaks, fine food, raucous nightlife and ambling milieu.

From left: Byron Bay pelicans; Byron Bay beach
FROM LEFT: SUZANNE MARSHALL / GETTY IMAGES ©;
MARCOS WELSH / DESIGN PICS / GETTY IMAGES ©

🎪 What's On

Byron Bay Bluesfest (www.bluesfest.com.au; Tyagarah Tea Tree Farm; ⊙Easter; 🎧) This jam attracts international performers and local heavyweights.

Splendour in the Grass (www.splendourinthegrass.com; North Byron Parklands; ⊙late Jul) Three-day festival featuring big-name indie artists.

Byron Bay Writers' Festival (www.byronbaywritersfestival.com.au; ⊙early Aug) Gathers top-shelf writers and literary followers from across Australia.

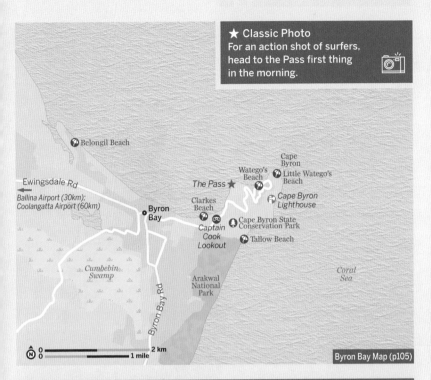

★ Classic Photo
For an action shot of surfers, head to the Pass first thing in the morning.

Belongil Beach

Ewingsdale Rd

Ballina Airport (30km);
Coolangatta Airport (60km)

Byron Bay

The Pass

Clarkes Beach

Captain Cook Lookout

Cumbebin Swamp

Byron Bay Rd

Arakwal National Park

Watego's Beach

Cape Byron

Little Watego's Beach

Cape Byron Lighthouse

Cape Byron State Conservation Park

Tallow Beach

Coral Sea

N

0   2 km
0   1 mile

Byron Bay Map (p105)

Byron Bay Lighthouse (p104)
PAWEL TOCZYNSKI / GETTY IMAGES ©

Learn to Surf

Whenever the surf is up, local swells fill with people. Learning to surf is an Australian rite of passage – if you feel like joining in, Byron Bay has a number of good surf schools.

Great For...

☑ **Don't Miss**

The Ben King Memorial Surf Classic, an annual competition that's been going for 40 years.

Surf Culture in Australia

Australia has been synonymous with surfing ever since the Beach Boys effused about 'Australia's Narrabeen', one of Sydney's northern beaches, in 'Surfin' USA'. Other surfing hot spots such as Bells Beach, Margaret River, the Pass at Byron Bay, the heavy-breaking Shipstern Bluff in Tasmania and Burleigh Heads on the Gold Coast also resonate with international wave addicts. Iron Man and Surf Lifesaving competitions are held on beaches around the country, attracting dedicated fans to the sand.

More than a few Australian surfers have attained 'World Champion' status. In the men's comp, legendary surfers include Mark Richards, Tom Carroll, Joel Parkin-

PETE SEAWARD / LONELY PLANET ©

son and 2013 champ Mick Fanning. In the women's competition, iconic Aussie surfers include Wendy Botha, seven-time champion Layne Beachley and 2014 champ (and six-time winner) Stephanie Gilmore.

If you're keen to learn, you'll find plenty of good waves, board hire and lessons available.

Surf Schools

Black Dog Surfing   Surfing
Intimate group lessons including women's and kids' courses. Highly rated. (02-6680 9828; www.blackdogsurfing.com; 11 Byron St; 3½hr lessons $60)

❶ Need to Know
Surfing is, obviously, dependent on the surf. A forecasting app such as Magic Seaweed can help you find the best waves.

✕ Take a Break
Nurse your sore limbs and recharge over an ale at the Byron Bay Brewing Co (p108).

✿ Surf Events
The **Byron Bay Surf Festival** (www. byronbaysurffestival.com; ◷ late Oct) is a three-day celebration of surf culture.

★ Top Tip
Belongil Beach, just 1km north of Byron's main beach, is quieter, and good for all levels.

Surfing Byron Bay   Surfing
Surfing lessons for adults and kids, plus a 'surf yoga' combo. (02-6685 7099; www. gosurfingbyronbay.com; 84 Jonson St; 2½hr lessons $60)

Byron Bay Surf School   Surfing
Lessons and surf camps. (1800 707 274; www.byronbaysurfschool.com; 29 Shirley St; 3½hr lessons $65)

Mojosurf   Surfing
Lessons and epic surf safaris. (1800 113 044; www.mojosurf.com; 9 Marvell St; 1/2 lessons $69/119)

Soul Surf School   Surfing
Half-day to five-day courses for beginners. (1800 089 699; www.soulsurfschool.com.au; 4hr lessons $59)

⊙ SIGHTS

Cape Byron State Conservation Park
State Park

The views from the summit are spectacular, rewarding those who have climbed up from the **Captain Cook Lookout** on the Cape Byron Walking Track. Ribboning around the headland, the track dips and (mostly) soars its way to the **lighthouse** (Lighthouse Rd; ☉10am-4pm). Along the way, look out for dolphins (year-round) and migrating whales during their northern (June to July) and southern (September to November) migrations. You're also likely to encounter brush turkeys and wallabies. Allow about two hours for the entire 3.7km loop. Inside the 1901 lighthouse there are maritime and nature displays. If you want to venture to the top you'll need to take one of the volunteer-run tours, which operate from around 10am to 3pm (gold-coin donation). There's also a cafe here and self-contained accommodation in the lighthouse-keeper's cottages.

You can drive right up to the lighthouse and pay $7 for the privilege of parking (or nothing at all if you chance upon a park in the small lot 300m below).
(www.nationalparks.nsw.gov.au/cape-byron-state-conservation-area)

Beaches

West of the town centre, wild **Belongil Beach** with its high dunes avoids the worst of the crowds and is clothing optional in parts. At its eastern end is the **Wreck**, a powerful right-hand surf break.

Directly in front of town, lifesaver-patrolled **Main Beach** is busy from sunrise to sunset with yoga classes, buskers and fire dancers. As it stretches east it merges into **Clarkes Beach**. The most popular surf break is at the **Pass** near the eastern headland.

Around the rocks is gorgeous **Watego's Beach**, a wide crescent of white sand surrounded by rainforest. A further 400m walk brings you to secluded **Little Watego's** (inaccessible by car), another lovely patch of sand directly under rocky Cape Byron.

Head here at sunset for an impressive moon rise. Tucked under the south side of the Cape (entry via Tallow Beach Rd) is **Cosy Corner**, which offers a decent-size wave and sheltered beach when the northerlies are blowing elsewhere.

Tallow Beach is a deserted sandy stretch that extends for 7km south from Cape Byron. This is the place to flee the crowds. Much of the beach is backed by **Arakwal National Park**, but the suburb of **Suffolk Park** sprawls along the sand near its southern end. **Kings Beach** is a popular gay beach, just off Seven Mile Beach Rd past the Broken Head Holiday Park.

✪ ACTIVITIES

About 3km offshore, **Julian Rocks Marine Reserve** is a meeting point for cold southerly and warm northerly currents, attracting a profusion of marine species including three types of turtle. You might spot leopard sharks and manta rays in summer, and grey nurse sharks in winter.

Sundive
Diving, Snorkelling

Two to three expeditions to Julian Rocks daily, plus various courses. (☎02-6685 7755; www.sundive.com.au; 8/9-11 Byron St; dives from $95, snorkelling tours $65)

Dive Byron Bay
Diving

Free-diving course $495 and Professional Association of Diving Instructors (PADI) courses from $325. (☎02-6685 8333; www.byronbaydivecentre.com.au; 9 Marvell St; dives from $99, snorkelling tours $65; ☉9am-5pm)

Byron Bay Ballooning
Ballooning

Sunrise flights including champagne breakfast. (☎1300 889 660; www.byronbayballooning.com.au; Tyagarah Airfield; adult/child $325/175)

Go Sea Kayaks
Kayaking

⊘ If you don't see a whale, turtle or dolphin, you can go again for free. (☎0416 222 344; www.goseakayakbyronbay.com.au; adult/child $69/59)

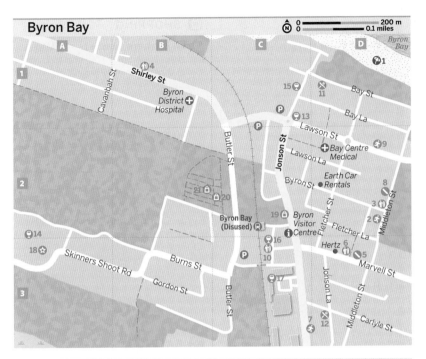

Byron Bay

⊙ Sights
1 Main Beach D1

⊕ Activities, Courses & Tours
2 Be Salon & Spa D2
3 Black Dog Surfing D2
4 Byron Bay Surf School B1
5 Dive Byron Bay D3
6 Mojosurf D3
7 Relax Haven C3
8 Sundive D2
9 Surf & Bike Hire D2
10 Surfing Byron Bay C3

⊗ Eating
11 Italian at the Pacific D1
12 Petit Snail D3

⊙ Drinking & Nightlife
13 Balcony Bar C1
14 Byron Bay Brewing Co A2
15 Miss Margarita C1
16 Railway Friendly Bar C3
17 Woody's Surf Shack C3

⊗ Entertainment
18 Pighouse Flicks A3

⊙ Shopping
19 Byron Bay Artisan Market C2
20 Byron Community Market C2
21 Byron Farmers' Market B2

Surf & Bike Hire   Bicycle Rental
Rents bikes and surfboards (from $10 per day) plus other active gear. (☏02-6680 7066; www.byronbaysurfandbikehire.com.au; 31 Lawson St; ☺9am-5pm)

Byron at Byron Spa   Spa
Six ultraluxurious treatment rooms nestled among the rainforest. Includes use of the resort swimming pool. (☏02-6639 2110; www.thebyronatbyron.com.au/spa; 77-97 Broken Head Rd; 1hr massages from $145)

John Byron, not Lord Byron

James Cook named Cape Byron, mainland Australia's most easterly point, after renowned navigator John Byron, grandfather of the poet Lord Byron. Later bureaucrats mistakenly planned out streets named after fellow poets such as Jonson, Burns and Shelley.

Be Salon & Spa   Spa
Manicures, pedicures, facials and waxing are offered alongside psychic readings, massage, re-balancing and naturopathy. (0413 432 584; www.besalonspa.com.au; 14 Middleton St; 30min massages $60)

Relax Haven   Spa
Flotation tanks (one hour $79), massage (one hour $89), kinesiology, quantum hypnotherapy and theta energy healing. (02-6685 8304; www.relaxhaven.com.au; 107 Jonson St; 10am-6.30pm)

TOURS

Numerous operators run tours to Nimbin and other interesting places in the hinterland. Most tour companies will pick you up from where you're staying.

Mountain Bike Tours   Mountain Biking
Environmentally aware bike tours into the rainforest and along the coast. (0429 122 504; www.mountainbiketours.com.au; half/full day $59/99)

Vision Walks   Wildlife Tour
See all manner of creatures in their natural habitat, including nocturnal animals (on the Night Vision Walk) and hippies (on the Hippie Trail Hinterland Tour). (02-6685 0059; www.visionwalks.com; night tours adult/child $99/75, other tours from $45/28)

SHOPPING

Byron Farmers' Market   Market
This open-air temple to regional food offers a wide variety of mainly organic stalls. Get in early for a terrific coffee and breakfast. (www.byronfarmersmarket.com.au; Butler Street Reserve; 8-11am Thu)

Byron Bay Artisan Market   Market
Local artists and designers flog their wares at this popular night market. Expect leather goods, jewellery, clothing and live entertainment. (www.byronmarkets.com.au; Railway Park, Jonson St; 4-9pm Sat Nov-Mar)

Byron Community Market   Market
The biggest market in the region with over 300 stalls covering several acres. Organic farmers and foodies meet alternative therapists, crafts people and musicians at this monthly extravaganza. (www.byronmarkets.com.au; Butler Street Reserve; 8am-2pm 1st Sun of the month)

EATING

The Roadhouse   Cafe $
A short trip out of town will find you at Byron's most atmospheric night spot. Rocking incredible, locally sourced wholefoods and elixirs by day, the Roadhouse transforms into a dimly lit, blues-infused bar at night with more than 500 types of whisky on the menu. Book ahead. (0403 355 498; byronbaycafebar.com.au; 6/142 Bangalow Rd; mains $14; 6am-3pm Mon, to 10pm Tue-Sun)

Top Shop   Cafe $
On the hill east of town, Top Shop has long been the choice of local surfers. Today it's an upmarket version of the old-school takeaway, with diners ripping into burgers, sausage rolls and quinoa kale salads on the lawn while chugging back ice coffees. (65 Carlyle St; mains $10-14; 6.30am-5pm)

Three Blue Ducks at the Farm   Restaurant $$
After the success of its Sydney cafe, the team from the Three Blue Ducks decided to

JOHN HAY / GETTY IMAGES ©

move up north and showcase its paddock-to-plate food philosophy on the grounds of this lovely cattle and chicken farm just out of Byron. (📞02-6684 7888; www.thefarm byronbay.com.au; 11 Ewingsdale Rd, Ewingsdale; ⏰7am-2.30pm Mon-Fri, 7am-3pm Sat & Sun, 5-10pm Fri-Sun)

Italian at the Pacific   Italian $$

Adjoining the Beach Hotel, this lively Italian offers a limited selection of pasta and larger dishes, but what it does do, it does well. Try the slow-cooked lamb-shank lasagne – it might just be the best you've ever tasted. (📞02-6680 7055; www.italianatthepacific.com. au; 2 Bay St; mains $28-36; ⏰6-10pm)

Byron Beach Cafe   Cafe $$

Step out of the surf and straight into this iconic Byron Bay cafe right on Clarkes Beach, the ideal spot for a lazy brunch. There are lots of interesting breakfast options; the menu gets more restaurant-like as the day progresses. (📞02-6685 8400; www.byronbeachcafe.com.au; Lawson St; mains breakfast $15-22, lunch & dinner $25-33; ⏰7.30am-5pm Sun-Wed, to 9pm Thu-Sat)

Byron at Byron Restaurant   Modern Australian $$$

With flickering candles and a rainforest backdrop this intimate resort restaurant offers light, Mediterranean-style dishes created around the best of Northern Rivers produce, such as sweet Bangalow pork and Yamba prawns. On Thursday night there's a good-value two-course Farmers' Market dinner ($49). (📞02-6639 2111; www.thebyron atbyron.com.au; 77-97 Broken Head Rd; mains $37-40; ⏰8am-9pm)

Petit Snail   French $$$

Get stuck into traditional Gallic fare such as steak tartare, duck confit and lots of fromage. There's outdoor dining on the verandah. Vegetarians get their own menu (mains $21 to $25). (📞02-6685 8526; www. thepetitsnail.com.au; 5 Carlyle St; mains $31-45; ⏰6.30-9.30pm Wed-Sat; 🍴)

Where to Stay

Book well in advance for January or during any of the annual music festivals. If you're not 17, Schoolies Week, which actually runs for about a month from mid-November, is one to avoid. During these periods, places taking one-night-only bookings are rare.

As you would expect, backpacker options are plentiful, but the town also has its share of guesthouses and resorts. If you are looking for an option out of the town centre, try for a spot near Clarkes Beach or Cape Byron.

Napping in Nature

Located right at the Byron Bay lighthouse, the historic 1901 **Lighthouse Keepers Cottages** (☎02-6685 6552; www.nationalparks.nsw.gov.au; 3-day rentals from $1200) have been renovated with polished wood floors and lovely furnishings. There are similar gems hidden in national parks, conservation areas and nature reserves along the coast. The NPWS website (www.environment.nsw.gov.au/NationalParks) has a wealth of info.

Above: Kookaburra
JAMES HARRISON / GETTY IMAGES ©

🍸 DRINKING & NIGHTLIFE

Byron Bay Brewing Co   Brewery
At this old piggery turned booze barn you can drink frosty glasses of house pale lager amid the brewing vats or sit outside in the tropical courtyard under the shade of a giant fig tree. Entertainment includes live music, DJs and trivia nights. Brewery tours are held at 4pm. (www.byronbaybrewery.com.au; 1 Skinners Shoot Rd; ⏰noon-late Mon-Sat, to 10pm Sun)

Balcony Bar   Bar
With its verandah poking out amid the palm trees overlooking the centre of town, this tapas and cocktail bar is a fine place to park yourself, particularly during the sunset happy hour. (☎02-6680 9666; www.balcony.com.au; Level 1, 3 Lawson St; ⏰8am-11pm) 🍴

Miss Margarita   Bar
A beach cantina offering seven versions of the classic margarita and an array of colourful, fruity cocktails. Soak up the tequila with enchiladas, salsa and creamy guacamole. (☎02-6685 6828; missmargarita.com.au; 2 Jonson St; ⏰12-3pm & 5pm-1am Mon-Fri, 11.30-1am Sat & Sun)

Railway Friendly Bar   Pub
This indoor-outdoor pub draws everyone from lobster-red British tourists to high-on-life earth mothers. The front beer garden, conducive to boozy afternoons, has live music and excellent food. (The Rails; ☎02-6685 7662; www.therailsbyronbay.com; 86 Jonson St; ⏰11am-late)

Woody's Surf Shack   Bar
Traditionally the last stop of the night, there's now a lockout for this clubby bar, so if you fancy shooting pool until 3am you'll need to get in before 1.30am. (www.woodysbyronbay.com; The Plaza, 90-96 Jonson St; ⏰8pm-3am Mon-Sat)

⭐ ENTERTAINMENT

For entertainment listings, check out the gig guide in Thursday's *Byron Shire News* (www.byronnews.com.au) or tune into Bay 99.9 FM.

Pighouse Flicks   Cinema
Attached to Byron Bay Brewing Co, this lounge cinema shows classic reruns and art-house flicks. (☎02-6685 5828; www.pighouseflicks.com.au; 1 Skinners Shoot Rd; tickets $10-14)

INFORMATION

Bay Centre Medical (02-6685 6206; www.byronmed.com.au; 6 Lawson St; ☺8am-5pm Mon-Fri, to noon Sat)

Byron District Hospital (02-6685 6200; www.ncahs.nsw.gov.au; cnr Wordsworth & Shirley Sts; ☺24hr)

Byron Visitor Centre (02-6680 8558; www.visitbyronbay.com; Stationmaster's Cottage, 80 Jonson St; admission by donation; ☺9am-5pm) Ground zero for tourist information, and last-minute accommodation and bus bookings.

GETTING THERE & AWAY

AIR

The closest airport is at Ballina and with its rapidly expanding service it is the best airport for Byron. It also has shuttle services and rental cars for Byron travellers.

Coolangatta airport on the Gold Coast has a greater range of services but can involve a traffic-clogged drive. **Byron Bay Shuttle** (www.byronbayshuttle.com.au) serves both Coolangatta ($37) and Ballina ($15) airports.

BUS

Coaches stop on Jonson St near the tourist office. Services include the following:

Greyhound (1300 GREYHOUND/ 1300 4739 46863; www.greyhound.com.au) Coaches to/from Sydney (from $95, 12 to 14 hours, three daily) and Brisbane ($38, four hours, five daily).

Byron Bay Express (www.byronbayexpress.com.au) Five buses a day to/from Gold Coast Airport (1¾ hours) and Surfers Paradise (2¼ hours) for $30/55 one way/return.

Byron Easy Bus (02-6685 7447; www.byronbayshuttle.com.au) Minibus service to Ballina Byron Gateway Airport ($20, 40 minutes), Gold Coast Airport ($39, two hours), Brisbane ($40, 3½ hours) and Brisbane Airport ($54, four hours).

GETTING AROUND

Byron Bay Taxis (02-6685 5008; www.byronbaytaxis.com.au)

Earth Car Rentals (02-6685 7472; www.earthcar.com.au; 1 Byron St)

Hertz (02-6680 7925; www.hertz.com.au; 5 Marvell St)

Main Beach (p104)

SUSAN BLICKMORE / GETTY IMAGES ©

AUSCAPE / UIG/GETTY IMAGES ©

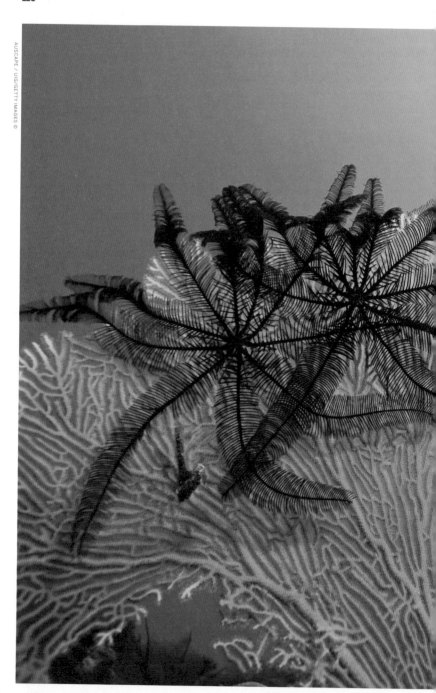

Feather stars on a sea fan, Great Barrier Reef

GREAT
BARRIER REEF

Great Barrier Reef

Each year, more than 1.6 million visitors experience the Great Barrier Reef – one of Australia's World Heritage–listed areas and one of nature's richest realms. Stretching more than 2000km from just south of the Tropic of Capricorn (near the Queensland city of Gladstone) to just south of Papua New Guinea, this fascinating offshore ecosystem is the most extensive reef system in the world, and is made entirely by living organisms.

There is a multitude of places along the Queensland coast to launch your reef adventure, and a range of ways to see the kaleidoscopic spectacle including diving, snorkelling, sailing and scenic flights. Get active under or over the water, or drift through your days exploring gateway towns or kicking back poolside at an island resort.

❶ In This Section

➡ Arriving in the Great Barrier Reef

Cairns is the major base for exploring the northern Reef, with daily boat tours and diving/snorkelling trips, plus good connections to Port Douglas, Lizard Island, Mission Beach and major Australian cities. Hamilton Island's airport connects the Whitsundays with Sydney, Melbourne, Brisbane and Cairns. Bundaberg, Gladstone and Town of 1770 offer boat and air connections to the southern reef islands.

From left: North Beach, Heron Island (p121); Brian Robinson's *Woven Fish*, Cairns Esplanade (p124)
FROM LEFT: BRUCE HOOD / GETTY IMAGES ©; ANDREW WATSON / GETTY IMAGES ©

From top: Yellow-crested cockatoo; clownfish, sea turtle and blue tang on the Great Barrier Reef

FROM TOP: CAROLYN HEBBARD / GETTY IMAGES ©; JEFF HUNTER / GETTY IMAGES ©

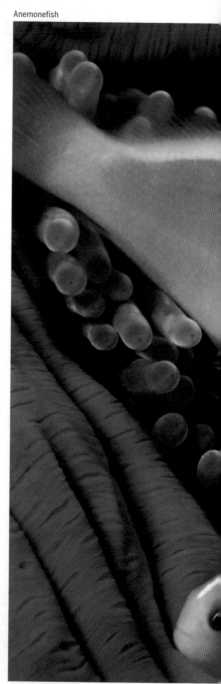
Anemonefish

Exploring the Reef

There are numerous ways to approach this massive undersea wonder: head to a gateway town and join an organised tour; sign up for a multiday sailing or diving trip exploring the reef's less-travelled outer reaches; or fly out to a remote island, where you'll have the gorgeous coral gardens largely to yourself.

Great For...

❶ Need To Know

June to November is the best time to visit: it's not too hot, and clear days mean good visibility.

STUART WESTMORLAND / GETTY IMAGES ©

Picking Your Spot

Given the reef's size, it follows that there are myriad popular spots from which to access it – but bear in mind that the qualities of individual areas do change over time, depending on the weather, tidal changes or any recent cyclone damage.

Mainland Gateways

The major mainland reef access points all offer slightly different experiences or activities. This list is organised from south to north:

- Agnes Water & Town of 1770 (p122)
- Airlie Beach (p137)
- Cairns (p124)
- Port Douglas (p148)

Island Gateways

Rising above the waterline throughout the reef are hundreds of islands and cays, offering instant access to the undersea marvels. Here is a list of some of our favourite islands, travelling from south to north:

- Lady Elliot Island (p120)
- Heron Island (p121)
- Hamilton Island (p135)

Island Resorts

The Great Barrier Reef is home to over a dozen island resorts, offering varying levels of comfort and style. Where to stay depends not only on your budget, but also what sort of activities you have in mind. Some resorts are small and secluded (and don't allow children), which can be ideal for

Hayman Island (p137)

a tropical getaway doing little more than sipping cocktails. If this sounds ideal, try Orpheus or Hayman Islands. Other resorts have a busier vibe and offer a wide range of activities, from sailing and kayaking to helicopter joy rides, plus restaurants and even some nightlife. If this is more to your liking, try Hamilton Island or Green Island.

Boat Excursions

Unless you're staying on a coral atoll in the middle of the Great Barrier Reef, you'll need to join a boat excursion to experience the reef's real beauty. Day trips set sail from many places along the coast, as

> ★ **Did You Know?**
> The Great Barrier Reef is around 8000 years old and around the size of Germany.

TANYA ANN PHOTOGRAPHY / GETTY IMAGES ©

well as from island resorts. Trips typically include the use of snorkelling gear, snacks and a buffet lunch, with scuba diving an optional extra. On some boats a naturalist or marine biologist presents a talk on reef ecology.

Boat trips vary dramatically in passenger numbers, type of vessel and quality – which is reflected in the price – so it's worth getting all the details before committing. When selecting a tour, consider the vessel (motorised catamaran or sailing ship), the number of passengers (anywhere from six to 400), and what kind of extras are offered (food, talks, hotel transfers etc). The destination is also key: outer reefs are usually more pristine; inner reefs often show signs of damage from humans, coral bleaching and the coral-eating crown-of-thorns starfish. Some operators offer the option of a trip in a glass-bottomed boat or semisubmersible.

Many boats have underwater cameras for hire – although you'll save money by hiring these back on the mainland (or using your own waterproof camera or underwater housing). Some boats also have professional photographers on board who will dive with you and take high-quality shots of you as you bubble away underneath the surface.

Diving & Snorkelling the Reef

Much of the diving and snorkelling on the reef is boat-based, although on some islands you can walk straight off the beach and dip into the coral kingdom just offshore. Free use of snorkelling gear is usually part of any cruise to the reef; cruises generally involve around three hours of underwater wandering. Overnight or 'live-aboard' trips provide a more in-depth experience and greater coverage of the reefs.

> ✗ **Take a Break**
> At **Heron Island Resort** (p121), 89km off the coast, you can simply wake up and dive into the coral-festooned sea.

If you're keen to experience scuba diving but don't have a diving certificate, many operators provide introductory dives – a guided dive where an experienced diver conducts an underwater tour. A lesson in safety and procedure is given beforehand and you don't require a five-day Professional Association of Diving Instructors (PADI) course or a 'buddy'.

Top Reef Dive Spots

The Great Barrier Reef is home to some of the planet's best reef-diving sites. Here are a few top spots to get you started:

SS Yongala A sunken shipwreck that has been home to a vivid marine community for more than 90 years.

Cod Hole Nose-to-nose with potato cods.

Heron Island Join a crowd of colourful fish, straight off the beach.

Lady Elliot Island Has 19 highly regarded dive sites.

Pixie Bommie Delve into the reef's after-five world on a night dive.

Top Snorkelling Sites

Non-divers may wonder if it's worth going to the Great Barrier Reef 'just to snorkel'. The answer is a resounding 'Yes!', as much of the rich, colourful coral lies just underneath the surface. Here's a round-up of the top snorkelling sites:

Fitzroy Reef Lagoon (Town of 1770)

Heron Island (Capricorn Coast)

Great Keppel Island (Capricorn Coast)

Lady Elliot Island (Capricorn Coast)

Lady Musgrave Island (Capricorn Coast)

Lizard Island (Cairns)

Michaelmas Reef (Cairns)

Hastings Reef (Cairns)

Norman Reef (Cairns)

Saxon Reef (Cairns)

Green Island (Cairns)

Trips from Cairns

Reef trips generally include transport, lunch, stinger-suits and snorkelling gear. When choosing a tour, consider the vessel type, its capacity, inclusions and destination: outer reefs are more pristine but further afield; inner reefs can be patchy and show signs of decay. Some prefer smaller, less-crowded vessels, while others go for the wide range of inclusions bigger boats promise.

Vendors with their own pontoon offer all-round value: pontoons are a great way for families to experience the reef – those who aren't keen on getting in the water can enjoy the pontoon's facilities, or a trip in a glass-bottomed boat or semisubmersible.

Almost all boats depart from the Marlin Wharf (with check-in and booking facilities located inside the Reef Fleet Terminal)

around 8am, returning around 6pm. Smaller operators may check-in boat-side at their berth on the wharf itself; check with your operator. Operators include:

Tusa Dive (07-4047 9100; www.tusadive. com; cnr Shields St & the Esplanade; adult/ child day trips from $185/110) A maximum of 60 passengers aboard Cairns' newest, custom-designed reef vessel (the T6), a roving outer reef permit and a high staff-to-passenger ratio make this operator an excellent choice for day trips.

Silverswift (07-4044 9944; www.silver series.com.au; 1 Spence St; adult/child day trips from $202/152) High speed, ride comfort (maximum 85 passengers) and facilities make Silverswift one of Cairns' most popular reef cruises for those able to spend a little more. You get around five hours of reef time at three of 16 outer reef locations.

Passions of Paradise (1800 111 346; www. passions.com.au; 1 Spence St; adult/child day trips from $159/109) This award-winning high-speed catamaran takes you to Michaelmas Cay, where you can snorkel from a white sandy beach in the middle of the reef, and then to its exclusive mooring on Paradise Reef, away from the madding crowds.

☑ **Don't Miss**

The chance to swim with (harmless) reef sharks – this is one experience definitely not to be passed up.

★ **Top Tip**

Remember never to walk on the coral: not only can it cut you badly, it's very fragile. For more responsible practices, see p121.

JEFF HUNTER / GETTY IMAGES ©

Southern Reef Islands

If you've ever had 'castaway' dreams of tiny coral atolls fringed with sugary white sand and turquoise-blue seas, you've found your island paradise in the southern Great Barrier Reef islands. From beautiful Lady Elliot Island, 80km northeast of Bundaberg, secluded and uninhabited coral reefs and atolls dot the ocean for about 140km up to Tryon Island. Access is from Town of 1770 and Gladstone.

Lady Elliot Island

On the southern frontier of the Great Barrier Reef, Lady Elliot is a 40-hectare vegetated coral cay populated with nesting sea turtles and an impressive number of seabirds. It's considered to have the best snorkelling in the southern Great Barrier Reef and the diving is good too: explore an ocean-bed of shipwrecks, coral gardens, bommies (coral pinnacles or outcroppings) and blowholes, and abundant marine life including barracuda, giant manta rays and harmless leopard sharks.

Lady Elliot Island is not a national park, and camping is not allowed; your only option is the low-key **Lady Elliot Island Resort** (📞1800 072 200; www.ladyelliot.com.au; per person $147-350). Accommodation is in tent cabins, simple motel-style units or more expensive two-bedroom, self-contained suites. Rates include breakfast and dinner, snorkelling gear and some tours.

The only way to reach the island is in a light aircraft. Resort guests are flown in from Bundaberg, the Gold Coast and Hervey Bay. The resort also manages fantastic, great-value day trips for around $300, including a scenic flight, a snorkelling tour and lunch; see the website for more info. Flights and day trips can be booked through local travel booking agencies.

Lady Musgrave Island

Wannabe castaways look no further. This tiny, 15-hectare cay, 100km northeast of Bundaberg, sits on the western rim of a stunning, turquoise-blue reef lagoon renowned for its safe swimming, snorkelling and diving. A squeaky, white-sand beach

Pisonia forest, Lady Musgrave Island

TED MEAD/GETTY IMAGES ©

fringes a dense canopy of pisonia forest brimming with roosting bird life, including terns, shearwaters and white-capped noddies. Birds nest from October to April while green turtles nest from November to February.

Day trips ($190) to Lady Musgrave depart from the Town of 1770 marina.

Heron & Wilson Islands

With the underwater reef world accessible directly from the beach, Heron Island is famed for the best easily accessed scuba diving in the southern reef islands, and also for great snorkelling, although you'll need a fair amount of cash to visit. A true coral cay, it is densely vegetated with pisonia trees and surrounded by 24 sq km of reef. There's a resort and research station on the northeastern third of the island; the remainder is national park.

Heron Island Resort (1300 863 248; www.heronisland.com; d/f/beach houses from $434/798/3198) offers comfortable accommodation suited to families and couples; the Point Suites have the best views. Great deals are often available online. Meal packages are extra, and guests pay $50/25 per adult/child for a launch transfer (one way), $291 for a seaplane transfer or $395 for a helicopter transfer. Transfers are from Gladstone.

Wilson Island, part of a national park, is an exclusive **wilderness retreat** (1300 863 248; www.wilsonisland.com; d per person $463) with six permanent 'tents' and solar-heated showers. Access is from Heron Island; you'll need to buy a combined Wilson-Heron package and spend at least two nights on Wilson Island. Transfers between Wilson and Heron are included, as are meals and drinks.

The island has excellent beaches, superb snorkelling and, during the season, turtle watching.

GETTING THERE & AWAY

Depending on their remoteness, the southern reef islands are accessible from mainland by boat (from Town of 1770) or plane or helicopter (from Bundaberg, Gladstone or Hervey Bay).

Looking After the Reef

The Great Barrier Reef is incredibly fragile: it's worth taking some time to educate yourself on responsible practices to minimise the impact of your visit.

o It is an offence to damage or remove coral in the marine park.

o If you touch or walk on coral you'll damage it (and probably get some nasty cuts).

o Don't touch or harass marine animals, and don't enter the water near a dugong.

o If you have a boat, be aware of the rules in relation to anchoring around the reef, including 'no anchoring areas' to avoid coral damage.

o If you're diving, check that you are weighted correctly before entering the water and keep your buoyancy control well away from the reef. Ensure that equipment such as secondary regulators and gauges aren't dragging over the reef.

o If you're snorkelling (especially if you're a beginner) practice your technique away from coral until you've mastered control in the water.

o Hire a wetsuit or a 'rashie' rather than slathering on sunscreen, which can damage the reef.

o Watch where your fins are – try not to stir up sediment or disturb coral.

o Note that there are limits on the amount and types of shells that you can collect.

o Take all litter away with you – even biodegradable materials like apple cores – and dispose of it back on the mainland.

GETTING AROUND

Once on the islands, boats organised by the resorts or local operators are the only means of transport.

Agnes Water & Town of 1770

Surrounded by national parks and the Pacific Ocean, the twin coastal towns of Agnes Water and Town of 1770 are among Queensland's loveliest and least hectic seaside destinations. The tiny settlement of Agnes Water has the east coast's most northerly surf beach, while the even tinier Town of 1770 (little more than a marina!) marks Captain Cook's first landing in the state, and is great for kayaking and stand-up paddleboarding.

 ACTIVITIES

Reef 2 Beach
Surf School   Surfing
Learn to surf on the gentle breaks of the main beach with this highly acclaimed surf school. A three-hour group lesson is $17 per person; surfboard hire is $20 for four hours. (07-4974 9072; www.reef2beachsurf. com; Agnes Water Shopping Centre, Agnes Water)

1770 Liquid Adventures   Kayaking
Paddle off on a spectacular twilight kayak tour. For $55 you ride the waves off 1770, before retiring to the beach for drinks and snacks as the sun sets – keep an eye out for dolphins. You can also rent kayaks (from $20 per hour). (0428 956 630; www.1770 liquidadventures.com.au)

TOURS

Lady Musgrave Cruises   Cruise
This family-owned company has excellent day trips to Lady Musgrave Island. Groups spend five hours at the island, and cruises include coral viewing in a semisubmersible, lunch, morning and afternoon tea, and snorkelling gear. For an extra cost you can go diving or reef fishing. Island camping transfers are also available for $450 per person. (07-4974 9077; www.1770reef cruises.com; Captain Cook Dr, Town of 1770; adult/child $190/90; departs daily 8.30am)

ThunderCat 1770   Adventure Tour
Go wave-jumping on a surf-racing craft, slingshot over the waves on the Tube Rider Xpress or – best of all – bounce and spin through the water in a sumo suit. For those less in need of an adrenaline hit, explore calmer waterways on a Wilderness Explorer ecotour. (0411 078 810; tours from $70)

EATING

Getaway
Garden Café   Modern Australian $$
An airy cafe with views of lily ponds, just a short walk from some deserted beaches. Everything is delectable, from the salmon Benedict breakfasts to burgers at lunch. The lamb spit roasts on Wednesday and Sunday nights are very popular with locals (book ahead). Stop in for cake and coffee outside of main meal times. (07-4974 9232; 303 Bicentennial Dr, Agnes Water; break-fast $7-19, lunch $10-22, dinner $20-25; 8am-4pm Sun-Thu & 5.30pm-late Wed & Sun)

Tree Bar   Modern Australian $$
This little salt-encrusted waterfront diner and bar is simple, with plastic tables, but it marvellously catches sea views and breezes from the beach through the trees. Local seafood is a winner here, though breakfasts (from $8) are pretty damn fine as well. (07-4974 7446; 576 Captain Cook Dr, Town of 1770; mains $16-34; breakfast, lunch & dinner)

INFORMATION

Agnes Water Visitors Centre (07-4902 1533; 71 Springs Rd, Town of 1770; 9am-5pm Mon-Fri, to 4pm Sat & Sun) Staffed by above-and-beyond volunteers who even leave out information and brochures when it's closed, just in case a lost soul blows into town.

GETTING THERE & AWAY

A handful of **Greyhound** (1300 4739 46863; www.greyhound.com.au) buses detour off the Bruce Hwy to Agnes Water; daily services include

Swimming lagoon, Cairns Esplanade (p124)

Cairns ($224, 21 hours). **Premier Motor Service** (13 34 10; www.premierms.com.au) also goes in and out of town.

Magnetic Island

It's hard not to love Maggie, as she's affectionately known, with her coastal, rocky walking trails, gum trees full of dozing koalas (you're likely to spot some), and surrounding bright turquoise seas. While she may rake in the tourists, there are also plenty of permanent residents who live and work here, making it feel more like a laid-back community than a holiday hot spot.

More than half of this mountainous, triangle-shaped island's 52 sq km is national park, with scenic walks and abundant wildlife, including a large (and adorable) rock wallaby population. Inviting beaches offer adrenaline-pumping water sports, and the chance to just bask in the sunshine. The granite boulders, hoop pines and eucalyptuses are a fresh change from the clichéd tropical island paradise.

The meticulously maintained Boardwalk, Esplanade and Lagoon are well loved

GETTING THERE & AWAY

All ferries arrive and depart Maggie from the terminal at Nelly Bay. Both Townsville ferry terminals have car parking.

Fantasea (www.magnetic-islandferry.com.au; foot passengers adult/child return $29/17) Operates a car ferry crossing eight times daily (seven on weekends) from the south side of Ross Creek, taking 35 minutes. It costs $178 (return) for a car and up to three passengers. Bookings essential.

Sealink (www.sealinkqld.com.au; adult/child return $32/16) Operates a frequent passenger ferry between Townsville and Magnetic Island, which takes around 20 minutes. Ferries depart Townsville from the Breakwater Terminal on Sir Leslie Thiess Dr.

Cairns

Gateway to the Great Barrier Reef and Daintree Rainforest Unesco World Heritage Sites, and starting point for serious 4WD treks into Cape York Peninsula's vast wilderness, Cairns (pronounced 'Cans') depends on tourism for survival. For many, it marks the end of a long journey up the east coast; for others, the beginning of an Aussie adventure. Whichever way you're swinging, you're bound to meet like-minded nomads.

Cairns' tidy CBD is more board shorts than briefcases, although there's no beach in town. The lush, meticulously maintained Boardwalk, Esplanade and Lagoon are well loved, while the Great Barrier Reef, the northern beaches and a bottomless swag of activities are never far away.

◎ SIGHTS & ACTIVITIES

Cairns Esplanade, Boardwalk & Lagoon — Waterfront

Sun- and fun-lovers flock to Cairns' Esplanade's spectacular swimming lagoon on the city's reclaimed foreshore. The artificial, sandy-edged, 4800-sq-metre chlorinated saltwater pool is lifeguard patrolled and illuminated nightly. The adjacent 3km foreshore boardwalk has picnic areas, free barbecues and fitness equipment. Families should follow it north to the play-mazing Muddy's playground. Check the website to see what free, fun events are planned. (www.cairnsesplanade.com.au; ⊙lagoon 6am-9pm Thu-Tue, noon-9pm Wed)

Reef Teach — Interpretive Centre

⬚ Take your knowledge to new depths at this fun, informative centre, where marine experts explain how to identify specific species of fish and coral, and how to approach the reef respectfully. (☑07-4031 7794; www.reefteach.com.au; 2nd fl, Main Street Arcade, 85 Lake St; adult/child $18/9; ⊙lectures 6.30-8.30pm Tue-Sat)

Tjapukai Aboriginal Cultural Park — Cultural Centre

Managed by the area's original custodians, this award-winning cultural extravaganza 15km north of downtown

White Heron on Heron Island (p121)

Blue sea star on brain coral

Spectacled flying fox

BOB CHARLTON / GETTY IMAGES ®

PTEROPUS CONSPICILLATUS / GETTY IMAGES ®

HOLGER LEUE / GETTY IMAGES ®

was extensively renovated in 2015. It tells the story of creation using giant holograms and actors. There's a dance theatre and a gallery, as well as boomerang- and spear-throwing demonstrations and turtle-spotting canoe rides. The Tjapukai by Night dinner-and-show package (adult/child $109/59, from 7pm to 9.30pm) culminates in a fireside corroboree. (07-4042 9999; www.tjapukai.com.au; Cairns Western Arterial Rd, Caravonica; adult/child $40/25; ⊙9am-5pm)

🅐 SHOPPING

Rusty's Markets
Market

No weekend in Cairns is complete without a visit to this fresh produce market where stallholders have mangoes, bananas, pineapples and all manner of tropical fruits piled high, plus farm-fresh honey. You'll also find hot chips, curries and cold drinks. (📞07-4040 2705; www.rustysmarkets.com.au; 57 Grafton St; ⊙5am-6pm Fri & Sat, to 3pm Sun)

EATING

Tokyo Dumpling
Japanese $

Come to this spotless little takeaway for the best *tantanmen* (a kind of spicy sesame ramen) outside Japan and some seriously drool-worthy *gyoza* (dumplings): the cheese and potato variety are to die for. We predict you won't be able to eat here just once. (📞07-4041 2848; 46 Lake St; dumplings from $7, bowls from $10.80; ⊙11.30am-8.30pm)

Meldrum's Pies in Paradise
Bakery $

Multi-award-winning Meldrum's Pies deserves the accolades bestowed upon the seemingly innumerable renditions of the humble Aussie pie it's been baking since 1972. From chicken and avocado, to pumpkin gnocchi and tuna mornay. We loved the steak and mushroo-mmm in creamy pepper sauce! (📞07-4051 8333; 97 Grafton St; pies $4.70-5.90; ⊙7am-4.30pm Mon-Fri, to 2.30pm Sat; 🌱)

Fire-making, Tjapukai Aboriginal Cultural Park

HOLGER LEUE / GETTY IMAGES ©

Where to Stay

As the Great Barrier Reef covers such a vast area, your accommodation choices along the coast are varied. See p116 for a list of the main gateways.

Base yourself on an island or boat in the Whitsundays, grab a backpacker room in carefree Cairns, enjoy a beach retreat on Magnetic Island (outside Townsville), or book a resort room in upmarket Port Douglas.

Above: Palm Cove, Cairns
ANDREW WATSON / GETTY IMAGES ©

Candy   Cafe $$
This quirky, licensed cafe has some seriously sweet treats on its more-than-tempting menu: eggs Benedict with light, fluffy hollandaise; caramelised French toast with poached pears and mascarpone; and the infamous Wagyu beef candy burger with egg, bacon, beetroot jam and vintage cheddar. (☎07-4031 8816; 70 Grafton St; ⊙7am-2.30pm)

Waterbar & Grill   Steakhouse $$$
Cairns' award-winning steakhouse shouldn't fail to deliver on its promise of succulent, juicy steaks and tender burgers. In the unlikely event that you do leave a crabby carnivore, be sure to let them know so they can make it right. Save room for the homemade sticky date pudding... (☎07-4031 1199; www.waterbarandgrill.com.au; Pier Shopping Centre, 1 Pierpoint Rd; mains $19-42; ⊙11.30am-11pm Mon-Sat, to 9pm Sun)

🍷 DRINKING & NIGHTLIFE

Salt House   Bar
Located near the yacht club, Cairns' coolest and classiest bar caters to a twenty-to-thirty-something crowd. Killer cocktails are paired with occasional live music and DJs. The restaurant serves up excellent modern Australian food. Come with cash to burn. (☎07-4041 7733; www.salthouse.com.au; 6/2 Pierpoint Rd; ⊙9am-2am Fri-Sun, noon-midnight Mon-Thu)

Jack   Pub
The Jack is a kick-ass pub by any standards, housed in an unmissable heritage Queenslander with an enormous shaded beer garden. There are nightly events, including live music and DJs, killer pub grub, and an adjacent backpackers, for those who just can't tear themselves away. (☎07-4051 2490; www.thejack.com.au; cnr Spence & Sheridan Sts; ⊙10am-late)

Pier Bar & Grill   Bar
Thoroughly refurbished in 2014, this local institution is loved for its killer waterfront location and daily happy hour (5pm to 7pm). The still-going-strong Sunday Sesh is the place to see and be seen, with live music, food and drink specials and an always happening crowd. (☎07-4031 4677; www.pierbar.com.au; Pier Shopping Centre, 1 Pierpoint Rd; ⊙11.30am-late)

ℹ GETTING THERE & AWAY

AIR
Qantas (www.qantas.com.au), **Virgin Australia** (www.virginaustralia.com) and **Jetstar** (www.jetstar.com.au) arrive and depart **Cairns Airport** (www.cairnsairport.com; Airport Ave), with direct services to all capital cities except Canberra and Hobart. Direct international connections from Cairns include Bali, Shanghai, Guam, Tokyo and Port Moresby.

BUS
Sun Palm (☎07-4087 2900; www.sunpalmtransport.com.au) Operates scheduled and

Kookaburra, Magnetic Island (p123)

charter services between Cairns CBD, the airport ($15, 20 minutes) and Port Douglas (from $40, 1½ hours) via Palm Cove and the northern beaches (from $20).

CAR & MOTORCYCLE

Major car-rental companies have downtown and airport branches. Daily rates start at around $45 for a compact auto and $80 for a 4WD.

TRAIN

New in 2015, **Queensland Rail's** (1800 872 467; www.traveltrain.com.au) scenic, state-of-the-art *Spirit of Queensland* train offers Railbed class, reminiscent of business class on a plane, and standard Premium Economy class seats, with personal entertainment systems. Departs **Cairns Central Railway Station** (Bunda St) on Monday, Wednesday, Thursday, Friday and Sunday for Brisbane (one-way from $222, 24 hours).

The **Kuranda Scenic Railway** (07-4036 9333; www.ksr.com.au; adult/child one-way $49/25, return $79/37) runs daily.

GETTING AROUND

TO/FROM THE AIRPORT

The airport is about 6km north of central Cairns; many accommodation places offer courtesy pickup. **Sun Palm** (07-4087 2900; www.sun palmtransport.com.au) meets all incoming flights and runs a shuttle bus (adult/child $15/7.50) to the CBD. The cheapest shuttle service is operated by **Cairns Airport Shuttle** (0432 488 783; www.cairnsairportshuttle.com.au; per person from $12): the more passengers, the cheaper the fare – online bookings recommended.

Taxis to the CBD are around $25.

BUS

Sunbus (07-4057 7411; www.sunbus.com. au; rides from $2.20) runs local buses all around Cairns.

TAXI

Cairns Taxis (13 10 08; www.cairnstaxis. com.au)

HOLGER LEUE / GETTY IMAGES ©

Aerial view over the Great Barrier Reef in the Whitsundays

THE
WHITSUNDAYS

The Whitsundays

Spread majestically through the Coral Sea, the sandy fringes of these 74 islands disappear into beautiful shades of aqua and indigo ocean. Sheltered by the Great Barrier Reef, there are no crashing waves or deadly undertows, and the waters are particularly perfect for sailing.

Of the numerous stunning beaches and secluded bays, Whitehaven Beach stands out for its pure white silica sand. It is undoubtedly the finest beach in the Whitsundays and, many claim, in the world.

Airlie Beach, on the mainland, is the coastal hub and major gateway to the islands. Only seven of the islands have tourist resorts: options range from the basic accommodation at Hook Island right up to the exclusive luxury of Hayman Island. Most of the Whitsunday Islands are uninhabited, and several offer back-to-nature beach camping and bushwalking.

❶ In This Section

➡ Arriving in the Whitsundays

The two main entry points for the Whitsundays are Airlie Beach, on the mainland, and the resort island of Hamilton Island (which has a major domestic airport, with connections to Sydney, Melbourne, Brisbane and Cairns). If you don't intend basing yourself in either Hamilton or Airlie, it's easy to grab a boat (Cruise Whitsundays is the main operator) to ferry you to your island(s) of choice.

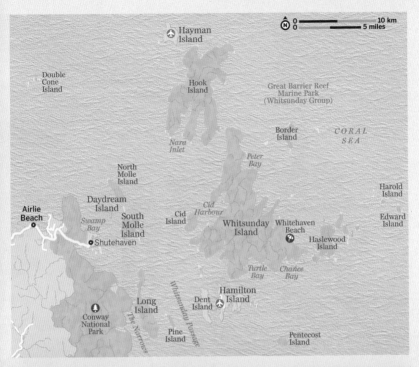

From left: Sea life; *Resonance* by Bonney Bombach, Airlie Beach (p137); Humpback whale

TANYA PUNTTI / GETTY IMAGES ©; GLENN VAN DER KNIJFF / GETTY IMAGES ©; TANYA PUNTTI / GETTY IMAGES ©

Sailing in the Whitsundays

The Whitsundays are the place to skim across fantasy-blue waters on a tropical breeze. Most vessels offer snorkelling on the colourful fringing reefs, while diving and other activities are often optional extras.

Great For...

☑ Don't Miss

The staggeringly photogenic Whitehaven Beach, often acclaimed as Australia's finest.

Day Trips

Other than the superfast Camira, sailing boats aren't able to make it all the way to destinations like Whitehaven Beach on a day trip. Instead they usually go to the lovely Langford Reef and Hayman Island; check before booking.

Multiday Trips

Most overnight sailing packages are for three days and two nights, or two days and one night.

Crewing

In return for a free bunk, meals and a sailing adventure, crewing will get you hoisting the mainsail and cleaning the head. Look for 'Crew Wanted' signs around the marina. Be sure to let someone know where you're

TIM GERARD BARKER / GETTY IMAGES ©

ℹ Need to Know

Sailing the Whitsundays is best between August and October, when the weather is mild and the waters calm.

✕ Take a Break

Daydream Island Resort (p135) has a clutch of bars and restaurants open to non-residents.

★ Top Tip

If you're aboard a smaller boat without a bar, you can usually bring your own bottle along.

keen on wildlife than the wild life. (www. tallshipadventures.com.au; day trips $179)

SV Domino   Sailing

Takes a maximum of eight guests to Bali Hai Island, a little-visited 'secret' of the Whitsundays. Includes lunch and a good two-hour snorkel. The boat is also available for private charters. (www.aussie yachting.com; day trips $180)

Illusions   Sailing

A 12m catamaran that offers the least expensive, yet consistently good, sailing tours to the islands. (☏0455 142 021; www.illusion. net.au; day trips $125)

Booking Your Trip

Once you've decided on your trip, book at one of the many booking agencies or management companies in Airlie Beach, including the following:

Whitsundays Central Reservation Centre (☏1800 677 119; www.airliebeach.com; 259 Shute Harbour Rd)

Whitsunday Sailing Adventures (☏07-4946 4999; www.whitsundaysailing.com; The Esplanade)

Explore Whitsundays (☏07-4946 5782; www.explorewhitsundays.com; 4 The Esplanade)

going, with whom and for how long. Your experience will depend on the vessel, skipper, other crew members.

Recommended Experiences

Camira   Sailing

One of the world's fastest commercial sailing catamarans is now a lilac-coloured Whitsunday icon. This good-value day trip includes Whitehaven Beach, snorkelling, morning and afternoon tea, a barbecue lunch and all refreshments (including wine and beer). (www.cruisewhitsundays.com; day trips $195)

Derwent Hunter   Sailing

A deservedly popular sailing safari on a beautiful timber gaff-rigged schooner. A good option for couples and those more

Long Island

Long Island has secluded, pretty white beaches, lots of adorable, wild rock wallabies and 13km of walking tracks. Some very good deals can be found online to stay at the **Break Free Long Island Resort** (📞1800 075 125; www.oceanhotels.com.au/longisland; ❄ @ ⛱). It's an easy-going, remote place, great for splashing around in the pool with the kids, drinking beer on the gorgeous beach or swinging in a hammock in the shade of a palm tree. Several forest walking trails start at the resort. Kayaks and peddle boats are free, there's minigolf, and plenty of other water-sports equipment is available for hire. Check online for the latest news about the resort's renovations.

Day trippers can also use the facilities at Break Free Long Island Resort.

Cruise Whitsundays connects Long Island with the Port of Airlie with frequent daily services. The direct trip takes about 20 minutes, and costs $48 each way.

South Molle Island

The largest of the Molle group of islands at 4 sq km, South Molle is virtually joined to Mid and North Molle Islands. Apart from the private residence area and golf course at Bauer Bay in the north, the island is all national park and is criss-crossed by 15km of walking tracks, with some superb lookout points.

Day trippers can get to South Molle with **Whitsunday Island Camping Connections – Scamper** (📞07-4946 6285; www.whitsundaycamping.com.au) for $65 return.

Daydream Island

Daydream Island, just over 1km long and 200m wide, would live up to its name a bit more if it wasn't quite so busy; one could be forgiven for mistaking it for a floating theme park. The closest resort to the mainland, it's a very popular day-trip destination and is suitable for everybody, especially busy families, swinging singles and couples looking for a romantic island wedding.

Daydream Island

GLENN VAN DER KNIJFF / GETTY IMAGES ©

The large and delightfully kitsch **Daydream Island Resort & Spa** (1800 075 040; www.daydreamisland.com; d from $368) is surrounded by beautifully landscaped tropical gardens, with a stingray-, shark- and fish-filled lagoon running through it. It has tennis courts, a gym, catamarans, windsurfers, three swimming pools and an open-air cinema all included in the tariff. There's also a club with constant activities to keep children occupied. The resort occupies the entire island; Daydream is not the place to head if you're seeking isolation.

Cruise Whitsundays (07-4946 4662; www.cruisewhitsundays.com; one-way adult/child $36/24) connects Daydream Island to Abel Point Marina and Shute Harbour with frequent daily services.

Whitsunday Island

Whitehaven Beach, on Whitsunday Island, is a pristine 7km-long stretch of blinding sand (at 98% pure silica, some of the whitest sand in the world), bounded by lush tropical vegetation and a brilliant blue sea. From Hill Inlet at the northern end of the beach, the swirling pattern of dazzling sand through the turquoise and aquamarine water paints a magical picture. There's excellent snorkelling from its southern end. Whitehaven is one of Australia's most beautiful beaches.

Whitsunday Island Camping Connections – Scamper (07-4946 6285; www.whitsundaycamping.com.au) can get you there from $105 return.

Hamilton Island

Welcome to a little slice of resort paradise where the paved roads are plied by golf buggies, steep, rocky hills are criss-crossed by walking trails blessed with magnificent sea views, and the white beaches are buzzing with water-sports action. Though it's not everyone's idea of a perfect getaway, it's hard not to be impressed by the selection of high-end accommodation options, restaurants, bars and activities – if

Boat Trips

Ecojet Safari (07-4948 2653; www.ecojetsafari.com.au; per person $195) Explore the islands, mangroves and marine life of the northern Whitsundays on these three-hour, small-group jet-ski safaris (two people per jet ski).

Ocean Rafting (07-4946 6848; www.oceanrafting.com.au; adult/child/family from $134/87/399) Visit the 'wild' side of the islands in a very fast, big yellow speedboat. Swim at Whitehaven Beach, regain your land legs with a guided national park walk, or snorkel the reef at Mantaray Bay and Border Island.

Big Fury (07-4948 2201; adult/child/family $130/70/350) Speed out to Whitehaven Beach on an open-air sports boat, and follow up with lunch and snorkelling at a secluded reef nearby. Great value and bookable through Airlie Beach travel agencies.

PHOTOLIBRARY / GETTY IMAGES ©

you've got the cash, there's something for everyone. Day trippers can use some resort facilities including tennis courts, a golf driving range and a minigolf course and enjoy the island on a relatively economical budget.

From **Catseye Beach**, in front of the resort area, you can hire stand-up paddleboards, kayaks, windsurfers, catamarans, jet skis and other equipment, and go parasailing or waterskiing. Nonmotorised equipment costs around $12 for half-hour rental, $20 for an hour.

From left: *Mermaid sculpture* by David Joffe, Daydream Island (p134); emu, Airlie Beach; Whitehaven Beach, Whitsunday Island (p135)

A few shops by the harbour organise dives and certificate courses, and just about everyone is ready to sign you up for a variety of cruises to other islands and the outer reef.

If you only have time for one walk, make it the clamber up to **Passage Peak** (239m) on the northeastern corner of the island.

✖ EATING

The main resort complex has a number of restaurants. The marina also offers plenty of choices including a good **bakery-deli** (Front St; sandwiches from $9; ⏱7am-4pm), a **fish and chip shop** (Front St; fish & chips $11.50; ⏱10am-9pm Sun-Thu, 11.30am-9pm Fri & Sat), a **tavern** (☎07-4946 8839; Marina Village; mains from $17.50; ⏱11am-midnight) and a general store for self-caterers.

Bommie
Restaurant   Modern Australian $$$
Upmarket Mod Oz cuisine with water views as exclusive as the prices. It's within the resort complex. (☎07-4948 9433; mains $38-50; ⏱6pm-midnight Tue-Sat)

Romano's   Italian $$$
Popular Italian restaurant with a large enclosed deck jutting over the water. (☎07-4946 8212; Marina Village; mains $33-40; ⏱6pm-midnight Thu-Mon)

Mariners Seafood
Restaurant   Seafood $$$
While the emphasis is on seafood, grills are also available. (☎07-4946 8628; Marina Village; mains $38-48; ⏱6pm-late Sat-Wed)

ℹ GETTING THERE & AWAY

AIR
Hamilton Island Airport is the main arrival centre for the Whitsundays, and is serviced by **Qantas** (www.qantas.com.au), **Jetstar** (www.jetstar.com.au) and **Virgin** (www.virginaustralia.com.au).

BOAT
Cruise Whitsundays (☎07-4946 4662; www.cruisewhitsundays.com) Connects Hamilton Island Airport and the marina with the Port of Airlie in Airlie Beach ($48).

GLENN VAN DER KNIJFF / GETTY IMAGES ©

Hayman Island

The most northern of the Whitsunday group, little Hayman is just 4 sq km in area and rises to 250m above sea level. It has forested hills, valleys and beaches, and a luxury five-star resort.

An avenue of stately date palms leads to the main entrance of the gorgeous **One&Only Hayman Island Resort** (☏07-4940 1838; www.hayman.com.au). It's one of the most gilded playgrounds on the Great Barrier Reef with a hectare of swimming pools, landscaped gardens and grounds, and exclusive boutiques.

Resort guests must first fly to Hamilton Island Airport before being escorted to Hayman's fleet of luxury cruisers for a pampered transfer to the resort.

Airlie Beach

Aside from being the jumping-off point for the dreamy Whitsunday Islands, Airlie Beach is a backpacker's good-time town of the highest order. But the 2014 opening of the new, slick Port of Airlie marina, hotel and restaurant complex is an unmissable sign that the village is going more upscale; there are now more options than ever to attract older, more sophisticated travellers wanting a little of the wild life before lifting anchor for the serenity of the sparkling seas and jungle-clad isles in the distance. Those looking to avoid the party scene all together will have no trouble finding quieter lodgings near town.

The Port of Airlie, from where the Cruise Whitsundays ferries depart and where many of the cruising yachts are moored, is about 750m east along a pleasant board-walk. Many other vessels leave from Abel Point Marina (1km west) or Shute Harbour (about 12km east); most cruise companies run courtesy buses into town.

🜨 ACTIVITIES

There are seasonal operators in front of the Airlie Beach Hotel that hire out jet skis, catamarans, sailboards and paddle skis.

MANFRED GOTTSCHALK / GETTY IMAGES ©

Lagoon, Airlie Beach

Lagoon   Swimming
Take a dip year-round in the stinger-croc-
and-tropical-nasties-free lagoon in the
centre of town. (Shute Harbour Rd)

Tandem Skydive
Airlie Beach   Skydiving
Jump out of a plane from 6000ft, 8000ft
or 14,000ft up. (📞07-4946 9115; www.sky
diveairliebeach.com.au; from $199)

Salty Dog Sea Kayaking   Kayaking
Offers guided full-day tours and kayak rental ($50/80 per half-/full day), plus longer
kayak/camping missions (the six-day
challenge costs $1650). It's a charming and
healthy way to see the islands. (📞07-4946
1388; www.saltydog.com.au; Shute Harbour;
half-/full-day trips $80/130)

⊕ TOURS

Cruise Whitsundays   Cruise
Transfers between the Port of Airlie and
Hamilton, Daydream and Long Islands
are provided by Cruise Whitsundays. Also

offers dives on day trips to its reef pontoon.
(📞07-4946 4662; www.cruisewhitsundays.com)

Air Whitsunday   Scenic Flights
Offers a range of tours, including day trips
to Whitehaven ($255), scenic flights and
snorkelling tours of the Great Barrier Reef
($375). (📞07-4946 9111; www.airwhitsunday.
com.au; Terminal 1, Whitsunday Airport)

Whitsunday Crocodile Safari   Tour
Spy on wild crocs, explore secret estuaries and eat real bush tucker. (📞07-4948
3310; www.crocodilesafari.com.au; adult/child
$120/60)

⊗ EATING

Easy Cafe   Cafe $
A hidden-away, modern cafe-deli escape
from Airlie's busy streets. Find the town's
best salad selections, as well as lauded
eggs Benedict on delicious fresh bread.
(Pavillion Arcade; mains $9.50-16; ⊕7.30am-
3pm Thu-Tue; 🛜)

Mr Bones   Pizza $$

Mr Bones is the standard bearer in Airlie Beach for hip, affordable dining. It's rightfully gained a reputation for its perfect thin-based pizzas – try the prawn and harissa. The 'not pizzas' (appetisers including lip-licking blackened fish skewers with pineapple and mint salsa) are also spectacular. (0416 011 615; Lagoon Plaza, 263 Shute Harbour Rd; shared plates $12-17, pizzas $15-23; 9am-9pm Tue-Sat)

Fish D'vine   Seafood $$

Pirates were definitely onto something: this fish-and-rum bar is shiploads of fun, serving up all things nibbly from Neptune's realm and lashings and lashings of rum (over 200 kinds of the stuff). Yo-ho-ho! (07-4948 0088; 303 Shute Harbour Rd; mains $16-30; 5pm-late)

Denman Cellars
Beer Cafe   Tapas $$

Solid Mod Oz food – including lamb meatballs, very small shared seafood tapas, and a stock breakfast menu – pales in comparison to the beer menu (over 700 brews!). (07-4948 1333; Shop 15, 33 Port Dr; tapas $10, mains $18-36; 11am-10pm Mon-Fri, 8am-11pm Sat & Sun)

🍷 DRINKING & NIGHTLIFE

It's said that Airlie Beach is a drinking town with a sailing problem. The bars at Magnums and Beaches, the two big backpackers in the centre of town, are always crowded, and are popular places to kick off a ribald evening.

Phoenix Bar   Bar

Dance and DJ hot spot with drink specials and free pizzas nightly (from 6pm to 8pm). (390 Shute Harbour Rd; 7pm-3am)

Paddy's Shenanigans   Irish Pub

As one would expect. (352 Shute Harbour Rd; 5pm-3am)

Just Wine & Cheese   Wine Bar

Showing that Airlie Beach is going more upscale, this place serves fine examples of

Where to Stay

The ultimate bed in the Whitsundays is a berth aboard a yacht. For those without sea legs, Hamilton and Hayman Islands offer high-end resorts, or there are numerous backpacker and mid-range options in Airlie Beach.

Camping – either independently or as part of an organised group – on beaches such as beautiful Whitehaven Beach on Whitsunday Island is possible; see www.nprsr.qld.gov.au for details.

Above: Rainbow lorikeet
OHN W BANAGAN / GETTY IMAGES ©

what it promises, with a view of the Port of Airlie marina. (Shop 8, 33 Port Dr; wines by the glass $7-18; 3-10pm)

ℹ GETTING THERE & AWAY

AIR

The closest major airports are Whitsunday Coast (Proserpine) and Hamilton Island.

BOAT

Transfers between the **Port of Airlie** (www.portofairlie.com.au) and Hamilton, Daydream and Long Islands are provided by **Cruise Whitsundays** (07-4946 4662; www.cruisewhitsundays.com).

BUS

Whitsunday Transit (07-4946 1800; www.whitsundaytransit.com.au) connects Proserpine (Whitsunday Airport), Cannonvale, Abel Point, Airlie Beach and Shute Harbour.

RON CHAPPLE STUDIOS / GETTY IMAGES ©

THE DAINTREE

The Daintree

The Daintree is many entities in one: it's a Unesco-listed rainforest, a river, a reef, a village and the home of its traditional custodians, the Kuku Yalanji people. Once threatened by logging, this fragile, ancient ecosystem is now a protected national park that encompasses the coastal lowland area between the Daintree and Bloomfield Rivers.

Reasons to visit are as varied as its environs: 4WD trekking through its humid gorges and canopies; hiking through rainforests that trace their lineage back to Gondwanaland; encountering rare and wonderful wildlife; learning firsthand about the ancient culture of its traditional owners; or just checking into a secluded lodge and kicking back with nothing but the sound of the tropics to intrude on your sleep.

❶ In This Section

➡ Arriving in the Daintree

Port Douglas, an hour's bus ride from Cairns on the southern fringe of the park, is the natural jumping-off point for any Daintree adventure. There are plenty of bars, restaurants, hostels, hotels and other comforts here, plus any number of tour operators happy to take you into the wild. Getting to Cow Bay or Cape Tribulation will require your own wheels.

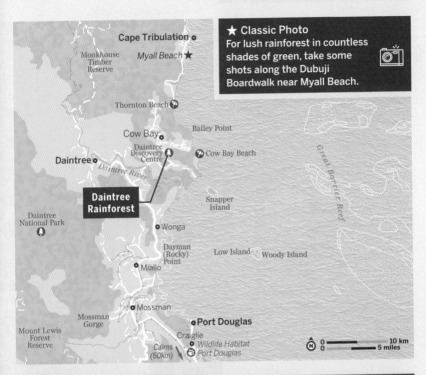

★ **Classic Photo**
For lush rainforest in countless shades of green, take some shots along the Dubuji Boardwalk near Myall Beach.

Cape Tribulation
Monkhouse Timber Reserve
Myall Beach ★
Thornton Beach
Bailey Point
Cow Bay
Daintree Discovery Centre
Cow Bay Beach
Daintree
Daintree River
Daintree Rainforest
Snapper Island
Great Barrier Reef
Daintree National Park
Wonga
Dayman (Rocky) Point
Low Island
Woody Island
Miallo
Mossman
Mossman Gorge
Port Douglas
Mount Lewis Forest Reserve
Craiglie
Wildlife Habitat
Cairns (60km)
Port Douglas

0 — 10 km
0 — 5 miles

From left: Fan palms; Daintree 4WDing; Mangroves in the Daintree
PAUL NEVIN / GETTY IMAGES ©; SILKENPHOTOGRAPHY / GETTY IMAGES ©; MILAN FISCHER / 500 PX ©

Daintree Discovery Centre (p146)

PAUL DYMOND / GETTY IMAGES ©

Daintree Rainforest

Lush green forest, replete with fan palms, prehistoric-looking ferns and twisted mangroves, tumbles down towards a brilliant white-sand coastline in the ancient, World Heritage–listed Daintree rainforest.

Great For...

☑ Don't Miss

The Marrdja Botanical Walk, which lets you walk through a mangrove without getting your feet wet.

Upon entering the forest, you'll be enveloped by a cacophony of birdsong, frog croaking and the buzz of insects. Continue exploring the area via wildlife-spotting night tours, mountain treks, interpretive boardwalks, canopy walks, self-guided walking trails, 4WD trips, horse riding, kayaking, croc-spotting cruises, tropical-fruit orchard tours and tastings...Whew! If you're lucky, you might even spot a cassowary.

History

The greater Daintree Rainforest is protected as part of Daintree National Park, but this protection is not without controversy. In 1983, despite conservationist blockades, what's now the Bloomfield Track was bulldozed through lowland rainforest from Cape Tribulation to the Bloomfield River. Ensuing publicity led to the federal govern-

❶ Need to Know

May to September has the best weather and fewest marine stingers, but also the most tourists.

✕ Take a Break

Heritage Lodge (www.heritagelodge .net.au) in Cape Trib is a delightful spa-resort between rainforest and reef.

★ Top Tip

The water of the Daintree looks inviting; that's just what its population of saltwater crocs thought.

Tours of the Daintree

Daintree
Rainforest Tours   Walking Tour

Book ahead for expert guided rainforest walks that include a dip in Cooper Creek. A variety of itineraries are available. (☏07-4098 9126; www.daintreerainforest.net.au; Cape Tribulation Rd; guided walks $55-300)

Cape Tribulation
Wilderness Cruises   Boat Tour

Join the only tour boat permitted in the Cape Trib section of the Daintree National Park for insightful mangrove and croc-spotting tours. (☏0457 731 000; www.capetribcruises.com; Cape Tribulation Rd; adult/child from $30/22)

Tony's Tropical Tours   Tour

This luxury, small-group (eight to 10 passengers) tour operator specialises in trips to out-of-the-way sections of the Mossman Gorge and Daintree Rainforest (Tour A, adult/child $185/155), and Bloomfield Falls and Cape Trib (Tour B, adults only $210 – good mobility required). Highly recommended. (☏07-4099 3230; www.tropicaltours.com.au; Lot 2, Captain Cook Hwy; day tours from $185)

ment nominating Queensland's wet tropical rainforests for World Heritage listing, generating state government and timber industry opposition. In 1988 the area was inscribed on the World Heritage List and commercial logging here was banned.

Unesco World Heritage listing (http:// whc.unesco.org) doesn't affect ownership rights or control. Since the 1990s the Queensland Government and conservation agencies have attempted to buy back and rehabilitate freehold properties in the area, adding them to the Daintree National Park. Sealing the road to Cape Tribulation in 2002 triggered the buy back of even more land, which, coupled with development controls, now bears the fruits of forest regeneration. Check out **Rainforest Rescue** (www.rainforestrescue.org.au) for more information.

Daintree River to Cape Tribulation

Part of the Wet Tropics World Heritage Area, the spectacular region from the Daintree River north to Cape Tribulation features ancient rainforest, sandy beaches and rugged mountains. North of the Daintree River, electricity is supplied by generators or, increasingly, solar power. Shops and services are limited, and mobile-phone reception is largely nonexistent. The **Daintree River Ferry** (www.douglas.qld.gov.au/community/daintree-ferry; car/motorcycle $13.50/5, bicycle & pedestrian $1; ☺6am–midnight) carries wanderers and their wheels across the river every 15 minutes or so; no bookings.

Cow Bay & Around

Surprisingly, given its tropical-rainforest surrounds, Daintree Village is not tree-covered; cattle farms operate in large clearings next to the Daintree River. Most folk come here to see crocodiles, and there are several small operators who will take you on croc-spotting boat tours.

◉ SIGHTS

The white-sand **Cow Bay Beach**, at the end of Buchanan Creek Rd, rivals any coastal paradise.

Daintree Discovery Centre   Nature Reserve

This award-winning attraction's aerial walkway, which includes a 23m tower used to study carbon levels, takes you high into the forest canopy. A theatre screens films on cassowaries, crocodiles, conservation and climate change. An excellent Aboriginal audio-guide tour is included in the admission fee; tickets are vaild for seven days. (☎07-4098 9171; www.discoverthedaintree.com; Tulip Oak Rd; adult/child/family $32/16/78; ☺8.30am–5pm)

✴ EATING

Cow Bay Hotel   Pub Food $$

If you're craving a decent counter meal, a coldie and that Aussie country pub atmosphere, the Cow Bay (adjacent to the turn-off to the beach) is your only option:

Cape Tribulation Beach

AUSTRALIAN SCENICS / GETTY IMAGES ©

thankfully, it delivers on expectations. (07-4098 9011; Cape Tribulation Rd; mains from $14; 11am-9.30pm)

Daintree Village

You may be racing to the beaches of Cape Trib, but for wildlife lovers it's worth taking the 20km each-way detour to tiny Daintree Village. Croc-spotting cruises on the Daintree River are the main event. Try **Crocodile Express** (07-4098 6120; www.crocodileexpress.com; 1hr cruises adult/ child $23/12; from 8.30am) or **Daintree River Wild Watch** (0447 734 933; www. daintreeriverwildwatch.com.au; 2hr cruises adult/child $60/35), which has informative sunrise birdwatching cruises and sunset photography nature cruises.

The 15 boutique 'banyans' (treehouses) of **Daintree Eco Lodge & Spa** (07-4098 6100; www.daintree-ecolodge.com.au; 20 Daintree Rd; treehouses from $215;) sit high in the rainforest a few kilometres south of the village. Nonguests are welcome at its superb **Julaymba Restaurant** (07-4098 6100; www.daintree-ecolodge.com. au; 20 Daintree Rd; mains $26.50-40; breakfast, lunch & dinner), where the menu makes tasty use of local produce.

No fuel is available in Daintree Village.

Cape Tribulation

This little piece of paradise retains a frontier quality, with low-key development, road signs alerting drivers to cassowary crossings, and crocodile warnings that make beach strolls that little bit less relaxing.

The rainforest tumbles right down to two magnificent, white-sand beaches – Myall and Cape Trib – separated by a knobby cape.

TOURS

Ocean Safari   Snorkelling
Ocean Safari leads small groups (25 people maximum) on snorkelling cruises

 Cape Tribulation Dining

Cape Trib's coolest address and undisputed best dining, **Whet** (07-4098 0007; www.whet.net.au; 1 Cape Tribulation Rd; mains from $16.50; 11.30am-3pm & 5.30-9.30pm) offers trendy Mod Oz cuisine and occasional themed nights and events.

to the Great Barrier Reef, just half an hour offshore. (07-4098 0006; www.ocean safari.com.au; Cape Tribulation Rd; adult/child $128/82)

Jungle Surfing   Outdoors, Hiking
Get right up into the rainforest on an exhilarating flying fox (zipline) ride through the canopy. Guided night walks follow biologist-guides, who shed light on the dark jungle. Rates include pickup from Cape Trib accommodation (self-drive not allowed). (07-4098 0043; www.junglesurfing.com. au; ziplines $90, night walks $40, combo $120; night walks 7.30pm)

Paddle Trek Kayak Tours   Kayaking
Guided sea-kayaking trips and kayak hire. (07-4098 0062; www.capetribpaddletrek. com.au; Lot 7, Rykers Rd; kayak hire per hour $16-55, trips $69-79)

Cape Trib Horse Rides   Horse Riding
Leisurely rides along the beach and into the forest. (07-4098 0043; www.capetrib-horserides.com.au; per person from $99; 8am & 2.30pm)

🛈 GETTING THERE & AWAY

There is no public transport to Cape Tribulation, nor are there airport shuttles to any accommodation beyond the Daintree River. To get here, rent your own wheels or join a day tour.

PAUL DYMOND / GETTY IMAGES ©

NATPHOTOS / GETTY IMAGES ©

From left: Bridge in Mossman Gorge; Roots of a rainforest tree, Mossman Gorge; Rainforest fungus; Boyd's forest dragon

Port Douglas

From its humble origins as a sleepy 1960s fishing village, Port Douglas has grown into a sophisticated alternative to Cairns' hectic tourist scene. With the outer Great Barrier Reef located less than an hour offshore, the Daintree Rainforest practically in the backyard, and more resorts than you can poke a stick at, a growing number of flashpackers, cashed-up couples and fiscally flush families now choose Port Douglas as their base, leaving Cairns at the airport.

The town's main attraction is **Four Mile Beach**, a pristine strip of palm-fringed, white sand which begins at the eastern end of Macrossan St, the main drag for shopping, wining and dining. On the western end of Macrossan you'll find the picturesque Dickson Inlet and Reef Marina, where the rich and famous park their aquatic toys.

⊙ SIGHTS

St Mary's by the Sea   Church
Worth a peek inside (when it's not overflowing with wedding parties), this quaint, nondenominational, white timber church was built in 1911. (✆0418 456 880; 6 Dixie St)

**Wildlife Habitat
Port Douglas**   Zoo
This sanctuary endeavours to keep and showcase native animals in enclosures that mimic their natural environment, while allowing you to get up close to koalas, kangaroos, crocs, cassowaries and more. Tickets are valid for three days. It's 4km from town; head south along Davidson St. (✆07-4099 3235; www.wildlifehabitat. com.au; Port Douglas Rd; adult/child $33/16.50; ⊙8am-5pm)

Trinity Bay Lookout   Viewpoint
Head to Trinity Bay Lookout for spectacular views of the Coral Sea and nearby coral cays. (Island Point Rd)

YEN TEOH / GETTY IMAGES ©

ANDREW WATSON / GETTY IMAGES ©

🕈 ACTIVITIES

Ballyhooley
Steam Railway　　　　Miniature Train
Kids will get a kick out of this cute mini-ature steam train. Every Sunday (and some public holidays), it runs from the little sta-tion at Reef Marina to St Crispins Station. A round trip takes about one hour; discounts are available for shorter sections. (www.ballyhooley.com.au; 44 Wharf St; adult/child day passes $10/5)

Port Douglas Boat Hire　　　Boating
Rents dinghies ($33 per hour) and cano-pied, family-friendly pontoon boats ($43 per hour), plus fishing gear. (www.pdboathire.com.au; Berth C1, Reef Marina)

🕈 TOURS

Quicksilver　　　　　Boat Tour
Major operator with fast cruises to its own pontoon on Agincourt Reef. Try an 'ocean walk' helmet dive ($158) on a submerged platform. Also offers 10-minute scenic helicopter flights ($165, minimum two passengers). (☏ 07-4087 2100; www.quicksilver-cruises.com; Reef Marina; adult/child $225/113)

Poseidon　　　　　Snorkelling
Now part of the Quicksilver group, this luxury catamaran specialises in trips to the Agincourt Ribbon Reefs. (☏ 07-4087 2100; www.poseidon-cruises.com.au; Reef Marina; adult/child $226/158)

Daintree Discovery Tours　　　Tour
Runs half- and full-day tours (adult/child $180/160) of Mossman Gorge, Cassowary Falls and Cape Trib, including waterfalls, river cruises and friendly, knowledgeable guides. (☏ 07-4098 2878; www.daintreediscov-erytours.com.au; 12 Thooleer Close, Mossman; half-day tours from adult/child $90/70)

Reef Sprinter　　　　Snorkelling
This 2¼-hour round trip gets to the Low Isles in just 15-minutes for one to 1½ hours in the water. Half-day outer reef trips are also available (from $200). (☏ 07-4099 6127;

www.reefsprinter.com.au; Shop 3, Reef Marina; adult/child $120/100)

Blue Dive   Diving
Port Douglas' most acclaimed dive operator offers a range of programs including live-aboard trips and PADI certification. Private, guided scuba dives of the reef are available. (📞0427 983 907; www.bluedive.com.au; 32 Macrossan St; reef intro diving courses from $285)

Lady Douglas   Boat Tour
Lovely paddle steamer running four daily croc-spotting tours (including a sunset cruise) along the Dickson Inlet. (📞07-4099 1603; www.ladydouglas.com.au; 1½hr cruises adult/child $30/20)

Bike N Hike   Bicycle Tour
Mountain-bike down the aptly named Bump Track on a cross-country bike tour, or take on an action-packed berserk night tour. (📞0477 774 443; www.bikenhiketours .com.au; bike adventures from $99)

> *a sophisticated alternative to the hectic tourist scene*

🅰 SHOPPING

Port Douglas Markets   Market
These Sunday markets feature handmade crafts and jewellery, local tropical fruits and fresh produce. (Anzac Park, Macrossan St; ⏰8am-1pm Sun)

✖ EATING

Port 'O Call   Australian $$
The kitchen of this equally regarded hostel turns out some seriously good grub at reasonable prices, in a cheery casual environment. Standard staples of fish, steak, pastas and salads are anything but ordinary, and the talented chef's daily specials (including Mexican nights!) are well worth a look-see. Fettuccine carbonara, which can so often be way too creamy, is just right. (📞07-4099 5422; www.portocall. com.au; cnr Port St & Craven Close; mains from $16; ⏰6pm-9.30pm Tue-Sun)

Cafe Fresq   Cafe $$
Best for breakfast (though you'll likely have to wait for a table) this alfresco cafe

Julaymba Restaurant, Daintree Eco Lodge & Spa (p147)

ANDREW WATSON / GETTY IMAGES ©

on Macrossan serves up big helpings of deliciousness, killer coffee and kick-start-your-day fresh juices. (07-4099 6111; 27 Macrossan St; breakfast from $10, mains from $15; 7.30am-3pm)

Salsa Bar & Grill   Modern Australian $$$

Salsa is a stayer on Port's fickle scene. For something a little different try the Creole jambalaya (rice with prawns, squid, crocodile and smoked chicken), or the kangaroo with tamarillo marmalade. We think you'd like a cocktail with that. (07-4099 4922; www.salsaportdouglas.com.au; 26 Wharf St; mains from $22.50; noon-3pm & 5.30-9.30pm;)

On the Inlet   Seafood $$$

Jutting out over Dickson Inlet, tables here are spread out along a huge deck, where you can await the 5pm arrival of George the 250kg groper, who comes to feed most days. Take up the bucket-of-prawns-and-a-drink deal ($18 from 3.30pm to 5.30pm). (07-4099 5255; www.portdouglasseafood.com; 3 Inlet St; mains from $24; noon-11.30pm)

Flames of the Forest   Modern Australian $$$

This unique experience goes way beyond the traditional concept of 'dinner and a show', with diners escorted deep into the rainforest for a truly immersive night of theatre, culture and gourmet cuisine. Bookings essential. (07-4099 5983; www.flamesoftheforest.com.au; Mowbray River Rd; dinner with show, drinks & transfers from $182)

🌀 ENTERTAINMENT

Moonlight Cinema   Cinema

Bring a picnic or hire a bean bag for the Moonlight Cinema's twilight outdoor movie screenings. Check the website for details. (www.moonlight.com.au/port-douglas; QT Resort, 87-109 Port Douglas Rd; adult/child $16/12; Jun-Oct)

Drinking & Nightlife

Tin Shed (07-4099 5553; www.thetin-shed-portdouglas.com.au; 7 Ashford Ave; 10am-10pm) Port Douglas' Combined Services Club is a rare find: bargain dining on the waterfront. Even the drinks are cheap.

Iron Bar (07-4099 4776; www.iron-barportdouglas.com.au; 5 Macrossan St; 11am-3am) Wacky outback decor sets the scene for a wild night out. Nightly 8pm cane-toad races ($5) are a must.

Court House (07-4099 5181; www.courthousehotelportdouglas.com.au; cnr Macrossan & Wharf Sts; 11am-late) Hotel Elegant and unmissable, the old 'Courty' is a lively local, with bands on weekends. There's good pub grub too.

ℹ INFORMATION

The *Port Douglas & Mossman Gazette* comes out every Thursday and has heaps of local info, gig guides and more.

There's no official, impartial visitor information centre in Port Douglas.

ℹ GETTING THERE & AWAY

Coral Reef Coaches (07-4098 2800; www.coralreefcoaches.com.au; adult from $44) Connects Port Douglas with Cairns (1¼ hours) via Palm Cove and Cairns Airport, and offers a local shuttle around town.

Port Douglas Bus (07-4099 5665; www.portdouglasbus.com.au; one-way adult/child $34/20) Operates daily services (1½ hours) between Port Douglas and Cairns via Palm Cove and Cairns Airport.

Sun Palm (07-4087 2900; www.sunpalm transport.com.au; adult from $44) Has frequent daily services between Port Douglas and Cairns (1½ hours) via the northern beaches and the airport.

JOON WEI OOI / 500PX PRIME ©

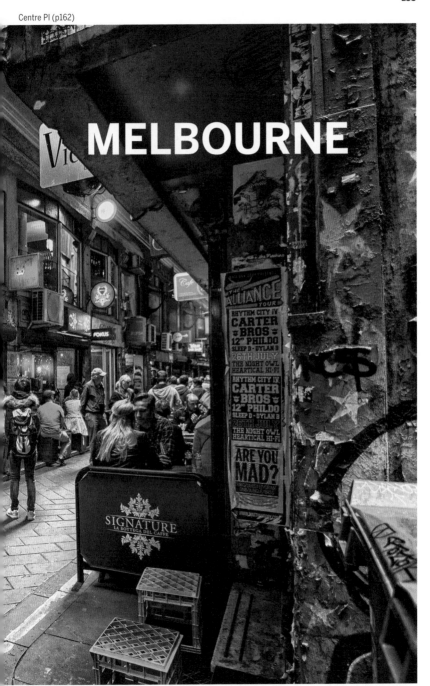

Centre Pl (p162)

MELBOURNE

Melbourne

Stylish, arty Melbourne is a city that's both dynamic and cosmopolitan. Its stately gold-rush-era architecture and multicultural make-up reflect the city's recent history, while edgy street art, top museums and sticky-carpeted band venues point to its present-day personality.

The city's character is largely reliant upon its collection of inner-city neighbourhoods. Despite a long-standing north–south divide (flashy St Kilda versus hipster Fitzroy), there's a coolness about its bars, cafes, restaurants, festivals and inhabitants that transcends the borders. The city centre has meanwhile reinvented itself, with chic eateries and rooftop bars opening in former industrial buildings.

Sport is also crucial to the fabric of the town. Melburnians are passionate about AFL football ('footy'), cricket and horse racing, and also love their Grand Slam tennis and Formula One car racing.

ℹ In This Section

➡ Arriving in Melbourne

Melbourne Airport Most arrivals come through Melbourne Airport, which handles international and domestic flights. Options for the 25-minute trip into the city are taxis, which cost around $65, or the SkyBus, which costs $18 and drops you at Southern Cross Station.

Southern Cross Station The city's long-distance terminus, where you'll arrive if travelling by bus or train. It's a major transport hub, allowing forward travel to most parts of Melbourne.

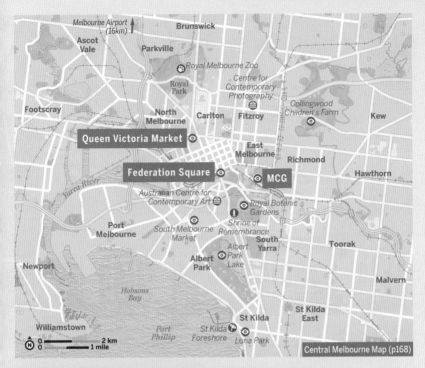

Melbourne Airport
(16km)

Brunswick

Ascot
Vale

Parkville

Royal Melbourne Zoo

Centre for
Contemporary
Photography

Royal
Park

Footscray

North
Melbourne

Carlton

Fitzroy

Collingwood
Children's Farm

Kew

Queen Victoria Market

East
Melbourne

Richmond

Hawthorn

Federation Square

MCG

Yarra River

Australian Centre for
Contemporary Art

Royal Botanic
Gardens

Port
Melbourne

South Melbourne
Market

Shrine of
Remembrance

South
Yarra

Toorak

Newport

Albert
Park

Albert
Park
Lake

Malvern

Hobsons
Bay

St Kilda
East

Williamstown

Port
Phillip

St Kilda
Foreshore

St Kilda

Luna Park

N

0 ___ 2 km
0 ___ 1 mile

Central Melbourne Map (p168)

➡ Melbourne in Two Days

Check out the galleries at **Federation Square** (p156), then join **Melbourne by Foot** (p174) to see the city's streetscapes or chill in a rooftop bar. Next day, stroll along **Birrarung Marr** (p164) and into the **Royal Botanic Gardens** (p171), then shop your way to the **Queen Victoria Market** (p158). Head to the **St Kilda Foreshore** (p172) for an afternoon stroll and later catch a band at the **Esplanade Hotel** (p187).

➡ Melbourne in Four Days

On day three, spend a couple of hours at the **Melbourne Museum** (p171), then revive with a coffee at **D.O.C** (p180) in Lygon St. Back in the city centre, wander through **Chinatown** (p165), and check out Ned Kelly's armour at the **State Library** (p166). On day four, catch a footy game at the **MCG** (p160). Make sure to save time to hit **Mamasita** (p177) for tacos and the **Tote** (p186) in Collingwood for live music.

From left: Gourmet pizza; Southern Cross Station; the Yarra River; Melbourne Museum (p171)

COLIN ANDERSON / GETTY IMAGES ©; ALLAN BAXTER / GETTY IMAGES ©; JUSTIN MCMANUS / GETTY IMAGES ©; PHILIP GAME / GETTY IMAGES ©

Federation Square

While it's taken some time, Melburnians have finally come to embrace Federation Sq, accepting it as a place for congregating – somewhere to celebrate, protest, watch major sporting events or hang out on its deckchairs.

Great For...

☑ Don't Miss

The buzz in Fed Square when major sporting events are broadcast on its giant screen.

Occupying a prominent city block, 'Fed Square' is far from square: its undulating and patterned forecourt is paved with 460,000 hand-laid cobblestones from the Kimberley region, with sight lines to Melbourne's iconic landmarks; its buildings are clad in a fractal-patterned reptilian skin.

Within are cultural heavyweights such as the Ian Potter Centre and the Australian Centre for the Moving Image (ACMI), plus restaurants, bars and the subterranean Melbourne Visitor Centre (p188). The square has free wi-fi, and there are always free public events going on here, particularly on weekends – as well as free daily tai chi from 7.30am and meditation at 12.30pm on Tuesday.

Ian Potter Centre: NGV Australia

Hidden away in the basement of Federation Sq, the **Ian Potter Centre** (🖉 03-8620

JOHN W BANAGAN / GETTY IMAGES ©

Swanston St

Flinders St

Flinders St ⊛

◉ **Federation Square**

Yarra River

Princes Bridge

❶ Need to Know

www.fedsquare.com.au; cnr Flinders & Swanston Sts; ☎; 🚊1, 3, 5, 6, 8, 16, 64, 67, 72, 🚆Flinders St

✕ Take a Break

MoVida (p177), the genre-defining Melbourne Spanish restaurant, is just over Flinders St, should you get peckish.

★ Top Tip

Highly recommended free tours of Fed Square depart Monday to Saturday at 11am; spaces are limited, so arrive 10 to 15 minutes early.

2222; www.ngv.vic.gov.au; exhibition costs vary; ⏱10am-5pm Tue-Sun) is the other half of the National Gallery of Victoria (NGV), set up to showcase its impressive collection of Australian works. Set over three levels, it's a mix of permanent (free) and temporary (ticketed) exhibitions, comprising paintings, decorative arts, photography, prints, sculpture and fashion. There's also a great museum gift shop. Free tours are conducted daily at 11am, noon, 1pm and 2pm.

Australian Centre for the Moving Image

Managing to educate, enthrall and entertain in equal parts, **ACMI** (☎03-8663 2200; www.acmi.net.au; ⏱10am-6pm) is a visual feast that pays homage to Australian cinema and TV, offering an insight into the modern-day Australian psyche perhaps

like no other museum can. Its floating screens don't discriminate against age, with TV shows, games and movies on-call – making it a great place to waste a day watching TV and not feel guilty about it. Free tours are conducted daily at 11am and 2.30pm. **Screenworld** is the main focus here, an interactive exhibition that celebrates the work of Australian cinema and TV; its exhibitions, games lab and zoetrope will interest anyone, whether they're clued in about Dexter from *Perfect Match* or not.

Upstairs, you'll find the **Australian Mediatheque**, a venue set aside for the viewing of programs from the National Film and Sound Archive and ACMI, the perfect hideaway on a rainy day. Mini-festivals of cinema classics and the occasional Pixar blockbuster are screened throughout the year; also keep an eye out for **Melbourne Cinémathèque** (www.melbourne cinematheque.org) screenings.

GLENN BEANLAND / GETTY IMAGES ©

Queen Victoria Market

With over 600 traders, the noisily vibrant Queen Vic Market is the largest open-air market in the southern hemisphere and attracts thousands of shoppers.

Great For...

☑ Don't Miss

Stallholders spruking discounted meat and seafood (still perfectly fresh) just before closing time.

This is where Melburnians sniff out fresh produce among the booming cries of spruiking fishmongers and fruit-and-veg vendors. The wonderful deli hall (with art deco features) is lined with everything from soft cheeses, wines and Polish sausages to Greek dips, truffle oil and kangaroo biltong. Plans for a major overhaul are afoot, although the market's core is unlikely to change much.

The market has been on this site for more than 130 years; before that, from 1837 to 1854, it was the old Melbourne Cemetery (remarkably, around 9000 bodies remain buried here, from underneath Shed F to the carpark leading to Franklin St). There's a small memorial on the corner of Queen and Therry Sts.

As well as the deli hall, make sure you check out the food court, the shops on Elizabeth and Victoria Sts, and the latest

❶ Need to Know

www.qvm.com.au; 513 Elizabeth St; ⏱6am-2pm Tue & Thu, to 5pm Fri, to 3pm Sat, 9am-4pm Sun; 🚆Tourist Shuttle, 🚌19, 55, 57, 59

✖ Take a Break

The market's outpost of the **Padre Coffee Empire** (String Bean Alley, M Shed near Peel St; ⏱7am-2pm Tue & Thu, to 4pm Fri-Sun; 🚌55) is the perfect pit stop when wandering around the market.

★ Top Tip

On busier weekend days many of the deli stalls entice customers with free samples of cheese and other comestibles.

addition to the market, String Bean Alley, a series of shipping containers housing artisans and traders (open Friday, Saturday and Sunday).

Join the thronging locals and snatch up some classic Vic Market treats:

○ A bratwurst from the Bratwurst Stall (step up for a spicy one with German mustard and sauerkraut).

○ Terrine from the French Shop (best enjoyed with French butter and cornichons, from the same source).

○ African hot-smoked blue-eye cutlets from Tribal Tastes (or biltong, or *shitto* – Ghanaian smoked fish and chilli sauce).

○ Superb 'wedding sausage', ham, brawn or bacon from the Polish deli (and perhaps a Polish doughnut or a poppy-seed strudel).

○ A perfectly blended *ras el hanout* from Gewürzhaus (or any spice mix you might possibly need).

What's On

Saturday mornings are particularly buzzing, with marketgoers having breakfast to the sounds and shows of buskers. Clothing and knick-knack stalls dominate on Sundays; these stalls are big on variety, but don't necessarily come looking for style. (If you're in the market for sheepskin moccasins or cheap T-shirts, you'll be in luck.)

On Wednesday evenings from mid-November to the end of February the Summer Night Market takes over. It's a lively social event featuring hawker-style food stalls, bars, and music and dance performances. There's also a winter night market each Wednesday evening in August.

A number of tours are run from the market, including heritage, cultural and foodie tours; check the website for details.

Melbourne Cricket Ground

With a capacity of 100,000 people, the MCG (or 'G') is one of the world's great sporting venues, hosting cricket in the summer, and AFL footy in the winter – for many Australians it's considered hallowed ground.

Great For...

☑ **Don't Miss**

Catching an AFL match – footy season runs from April to September.

History

In 1858 the first game of Australian Rules football was held where the MCG and its car parks now stand; in 1877 it was the venue for the first Test cricket match between Australia and England. The MCG was the main stadium for the 1956 Melbourne Olympics and the 2006 Commonwealth Games. It was also used as army barracks during WWII.

MCG Dreaming

Where did Australian Rules football come from? There's plenty of evidence to suggest that Aboriginal men and women played a form of football (called 'marngrook') prior to white settlement. Did they play it at the MCG site pre-settlement? The MCG has two scar trees from which bark was removed by Aboriginal people to make canoes. These reminders make it clear that Melbourne's

An AFL match at the Melbourne Cricket Ground

MICHAEL DODGE / STRINGER / GETTY IMAGES ©

ⓘ Need to Know

MCG; 📞 03-9657 8888; www.mcg.org.au; Brunton Ave; 🚌 Tourist Shuttle, 🚌 48, 70, 75, 🚆 Jolimont or Richmond

✕ Take a Break

Richmond Hill Cafe & Larder (📞 03-9421 2808; www.rhcl.com.au; 48-50 Bridge Rd; lunch $12-30; ⏰ 8am-5pm; 🚌 75, 🚆 West Richmond) is a 10-minute walk away.

> ★ **Top Tip**
> Never try to drive to the ground on a big match day. You'll surely regret it.

footy fans (and perhaps players) were not the first to gather at the site of the MCG – or the Melbourne Corroboree Ground, as some Indigenous Australians like to call it.

Visiting the Ground

Make it to a game if you can (highly recommended), but otherwise you can still make your pilgrimage on non-match-day **tours** (📞 03-9657 8879; adult/child/family $20/10/50; ⏰ 10am-3pm) that take you through the stands, media and coaches' areas, change rooms and out onto the ground (though unfortunately not beyond the boundary).

Sports fans can also visit the on-site **National Sports Museum** (📞 03-9657 8856; www.nsm.org.au; MCG, Olympic Stand, Gate 3; adult/concession/family $20/10/50, with MCG tour $30/15/70; ⏰ 10am-5pm), which features

five permanent exhibitions focusing on Australia's favourite sports and celebrates historic sporting moments. Kids will love the interactive sports section where they can test their footy, cricket or netball skills. There are some choice sports objects on display: the handwritten notes used to define the rules of Australian Rules football in 1859; a who's who of Aussie cricket's baggy green caps (including Don Bradman's); Brownlow medals; olive branches awarded to Edwin Flack, Australia's first Olympian in 1886; and Cathy Freeman's famous Sydney Olympics swift suit. The museum also incorporates the Champions horse-racing gallery.

Events Held at the MCG

○ **Boxing Day Test** Day one of Melbourne's annually scheduled international Test cricket match, drawing out the cricket fans. Expect some shenanigans from Bay 13.

○ **AFL Grand Final** It's not hard to get your share of finals fever anywhere in Melbourne (particularly at pubs) in September.

Hosier Lane

Walking Tour: Arcades & Lanes

Central Melbourne is a warren of 19th-century arcades and gritty-turned-hip cobbled bluestone lanes featuring street art, basement restaurants, boutiques and bars.

Distance: 3km
Duration: 2½ hours

✕ Take a Break
Hopetoun Tea Rooms (p179) in Block Arcade is perfect for a refreshing pot of Darjeeling and a slice of something sweet.

Start Campbell Arcade, ⬛Flinders St

❶ Campbell Arcade

Start off underground at the art deco Campbell Arcade, also known as Degraves Subway, built for the '56 Olympics and now home to indie stores. There are often contemporary art exhibitions in the glass cases lining the arcade.

❷ Degraves St

Head upstairs to Degraves St, grab a coffee at **Degraves Espresso** (⏱7am-9pm Mon-Fri, 8am-9pm Sat, 8am-6pm Sun) and then continue north, crossing over Flinders Lane to cafe-filled **Centre Place**. This is a good place to start spotting street art, including some excellent examples of stencil graffiti.

❸ Block Arcade

Cross over Collins St, turn left and enter the **Block Arcade** (www.theblockarcade.com.au; 282 Collins St), which runs between Collins and Elizabeth Sts. Built in 1891 and featuring etched-glass ceilings and mosaic floors, it's based on the Galleria Vittorio Emanuele in Milan. Ogle the window display at the Hopetoun Tea Rooms, or pick up a sample or two from Haigh's Chocolates. Exit the other end of the arcade into Little Collins St and perhaps grab an afternoon cocktail at Chuckle Park.

❹ Royal Arcade

Across Little Collins, head into **Royal Arcade** (www.royalarcade.com.au; 335 Bourke St Mall) for a potter. This Parisian-style shopping arcade was built between 1869 and 1870 and is Melbourne's oldest; the

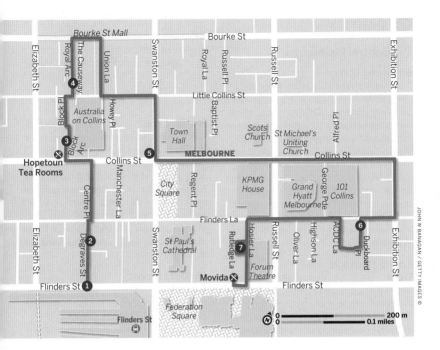

upper walls retain much of the original 19th-century detail. Check out the 1892 Gaunt's Clock with Gog and Magog striking the hour. Wander through to Bourke St Mall, then turn right and walk until you find street-art-covered Union Lane on the right. Follow Union Lane out and turn left onto Little Collins St, then take a right on Swanston St.

➎ Manchester Unity Arcade

Walk south to the Manchester Unity Arcade (1932) on the corner of Collins St. Take a look in this beautiful art deco arcade and landmark Melbourne building, then go back out to Swanston and head east, up the hill, to the 'Paris End' of Collins St.

➏ Duckboard Place

Turn right into Exhibition St, then right into Flinders Lane and continue until you see Duckboard Pl. Head down the lane, taking time to soak up the street art before horseshoeing around into ACDC Lane, named after iconic Australian rockers, and head past rock 'n' roll dive bar **Cherry** (www. cherrybar.com.au; ⊙6pm-3am Tue & Wed, 5pm-5am Thu-Sat, 2-6.30pm Sun).

➐ Hosier Lane

Continue down Flinders Lane to the street-art meccas of Hosier Lane and Rutledge Lane before finishing with tapas and a hard-earned drink at MoVida (p177).

Finish Movida, 🚇Flinders St

◎ SIGHTS

◎ Central Melbourne

Birrarung Marr   Park

The three-terraced Birrarung Marr is a welcome addition to Melbourne's patchwork of parks and gardens, featuring grassy knolls, river promenades, a thoughtful planting of indigenous flora and great viewpoints of the city and the river. There's also a scenic route to the Melbourne Cricket Ground (p160; MCG) via the 'talking' William Barak Bridge – listen out for songs, words and sounds representing Melbourne's cultural diversity as you walk. (btwn Federation Sq & Yarra River; 🚊1, 3, 5, 6, 8, 16, 64, 67, 72, 🚉Flinders St)

**Koorie Heritage
Trust**   Cultural Centre

Devoted to southeastern Aboriginal culture, this centre displays interesting artefacts and oral history. Its gallery spaces show a variety of contemporary and traditional work, a model scar tree at the centre's heart, and a permanent chronological

display of Victorian Koorie history. Behind the scenes, significant objects are carefully preserved; replicas that can be touched by visitors are used in the displays. (📞03 8662 6300; www.koorieheritagetrust.com; Yarra Bld, Federation Sq; gold coin donation, tours $15; ⏰10am-5pm; 🚊24,30, 🚉Flagstaff) ♿

Hosier Lane   Street

Melbourne's most celebrated laneway for street art, Hosier Lane's cobbled length draws camera-wielding crowds snapping edgy graffiti, stencils and art installations. Subject matter runs to the mostly political and counter culture, spiced with irreverent humour; pieces change almost daily (not even a Banksy is safe here). Be sure to see Rutledge Lane (which horseshoes around Hosier), too. (🚊75, 70)

**Flinders Street
Station**   Historic Building

If ever there was a true symbol of the city, Flinders Street Station would have to be it. Built in 1854, it was Melbourne's first railway station, and you'd be hard-pressed to find a Melburnian who hasn't uttered the phrase 'Meet me under the clocks' at one

Birrarung Marr and the Yarra River

RACHEL LEWIS / GETTY IMAGES ©

time or another (the popular rendezvous spot is located at the front entrance of the station). Stretching along the Yarra, it's a beautiful neoclassical building topped with a striking octagonal dome. (cnr Flinders & Swanston Sts; 🛜)

Young & Jackson's   Historic Building

Across the street from Flinders Street Station is a pub (www.youngandjacksons. com.au; cnr Flinders & Swanston Sts; 🚉Flinders St) known less for its beer (served since 1861) than its iconic nude portrait of the teenaged **Chloe**, painted by Jules Joseph Lefebvre. Chloe's yearning gaze, cast over her shoulder and out of the frame, was a hit at the Paris Salon of 1875. (www.youngand jacksons.com.au; cnr Flinders & Swanston Sts; 🕑11am-late; 🚋Tourist Shuttle, 🚋City Circle, 1, 3, 5, 6, 8, 16, 64, 67, 72, 🚉Flinders St)

Sea Life Melbourne
Aquarium   Aquarium

This aquarium is home to rays, gropers and sharks, all of which cruise around a 2.2-million-litre tank, watched closely by visitors in a see-through tunnel. See the penguins in icy 'Antarctica' or get up close to one of Australia's largest saltwater crocs in the crocodile lair. Divers are thrown to the sharks three times a day; for between $210 and $300 you can join them. Admission tickets are cheaper online. (🗗03-9923 5999; www.melbourneaquarium. com.au; cnr Flinders & King Sts; adult/child/family $38/22/96; 🕑9.30am-6pm, last entry 5pm; 🚋70, 75)

Immigration Museum   Museum

The Immigration Museum uses personal and community voices, images and memorabilia to tell the many stories of Australian immigration. Symbolically housed in the old Customs House, the restored building alone is worth the visit: the Long Room is a magnificent piece of Renaissance revival architecture. (🗗13 11 02; www.museumvictoria. com.au/immigrationmuseum; 400 Flinders St; adult/child $12/free; 🕑10am-5pm; 🚋70, 75)

Melbourne for Children

Australian Centre for the Moving Image (ACMI; p157) Free access to computer games and movies may encourage square eyes, but it's a great spot for a rainy day.

Royal Melbourne Zoo (p171) A broad range of animals are housed in nature-like enclosures.

National Sports Museum (p161) Just walking in will get your junior champion's heart rate up.

Melbourne Museum (p171) Head to the Children's Museum for hands-on exhibits that make kids squeal.

Above: Orang-utans at the Royal Melbourne Zoo
ALEX DISSANAYAK / GETTY IMAGES ©

Chinatown   Area

Chinese miners arrived in search of the 'new gold mountain' in the 1850s and settled in this strip of Little Bourke St, now flanked by traditional red archways. The **Chinese Museum** (🗗03-9662 2888; www. chinesemuseum.com.au; 22 Cohen Pl; adult/child $8/6; 🕑10am-5pm) here does a wonderful job of putting it into context with five floors of displays, including artefacts from the gold-rush era, dealings under xenophobic White Australia Policy and the stunning 63m-long, 200kg Millennium Dragon that bends around the building; in full flight it needs eight people just to hold up its head alone. (Little Bourke St, btwn Spring & Swanston Sts; 🚋1, 3, 5, 6, 8, 16, 64, 67, 72)

Seaside Williamstown

Williamstown is a yacht-filled gem just a short boat ride (or drive or train ride) from Melbourne's CBD. It has stunning views of Melbourne, and a bunch of touristy shops along its esplanade. The park by the marina is made for picnics or takeaway fish and chips.

Gem Pier is where passenger ferries dock to drop off and collect those who visit Williamstown by boat. It's a fitting way to arrive, given the area's maritime ambience.

Williamstown Ferries (03-9682 9555; www.williamstownferries.com.au; Williamstown-Southbank adult/child $18/9, return $28/14) Plies Hobsons Bay daily, stopping at Southgate and visiting a number of sites along the way, including Docklands.

Melbourne River Cruises (03-8610 2600; www.melbcruises.com.au; Williamstown-City adult/child $22/11) Also docks at Gem Pier, travelling up the Yarra River to Southgate. Pick up a timetable from the very useful visitors centre in Williamstown or at Federation Sq, or contact the companies directly; bookings are advised.

Above: Melbourne city views from Williamstown
RACHEL LEWIS / GETTY IMAGES ©

State Library of Victoria Library

A big player in Melbourne's achievement of being named Unesco City of Literature in 2008, the State Library has been the forefront of Melbourne's literary scene since it opened in 1854. With over two million books

in its collection, it's a great place to browse. Its epicentre, the octagonal La Trobe Reading Room, was completed in 1913; its reinforced-concrete dome was the largest of its kind in the world and its natural light illuminates the ornate plasterwork and the studious Melbourne writers who come here to pen their works. Another highlight is the collection of Ned Kelly memorabilia, including his suit of armour. (03-8664 7000; www.slv.vic.gov.au; 328 Swanston St; 10am-9pm Mon-Thu, to 6pm Fri-Sun; ; 1, 3, 5, 6, 8, 16, 64, 67, 72, Melbourne Central)

Southbank & Docklands

NGV International Gallery
Beyond the water-wall facade you'll find an expansive collection set over three levels, covering international art that runs from the ancient to the contemporary. Key works include a Rembrandt, a Tiepolo and a Bonnard. You might also bump into a Monet, a Modigliani, or a Bacon. It's also home to Picasso's *Weeping Woman,* which was the victim of an art heist in 1986. Free 45-minute tours occur hourly from 11am to 2pm, which alternate to different parts of the collection. (03-8662 1555; www.ngv. vic.gov.au; 180 St Kilda Rd; exhibition costs vary; 10am-5pm Wed-Mon; ; Tourist Shuttle, 1, 3, 5, 6, 8, 16, 64, 67, 72)

Arts Centre Melbourne Arts Centre
The Arts Centre is made up of two separate buildings: Hamer Hall (the concert hall) and the theatres building (under the spire). Both are linked by a series of landscaped walkways. The George Adams Gallery and St Kilda Road Foyer Gallery are free gallery spaces with changing exhibitions. In the foyer of the theatres building, pick up a self-guided booklet for a tour of art commissioned for the building and including works by Arthur Boyd, Sidney Nolan and Jeffrey Smart. (bookings 1300 182 183; www.artscentremelbourne.com.au; 100 St Kilda Rd; box office 9am-8.30pm Mon-Fri, 10am-5pm Sat; Tourist Shuttle, 1, 3, 5, 6, 8, 16, 64, 67, 72, Flinders St)

Eureka Skydeck — Viewpoint

Melbourne's tallest building, the 297m-high Eureka Tower was built in 2006, and a wild elevator ride takes you up to its 88 floors in less than 40 seconds (check out the photo on the elevator floor if there's time). The 'Edge' – a slightly sadistic glass cube – cantilevers you out of the building; you've got no choice but to look down. (www.eureka skydeck.com.au; 7 Riverside Quay; adult/child/family $19.50/11/44, The Edge extra $12/8/29; ⏰10am-10pm, last entry 9.30pm; 🚆Tourist Shuttle)

Australian Centre for Contemporary Art — Gallery

ACCA is one of Australia's most exciting and challenging contemporary galleries, showcasing a range of local and international artists. The building is, fittingly, sculptural, with a rusted exterior evoking the factories that once stood on the site, and a soaring interior designed to house often massive installations. From Flinders Street Station, walk across Princes Bridge and along St Kilda Rd. Turn right at Grant St, then left to Sturt. (ACCA; 📞03-9697 9999; www.accaonline.org.au; 111 Sturt St; ⏰10am-5pm Tue & Thu-Sun, to 8pm Wed; 🚆1) FREE

◎ East Melbourne

Fitzroy Gardens — Park

The city drops away suddenly just east of Spring St, giving way to Melbourne's beautiful backyard, the Fitzroy Gardens. The stately avenues lined with English elms, flowerbeds, expansive lawns, strange fountains and a creek are a short stroll from town. The highlight is **Cooks' Cottage** (📞03-9419 5766; adult/child/family $6/3/16.50; ⏰9am-5pm), shipped brick by brick from Yorkshire and reconstructed in 1934 (the cottage actually belonged to the navigator's parents). It's decorated in mid-18th-century style, with an exhibition about Captain James Cook's eventful, if controversial, voyages to the Southern Ocean. (www.fitzroygardens.com; Wellington Pde, btwn Lansdowne & Albert Sts; 🚆Tourist Shuttle, 🚋75, 🚆Jolimont)

Royal Exhibition Building (p171)

DAVID HANNAH / GETTY IMAGES ©

Central Melbourne

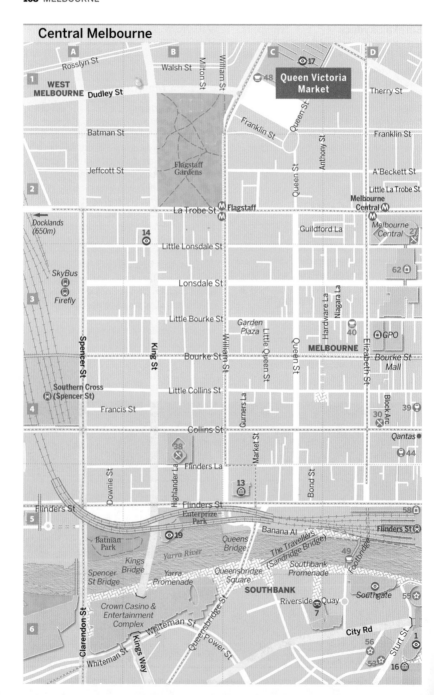

A

1 WEST
MELBOURNE

Rosslyn St

Walsh St **B**

Milton St

William St

Dudley St

Batman St

Jeffcott St

2

Flagstaff
Gardens

La Trobe St Ⓜ Flagstaff
Ⓜ

C ⊙17

🍴48 **Queen Victoria
Market**

Queen St

Franklin St

Therry St **D**

Franklin St

Anthony St

A'Beckett St

Queen St

Little La Trobe St

Melbourne
Central Ⓜ

Docklands
(650m)

14
⊙

Little Lonsdale St

Guildford La

Ⓜ
Melbourne
Central 27
✕

SkyBus

Firefly

3

Lonsdale St

Little Bourke St

Garden
Plaza

62 🏛

Hardware La

Niagara La

Spencer St

King St

William St

Little Queen St

Queen St

40

MELBOURNE

🔒GPO

Southern Cross
(Spencer St)

4

Bourke St

Little Collins St

Francis St

Gurners La

Elizabeth St

Bourke St
Mall

Block Arc

30
⊗

39

Collins St

38
⊗

Flinders La

Market St

Bond St

Qantas ●

44

13

Downie St

Highlander La

Flinders St

Flinders St

Enterprize
Park

Flinders St 🚆

58 🔒

5

⊙19

Batman
Park

Kings
Bridge

Spencer
St Bridge

Banana Al

Queens
Bridge

Yarra River

Yarra
Promenade

Queensbridge
Square

The Travellers
(Sandridge Bridge)

Southbank
Promenade

49

Footbridge

Southgate 55

6

Crown Casino &
Entertainment
Complex

Clarendon St

Kings Way

Whiteman St

Whiteman St

Queensbridge St

Power St

City Rd

SOUTHBANK

Riverside Quay
7

Southbank

Southgate

56
☆

53
☆

16 🏛

Sturt St

1

⊙

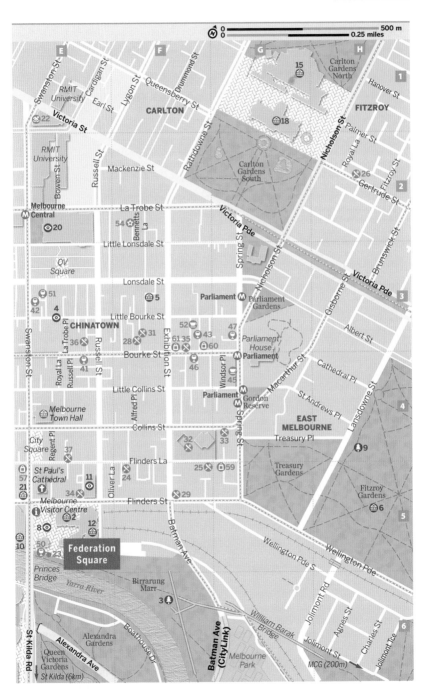

Central Melbourne

⊙ Fitzroy & Around

Collingwood Children's Farm   Farm
The inner city melts away at this rustic riverside retreat that's beloved not just by children. There's a range of frolicking farm animals that kids can help feed, as well as rambling gardens and grounds for picnicking on warm days. The farm cafe is open early and can be visited without entering the farm itself. The monthly **farmers market** (www.mfm.com.au; adult/child $2/ free; ◷8am-1pm 2nd Sat of the month), held right by the river, is a local highlight, with everything from rabbits to roses to organic milk hoisted into baskets. (www.farm.org.au; 18 St Heliers St, Abbotsford; adult/child/family $9/5/18; ◷9.15am-4.30pm; 🚌200, 201, 207, 🚉Victoria Park)

Centre for Contemporary Photography   Gallery
This not-for-profit centre has a changing schedule of photography exhibitions across

a couple of galleries. Shows traverse traditional technique and the highly conceptual. There's a particular fascination with work involving video projection, including a nightly after-hours screening in a window. Also offers photography courses. (CCP; ☏03-9417 1549; www.ccp.org.au; 404 George St, Fitzroy; ⊘11am-6pm Wed-Fri, noon-5pm Sat & Sun; 🚌86) FREE

◎ Carlton & Around

Melbourne Museum   Museum
This museum provides a grand sweep of Victoria's natural and cultural histories, with exhibitions covering everything from dinosaur fossils and giant squid specimens to the taxidermy hall, a 3D volcano and an open-air forest atrium of Victorian flora. Become immersed in the legend of champion racehorse and national hero Phar Lap. The excellent Bunjilaka, on the ground floor, presents Indigenous Australian stories and history told through objects and Aboriginal voices with state-of-the-art technology. There's also an IMAX cinema on-site. (☏13 11 02; www.museumvictoria.com.au; 11 Nicholson St, Carlton; adult $12, child & student free, exhibitions extra; ⊘10am-5pm; 🚌Tourist Shuttle, 🚋City Circle, 86, 96, 🚉Parliament)

Royal Exhibition Building   Historic Building
Built for the International Exhibition in 1880, and winning Unesco World Heritage status in 2004, this beautiful Victorian edifice symbolises the glory days of the Industrial Revolution, the British Empire and 19th-century Melbourne's economic supremacy. It was the first building to fly the Australian flag, and Australia's first parliament was held here in 1901; it now hosts everything from trade fairs to car shows, as well as the biennial Melbourne Art Fair. Tours of the building leave from the Melbourne Museum at 2pm. (☏13 11 02; www.museumvictoria.com.au/reb; 9 Nicholson St, Carlton; tours adult/child $10/7; 🚌Tourist Shuttle, 🚋City Circle, 86, 96, 🚉Parliament)

Royal Melbourne Zoo   Zoo
Established in 1861, this is the oldest zoo in Australia and the third-oldest in the world. Today it's one of the city's most popular attractions. Set in spacious, prettily landscaped gardens, the zoo's enclosures aim to simulate the animals' natural habitats. Walkways pass through the enclosures: you can stroll through the bird aviary or enter a tropical hothouse full of colourful butterflies. (☏03-9285 9300; www.zoo.org. au; Elliott Ave, Parkville; adult/child $30/13.20, children free on weekends & holidays; ⊘9am-5pm; 🚌505, 🚋55, 🚉Royal Park)

◎ South Yarra

Royal Botanic Gardens   Gardens
One of the finest botanic gardens in the world, the Royal Botanic Gardens are one of Melbourne's most glorious attractions. Sprawling beside the Yarra River, the beautifully designed gardens feature a global selection of plantings and specifically endemic Australian flora. Mini-ecosystems, such as a cacti and succulents area, a herb garden and an indigenous rainforest, are set amid vast lawns. Take a book, picnic or Frisbee – but most importantly, take your time. (www.rbg.vic.gov.au; Birdwood Ave, South Yarra; ⊘7.30am-sunset, Children's Garden open Wed-Sun, closed mid-Jul–mid-Sep; 🚌Tourist Shuttle, 🚋1, 3, 5, 6, 8, 16, 64, 67, 72) FREE

Shrine of Remembrance   Monument
Beside St Kilda Rd stands the massive Shrine of Remembrance, built as a memorial to Victorians killed in WWI. It was built between 1928 and 1934, much of it with depression-relief, or 'susso', labour. Its bombastic classical design is partly based on the Mausoleum of Halicarnassus, one of the seven ancient wonders of the world. The shrine is visible from the other end of town, and planning regulations continue to restrict any building that would obstruct the view of it from Swanston St as far back as Lonsdale St. (www.shrine.org.au; Birdwood Ave, South Yarra; ⊘10am-5pm; 🚌Tourist Shuttle, 🚋1, 3, 5, 6, 8, 16, 64, 67, 72) FREE

What's On

Australian Open (www.australianopen.
com; National Tennis Centre; ⊙Jan) The
world's top tennis players and huge,
merry-making crowds descend for
Australia's Grand Slam tennis
championship.

Melbourne Food & Wine Festival (www.
melbournefoodandwine.com.au; ⊙Mar)
Market tours, cooking classes and
presentations by celeb chefs take place
at venues across the city.

**Melbourne International Comedy
Festival** (www.comedyfestival.com.au;
Melbourne Town Hall; ⊙Mar-Apr) An enormous range of local and international
comic talent hits town with four weeks
of laughs.

Melbourne International Film Festival
(MIFF; www.miff.com.au; ⊙Jul-Aug) This
cinema-fest, one of the world's biggest,
makes winter more than bearable.

Above: Band at Melbourne Food & Wine Festival
JOHN HAY / GETTY IMAGES ©

◎ St Kilda

St Kilda Foreshore   Beach
While there are palm-fringed promenades,
a parkland strand and a long stretch of
sand, St Kilda's seaside appeal is more
Brighton, England, than Baywatch, despite
20-odd years of glitzy development. The
kiosk at the end of St Kilda Pier (an exact
replica of the original, which burnt down in
2003, a year short of its centenary) is as
much about the journey as the destination.
(Jacka Blvd; 🚊16, 96)

Luna Park   Amusement Park
It opened in 1912 and still retains the feel of
an old-style amusement park, with creepy
Mr Moon's gaping mouth swallowing you
up as you enter. There's a heritage-listed
'scenic railway' (the oldest operating roller
coaster in the world) and a beautifully bar-
oque carousel with hand-painted horses,
swans and chariots, as well as the full complement of gut-churning rides. (🕿03-9525
5033; www.lunapark.com.au; 18 Lower Esplanade,
St Kilda; single ride adult/child $11/9, unlimited
rides $49/39; 🚊16, 96)

◎ South Melbourne &
Albert Park

South Melbourne Market   Market
The market's labyrinthine interior is packed
with stalls ranging from old-school to
boutique. It's been on this site since 1864
and is a neighbourhood institution, as are
its famous dim sims (sold here since 1949).
There are plenty of atmospheric eateries
and a lively night market on Thursdays
from mid-January to early March. There's
a cooking school here, too – see website
for details. (www.southmelbournemarket.com.
au; cnr Coventry & Cecil Sts, South Melbourne;
⊙8am-4pm Wed, Sat & Sun, to 5pm Fri; 🚊96)

Albert Park Lake   Lake
Elegant black swans give their inimitable
bottoms-up salute as you jog, cycle or walk
the 5km perimeter of this constructed lake.
Lakeside Dr was used as an international
motor-racing circuit in the 1950s, and since
1996 the revamped track has been the venue for the Australian Formula One Grand
Prix each March. Also on the periphery is
the Melbourne Sports & Aquatic Centre,
with an Olympic-size pool and child-
delighting wave machine. (btwn Queens Rd,
Fitzroy St, Aughtie Dr & Albert Rd; 🚊96)

✪ ACTIVITIES

Stand Up Paddle HQ   Water Sports
Arrange a lesson or hire SUP equipment from
St Kilda Pier, or join one of the Yarra River

Flinders Street Station (p164)

tours. (☎0416 184 994; www.supb.com.au; St Kilda Pier; hire per hour $30, 2hr tours $89; 🚇96)

Melbourne City Baths   Swimming
The City Baths were literally public baths when they opened in 1860 and were intended to stop people bathing in and drinking from the seriously polluted Yarra River. They now boast the city centre's largest pool (30m), where you can do laps in a 1903 heritage-listed building. (☎03-9663 5888; www.melbourne.vic.gov.au/melbournecity baths; 420 Swanston St, Melbourne; adult/child $6.10/3.60; ☉6am-10pm Mon-Thu, to 8pm Fri, 8am-6pm Sat & Sun; 🚇Melbourne Central)

🅖 TOURS

Real Melbourne
Bike Tours   Bicycle Tour
🚲 These bike tours allow you to cover more ground on a well-thought-out itinerary that provides a local's insight to Melbourne, with a foodie focus. Rents bikes, too. (☎0417 339 203; www.rentabike.net.au/biketours; Federation Sq; 4hr tour incl lunch adult/child $110/79; ☉10am; 🚇Flinders St)

Aboriginal
Heritage Walk   Cultural Tour
🚶 The Royal Botanic Gardens are on a traditional camping and meeting place of the original Indigenous owners, and this tour takes you through their story – from songlines to plant lore, all in 90 fascinating minutes. The tour departs from the visitor centre. (☎03-9252 2300; www.rbg.vic.gov.au; adult/child $25/10; ☉11am Sun-Thu; 🚌Tourist Shuttle, 🚇8)

City Circle Trams   Tram
FREE Designed primarily for tourists, this free tram service travels around the city centre, passing many city sights along the way with an audio commentary. It runs every 10 minutes or so. (Tram 35; ☎13 16 38; www.ptv.vic.gov.au; ☉10am-6pm Sun-Wed, to 9pm Thu-Sat;)

Hidden Secrets Tours   Walking Tour
🚶 Offers a variety of walking tours covering subjects such as lanes and arcades, wine, architecture, coffee and cafes, and vintage Melbourne. (☎03-9663 3358; www.hiddensecretstours.com; tours $29-150)

Kayak Melbourne
Kayaking

Don't miss the chance to see the Yarra River by kayak. These two-hour tours take you past Melbourne's newest city developments and explain the history of the older ones. Moonlight tours are most evocative and include a dinner of fish and chips. Tours usually depart from Victoria Harbour, Docklands – check website for directions. (0418 106 427; www.kayakmelbourne.com.au; tours $72-117; 11, 31, 48)

Melbourne By Foot
Walking Tour

Take a few hours out and experience a mellow, informative 4km walking tour that covers laneway art, politics, Melbourne's history and diversity. Tour includes a refreshment break. Highly recommended; book online. (0418 394 000; www.mebournebyfoot.com; tours $40; Flinders St)

Melbourne Visitor Shuttle
Bus Tour

This bus shuttle runs a 1½-hour round-trip with audio commentary and 13 stops that take passengers to all Melbourne's main sights. (Tourist Shuttle; www.thatsmelbourne.com.au; daily ticket $5, children under 10 yr free; 9.30am-4.30pm)

SHOPPING

Central Melbourne

Craft Victoria Shop
Crafts

This retail arm of Craft Victoria showcases the best of handmade, mainly by local Victorian artists. Its range of jewellery, textiles, accessories, glass and ceramics bridges the art/craft divide and makes for some wonderful mementos of Melbourne. There are also a few galleries with changing exhibitions; admission is free. (03-9650 7775; www.craft.org.au; 31 Flinders Lane; 11am-6pm Mon-Sat; City Circle, 70, 75)

Alice Euphemia
Fashion, Jewellery

Art-school cheek abounds in the Australian-made and designed labels sold here – Romance was Born, Karla Spetic and Kloke, to name a few. Jewellery sways between the shocking and exquisitely pretty, and the upstairs space hosts regular events and exhibitions. (Shop 6, Cathedral Arcade, 37 Swanston St; 10am-6pm Mon-Thu & Sat, to 7pm Fri, noon-5pm Sun; Flinders St)

RAY WARREN / GETTY IMAGES ©

Melbournalia   Gifts, Souvenirs
Pop-up store turned permanent, this is the place to stock up on interesting souvenirs by local designers – from tram tote bags and city-rooftop honey to prints of the city's icons and great books on Melbourne. (www.melbournalia.com.au; Shop 5, 50 Bourke St; ⊙10am-6pm Mon-Thu, to 8pm Fri, 11am-5pm Sat & Sun; 🚃86, 96)

City Hatters   Accessories
Located beside the main entrance to Flinders Street Station, this is the most convenient place to purchase an iconic Akubra hat, kangaroo-leather sun hat or something a little more unique. (🖉03-9614 3294; www.cityhatters.com.au; 211 Flinders St; ⊙9.30am-6pm Mon-Fri, 9am-5pm Sat, 10am-4pm Sun; 🚉Flinders St)

**Original & Authentic
Aboriginal Art**   Arts, Crafts
Open for 25 years this centrally located gallery has a good relationship with its Indigenous artists across Australia and offers stunning and affordable pieces, all with author profiles. (🖉03-9663 5133; www.

originalandauthenticaboriginalart.com; 90 Bourke St; ⊙11am-6pm; 🚃86, 96)

RM Williams   Clothing
An Aussie icon, even for city slickers, this brand will kit you up with stylish essentials for working the land, including a pair of those famous boots. (🖉03-9663 7126; www.rmwilliams.com.au; Melbourne Central, Lonsdale St; ⊙10am-6pm Mon-Thu & Sat, to 9pm Fri, to 5pm Sun; 🚉Melbourne Central)

🅰 Fitzroy

Third Drawer Down   Homewares
It all started with their signature tea towel designs (now found in MOMA in New York) at this 'museum of art souvenirs'. Third Drawer Down make life beautifully unusual by stocking absurdist pieces with a sense of humour as well as high-end art by well-known designers. (www.thirddrawerdown.com; 93 George St, Fitzroy; ⊙11am-5pm Mon-Sat; 🚃86)

Aesop   Beauty
This homegrown empire specialises in citrus-and-botanical-based aromatic

★ **Top Five Cocktail Bars**
Lui Bar (p182)
Bar Americano (p182)
Everleigh (p184)
Panama Dining Room (p184)
Cookie (p182)

From left: Ponyfish Island (p183); Chinatown (p165); Degraves St (p162)

CHERYL FORBES / GETTY IMAGES ©

DAVID HANNAH / GETTY IMAGES ©

Don't Miss
Markets

Rose Street Artists' Market (www.rosest market.com.au; 60 Rose St, Fitzroy; ⊙11am-5pm Sat; 🚊112) One of Melbourne's most popular art-and-craft markets showcases the best local designers, just a short stroll from Brunswick St. Here you'll find up to 70 stalls selling matte silver jewellery, clothing, milk-bottle ceramics, iconic Melbourne screen prints, wild fig candles and ugly-cute toys.

Esplanade Market (www.esplanade market.com; btwn Cavell & Fitzroy Sts, St Kilda; ⊙10am-4pm Sun May-Sep, to 5pm Oct-Apr; 🚊96) Fancy a Sunday stroll shopping by the seaside? Well, here's the place, with a kilometre of trestle tables joined end-to-end carrying individually crafted products, from toys and organic soaps to large metal sculptures of fishy creatures.

Above: Esplanade Market, St Kilda
JOHN W BANAGAN / GETTY IMAGES ©

balms, hair masques, scents, cleansers and oils in beautifully simple packaging for both men and women. There are plenty of branches around town (and plenty of opportunity to sample the products in most of Melbourne's cafe bathrooms). (📞03-9419 8356; www.aesop.com; 242 Gertrude St, Fitzroy; ⊙11am-5pm Mon & Sun, 10am-6pm Tue-Fri, 10am-5pm Sat; 🚊86)

Crumpler   Accessories
Crumpler's bike-courier bags started it all, designed by two former couriers looking for a bag they could hold their beer in while

cycling home. Its durable, practical designs now extend to bags for cameras, laptops and iPods, and can be found around the world. (📞03-9417 5338; www.crumpler.com; 87 Smith St, cnr Gertrude St, Fitzroy; ⊙10am-6pm Mon-Sat, to 5pm Sun; 🚊86)

🅐 Carlton

Readings   Books
A potter around this indie bookshop can occupy an entire afternoon if you're so inclined. There's a dangerously loaded (and good-value) specials table, switched-on staff and everyone from Lacan to Charlie & Lola on the shelves. Its exterior 'house-mate wanted' board is legendary. Also in St Kilda (112 Acland St; 🚊96) and the city centre (State Library, cnr La Trobe & Swanston Sts; 🚊Melbourne Central). (www.readings.com. au; 309 Lygon St, Carlton; ⊙8am-11pm Mon-Fri, 9am-11pm Sat, 9am-9pm Sun; 🚊Tourist Shuttle, 🚊1, 8)

🅧 EATING

🅧 Central Melbourne
ShanDong MaMa   Asian $
Melbourne's passion for dumplings finds its truest expression in this simple little place. The dumplings here are boiled, rather than steamed as they are elsewhere, and arrive any later than noon for lunch and you'll have to wait. Our favourite order for two is a plate of Little Rachaels and another of King Prawn dumplings. Bliss. (📞03-9650 3818; Shop 7, Mid City Arcade, 200 Bourke St; mains from $11; ⊙11am-9pm; 🚊86, 96)

Don Don   Japanese $
Due to its popularity, Don Don had to move digs to a bigger space, yet it still fills up fast. Grab a big bowl or bento box full of Japanese goodness and wolf it down indoors, or join the masses eating it on the State Library's lawns. (198 Little Lonsdale St; mains $6-9; ⊙11am-9pm Mon-Sat, to 8.30pm Sun; 🚊3, 5, 6, 16, 64, 67, 72, 🚊Melbourne Central)

PHIL WEYMOUTH / GETTY IMAGES ©

Live music in the city centre

MoVida   Spanish $$

MoVida sits in a cobbled laneway embla-zoned with one of the world's densest collections of street art – it doesn't get much more Melbourne than this. Line up along the bar, cluster around little window tables or, if you've booked, take a table in the dining area for fantastic Spanish tapas and raciones. (📞03-9663 3038; www.movida. com.au; 1 Hosier Lane; tapas $4-6, raciones $8-30; 🕑noon-late; 🚋70, 75, 🚉Flinders St)

Supernormal   Asian $$

Andrew McConnell can, it seems, do no wrong. Drawing on his years spent living and cooking in Shanghai and Hong Kong, McConnell presents a creative selection from dumplings to raw seafood or mains such as slow-cooked Szechuan lamb. Even if you don't dine in, stop by for his now-famous takeaway New England lobster roll – lobster in a small brioche...what's not to like? No dinner bookings for five or less at dinner. (📞03-9650 8688; www. supernormal.net.au; 180 Flinders Lane; mains $15-37; 🕑11am-11pm Sun-Thu, to midnight Fri & Sat; 🚉Flinders St)

Mamasita   Mexican $$

The restaurant responsible for kicking off Melbourne's obsession with authentic Mexican street food, Mamasita is still one of the very best – as evidenced by the perpetual queues to get into the place. The chargrilled corn sprinkled with cheese and chipotle mayo is a legendary starter, and there's a fantastic range of corn-tortilla tacos and 180 types of tequila. No reservations, so prepare to wait. (📞03-9650 3821; www.mamasita.com.au; 1/11 Collins St; tacos from $5, shared plates from $19; 🕑noon-late Mon-Sat, from 1pm Sun; 🚋City Circle, 11, 31, 48, 112)

Cumulus Inc   Modern Australian $$

One of Melbourne's best for any meal; it gives you that wonderful Andrew McCon-nell style along with reasonable prices. The focus is on beautiful produce and simple but artful cooking: from breakfasts of sardines and smoked tomato on toast

JAMES BRAUND / GETTY IMAGES ©

The Tan running track, Royal Botanic Gardens (p171)

> *the Royal Botanic Gardens are one of Melbourne's most glorious attractions*

at the marble bar to suppers of freshly shucked clair de lune oysters tucked away on the leather banquettes. No reservations, so queues are highly probable. (www.cumulusinc.com.au; 45 Flinders Lane; mains $19-39; ⏱7am-11pm Mon-Fri, from 8am Sat & Sun; 🚃City Circle, 48)

Chin Chin   Asian $$
Yet another great option on Flinders Lane, Chin Chin does delicious Southeast Asian hawker-style food designed as shared plates. It's inside a busied-up shell of an old building with a real New York feel, and while there are no bookings, Go Go Bar downstairs will have you till there's space. (📞03-8663 2000; www.chinchinrestaurant.com.au; 125 Flinders Lane; mains $19-33; ⏱11am-late; 🚃City Circle, 70, 75)

HuTong Dumpling Bar   Chinese $$
HuTong's windows face out on the famed Flower Drum, and its reputation for divine *xiao long bao* (soupy dumplings) means getting a lunchtime seat anywhere in this three-level building isn't easy. Downstairs, watch chefs make the delicate dumplings, then hope they don't watch you making a mess eating them. There's also a branch in Prahran. (www.hutong.com.au; 14-16 Market Lane; mains $15-25; ⏱11.30am-3pm & 5.30-10.30pm; 🚃86, 96)

Gazi   Greek $$
An offering from George Calombaris of *MasterChef* fame, this rebadged side project to the fancier Press Club (located next door) is set in a cavernous industrial space with a menu inspired by Greek street food. Select from authentic shared starters and gourmet mini souvlakis filled with prawn or duck to wood-fire spit mains. He also owns the East Brunswick eatery Hellenic Republic. (📞03-9207 7444; www.gazirestaurant.com.au;

2 Exhibition St; shared plates from $11.50, mains $23; ⊙11.30am-11pm; 🚊48, 70, 75)

Pellegrini's Espresso Bar Italian $$

The iconic Italian equivalent of a classic '50s diner, Pellegrini's has remained genuinely unchanged for decades. Pick and mix from the variety of homemade pastas and sauces; from the table out the back you can watch it all being thrown together from enormous, ever-simmering pots. In summer, finish with a glass of watermelon granita. (📞03-9662 1885; 66 Bourke St; mains $15-18; ⊙8am-11.30pm Mon-Sat, noon-8pm Sun; 🚇Parliament)

Hopetoun Tea Rooms Teahouse $$

Since 1892 patrons have been nibbling pinwheel sandwiches here, taking tea (with pinkies raised) and delicately polishing off a lamington. Hopetoun's venerable status has queues almost stretching out the entrance of Block Arcade. Salivate over the window display while you wait. (📞03-9650 2777; www.hopetountearooms.com.au; 282 Collins St; dishes $13-23; ⊙8am-5pm Mon-Sat, 9am-5pm Sun; 🚊11, 31, 48, 109, 112)

Vue de Monde Modern Australian $$$

Sitting pretty in the old 'observation deck' of the Rialto, Melbourne's favoured spot for occasion dining has views to match its name. Visionary chef Shannon Bennett has moved away from its classic French style to a subtle Modern Australian theme that runs through everything from the decor to the menu. (📞03-9691 3888; www.vuedemonde.com.au; Level 55, Rialto, 525 Collins St; set menus $150-250; ⊙reservations from noon-2pm Tue-Fri & Sun, 6-9.15pm Mon-Sat; 🚊11, 31, 48, 109, 112, 🚇Southern Cross)

Kenzan Japanese $$$

One of numerous candidates for the title of Melbourne's best Japanese restaurant, Kenzan inhabits an unpromising setting but serves up sublime sashimi and sushi,

---

Food Trucks

Perhaps appealing to the current obsession with 'pop up' shops and bars, fabulous food trucks have begun plying the streets of Melbourne. Each day the different trucks use Twitter and Facebook to let their followers and friends know where they are, and dutiful, hungry folk respond by turning up street-side for a meal. Favourite Melbourne food trucks to chase down include the following:

Taco Truck (@tacotruckmelb)

Gumbo Kitchen (@GumboKitchen; serving New Orleans–style food)

Beatbox Kitchen (@beatboxkitchen; serving gourmet burgers and fries)

---

with the fine *nabe ryori* (which you cook at your table) another fine option. Can't choose? Lunch or dinner set menus are outstanding. Order the more expensive marbled beef when given the choice. (📞03-9654 8933; www.kenzan.com.au; 56 Flinders Lane; mains $30-45, lunch/dinner set menu from $36/85; ⊙noon-2.30pm & 6-10pm; 🚊City Circle, 48)

Flower Drum Chinese $$$

The Flower Drum continues to be Melbourne's most celebrated Chinese restaurant. The finest, freshest produce prepared with absolute attention to detail keeps this Chinatown institution booked out for weeks in advance. The sumptuous, but ostensibly simple, Cantonese food (from a menu that changes daily) is delivered with the slick service you'd expect in such elegant surrounds. (📞03-9662 3655; www.flower-drum.com; 17 Market Lane; mains $15-60; ⊙noon-3pm & 6-11pm Mon-Sat, 6-10.30pm Sun; 📶; 🚊86, 96)

Luna Park (p172)

🍴 Fitzroy

Charcoal
Lane   Modern Australian $$

🌿 Housed in an old bluestone former bank, this training restaurant for Indigenous and disadvantaged young people is one of the best places to try native flora and fauna; menu items may include kangaroo burger with bush tomato chutney and wallaby tartare. Weekend bookings advised. (🖉 03-9418 3400; www.charcoallane.com.au; 136 Gertrude St, Fitzroy; mains $19-31; ⏰noon-3pm & 6-9pm Tue-Sat; 🚋86)

Cutler & Co   Modern Australian $$$

Hyped for all the right reasons, this is another of Andrew McConnell's restaurants and though its decor might be a little over the top, its attentive, informed staff and joy-inducing dishes have quickly made this one of Melbourne's best. (🖉 03-9419 4888; www.cutlerandco.com.au; 55 Gertrude St, Fitzroy; mains $36-49; ⏰noon-late Fri & Sun, 6pm-late Mon-Thu; 🚋86)

🍴 Carlton & Around

D.O.C   Italian $$

Run by third-generation Italians, D.O.C is bringing authenticity, and breathing new life, back into Lygon St. The espresso bar features homemade pasta specials, Italian microbrewery beers and *aperitivo* time (4pm to 7pm), where you can enjoy a Negroni cocktail with complimentary nibble board, surrounded by dangling legs of meat and huge wheels of cheese behind glass shelves.

The **deli** (mains from $12; ⏰9am-8pm) next door does great cheese boards and panini, while around the corner is D.O.C's original **pizzeria** (295 Drummond St, Carlton; pizzas $13-18; ⏰5.30-10.30pm Mon-Wed, noon-10.30pm Fri-Sun), with excellent thin-crust pizzas and a convivial atmosphere. (🖉 03-9347 8482; www.docgroup.net; 326 Lygon St, Carlton; mains $12-20; ⏰7.30am-9.30pm Mon-Sat, 8am-9pm Sun; 🚌205, 🚋1, 8, 96)

Tiamo   Italian $$

When you've had enough of pressed, siphoned, Slayer-machined, poured-over, filtered and plunged coffee, head here to one of Lygon St's original Italian cafe-restaurants. There's the laughter and relaxed *joie de vivre* that only a well-established restaurant can have. Great pastas and pizza, too. Also has the up-market Tiamo 2 next door. (www.tiamo. com.au; 303 Lygon St, Carlton; mains $9-26; ⏱6.30am-11pm; 🚊Tourist Shuttle, 🚃1, 8)

Abla's
Lebanese $$
The kitchen here is steered by Abla Amad, whose authentic, flavour-packed food has inspired a whole generation of local Lebanese chefs. Bring a bottle of your favourite plonk and settle in for the compulsory banquet ($70) on Friday and Saturday night. (🖉03-9347 0006; www.ablas.com.au; 109 Elgin St, Carlton; mains $27-30; ⏱noon-3pm Thu & Fri, 6-11pm Mon-Sat; 🚊205, 🚃1, 8, 96)

Rumi
Middle Eastern $$
A fabulously well-considered place that serves up a mix of traditional Lebanese cooking and contemporary interpretations of old Persian dishes. The *sigara boregi* (cheese and pine-nut pastries) are a local institution, and tasty mains like meatballs are balanced with a large and interesting selection of vegetable dishes (the near-caramelised cauliflower and the broad beans are standouts). (🖉03-9388 8255; www.rumirestaurant.com.au; 116 Lygon St, East Brunswick; mains $12-24; ⏱6-10pm; 🚃1, 8)

St Kilda & Around

Monarch Cake Shop
Desserts, European $
St Kilda's Eastern European cake shops have long drawn crowds that come to peer at the sweetly stocked windows. Monarch is a favourite – its *kugelhopf* (marble cake), plum cake and poppy-seed cheesecake can't be beaten. In business since 1934, not much has changed here with its wonderful buttery aromas and old-time atmosphere. Also does good coffee. (🖉03-9534 2972; www.monarchcakes.com.au; 103 Acland St, St Kilda; slice of cake from $5; ⏱8am-10pm; 🚃96)

Monk Bodhi Dharma
Cafe $$
Monk Bodhi Dharma's hidden location, down an alley off Carlisle St (next to Safeway), means it doesn't get much passing foot traffic, which is lucky given that this cosy brick cafe has enough devotees as it is. A former 1920s bakehouse, these days it's all about transcendental vegetarian food, housemade Bircher muesli and house-roasted single-estate coffee. Book ahead for Friday night dinners. (🖉03-9534 7250; www.monkbodhidharma.com; rear 202 Carlisle St, Balaclava; breakfast $9-20; ⏱7am-5pm Mon-Fri, 8am-5pm Sat & Sun; 🖋; 🚃3, 16, 79)

Uncle
Vietnamese $$
Stellar Vietnamese cooking in a quintessentially St Kilda space (complete with rooftop dining area) is one of Melbourne's more exciting Asian openings in recent years. The drinks list includes Viet sangria, mains might include lemongrass and coconut scotch fillet, while traditionalists will love the traditional *pho* (Vietnamese noodle soup). (🖉03-9041 2668; www.unclestkilda.com.au; 188 Carlisle St, St Kilda; mains $24-34; ⏱5pm-late Tue, noon-late Wed-Sun; 🚃3, 16, 79)

Claypots
Seafood $$
A local favourite, Claypots serves up seafood in its namesake dish. Get in early to both get a seat and ensure the good stuff is still available, as hot items go fast. It also has a spot in the South Melbourne Market (p172). (🖉03-9534 1282; 213 Barkly St, St Kilda; mains $24-38; ⏱noon-3pm & 6pm-1am; 🚃96)

Mirka's at Tolarno
International, Italian $$
Beloved artist Mirka Mora's murals grace the walls in this dining room with a history (it's been delighting diners since the early '60s). Guy Grossi's Italian menu has some rustic classics, like veal satimbocca mixed with interesting surprises such as walnut and pear gnocchi with gorgonzola. There's also a four-course sharing menu ($60). (🖉03-9525 3088; www.mirkatolarnohotel.com;

LGBTI Melbourne

These days, Melbourne's gay and lesbian community is well and truly integrated into the general populace. Here are some highlights:

○ The **Midsumma Festival** (www. midsumma.org.au) has a diverse program of more than 100 cultural, community and sporting events.

○ *MCV* (www.gaynewsnetwork.com. au) is a free weekly newspaper; also available online.

○ Gay and lesbian community radio station JOY 94.9 FM (www.joy.org. au) is another important resource for visitors and locals.

○ Gay men are particularly welcomed at the **Peel Hotel nightclub** (☑ 03-9419 4762; www.thepeel.com.au; 113 Wellington St, Collingwood; ☺ 9pm-dawn Thu-Sat; 🚌 86), and **169 Drummond** (☑ 03-9663 3081; www.169drummond.com.au; 169 Drummond St, Carlton; d incl breakfast $120-145; ☏; 🚌 1, 8) has been offering gay-friendly accommodation for two decades.

Tolarno Hotel, 42 Fitzroy St, St Kilda; mains $18-38; ☺ 6pm-late; 🚌 16, 96, 112)

Attica
Modern Australian $$$

Consistent award-winning Attica is a suburban restaurant that serves Ben Shewry's creative dishes degustation-style. Many dishes are not complete on delivery; staff perform minor miracles on cue with a sprinkle of this or a drop of that. 'Trials' of Shewry's new ideas take place on Tuesday night's Chef's Table ($125 per head). Booking several months in advance is essential. Follow Brighton Rd south to Glen Eira Rd. (☑ 03-9530 0111; www.attica.com. au; 74 Glen Eira Rd, Ripponlea; 8-course tasting menu $190; ☺ 6.30pm-late Wed-Sat; 🚌 67, 🚉 Ripponlea)

🍷 DRINKING & NIGHTLIFE

🍷 Central Melbourne

Bar Americano
Cocktail Bar

A hideaway bar in a city alley, Bar Americano is a standing-room-only affair with black-and-white chequered floors complemented with classic 'do not spit' subway tiled walls and a subtle air of speakeasy. By day it serves excellent coffee but after dark it's all about the cocktails; they don't come cheap but they do come superb. (20 Pesgrave Pl, off Howey Pl; ☺ 8.30am-1am; 🚌 11, 31, 48, 109, 112)

Lui Bar
Cocktail Bar

One of the city's most sophisticated bars, Lui offers the chance to sample the views and excellent bar snacks (smoked ocean trout jerky!). Suits and jet-setters cram in most nights so get there early (nicely dressed), claim your table and order drinks from the 'pop-up book' menu containing serious drinks like macadamia martinis – vacuum distilled at the bar. (www.luibar.com.au; level 55, Rialto, 525 Collins St; ☺ 5.30pm-midnight Mon, noon-midnight Tue-Fri, 5.30pm-late Sat, noon-evening Sun; 🚌 11, 31, 48, 109, 112, 🚉 Southern Cross)

Melbourne Supper Club
Bar

Melbourne's own Betty Ford's (the place you go when there's nowhere left to go), the Supper Club is open very late and is a favoured after-work spot for performers and hospitality types. It's entered via an unsigned wooden door, where you can leave your coat before cosying into a chesterfield. Browse the encyclopaedic wine menu and relax; the sommeliers will cater to any liquid desire. (☑ 03-9654 6300; 1st fl, 161 Spring St; ☺ 5pm-4am Sun-Thu, to 6am Fri & Sat; 🚌 95, 96, 🚉 Parliament)

Cookie
Bar

Part swanky bar, part Thai restaurant, Cookie does both exceptionally well and is one of the more enduring rites of passage of the Melbourne night. The bar is unbelievably well stocked with fine whiskies, wines and plenty of craft beers among the more

Sunset at St Kilda Pier (p172)

than 200 on offer. They also know how to make a serious cocktail. (☏03-9663 7660; www.cookie.net.au; Level 1, Curtin House, 252 Swanston St; ☺noon-1am Sun-Thu, to 3am Fri & Sat; ☒3, 5, 6, 16, 64, 67, 72)

Hell's Kitchen   Bar
Original hidden laneway bar located in the beautiful Centre Place Arcade, Hell's is up a narrow flight of stairs where you can sip on classic cocktails (Negroni, whisky sour and martinis), beer or cider and people-watch from the large windows. Attracts a young, hip crowd and also serves food. (Level 1, 20 Centre Pl; ☺noon-10pm Mon & Tue, to late Wed-Sat, to 11pm Sun; ☒Flinders St)

Double Happiness   Bar
This stylish hole-in-the-wall is decked out in Chinese propaganda posters and Mao statues with an excellent range of Asian-influenced chilli- or coriander-flavoured cocktails. Upstairs is the bar **New Gold Mountain** (☏03-9650 8859; www.newgold mountain.org; ☺6pm-late Tue-Thu, to 5am Fri & Sat), run by the same owners with table

service. (☏03-9650 4488; www.double-happiness.com.au; 21 Liverpool St; ☺4pm-1am Mon-Wed, to 3am Thu & Fri, 6pm-3am Sat, to 1am Sun; ☒86, 96, ☒Parliament)

Ponyfish Island   Cafe, Bar
Laneway bars have been done to death; now Melburnians are finding creative new spots to do their drinkin'. Where better than a little open-air nook under a bridge arcing over the Yarra? From Flinders St Station underground passage, head over the pedestrian bridge towards South-gate, where steps head down to people knocking back beers with toasted sangas or cheese plates. (www.ponyfish.com.au; under Yarra Pedestrian Bridge; ☺8am-1am; ☒Flinders St)

Section 8   Bar
Enclosed within a cage full of shipping containers and wooden-pallet seating, Section 8 remains one of the city's hippest bars. It does great hot dogs, including vegan ones. (www.section8.com.au; 27-29 Tattersalls Lane; ☺10am-11pm Mon-Wed, to 1am Thu & Fri, noon-1am Sat & Sun; ☒3, 5, 6, 16, 64, 67, 72)

JOHN W BANAGAN / GETTY IMAGES ©

Riverland   Bar

Perched below Princes Bridge alongside the Yarra River, this bluestone beauty keeps things simple with good wine, beer on tap and bar snacks that hit the mark: charcuterie, cheese and BBQ sausages. Outside tables are a treat when the weather is kind. Be prepared for rowdiness pre- and post-footy matches at the nearby MCG. (03-9662 1771; www.riverlandbar. com; Vaults 1-9 Federation Wharf, under Princes Bridge; 10am-late Mon-Fri, 9am-late Sat & Sun; Flinders St)

Hotel Windsor   Teahouse

This grand hotel has been serving afternoon tea since 1883. Indulge in the delights of three-tier platters of finger sandwiches, scones, pastries and champagne, hosted in either its front dining room or the art nouveau ballroom. (www.thehotelwindsor.com. au; 111 Spring St; afternoon tea Mon-Fri $69, Sat & Sun $89; noon Mon & Tue, noon & 2.30pm Wed-Sun; Parliament)

Alumbra   Club

Great music and a stunning location will impress – even if the Bali-meets-Morocco follies of the decor don't. If you're going to do one megaclub in Melbourne (and like the idea of a glass dance floor), this is going to be your best bet. It's in one of the old sheds jutting out into Docklands' Victoria Harbour. Saturday is house, while Sunday is all about soul and R&B. (03-8623 9666; www.alumbra.com.au; Shed 9, Central Pier, 161 Harbour Esplanade, Docklands; 4pm-3am Fri & Sat, to 1am Sun; Tourist Shuttle, 70, City Circle)

Fitzroy

Everleigh   Cocktail Bar

Sophistication and bartending standards are off the charts at this upstairs hidden nook. Settle into a leather booth in the intimate setting with a few friends for conversation and oohing-and-ahhing over classic 'golden era' cocktails like you've never

tasted before. (www.theeverleigh.com; 150-156 Gertrude St, Fitzroy; 5.30pm-1am; 86)

Panama Dining Room   Bar

Gawp at the ersatz Manhattan views in this large warehouse-style space while sipping serious cocktails and snacking on truffled polenta chips or felafel balls with tahini. The dining area gets packed around 9pm for its Mod European menu. (03-9417 7663; www.thepanama.com.au; 3rd fl, 231 Smith St, Fitzroy; 5-11pm Sun-Wed, to midnight Thu, to 1am Fri & Sat; 86)

Industry Beans   Cafe

It's all about coffee chemistry at this warehouse cafe tucked in a Fitzroy side street. The coffee guide takes you through the specialty styles on offer (roasted on site) and helpful staff take the pressure off deciding. Pair your brew with some latte coffee pearls or coffee toffee prepared in the 'lab'. The food menu is ambitious but doesn't always hit the mark. (www.industry beans.com; cnr Fitzroy & Rose Sts, Fitzroy; 7am-4pm Mon-Fri, 8am-5pm Sat & Sun; ; 96, 112)

Napier Hotel   Pub

The recently refurbished Napier has stood on this corner for over a century; many pots have been pulled as the face of the neighbourhood changed, as demonstrated by the memorabilia of the sadly departed Fitzroy footy team. Worm your way around the central bar to the boisterous dining room for an iconic Bogan Burger. Head upstairs to check out its gallery, too. (03-9419 4240; www.thenapierhotel.com; 210 Napier St, Fitzroy; 3-11pm Mon-Thu, 1pm-1am Fri & Sat, 1-11pm Sun; 86, 112)

Rose   Pub

A much-loved Fitzroy backstreet local, the Rose has remained true to its roots with cheap counter meals and a non-pretentious crowd here to watch the footy. (406 Napier St, Fitzroy; noon-midnight Sun-Wed, to 1am Thu-Sat; 86, 112)

Carlton

Seven Seeds   Cafe

The most spacious of the Seven Seeds coffee empire; there's plenty of room to store your bike and sip a splendid coffee beside the other lucky people who've found this rather out-of-the-way warehouse cafe. Public cuppings are held Wednesday (9am) and Saturday (10am). Pop into **Traveller** (2/14 Crossley St; ☺7am-5pm Mon-Fri, 10am-5pm Sat; 🚌86, 96) and **Brother Baba Budan** (359 Little Bourke St; ☺7am-5pm Mon-Sat, 9am-5pm Sun; 📷; 🚌19, 57, 59) in the CBD for standing-room only. (www.sevenseeds.com.au; 114 Berkeley St, Carlton; ☺7am-5pm Mon-Sat, 8am-5pm Sun; 🚌19, 59)

St Kilda & Around

George Lane Bar   Bar

Hidden behind the hulk of the George Hotel, tucked away off Grey St, this little bar is a good rabbit hole to dive into. Its pleasantly ad-hoc decor is a relief from the inch-of-its-life design aesthetic elsewhere. There's DJs (and queues) on the weekends. (www.georgelanebar.com.au; 1 George Lane, St Kilda; ☺7pm-1am Thu-Sun; 🚌96, 16)

Carlisle Wine Bar   Wine Bar

Locals love this often rowdy, wine-worshipping former butcher's shop. The staff will treat you like a regular and find you a glass of something special, or effortlessly throw together a cocktail amid the weekend rush. The rustic Italian food is good, too. Carlisle St runs east off St Kilda Rd. (📞03-9531 3222; www.carlislewinebar.com.au; 137 Carlisle St, Balaclava; ☺3pm-1am Mon-Fri, 11am-1am Sat & Sun; 🚌3, 16, 🚆Balaclava)

Vineyard   Bar

An old favourite, the Vineyard has the perfect corner position and a courtyard BBQ that attracts crowds of backpackers and scantily clad young locals who enjoy themselves so much they drown out the neighbouring roller coaster. Sunday

⟲ Yarra Valley Wineries

The Yarra Valley, about an hour northeast of Melbourne, has more than 80 wineries and 50 cellar doors scattered around its rolling hills – the first vines were planted at Yering Station in 1838. The region produces cool-climate, food-friendly drops such as chardonnay and pinot noir.

Some top Yarra Valley wineries with cellar-door sales and tastings:

Domaine Chandon (📞03-9738 9200; www.chandon.com; 727 Maroondah Hwy, Coldstream; ☺10.30am-4.30pm) This slick operation is worth a visit for the free guided tours (11am, 1pm and 3pm). Tastings $5.

TarraWarra Estate (📞03-5957 3510; www.tarrawarra.com.au; 311 Healesville–Yarra Glen Rd, Healesville; tastings $4; ☺11am-5pm) TarraWarra has a striking and modern art gallery showing wonderful exhibitions. Refuel at the neighbouring bistro and cellar door. Tastings $4.

Yering Station (📞03-9730 0100; www.yering.com; 38 Melba Hwy, Yering; ☺10am-5pm Mon-Fri, to 6pm Sat & Sun) Taste wines in the original 1859 winery and walk through the lovely grounds to the modern fine-dining restaurant.

GREG ELMS / GETTY IMAGES ©

afternoon sessions are big here. (www.thevineyard.com.au; 71a Acland St, St Kilda; ☺10.30am-3.30am Mon-Fri, 10am-3.30am Sat & Sun; 🚌3a, 16, 96)

**Rooftop Drinking
& Entertainment**

If you like your brew with a view, swing up to these excellent Melbourne rooftop bars:

Naked for Satan (☑03-9416 2238; www.nakedforsatan.com.au; 285 Brunswick St, Fitzroy; ☺noon-midnight Sun-Thu, to 1am Fri & Sat; ☒112) Vibrant, loud and reviving an apparent Brunswick St legend (a man nicknamed Satan who would get down and dirty, naked because of the heat, in an illegal vodka distillery under the shop), this place packs a punch both with its popular *pintxos* (Basque tapas; $2), huge range of cleverly named beverages and unbeatable roof terrace with wraparound decked balcony.

Carlton Hotel (www.thecarlton.com.au; 193 Bourke St; ☺4pm-late; ☒86, 96) Over-the-top Melbourne rococo gets another workout here and never fails to raise a smile. Check out the rooftop **Palmz** if you're looking for some Miami-flavoured vice, or just a great view.

Rooftop Cinema (www.rooftop cinema.com.au; Level 6, Curtin House, 252 Swanston St; ☒Melbourne Central) This rooftop bar sits at dizzying heights on top of the happening Curtin House. In summer it transforms into an outdoor cinema with striped deckchairs and a calendar of new and classic favourite flicks.

Madame Brussels (www.madamebrussels.com; Level 3, 59-63 Bourke St; ☺noon-1am; ☒86, 96) Head here if you've had it with Melbourne-moody and all that dark wood. Although named for a famous 19th-century brothel owner, it feels like a camp '60s rabbit hole, with much Astroturfery and staff dressed à la the country club. It's just the tonic to escape the city for a jug of Madame Brussels–style Pimms on its wonderful rooftop terrace.

 ENTERTAINMENT

**Australian Centre
for the Moving Image**   Cinema
ACMI's cinemas screen a diverse range of films. It programs regular events and festivals for film genres and audiences, as well as screening one-offs. (ACMI; ☑03-9663 2583; www.acmi.net.au; Federation Sq; ☒1, 48, 70, 72, 75, ☒Flinders St)

Cinema Nova   Cinema
The latest in art-house, docos and foreign films. Cheap Monday screenings. (☑03-9347 5331; www.cinemanova.com.au; 380 Lygon St, Carlton; ☒Tourist Shuttle, ☒1, 8)

Moonlight Cinema   Cinema
Melbourne's original outdoor cinema, with the option of 'Gold Grass' tickets that include a glass of wine and a reserved bean-bag bed. (www.moonlight.com.au; Royal Botanic Gardens, Gate D, Birdwood Ave, South Yarra; ☒8)

Malthouse Theatre   Theatre
The Malthouse Theatre Company often produces the most exciting theatre in Melbourne. Dedicated to promoting Australian works, the company has been housed in the atmospheric Malthouse Theatre since 1990. From Flinders Street Station walk across Princes Bridge and along St Kilda Rd. Turn right at Grant St, then left into Sturt. (☑03-9685 5111; www.malthousetheatre.com.au; 113 Sturt St, Southbank; ☒1)

**Melbourne Theatre
Company**   Theatre
Melbourne's major theatrical company stages around 15 productions each year, ranging from contemporary and modern (including many new Australian works) to Shakespearean and other classics. Performances take place in a brand-new, award-winning venue in Southbank. (MTC; ☑03-8688 0800; www.mtc.com.au; 140 Southbank Blvd, Southbank; ☒1)

Tote   Live Music
One of Melbourne's most iconic live-music venues, not only does this divey Collingwood

RACHEL LEWIS / GETTY IMAGES ©

Pellegrini's Espresso Bar (p179)

pub have a great roster of local and international underground bands, but one of the best jukeboxes in the universe. Its temporary closure in 2010 saw people protesting on the city-centre streets against the liquor licensing laws that were blamed for its closure. (03-9419 5320; www.thetotehotel. com; cnr Johnston & Wellington Sts, Collingwood; 4pm-late Tue-Sun; 86)

Esplanade Hotel   Live Music

Rock-pigs rejoice. The Espy remains gloriously shabby and welcoming to all. A mix of local and international bands play nightly, everything from rock 'n' roll to hip hop either in the legendary Gershwin Room, the front bar or down in the basement. (The Espy; 03-9534 0211; www.espy.com.au; 11 The Esplanade, St Kilda; noon-1am Sun-Wed, to 3am Thu-Sat; 16, 96)

Corner Hotel   Live Music

The band room here is one of Melbourne's most popular midsized venues and has seen plenty of loud and live action over the years, from Dinosaur Jr to the Buzzcocks.

If your ears need a break, there's a friendly front bar. The rooftop has city views, but gets superpacked, and often with a different crowd from the music fans below. (03-9427 9198; www.cornerhotel.com; 57 Swan St, Richmond; 4pm-late Tue & Wed, noon-late Thu-Sun; 70, Richmond)

Bennetts Lane   Jazz

Bennetts Lane has long been the boiler room of Melbourne jazz. It attracts the cream of local and international talent and an audience that knows when it's time to applaud a solo. Beyond the cosy front bar, there's another space reserved for big gigs. (03-9663 2856; www.bennettslane.com; 25 Bennetts Lane; 9pm-late; City Circle, 24, 30)

Australian Ballet   Ballet

Based in Melbourne and now more than 40 years old, the Australian Ballet performs traditional and new works at the State Theatre in the Arts Centre. You can take an hour-long Australian Ballet Centre Tour ($18, bookings essential) that includes a visit to the production and wardrobe departments as well as the studios of both the company and the school. (1300 369 741; www.australianballet.com.au; 2 Kavanagh St, Southbank; 🚋1)

Opera Australia   Opera
The national opera company performs with some regularity at Melbourne's Victorian Arts Centre. (03-9685 3700; www.opera.org.au; cnr Fawkner & Fanning Sts, Southbank)

Melbourne Symphony Orchestra   Orchestra
The MSO has a broad reach: while not afraid to be populist (it's done sell-out performances with both Burt Bacharach and the Whitlams), it can also do edgy – such as performing with Kiss – along with its performances of the great masterworks of symphony. It performs regularly at venues around the city, including Melbourne Town Hall, the Recital Centre and Hamer Hall. Also runs a summer series of free concerts at the Sidney Myer Music Bowl. (MSO; 03-9929 9600; www.mso.com.au)

ℹ️ INFORMATION

MEDICAL SERVICES
Royal Melbourne Hospital (03-9342 7000; www.rmh.mh.org.au; cnr Grattan St & Royal Pde, Parkville; 🚋19, 59) The most central public hospital with an emergency department.

TOURIST INFORMATION
Melbourne Visitor Centre (MVC; 03-9658 9658; www.melbourne.vic.gov.au/tourist information; Federation Sq; 🕙9am-6pm; 📶; 🚉Flinders St) Located at Federation Sq, the centre has comprehensive tourist information on Melbourne and regional Victoria, including excellent resources for mobility-impaired travellers, and a travel desk for accommodation and tour bookings. There are power sockets for recharging phones, too.

There's also a booth on the Bourke St Mall (mostly for shopping and basic enquiries) and City Ambassadors (dressed in red) wandering around the city, who can help with info and directions.

ℹ️ GETTING THERE & AWAY

AIR
Two main airports serve Melbourne: **Avalon** (1800 282 566, 03-5227 9100; www.avalon airport.com.au; 80 Beach Rd, Lara) and **Melbourne Airport** (03-9297 1600; www.melbourneairport.com.au; Centre Rd, Tullamarine), though at present only **Jetstar** (www.jetstar.com) operates from Avalon. Tullamarine Airport also has some Jetstar flights, in addition to domestic and international flights offered by **Tiger** (www.tigerairways.com), **Qantas** (www.qantas.com), **Virgin Australia** (www.virginaustralia.com) and other carriers.

BOAT
Spirit of Tasmania (1800 634 906; www.spiritoftasmania.com.au; adult/car one way from $159/83) The *Spirit of Tasmania* crosses Bass Strait from Melbourne to Devonport, Tasmania, at least nightly; there are also day sailings during peak season. It takes 11 hours and departs from Station Pier, Port Melbourne.

BUS & TRAIN
Southern Cross Station (www.southern crossstation.net.au; cnr Collins & Spencer Sts) This is the main terminal for interstate bus services.

Firefly (1300 730 740; www.fireflyexpress.com.au) Day and overnight buses from Melbourne to Adelaide (from $55, 11 hours) and Sydney (from $60, 14 hours).

ℹ️ GETTING AROUND
TO/FROM THE AIRPORT
There are no direct trains or trams to Melbourne Airport. Taxis charge around $65 for the trip to Melbourne's CBD, or you can catch the **SkyBus** (03-9335 2811; www.skybus.com.au; adult one way $18), a 25-minute express bus service to/from Southern Cross Station; allow more time during peak hour.

BICYCLE

Melbourne Bike Share (📞1300 711 590; www.melbournebikeshare.com.au) Melbourne Bike Share began in 2010 and has had a slow start, mainly blamed on Victoria's compulsory helmet laws. Subsidised safety helmets are now available at 7-Eleven stores around the CBD ($5 with a $3 refund on return). Each first half-hour of hire is free. Daily ($2.80) and weekly ($8) subscriptions require a credit card and $300 security deposit.

CAR & MOTORCYCLE

CAR HIRE

Avis (📞13 63 33; www.avis.com.au)

Budget (📞1300 362 848; www.budget.com.au)

Europcar (📞1300 131 390; www.europcar.com.au)

TOLL ROADS

Drivers and motorcyclists will need to purchase a toll pass if they're planning on using one of the two toll roads: **CityLink** (📞13 26 29; www.citylink.com.au) from Melbourne Airport to the city and eastern suburbs; or **EastLink** (📞13 54 65; www.eastlink.com.au) which runs from Ringwood to Frankston. Pay online or via phone (within three days of using the toll road to avoid a fine).

PUBLIC TRANSPORT

Melbourne's much-maligned myki system is the key to all public transport, which is organised into a two-zone network covering much of the city. Buy a card at a machine (in train stations) or at a local store displaying the myki sign, top it up (at the same locations) and make sure you touch it to the reader before getting on or off any train, tram or bus. Ticket inspectors are everywhere, and can be ruthless.

Train Trains run from 5.30am to 12.30am on 15 lines.

Tram Trams run in the inner suburbs, and are useful for short trips. Trips within the central CBD are free.

Bus The main form of transport in more far-flung suburbs.

Flinders St Station is the main metro train station connecting the city and suburbs. The City Loop runs under the city, linking the four corners of town.

An extensive network of tram lines covers every corner of the city, running north–south and east–west along most major roads. Trams run roughly every 10 minutes Monday to Friday, every 10 to 15 minutes on Saturday, and every 20 minutes on Sunday. Tram travel is free within the city centre and Docklands area. Check **Public Transport Victoria** for more information. Also worth considering is the free **City Circle tram** (p173), which loops around town, and the **Melbourne City Tourist Shuttle bus** (www.melbourne.vic.gov.au/shuttle).

Melbourne's buses, trams and trains use **myki** (www.myki.com.au), a 'touch on, touch off' card. You must purchase a plastic myki card ($6) and put credit on it before you travel. Cards can be purchased from machines at stations, 7-Eleven stores or newsagents, but some hostels also collect myki cards from travellers who leave Melbourne. Travellers are best advised to buy a myki Visitor Value Pack ($14), which gets you one day's travel and discounts on various sights. It's available only from the airport, SkyBus terminal or the PTV Hub at Southern Cross Station.

The myki card can be topped up at 7-Eleven stores and myki machines at most train stations and some tram stops in the city centre. Frustratingly, online top-ups take at least 24 hours to process. For Zone 1, which is all that most travellers will need, the Myki Money costs $3.76 for two hours, or $7.52 for the day. Machines don't always issue change, so bring exact money. The fine for travelling without a valid myki card is $212 (or $75 if you pay on the spot) – ticket inspectors are vigilant and unforgiving.

TAXI

Melbourne's taxis are metered and require an estimated prepaid fare when hailed between 10pm and 5am. You may need to pay more or get a refund depending on the final fare. Toll charges are added to fares. A small tip is usual but not compulsory.

13 Cabs (📞13 22 27; www.13cabs.com.au)

Silver Top (📞131 008; www.silvertop.com.au)

⌐⮕ The Great Ocean Road

When you've had your fill of city sightseeing, jump in the car and head to the Great Ocean Road, one of Australia's most rewarding road trips. Covering 240km from Torquay and Warrnambool, the road sidles past world-class surf spots, thick eucalypt forest, buzzy seaside towns and koala hang-outs, all the time following Southern Ocean waves pounding onto isolated beaches. And, of course, there are the mighty limestone stacks standing just offshore, including the famous Twelve Apostles.

While you can see the highlights of this coast in a very long day trip from Melbourne, it's more enjoyable to allow a couple of days. If you don't want to drive the narrow, winding roads yourself, join one of the many tours from Melbourne.

Travelling from Melbourne, **Torquay** is the first seaside town you'll come to. Surfing is its lifeblood and it's only a short detour to the surfing mecca of **Bells Beach**. The Great Ocean Road officially begins on the stretch between Torquay and Anglesea – watch out for the Diggers sculpture that sits under the Memorial Arch, depicting one of the ex-WWI soldiers who laboured on the road. You'll roll through the pretty beachside towns of **Anglesea** and **Airey's Inlet** before arriving in charming **Lorne**, then more coast-hugging curves wind along towards **Apollo Bay**. With lovely beaches and some funky cafes, both Lorne and Apollo Bay make a good overnight stop.

Next up is the most rugged, sea-scoured stretch of the coast with **Cape Otway** and its lighthouse giving a glimpse of the untamed elements that made this the Shipwreck Coast. The highlights here are the towering sculpted rock stacks and archways jutting from the churning surf. The most famous of these are the **Twelve Apostles** (though, for the record, there are not twelve of them) but make every effort to travel a few extra kilometres to the powerful, canyon-like **Loch Ard Gorge**, **London Bridge** and the **Grotto**.

There's not just spectacular scenery; the Great Ocean Road is a top opportunity for some wildlife-spotting too. **Kangaroos** often loll on the fairways of the Anglesea Golf Club and there's a great chance of a **koala** sighting at either Kennett River or on the way to the Cape Otway lighthouse. You may spot tiny **penguins** at sunset around the rocks of the Twelve Apostles and **southern right whales** in the waters off Warrnambool as they migrate between May and September.

Above: The Twelve Apostles
MANFRED GOTTSCHALK / GETTY IMAGES ©

Where to Stay

While you'll have no trouble finding a place to stay that suits your taste and budget, for a city that's big on style Melbourne has only a handful of small, atmospheric hotels. Prices peak for major sporting events and over the summer.

Neighbourhood	Atmosphere
Central Melbourne	Lot of places across all price ranges and for all tastes, whether you've come to town and want to shop, party, catch a match or take in some culture. Backpacker options and the major hotel chains abound.
East Melbourne	Leafy East Melbourne takes you out of the action, yet is still walking distance from the city and offers ready access to the MCG and the city's other sporting hubs.
Fitzroy	Vibrant Fitzroy hums with attractions day and night, and is a walk or short tram ride away from the city. Some good serviced apartments and boutique options.
Carlton	Carlton is home to Melbourne's Italian community, mixed in with students, a literary flavour and some outstanding sights. Public transport to the city centre is good, but sleeping options are light on.
South Yarra	South of the river, South Yarra has boutique, upmarket places set in pretty, tree-lined residential streets.
St Kilda	St Kilda is a budget-traveller enclave but there are some stylish options a short walk from the beach, too. Lives up to its reputation as party central.

GRANT DIXON / GETTY IMAGES ©

Constitution Dock (p203)

HOBART

Hobart

No doubt about it, Hobart's future is looking rosy. Tourism is booming and the old town is brimming with new-found self-confidence. It's worth planning on staying awhile – you'll need at least a few days to savour the full range of beers flowing from the city's pubs.

Riding high above the city is Mt Wellington, a rugged monolith seemingly made for mountain biking and bushwalking. Down on the waterfront, the cafes, bars and restaurants along historic Salamanca Pl and in nearby Battery Point showcase the best of Tassie produce. There's more great eating and boozing in cashed-up Sandy Bay and along Elizabeth St in bohemian North Hobart.

❶ In This Section

☼ What's On

Spring THAW (🕙Sep) Launching in 2016, this five-day Hobart festival celebrates Tasmania's Antarctic links.

Taste of Tasmania (www.thetasteof tasmania.com.au; 🕙Dec-Jan) On either side of New Year's Eve, this week-long harbourside event is a celebration of Tassie's gastronomic prowess.

Falls Festival (www.fallsfestival.com.au; 🕙29 Dec-1 Jan) Three nights and four days of live Oz and international tunes at Marion Bay, an hour east of Hobart.

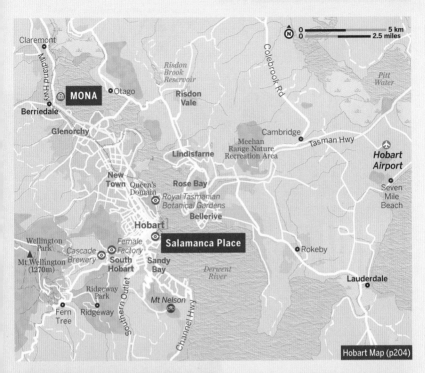

From left: Tasmanian devil; Breakfast in Salamanca Place (p198); Fishing floats
VMJONES / GETTY IMAGES ©; SALLY DILLON / GETTY IMAGES © ; MARIUSZ_PRUSACZYK/ GETTY IMAGES ©

Chapel by Belgian artist Wim Delvoye, MONA

MONA / REMI CHAUVIN. IMAGE COURTESY MONA MUSEUM OF OLD AND NEW ART, HOBART ©

MONA

Subversive, confronting, funny and downright weird, this is art for grown-ups. Laugh, be appalled, be turned on, then have a glass of wine...there's nothing quite like it anywhere else in the country.

Great For...

☑ Don't Miss

Bit.fall: Julius Popp's two-storey high installation that drips phrases randomly selected from news websites.

Visiting MONA

The brainchild of Hobart philanthropist David Walsh, MONA has turned the Australian art world on its head. Twelve kilometres north of Hobart's city centre, the gallery occupies a saucepan-shaped peninsula on the Derwent River. Arrayed across three underground levels, abutting a sheer rock face, the $75-million museum has been described by its owner as 'a subversive adult Disneyland'. You'll find ancient antiquities showcased next to contemporary works: the experience is sexy, provocative, disturbing and deeply engaging.

Give yourself half a day to explore the darkened underground galleries. To get here, catch a ferry upriver from the Hobart waterfront and eyeball the museum, carved out of a sandstone headland like a vast rusty bunker, from the water.

❶ Need to Know

Museum of Old & New Art; www.mona.net.
au; 655 Main Rd, Berriedale; ⏱10am-6pm
Wed-Mon Dec & Feb-Apr, 10am-6pm daily Jan,
10am-5pm Wed-Mon May-Nov; adult/child
$20/free)

✕ Take a Break

It's hard to beat the outstanding on-site
restaurant, **The Source** (📞03-6277
9900; www.mona.net.au/mona/restaurant;
lunch mains $27-38, dinner degustation from
$75; ⏱7.30-10am & noon-2pm Wed-Mon,
6pm-late Wed-Sat).

★ Top Tip

If you're from Tasmania, entry is free;
if you're not, it's cheaper between
March and November.

Exhibitions

The permanent exhibits bear the stamp
of David Walsh, whose private collection
they once formed. You can expect plenty of
playful, attention-grabbing works, including
Chris Ofili's controversial *The Holy Virgin
Mary* (which includes elephant dung and
snippets of pornography) and a version
of Wim Delvoye's *Cloaca* machine, which
turns food intro excrement as you watch.

While You're Here

As well as the gallery, MONA is home to the
cellar door for **Moorilla** (📞03-6277 9960;
www.moorilla.com.au; tastings $10, redeemable
with purchase; ⏱9.30am-5pm Wed-Mon, daily
Jan), a winery established here in the 1950s;
duck in for a wine or **Moo Brew** (www.moo
brew.com.au) beer tasting. You can also catch

a summer concert on the lawns, or maybe
splash out for a stay overnight in the uber-
swish **Pavilions** (www.mona.net.au/mona/
accommodation/the-pavilions; d from $490).

Festivals at MONA

MONA FOMA   Music, Art

On the grounds of MONA, January's wonderfully eclectic Festival of Music & Arts
features a high-profile 'Eminent Artist in
Residence' (EAR) every year. Previous EARs
have included John Cale and Nick Cave.
Stirring stuff. (MOFO; www.mofo.net.au; ⏱Jan)

Dark MOFO   Music, Art

The sinister sister of MONA FOMA, Dark
MOFO broods in the half-light of June's winter solstice. Expect live music, installations,
readings, film noir and midnight feasts, all
tapping into Tasmania's edgy gothic under-
currents. (www.darkmofo.net.au; ⏱Jun)

Buskers at Salamanca Place

CHRIS TAYLOR/ 500PX PRIME ©

Salamanca Place

Dating back to the whaling days of the 1830s, Salamanca was the hub of Hobart's trade and commerce. These days Salamanca hosts myriad restaurants, cafes, bars and shops, and the unmissable Saturday morning Salamanca Market.

Great For...

☑ Don't Miss

Fine woodwork carved from salvaged Huon pine, the beautiful conifer, endemic to Tassie, known as 'green gold'.

Exploring Salamanca Place

This picturesque row of four-storey sandstone warehouses is a classic example of Australian colonial architecture. By the mid-20th century many of the warehouses had fallen into ruin, before restorations began in the 1970s. The development of the quarry behind the warehouses into **Salamanca Sq** has bolstered the atmosphere, while at the eastern end of Salamanca the conversion of four old wheat silos into plush apartments has also been a hit.

There are plenty of cafes in Salamanca Pl. Our picks include Retro Café (p209), Machine Laundry Café (p210) and Tricycle Café Bar (p210). Nightlife options include pubs Knopwood's Retreat (p211) and Jack Greene (p212).

Operating behind the scenes is a vibrant and creative arts community. The nonprofit

Salamanca Market produce

ANDREW WATSON / GETTY IMAGES ©

ℹ Need to Know

Salamanca Place is closed to traffic on market days: get a Salamanca Shuttle or Hobart Hopper bus or, ideally, walk!

✗ Take a Break

Knopwood's (p211), right on Salamanca Place, is the classic spot for a post-browse beverage.

★ Top Tip

While the market is open every Saturday, Hobart's winter weather can drive some stallholders to pack up early.

Salamanca Arts Centre (☎03-6234 8414; www.salarts.org.au; 77 Salamanca Pl; ⏰shops & galleries 9am-5pm) occupies seven Salamanca warehouses, home to 75-plus arts organisations and individuals, including shops, galleries, performing-arts venues and versatile public spaces. Check the website for happenings.

To reach Salamanca from Battery Point, descend the well-weathered **Kelly's Steps** (1839), wedged between warehouses half-way along the main block of buildings.

Salamanca Market

Every Saturday morning since 1972, the open-air **Salamanca Market** (www.salamanca.com.au; ⏰8am-3pm Sat) has lured hippies and craft merchants from the foothills to fill the tree-lined expanses of Salamanca Pl with their stalls. Fresh organic produce, secondhand clothes and books, tacky tourist souvenirs, ceramics and woodwork, cheap sunglasses, antiques, exuberant buskers, quality food and drink... It's all here, but people-watching is the real name of the game. Rain or shine – don't miss it!

Friday Night Fandango

Some of Hobart's best live tunes get an airing every Friday night at the **Salamanca Arts Centre Courtyard** (www.salarts.org.au/portfolio/rektango; 77 Salamanca Pl; ⏰5.30-7.30pm), just off Woobys Lane. It's a free community event that started in about 2000, with the adopted name 'Rektango', borrowed from a band that sometimes graces the stage. Acts vary from month to month – expect anything from African beats to rockabilly, folk and gypsy-Latino. Drinks essential (sangria in summer, mulled wine in winter); dancing near-essential.

Walking Tour: Hobart's Harbour & History

Get to know Hobart's history with this walking tour around the city centre.

Distance: 3km
Duration: 3 hours

✕ Take a Break

Recharge your batteries with a coffee and pie at Jackman & McRoss (p209) in Battery Point.

Window, Battery Point

Start Franklin Sq

❶ Franklin Sq

Launch your expedition at Franklin Sq under the statue of Sir John Franklin, rear admiral, Arctic explorer and lieutenant-governor of Van Diemen's Land (as Tasmania was once known).

Trek down Macquarie St past the 1906 sandstone clock tower of the General Post Office, the 1864 Town Hall and into the Tasmanian Museum & Art Gallery.

❷ Victoria Dock

Navigate across Campbell St and Davey St to the fishing boats at Victoria Dock. Built in 1804, the dock is one of Tasmania's oldest, and now hosts regular visits from Australia's Antarctic supply vessels and Tasmania's fleet of commercial fishing boats.

❸ Henry Jones Art Hotel

Check out the renovated Henry Jones Art Hotel. Formerly the IXL jam factory, it was once Tasmania's largest private employer, and now houses one of the city's most sophisticated boutique hotels. Cross the swing bridge and fishtail towards Constitution Dock for fish and chips.

❹ Sullivans Cove

Next stop is the slickly reworked Elizabeth St Pier jutting into Sullivans Cove, which features a range of classy accommodation upstairs, plus restaurants and bars downstairs. If the tide is out, take the low-road steps around Watermans Dock. Cross Morrison St then wander through Parliament Sq in front of Parliament House.

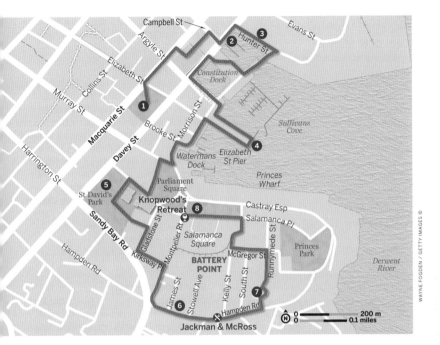

❺ St David's Park

Resist the photogenic frontage of Salamanca Pl for now, turning right instead to detour through St David's Park. This lovely park was the site of Hobart Town's original cemetery and Tasmania's first church, and dates to the founding of the colony in 1804. Take your time to stroll past the picturesque pergola and walls of colonial gravestones.

❻ Battery Point

Cut through Salamanca Mews, jag right onto Gladstone St, left onto Kirksway Pl, then right onto Montpellier Retreat, arcing uphill into Battery Point, Hobart's oldest residential area.

❼ Arthur Circus

Turn left into Runnymede St to check out Arthur Circus, an improbably quaint round-

about lined with eave-free Georgian cottages. Built for the officers of the Battery Point garrison, these cottages were originally just two rooms and were dwarfed by more genteel neighbouring residences.

Continue down Runnymede St and turn left into McGregor St, casting an eye up well-preserved South St.

❽ Salamanca Place

Turn right onto Kelly St and bumble down Kelly's Steps, an 1839 sandstone link between Battery Point and the redeveloped warehouses of Salamanca Pl. Nearby is our favourite Hobart pub, Knopwood's Retreat, and a well-earned cold beer.

Finish Knopwood's Retreat

⊙ SIGHTS

Farm Gate Market   Market

Salamanca Market on the waterfront has been a success for decades, but this hyper-active new foodie street-mart might just give it a run for its money. Trading commences with the ding of a big brass bell at 9am. Elbow your way in for the best buys, or take your time to browse the fruit, veg, honey, wine, baked goods, beer, smoked meats, coffee, nuts, oils, cut flowers and jams... Terrific! (www.farmgatemarket.com.au; Bathurst St, btwn Elizabeth & Murray Sts; ☺9am-1pm Sun)

Tasmanian Museum & Art Gallery   Museum

Incorporating Hobart's oldest building, the Commissariat Store (1808), this revamped museum features colonial relics and excellent Aboriginal and wildlife displays. The gallery curates a collection of Tasmanian colonial art. There are free guided tours at 1pm and 2pm from Wednesday to Sunday (hordes of school kids might be a little less interested in proceedings than you are), plus tours of a historic cottage within the museum grounds at 11am on Wednesdays. There's a cool cafe, too. (www.tmag.tas.gov.au; Dunn Pl; ☺10am-4pm Tue-Sun) FREE

Penitentiary Chapel Historic Site   Historic Site

Ruminating over the courtrooms, cells and gallows here, writer TG Ford mused: 'As the Devil was going through Hobart Gaol, he saw a solitary cell; and the Devil was pleased for it gave him a hint, for improving the prisons in hell'. Take the excellent National Trust–run **tour** (adult/child/family $12/5/25; ☺10am, 11.30am, 1pm & 2.30pm Sun-Fri, 1pm & 2.30pm Sat), or the one-hour **Penitentiary Chapel Ghost Tour** (adult/child/family $15/10/50; ☺8.30pm Mon & Fri) held twice weekly (bookings essential). (📞03-6231 0911; www.penitentiarychapel.com; cnr Brisbane & Campbell Sts; tours

Maritime Museum of Tasmania   Museum

Highlighting shipwrecks, boat building, whaling and Hobart's unbreakable bond with the sea, the Maritime Museum of Tasmania has an interesting (if a little static) collection of photos, paintings, models and

Sculpture at the Royal Tasmanian Botanical Gardens (p207)

GRANT DIXON / GETTY IMAGES ©

relics (try to resist ringing the huge brass bell from the *Rhexenor*). Upstairs is the council-run **Carnegie Gallery** (10am-5pm) FREE, exhibiting contemporary Tasmanian art, craft, design and photography. (03-6234 1427; www.maritimetas.org; 16 Argyle St; adult/child/family $9/5/18; 9am-5pm)

Waterfront   Historic Site

Hobartians flock to the city's waterfront like seagulls to chips. Centred around **Victoria Dock** (a working fishing harbour) and **Constitution Dock** (chock-full of floating take-away-seafood punts), it's a brilliant place to explore. The obligatory Hobart experience is to sit in the sun, munch some fish and chips and watch the harbour hubbub. If you'd prefer something with a knife and fork, there are some superb restaurants here, too – head for **Elizabeth St Pier**.

Celebrations surrounding the finish of the annual **Sydney to Hobart Yacht Race** (www.rolexsydneyhobart.com; Dec) also revolve around Constitution Dock at New Year. The fab food festival **Taste of Tasmania** (www.thetasteoftasmania.com.au) is also in full swing around this time. There are so many people around the waterfront, Hobart could be Monaco! The waterfront on New Year's Eve can be both exhilarating and nauseating (depending on how late you stay out).

Hunter St has a row of fine Georgian warehouses, most of which comprised the old Henry Jones IXL jam factory. It's occupied these days by the University of Tasmania's Art School and the uber-swish Henry Jones Art Hotel (p200), both retaining their original heritage facades.

Most of the Hobart waterfront area is built on reclaimed land. When the town was first settled, Davey St marked the shoreline and the Hunter St area was an island used to store food and imported goods. Subsequent projects filled in the shallow waters and created the land upon which the Hunter St and Salamanca Pl warehouses were constructed. On Hunter St itself, markers indicate the position of the original causeway, built in 1820 to link Hunter Island with the long since demolished suburb of Wapping.

Hobart for Children

Parents won't break the bank keeping the troops entertained in Hobart. The free Friday-night **Rektango** (p198) music event in the courtyard at the Salamanca Arts Centre is a family-friendly affair, while the street performers, buskers and visual smorgasbord of Saturday's **Salamanca Market** (p198) captivate kids of all ages.

There's always something going on around the **waterfront** – fishing boats chugging in and out of Victoria Dock, yachts tacking in Sullivans Cove...and you can feed the tribe on a budget at the floating fish punts on Constitution Dock.

Rainy-day attractions to satisfy your child (or inner child) include the **Tasmanian Museum & Art Gallery**, the **Maritime Museum of Tasmania** and the excellent new **Mawson's Huts Replica Museum** (p205).

Hobart is an active kinda town: take a boat cruise up or down the river; assail the heights of **Mt Wellington** (p206) or **Mt Nelson**; hire a bike and explore the cycling paths; or pack the teens into the Kombi and go surfing at **Clifton Beach**. And beyond the edge of town there's a plethora of animal parks, beaches, caves, nature walks and mazes to explore.

If you're in need of a romantic dinner for two, contact the **Mobile Nanny Service** (03-6273 3773, 0437 504 064; www.mobilenannyservice.com.au).

Above: Tasmanian Museum & Art Gallery
OLIVER STREWE / GETTY IMAGES ©

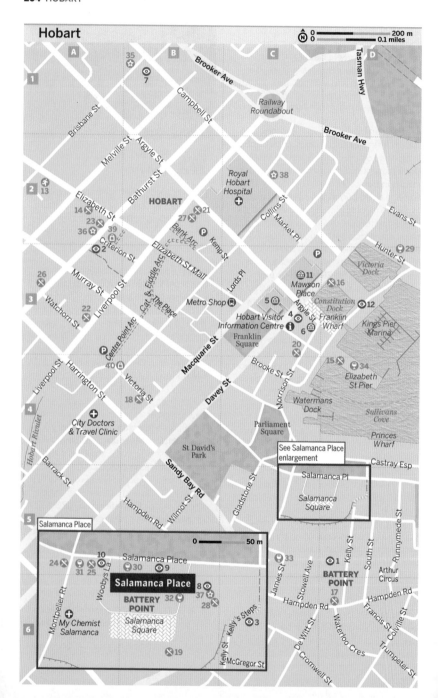

Hobart

N 0 — 200 m
0 — 0.1 miles

Brooker Ave

Campbell St

Railway Roundabout

Brooker Ave

Tasman Hwy

Brisbane St

Melville St

Argyle St

Bathurst St

Elizabeth St

Evans St

35
7

38

Royal Hobart Hospital

Collins St

Market Pl

HOBART

14
23
36
39
2
Criterion St

27
Bank Arc
Kemp St

21

Elizabeth St Mall

Lords Pl

Hunter St

29

Victoria Dock

13

26

Murray St

Liverpool St

Cat & The Place

Eddie Arc

Metro Shop

11
Mawson Place

16

Constitution Dock

12

22

Watchorn St

Centre Point Arc

40

Harrington St

Liverpool St

Victoria St

18

Macquarie St

Hobart Visitor Information Centre

5
4
6

Argyle St
Franklin Wharf

Franklin Square

Kings Pier Marina

20

Brooke St

Morrison St

15
34

Elizabeth St Pier

City Doctors & Travel Clinic

Davey St

Watermans Dock

Sullivans Cove

Parliament Square

Princes Wharf

Hobart Rivulet

Barrack St

Sandy Bay Rd

St David's Park

Gladstone St

See Salamanca Place enlargement

Castray Esp

Salamanca Pl

Salamanca Square

Hampden Rd

Wilmot St

Salamanca Place

24
31 25

10
30
9

Salamanca Place

Salamanca Place

BATTERY POINT

32

8
37
28

33

James St

Stowell Ave

1

BATTERY POINT

Kelly St

South St

Runnymede St

Arthur Circus

17

Hampden Rd

My Chemist Salamanca

Montpelier Rt

Woobys La

Salamanca Square

Kelly's Steps

3

Francis St

Colville St

Trumpeter St

19

Kelly St

McGregor St

De Witt St

Cromwell St

Waterloo Cres

Hobart

Mawson's Huts Replica Museum   Museum
This excellent new waterfront installation is an exact model of the hut in which Sir Douglas Mawson hunkered down on his 1911–14 Australasian Antarctic Expedition, which set sail from Hobart. Inside it is 100% authentic, right down to the matches, the stove and the bunks. A knowledgeable guide sits at a rustic table, ready to answer your Antarctic enquiries. Entry fees go towards the upkeep of the original hut at Cape Denison in the Antarctic. (www.mawsons-huts-replica.org.au; cnr Morrison & Argyle Sts; adult/child/family $12/4/26; ⌚9am-6pm Oct-Apr, 10am-5pm May-Sep)

Lark Distillery   Distillery
The Lark Distillery, next door to the visitor information centre, is at the fore of Tasmania's surge into the world of single malt whisky. Enjoy a wee dram via a tasting session, or a longer tour of the distillery that's 20 minutes' drive from the cellar door. On Friday and Saturday nights there's live music from 6pm, plus cheese-and-dip platters and Moo Brew on tap, if you're more of a beer boffin. (☎03-6231 9088; www.larkdistillery.com.au; 14 Davey St; tastings per person $15, 3hr whisky tours per person $75; ⌚9am-7pm Sun-Thu, to 10pm Fri & Sat)

Battery Point   Historic Site
An empty rum bottle's throw from the waterfront, the old maritime village of **Battery Point** (www.batterypoint.net) is a tight nest of lanes and 19th-century cottages, packed together like shanghaied landlubbers in a ship's belly. Spend an afternoon exploring: stumble up Kelly's Steps from Salamanca Pl and dogleg into South St, where the red lights once burned night and day. Spin around picturesque **Arthur Circus**, refuel in the cafes on Hampden Rd, then ogle **St George's Anglican Church** on Cromwell St. Battery Point's name derives from the 1818 gun battery that stood on the promontory, protecting Hobart Town from nautical threats both real and imagined. The guns were never used in battle and the

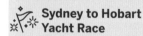

Sydney to Hobart Yacht Race

Arguably the world's greatest and most treacherous open-ocean yacht race, the **Sydney to Hobart Yacht Race** (www.rolexsydneyhobart.com; ☉Dec) winds up at Hobart's Constitution Dock some time around New Year's Eve. As the storm-battered maxis limp across the finish line, champagne corks pop and weary sailors turn the town upside down. On New Year's Day, find a sunny spot by the harbour, munch some lunch from the Taste of Tasmania food festival and count spinnakers on the river. New Year's resolutions? What New Year's resolutions?

only damage they inflicted was on nearby windowpanes when fired during practice.

Architectural styles here reflect the original occupants' varying jobs (and salaries), ranging from one- and two-room fishermen's cottages to the lace-festooned mansions of merchants and master mariners. Most houses are still occupied by Hobartians, and many are now guesthouses where you can stay (usually for a pretty penny) and absorb the village atmosphere. For a fortifying stout, duck into the **Shipwright's Arms Hotel** (✆03-6223 5551; www.shipwrightsarms.com.au; 29 Trumpeter St, Battery Point).

Cascade Brewery   Brewery
Standing in startling, gothic isolation next to the clean-running Hobart Rivulet, Cascade is Australia's oldest brewery (1832) and is still pumping out superb beers. Tours involve plenty of history, with tastings at the end, Note that under-16s aren't permitted on the main brewery tour (take the family-friendly Heritage Tour instead), and that brewery machinery doesn't operate on weekends (brewers have weekends, too). Bookings essential. To get here, take bus 44, 46, 47 or 49. (✆03-6224 1117; www.cascadebrewery.com.au; 140 Cascade Rd, South Hobart; adult/family brewery tours $25/65,

heritage tours $15/37; ☉brewery tours 11am & 12.30pm daily, heritage tours 12.30pm Mon, Wed & Fri)

Female Factory   Historic Site
Finally being recognised as an important historic site (one in four convicts transported to Van Diemen's Land was a woman), this was where Hobart's female convicts were incarcerated. Explore the site under your own steam, or book a guided tour or 'Her Story' dramatisation. It's not far from the Cascade Brewery – combining the two makes an engaging afternoon. To get here by public transport, take bus 44, 46, 47 or 49 and jump off at stop 13. (✆03-6233 6656; www.femalefactory.org.au; 16 Degraves St, South Hobart; adult/child/family $5/5/15, tour $15/10/40, 'Her Story' dramatisation $20/12.50/60; ☉9.30am-4pm, tours hourly 10am-3pm, 'Her Story' dramatisation 11am)

Mt Wellington   Mountain
Cloaked in winter snow, Mt Wellington (1270m) towers over Hobart like a benevolent overlord. The citizens find reassurance in its constant, solid presence, while outdoorsy types find the space to hike and bike on its leafy flanks. And the view from the top is unbelievable! You can drive all the way to the summit on a sealed road; alternatively, the **Hobart Shuttle Bus Company** (✆0408 341 804; www.hobartshuttlebus.com; tours per adult/child $30/20, transfers per person $20) runs daily two-hour tours to the summit, plus one-way transfers for walkers. Hacked out of the mountainside during the Great Depression, the summit road winds up from the city through thick temperate forest, opening out to lunar rockscapes at the summit. If you don't have wheels, local buses 48 and 49 stop at Fern Tree halfway up the hill, from where it's a five- to six-hour return walk to the top via Fern Glade Track, Radfords Track, Pinnacle Track and then the steep Zig Zag Track. The Organ Pipes walk from the Chalet (en route to the summit) is a flat track below these amazing cliffs. Download maps at www.wellingtonpark.org.au/maps, or pick up the free *Wellington*

Park walk map or detailed *Wellington Park Recreation Map* ($9.90) from the visitor information centre.

Feeling more intrepid? Bomb down the slopes on a mountain bike with Mt Wellington Descent. Don't be deterred if the sky is overcast – often the peak rises above cloud level and looks out over a magic carpet of cotton-topped clouds. (Kunanyi; www.wellington park.org.au; Pinnacle Rd, via Fern Tree)

Royal Tasmanian Botanical Gardens   Gardens

On the eastern side of the Queens Domain, these small but beguiling gardens hark back to 1818 and feature more than 6000 exotic and native plant species. Picnic on the lawns, check out the Subantarctic Plant House or grab a bite at the Botanical Restaurant, which also houses a gift shop and kiosk. Across from the main entrance is the site of the former Beaumaris Zoo, where the last captive Tasmanian tiger died in 1936. (☎03-6236 3057; www.rtbg.tas.gov.au; Lower Domain Rd, Queens Domain; ⏰8am-6.30pm Oct-Mar, to 5.30pm Apr & Sep, to 5pm May-Aug) FREE

✪ ACTIVITIES

Mt Wellington Descent   Cycling

Take a van ride to the summit of Mt Wellington (1270m), and follow with 22km of downhill cruising on a mountain bike. It's terrific fun, with minimal energy output and maximum views! Tours start and end at Brooke St Pier on the Hobart waterfront. (☎1800 064 726; www.underdownunder.com. au; adult/child $75/65; ⏰10am & 1pm daily year-round, plus 4pm Jan & Feb)

Artbikes   Bicycle Rental

More than 140cm tall? You qualify for free city-bike hire from Artbikes. Just bring a credit card and some photo ID, and off you go. If you want to keep the bike overnight it's $22; for a weekend it's $44. (☎03-6165 6666; www.artbikes.com.au; 146 Elizabeth St; ⏰9am-4.30pm Mon-Fri)

> *Standing in startling, gothic isolation... Cascade is Australia's oldest brewery*

Cascade Brewery

RACHEL LEWIS / GETTY IMAGES ©

Mt Wellington (p206)

Gourmania   Walking Tour

Flavour-filled walking tours around Salamanca Pl and central Hobart, with plenty of opportunities to try local foods and chat to restaurant, cafe and shop owners. A tour of Hobart's best cafes was also mooted at the time of writing. (☎0419 180 113; www.gourmania foodtours.com.au; per person from $95)

🔒 SHOPPING

Fullers Bookshop   Books

Hobart's best bookshop has a great range of literature and travel guides, plus regular launches and readings, and a cool cafe in the corner. (www.fullersbookshop.com.au; 131 Collins St; ⏰8.30am-6pm Mon-Fri, 9am-5pm Sat, 10am-4pm Sun)

Cool Wine   Wine

Excellent selection of Tasmanian wine and global craft beers. (www.coolwine.com.au; Shop 8, MidCity Arcade, Criterion St; ⏰9.30am-6.30pm Mon-Sat, 10am-2pm Sun)

⊗ EATING

Hobart's city centre proffers some classy brunch and lunch venues, but when the sun sinks behind the mountain, there's not much going on here. Instead, head for Salamanca Pl and the waterfront, the epicentre of the city's culinary scene, with quality seafood everywhere you look.

For Hobart's best pub grub, head to the New Sydney Hotel (p212), the Shipwright's Arms Hotel (p206) or the Republic Bar & Café (p212).

Pilgrim Coffee   Cafe $

With exposed bricks, timber beams and distressed walls, L-shaped Pilgrim is Hobart's hippest cafe. Expect wraps, panini and interesting mains (Peruvian spiced alpaca with quinoa and beetroot!), plus expertly prepared coffee. Fall into conversation with the locals at big shared tables. Down a laneway around the back is the **Standard** (☎03-6234 1999; Hudsons Lane; burgers $7-12; ⏰11am-10pm daily),

STEFAN WILKSCH / GETTY IMAGES ©

a fab burger bar run by the same hipsters. (☑03-6234 1999; 48 Argyle St; mains $11-20; ⊙7am-5pm Mon-Fri)

Jackman & McRoss   Bakery $

Don't bypass this conversational, neighbourhood bakery-cafe, even if it's just to gawk at the display cabinet full of delectable pies, tarts, baguettes and pastries. Early-morning cake and coffee may evolve into a quiche for lunch, or perhaps a blackberry-and-wallaby pie. Staff stay cheery despite being run off their feet. The **city branch** (☑03-6231 0601; 4 Victoria St; ⊙7am-4.30pm Mon-Fri) has parallel prices. (☑03-6223 3186; 57-59 Hampden Rd, Battery Point; meals $8-13; ⊙7am-6pm Mon-Fri, to 5pm Sat & Sun)

Retro Café   Cafe $

So popular it hurts, funky Retro is ground zero for Saturday brunch among the market stalls (or any day, really). Masterful breakfasts, bagels, salads and burgers interweave with laughing staff, chilled-out jazz and the whirr and bang of the coffee machine. A classic Hobart cafe. (☑03-6223 3073; 31 Salamanca Pl; mains $10-18; ⊙7am-5pm)

Small Fry   Cafe $

☑ Hip Small Fry is now one of Hobart's best cafe-bars in its own right. Conversation comes naturally at the shared steel counter: sip a glass of wine, some soup or a coffee; talk, listen, laugh, crunch a salad... It's a flexible vibe designed to 'avoid labels'. Love the wooden menu cubes! (☑03-6231 1338; www.small-fryhobart.com.au; 129 Bathurst St; mains $6-25; ⊙7.30am-3.30pm Mon-Thu, to 9pm Fri, 8.30am-9pm Sat)

Raspberry Fool   Cafe $

The all-day menu here features dressed-up comfort food with a chef's spin. Try the cheesy leeks on toast with bacon and a fried egg, or the baked eggs with caramelised onion, ham and Gruyère. It gets as busy as a woodpecker when the Farm Gate Market (p202) is happening outside on Sunday mornings. Great coffee, too.

📖	**Hobart**
	Historic Tours

Informative, entertaining 90-minute walking tours of Hobart (3pm Thursday to Saturday and 9.30am Sunday) and historic Battery Point (5pm Wednesday and 1pm Saturday). There's also an Old Hobart Pub Tour (5pm Thursday to Saturday), which sluices through some waterfront watering holes. Reduced winter schedule, and bookings essential. (☑03-6238 4222, 03-6231 4214; www.hobart historictours.com.au; tours adult/child/family $30/14/75)

(☑03-6231 1274; 85 Bathurst St; mains $9-17; ⊙7.30am-4pm Mon-Fri, to 2.30pm Sat & Sun)

R. Takagi Sushi   Japanese $

Hobart's best sushi spot makes the most of Tasmania's great seafood. Udon noodles and miso also make an appearance at this sleek, compact eatery – a favourite of Hobart desk jockeys. (☑03-6234 8524; 155 Liverpool St; sushi from $3; ⊙10.30am-5.50pm Mon-Fri, to 4pm Sat, 11.30am-3pm Sun)

Flippers   Seafood $

With its voluptuous fish-shaped profile and alluring sea-blue paint job, floating Flippers is a Hobart institution. Not to mention the awesome fish and chips! Fillets of flathead and curls of calamari – straight from the deep blue sea and into the deep fryer. The local seagulls will adore you. (www.flippers fishandchips.com.au; Constitution Dock; meals $10-24; ⊙9.30am-8.30pm)

Salamanca Fresh   Supermarket $

Gourmet self-caterers alert: don't miss the fruit, veg, meats and groceries here, plus a suite of Tasmanian wines. (☑03-6223 2700; www.salamancafresh.com.au; 41 Salamanca Pl; ⊙7am-7pm)

Ginger Brown   Cafe $

When a food business is this well run, the mood infects the entire room: happy staff,

From left: Fish and chips at Fish Frenzy; Salamanca Place dining; St David's Park (p201)

happy customers and happy vibes. Try the slow-cooked lamb panini with cornichons and hummus. Very kid- and cyclist-friendly. Last orders 3pm. (03-6223 3531; 464 Macquarie St, South Hobart; mains $10-20; 7.30am-4pm Tue-Fri, 8.30am-4pm Sat & Sun;)

Machine Laundry Café   Cafe $

Hypnotise yourself watching the tumble dryers spin at this bright retro cafe, where you can wash your dirty clothes ($5) while discreetly adding fresh juice, soup or coffee stains to your clean ones. Don't miss the chilli-infused roti wrap for breakfast. (03-6224 9922; 12 Salamanca Sq; mains $7-17; 7.30am-5pm Mon-Sat, 8.30am-5pm Sun)

Tricycle Café Bar   Cafe $

This cosy red-painted nook inside the Salamanca Arts Centre serves up a range of cafe classics (BLTs, toasties, free-range scrambled eggs, salads, house-brewed chai and Fair Trade coffee), plus awesome daily specials (braised Wagyu rice bowl with jalapeño cream – wow!). Wines by the glass from the bar. (03-6223 7228; www.salarts.org.au/portfolio/tricycle;

71 Salamanca Pl; mains $8-15; 8.30am-4pm Mon-Sat)

Fish Frenzy   Seafood $$

A casual, waterside fish nook, overflowing with fish fiends and brimming with fish and chips, fishy salads (spicy calamari, smoked salmon and brie) and fish burgers. The eponymous 'Fish Frenzy' ($18) delivers a little bit of everything. Quality can be inconsistent, but good staff and buzzy harbourside vibes compensate. No bookings. (03-6231 2134; www.fishfrenzy.com.au; Elizabeth St Pier; mains $14-35; 11am-9pm)

Mill on   Spanish,
Morrison   Modern Australian $$

Inside the gorgeously renovated Gibson's City Mill (cast-iron columns, exposed timber ceilings, dark-wood furniture) is this sharp but relaxed tapas restaurant: a bit Spanish, a bit Mexican, a bit Mod Oz. Try the chargrilled calamari or the arancini balls. Terrific wines by the glass, from Coal River Valley to Catalonia. (03-6234 3490; www.themillonmorrison.com.au; 11 Morrison St;

STEVE WATERS / GETTY IMAGES ©

tapas $4-16; ⊘noon-2pm Mon-Fri, 5.30pm-late Mon-Sat)

Elizabeth St
Food + Wine   Modern Australian $$
🍴 Cafe, providore, wine room – take your pick at this vibrant North Hobart foodie space. Expect excellent breakfasts, big salads and classy mains (try the spicy beef cheek with potato and peperonata), all paired with local wines (except the breakfasts...). Communal tables and shelves crammed with 100% seasonal and sustainable Tasmanian produce. (🖉03-6231 2626; 285 Elizabeth St, North Hobart; mains $10-20; ⊘8am-6pm Sun-Thu, to 8pm Fri, to 4pm Sat)

Ethos   Modern Australian $$$
Hidden in a courtyard down a flagstone alley off Elizabeth St, Ethos rigorously supports local farmers and ethically produced Tasmanian food. The menu is very seasonal, with artisan-produced ingredients showcasing whatever's fresh. Servings are on the small side, but the flavours are innovative and delicious. Bookings essential.

There's also a moody new wine bar downstairs. (🖉03-6231 1165; www.ethoseatdrink.com; 100 Elizabeth St; 6/8-course menu $75/90; ⊘6pm-late Tue-Sat)

🍸 DRINKING & NIGHTLIFE

Knopwood's Retreat   Pub
Adhere to the 'when in Rome...' dictum and head for 'Knoppies', Hobart's best pub, which has been serving ales to seagoing types since the convict era. For most of the week it's a cosy watering hole with an open fire. On Friday nights, city workers swarm and the crowd spills across the street. (www.knopwoods.com; 39 Salamanca Pl; ⊘10am-late)

Preachers   Bar
Grab a retro sofa seat inside, or adjourn to the ramshackle garden bar – in which an old Hobart bus is now full of beer booths – with the hipsters. Lots of Tasmanian craft beers on tap, plus cool staff and a resident ghost. A steady flow of $15 burgers and $12

tapas keeps the beer in check. (5 Knopwood St, Battery Point; ☺noon-late)

Jack Greene   Bar
The gourmet burgers here cost up to $20 but atmospheric Jack Greene (a European hunting lodge on the run?) is worthwhile if you're a wandering beer fan. Glowing racks of bottled brews fill the fridges, and there are at least 16 beers on tap from around Australia and New Zealand. Occasional acoustic troubadors perch next to the stairs. (www.jackgreene.com.au; 47-48 Salamanca Pl; ☺11am-late)

IXL Long Bar   Bar
Take a seat at the glowing bar at the Henry Jones Art Hotel (p200) and check out Hobart's fashionistas over a whisky sour. If there are no spare stools at the not-so-long bar, flop onto the leather couches in the lobby. Moo Brew on tap, and live jazz Friday to Sunday. (www.thehenryjones.com; 25 Hunter St; ☺5-10.30pm Mon-Fri, 3pm-late Sat & Sun)

T-42°   Bar
Waterfront T-42° makes a splash with its food (mains $13 to $30), and draws late-week barflies with its minimalist interior, spinnaker-shaped bar and ambient tunes. If you stay out late enough, it also does breakfast. (www.tav42.com.au; Elizabeth St Pier; ☺7.30am-late Mon-Fri, from 8.30am Sat & Sun)

Nant Whisky Bar   Bar
Prop yourself at the bar in this compact, heritage-hued room off Salamanca Pl and see how whisky from the **Nant Distillery** in Tasmania's central highlands stacks up next to other peaty drops from around the globe. (www.nant.com.au; 63 Woobys Lane; ☺noon-midnight Sun-Fri, 10am to midnight Sat)

⊛ ENTERTAINMENT

State Cinema   Cinema
Saved from the wrecking ball in the 1990s, the multiscreen State shows independent and art-house flicks from local and international film-makers. There's a great cafe and bar on-site, a browse-worthy bookshop and the foodie temptations of North Hobart's restaurants right outside. (☎03-6234 6318; www.statecinema.com.au; 375 Elizabeth St, North Hobart; tickets adult/child $18/14; ☺10am-late)

Republic Bar & Café   Live Music
The Republic is a raucous art deco pub hosting live music every night (often free entry). It's the number-one live-music pub around town, with an always-interesting line-up, including international acts. Loads of different beers and excellent food – just the kind of place you'd love to call your local. (☎03-6234 6954; www.republicbar.com; 299 Elizabeth St, North Hobart; ☺11am-late)

Brisbane Hotel   Live Music
The bad old Brisbane has dragged itself up from the pit of old-man, sticky-carpet alcoholism to be reinvented as a pro-gressive live-music venue. This is where anyone doing anything original, offbeat or uncommercial gets a gig: punk, metal, hip hop and singer-songwriters. (3 Brisbane St; ☺noon-late Tue-Sat, 3pm-late Sun)

New Sydney Hotel   Live Music
Low-key folk, jazz, blues and comedy play to a mature crowd Tuesday to Sunday nights (usually free): see the website for gig listings. Great pub food and a terrific beer selection, including an ever-changing array of island microbrews. Irish jam session 2pm Saturdays. (www.newsydney hotel.com.au; 87 Bathurst St; ☺noon-midnight)

Theatre Royal   Theatre
This venerable old stager is Australia's oldest continuously operating theatre, with actors first cracking the boards here back in 1834. Expect a range of music, ballet, theatre, opera and university revues. (☎03-6233 2299, 1800 650 277; www.theatreroyal.com.au; 29 Campbell St; tickets $20-60; ☺box office 9am-5pm Mon-Fri)

ℹ INFORMATION

MEDICAL SERVICES
City Doctors & Travel Clinic (📞03-6231 3003; www.citydoctors.com.au; 188 Collins St; ⏰9am-5pm Mon-Fri) General medical appointments and travel immunisations.

My Chemist Salamanca (📞03-6235 0257; www.mychemist.com.au; 6 Montpelier Retreat, Battery Point; ⏰8.30am-6.30pm Mon-Fri, to 5pm Sat, 10am-4pm Sun) Handy chemist just off Salamanca Pl.

Royal Hobart Hospital (📞03-6222 8423; www.dhhs.tas.gov.au; 48 Liverpool St; ⏰24hr) Emergency entry on Liverpool St.

TOURIST INFORMATION
Hobart Visitor Information Centre (📞03-6238 4222; www.hobarttravelcentre.com.au; cnr Davey & Elizabeth Sts; ⏰9am-5pm daily, extended hours in summer) Information, maps and state-wide tour, transport and accommodation bookings.

ℹ GETTING THERE & AWAY

Hobart's 'international' airport has only domestic flights, operated by **Qantas** (www.qantas.com.au), **Virgin Australia** (www.virginaustralia.com.au), **Jetstar** (www.jetstar.com.au) and **Tiger Airways** (www.tigerairways.com.au).

ℹ GETTING AROUND
TO/FROM THE AIRPORT
Hobart Airport (📞03-6216 1600; www.hobartairport.com.au; Strachan St, Cambridge) is 19km east of the city. A taxi to the city will cost around $42 between 6am and 8pm weekdays, and around $50 at other times.

BICYCLE
There are a number of bike-hire options around the city.

BUS
Metro Tasmania (📞13 22 01; www.metrotas.com.au) operates the local bus network, which is

Where to Stay

The liveliest areas to stay in Hobart are the waterfront and Salamanca Pl, though prices here are usually sky-high and vacancy rates low. If you're visiting in January, book as far in advance as humanly possible.

The CBD has less atmosphere, but most of the backpacker hostels, pubs with accommodation and midrange hotels are here. To the north of the city centre are suburban North Hobart and New Town, with apartments and B&Bs within walking distance of the North Hobart restaurants. To the south, accommodation in Sandy Bay is surprisingly well priced.

reliable but infrequent outside of business hours. The **Metro Shop** (22 Elizabeth St; ⏰8am-6pm Mon-Fri) handles ticketing and enquiries: most buses depart from this section of Elizabeth St, or from nearby Franklin Sq.

One-way fares vary with distances ('sections') travelled (from $3 to $6.20). For $5.30 you can buy an unlimited-travel **Day Rover** ticket, valid after 9am from Monday to Friday, and all weekend. Buy one-way tickets from the Metro Shop, the driver (exact change required) or ticket agents (newsagents and post offices). Drivers don't sell Day Rover tickets.

CAR
Timed, metered parking predominates in the CBD and tourist areas such as Salamanca Pl and the waterfront. For longer-term parking, large CBD garages (clearly signposted) offer inexpensive rates.

The big-boy rental firms have airport desks and city offices. Cheaper local firms offer daily rental rates from as low as $30.

FEARGUS COONEY / GETTY IMAGES ©

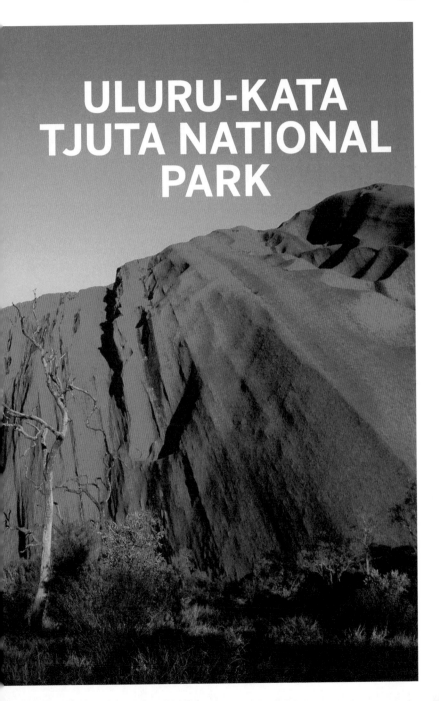

ULURU-KATA TJUTA NATIONAL PARK

Uluru-Kata Tjuta National Park

Nothing can really prepare you for the immensity, grandeur, changing colour and stillness of Uluru. It really is a sight that will sear itself onto your mind.

The World Heritage–listed icon has attained the status of a pilgrimage. Uluru, the equally (some say more) impressive Kata Tjuta (the Olgas), and the surrounding area are of deep cultural significance to the traditional owners, the Pitjantjatjara and Yankuntjatjara Aboriginal peoples (who refer to themselves as Anangu). The Anangu officially own the national park, which is leased to Parks Australia and jointly administered.

There's plenty to see and do: meandering walks, bike rides, guided tours, desert culture and simply contemplating the many changing colours and moods of the great monolith itself.

❶ In This Section

➡ Arriving in Uluru-Kata Tjuta National Park

The best ways to access Uluru are by direct flight from Melbourne or Sydney, or the 450km, six-hour bus trip from Alice Springs (also connected to Australia's major cities by air).

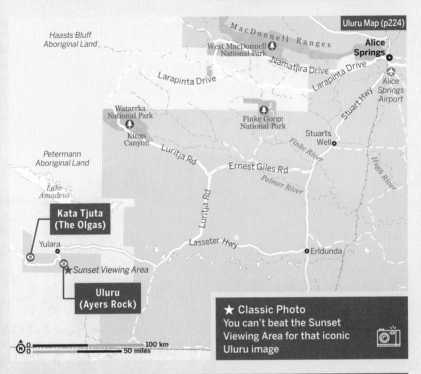

Uluru Map (p224)

Haasts Bluff
Aboriginal Land

MacDonnell Ranges

Alice Springs

West MacDonnell
National Park

Namatjira Drive

Larapinta Drive

Larapinta Drive

Stuart Hwy

Alice Springs Airport

Watarrka
National Park

Finke Gorge
National Park

Petermann
Aboriginal Land

Kings
Canyon

Luritja Rd

Stuarts Well

Finke River

Lake
Amadeus

Ernest Giles Rd

Palmer River

Hugh River

**Kata Tjuta
(The Olgas)**

Luritja Rd

Yulara

★ Sunset Viewing Area

Lasseter Hwy

Erldunda

**Uluru
(Ayers Rock)**

N
0 ——— 100 km
0 ——— 50 miles

★ Classic Photo
You can't beat the Sunset
Viewing Area for that iconic
Uluru image

From left: Cave at Uluru; No water sign near Uluru; Thorny devil, Uluru-Kata Tjuta National Park
MICHAEL DUNNING / GETTY IMAGES ©; ROBIN SMITH / GETTY IMAGES ©; AUSTRALIAN SCENICS / GETTY IMAGES ©

Late afternoon at Uluru

CHRIS MELLOR / GETTY IMAGES ©

Uluru (Ayers Rock)

Nothing in Australia is as readily identifiable as Uluru. No matter how many times you've seen it in postcards, nothing prepares you for the hulk on the horizon – so solitary and prodigious.

Great For...

☑ Don't Miss

The wonderful art in several rock shelters along the Mala Walk and Kuniya Walk to Mutitjulu Waterhole.

Uluru is 3.6km long and rises a towering 348m from the surrounding sandy scrubland (867m above sea level). If that's not impressive enough, it's believed that two-thirds of the rock lies beneath the sand.

Sacred sites are located around the base of Uluru; entry to and knowledge of the particular significance of these areas is restricted by Anangu law. The landscape of Uluru changes dramatically with the shifting light and seasons. In the afternoon, Uluru appears as an ochre-brown colour, scored and pitted by dark shadows. As the sun sets, it illuminates the rock in burnished orange, then a series of deeper and darker reds before it fades into charcoal. A performance in reverse, with marginally fewer spectators, is given at dawn.

Southwest face of Uluru

BETHUNE CARMICHAEL / GETTY IMAGES ©

• Yulara

Lasseter Hwy

◉ *Uluru*

❶ Need to Know

There are a number of tour companies that can take you from Alice to Uluru and back in a day: Viator, McCafferty's and Greyhound are the best known.

✕ Take a Break

While the park itself is understandably light on dining options, the **Tali Wiru** (📞02-8296 8010; www.ayersrockresort.com.au) outdoor dining experience can be magical.

★ Top Tip

Head to the end of the Mala Walk in time for a dazzling sunset on the walls of the Rock.

Exploring Uluru

The **Uluru-Kata Tjuta Cultural Centre**

(📞08-8956 1128; www.parksaustralia.gov.au/uluru/do/cultural-centre.html; ⏰7am-6pm) is 1km before Uluru on the road from Yulara and should be your first stop. Displays and exhibits focus on tjukurpa (Aboriginal law, religion and custom) and the history of the national park. The information desk in the Nintiringkupai building is staffed by park rangers who can supply the informative visitor guide, leaflets and walking notes.

The Cultural Centre encompasses the craft outlet Maruku Arts, owned by about 20 Anangu communities from across central Australia, selling hand-crafted wooden carvings, bowls and boomerangs.

A wonderful new way of experiencing the rock is by bike, available for hire at the Cultural Centre.

Walks

There are walking tracks around Uluru, and ranger-led walks explain the area's plants, wildlife, geology and cultural significance.

The excellent *Visitor Guide & Maps* brochure, which can be picked up at the Cultural Centre, gives details on a few self-guided walks.

Base Walk Circumnavigates the Rock, passing caves, paintings, sandstone folds and geological abrasions along the way (10.6km, three to four hours).

Liru Walk Links the Cultural Centre with the start of the Mala walk and climb, and winds through strands of mulga before opening up near Uluru (4km return, 1½ hours).

Mala Walk From the base of the climbing point (2km return, one hour), interpretive signs explain the tjukurpa of the Mala (hare-wallaby people), which is significant to the Anangu, as well as fine examples of rock art. A ranger-guided walk (free) along this route departs at 10am (8am from October to April) from the car park.

Kuniya Walk A short walk (1km return, 45 minutes) from the car park on the southern side leads to the most permanent waterhole, Mutitjulu, home of the ancestral watersnake. Great birdwatching and some excellent rock art are highlights.

Sunset Views

About halfway between Yulara and Uluru, the **sunset viewing area** has plenty of car and coach parking for that familiar post-card view. The **Talnguru Nyakunytjaku sunrise viewing area** is perched on a sand dune and captures both the Rock and Kata Tjuta in all their glory. It also has two great interpretive walks (1.5km) about women's and men's business. There's a shaded viewing area, toilets and a place to picnic.

A Question of Climbing

Many visitors consider climbing Uluru to be a highlight of a trip to the Centre. But for the traditional owners, the Anangu, Uluru is a sacred place. The path up the side of the Rock is part of the route taken by the Mala ancestors on their arrival at Uluru and has great spiritual significance. When you arrive at Uluru you'll see a sign from the Anangu saying 'We don't climb', and a request that you don't climb either.

The Anangu are the custodians of Uluru and take responsibility for the safety of visitors. Any injuries or deaths that occur are a source of distress and sadness to them. For similar reasons of public safety, Parks Australia would prefer that people didn't climb. It's a very steep ascent, not to be taken lightly, and each year there are air rescues, mostly for people suffering heart attacks.

A commitment has been made to close the climb for good, but only when there are adequate new visitor experiences in place or when the proportion of visitors climbing falls below 20%. Until then, it remains a personal decision and a question of respect. Before deciding, visit the Cultural Centre or take an Anangu guided tour.

Tours of Uluru

Uluru Aboriginal Tours Cultural Tour Owned and operated by Anangu from the Mutitjulu community, this company offers a range of trips to give you an insight into the significance of the Rock through the eyes of the traditional owners. Tours operate and depart from the Cultural Centre, as well as from Yulara Ayers Rock Resort (through AAT Kings) and from Alice Springs. There are a range of tours including the Rising Sun & Sacred Walk tour, which includes bush skills demonstrations such as spear throwing, a hot buffet breakfast around a campfire, and unparalleled insights into the area's traditional lore and legend from your local guide. (☎0447 878 851; www.uluruaboriginaltours.com.au; guided tours from $99)

Base Walk (p219), Uluru

Seit Outback Australia   Bus Tour

This small group-tour operator offers a sunset tour around Uluru (adult/child $149/121), and a sunrise tour at Kata Tjuta for the same price including breakfast and a walk into Walpa Gorge. (📞08-8956 3156; www.seitoutbackaustralia.com.au)

AAT Kings   Bus Tour

Operating the largest range of coach tours to Uluru, AAT offers a variety of half- and full-day tours from Yulara. Check the website or enquire at the Tour & Information Centre (p225) in Yulara. (📞08-8956 2171; www. aatkings.com)

Sounds of Silence   Tour

Waiters serve champagne and canapés on a desert dune with stunning sunset views of Uluru and Kata Tjuta. Then it's a buffet dinner (with emu, croc and roo) beneath the southern sky, which, after dinner, is dissected and explained with the help of a telescope. If you're more of a morning person, try the similarly styled Desert Awakenings 4WD Tour. Neither tour is suitable for children under 10 years. (📞08-8957 7448; www.ayersrockresort.com.au; adult/child Sounds of Silence tour $195/96, Desert Awakenings tour $168/130)

★ **When to Go**

Between May and September the weather is at its coolest, and you're more likely to encounter native fauna and flora.

ℹ **Need to Know**

Aboriginal people have been living in this part of Australia for over 30,000 years.

ANDREW WATSON / GETTY IMAGES ©

Kata Tjuta

RICHARD I ANSON / GETTY IMAGES ©

Kata Tjuta (The Olgas)

No journey to Uluru is complete without a visit to Kata Tjuta, a striking group of domed rocks huddled together about 35km west of the Rock.

Great For...

☑ **Don't Miss**

Kata Tjuta at sunset, when the boulders are at their glorious, blood-red best.

The Kata Tjuta site comprises 36 boulders sitting shoulder to shoulder, forming deep valleys and steep-sided gorges. Many visitors find them even more captivating than their prominent neighbour. The tallest rock, Mt Olga (546m; 1066m above sea level) is approximately 200m higher than Uluru. Trails weave in among the red rocks, leading to pockets of silent beauty and spiritual gravitas.

Indigenous Significance

The name 'Kata Tjuta' in the Pitjantjatjara language means 'many heads'. Sacred to the Anangu people, the 500-million-year-old rocks are said to be the home of the snake king Wanambi, who only comes down from his fastness atop Mt Olga in the dry season. This is, however, by no

Pale knob-tailed gecko babies

HENRY COOK / GETTY IMAGES ©

❶ Need to Know

Ayers Rock (Connellan) airport is the main entry-point for the park. Several different bus companies run services between Alice Springs, Uluru and Kata-Tjuta.

✕ Take a Break

There's a picnic and sunset-viewing area with toilet facilities just off the access road a few kilometres west of the base of Kata Tjuta.

★ Top Tip

The Valley of the Winds walk will get you away from the crowds, and reward you with sensational views.

means the only legend told about the site. The majority of myths about Kata Tjuta, and the ceremonies still practised by its traditional owners, are off-limits to women and outsiders.

Exploring Kata Tjuta

The 7.4km Valley of the Winds loop (two to four hours) is one of the most challenging and rewarding bushwalks in the park. It winds through the gorges, giving excellent views of the surreal domes and traversing varied terrain. It's not particularly arduous, but wear sturdy shoes, and take plenty of water. Starting this walk at first light often rewards you with solitude, enabling you to appreciate the sounds of the wind and bird calls carried up the valley.

The short signposted track beneath towering rock walls into pretty Walpa Gorge (2.6km return, 45 minutes) is especially beautiful in the afternoon, when sunlight floods the gorge.

Tours

Many companies offering tours of Uluru (see p220) also go to Kata Tjuta, including Seit Outback Australia, Sounds of Silence and Ayers Rock Helicopters.

Planning Ahead

Uluru-Kata Tjuta National Park is open from half an hour before sunrise to sunset daily (varying slightly between months – check the website for exact times). Entry permits are valid for three days and available at the drive-through entry station on the road from Yulara.

Yulara (Ayers Rock Resort)

Yulara is the service village for the national park and has turned one of the world's least hospitable regions into a comfortable place to stay. Lying just outside the national park, 20km from Uluru and 53km from Kata Tjuta, the complex is the closest base for exploring the park. Yulara supplies the only accommodation, food outlets and other services available in the region.

✖ EATING

Walpa Lobby Bar Modern Australian $$
If you want to treat yourself, this is the place to try. A recent makeover has given it the feel of a Hilton Hotel bar, but the excellent food and service make up for the slight sterility. Hot and cold seafood platters are a treat, and most dishes feature Australian bush ingredients. Salads and antipasto also available. 'Walpa' is the Pitjantjatjara name for wind. (Sails in the Desert; mains $30; ⊙11am-10pm)

Geckos Cafe Mediterranean $$
For great value, a warm atmosphere and tasty food head to this buzzing licensed cafe. The wood-fired pizzas, pastas, burgers and fish and chips go well with a carafe of sangria, and the courtyard tables are a great place to enjoy the desert night air. There are veggie and gluten-free options; meals can be made to takeaway. (Resort Shopping Centre; mains $20-30; ⊙11am-9pm; 🖭)

Outback
Pioneer Barbecue Barbecue $$
For a fun, casual night out, this tavern is the popular choice for everyone from backpackers to grey nomads. Choose between kangaroo skewers, prawns, veggie burgers, steaks and emu sausages, and grill them yourself at the communal BBQs. In the same complex is the **Pioneer Kitchen** (meals $10-22; ⊙6-9pm), doing brisk business in burgers, pizza and kiddie meals. (Outback Pioneer Hotel & Lodge; burgers $18, meat $30, salad bar only $17; ⊙6-9pm)

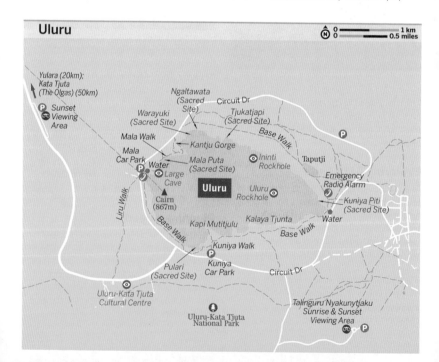

Bough House   Australian $$$

This family-friendly, country-style place overlooks the pool at the Outback Pioneer. Intimate candlelit dining is strangely set in a barnlike dining room. Bough House specialises in native ingredients such as lemon myrtle, Kakadu plums and bush tomatoes. Try the native tasting plate for a selection of Australian wildlife meats, and follow up with the braised wallaby shank for your main. The dessert buffet is free with your main course. (Outback Pioneer Hotel & Lodge; mains $30-40; ⏰6.30-10am & 6.30-9.30pm)

ℹ️ INFORMATION

Tour & Information Centre (📞08-8957 7324; Resort Shopping Centre; ⏰8am-8pm) Most tour operators and car-hire firms have desks at this centre.

Visitor Information Centre (📞08-8957 7377; ⏰8.30am-4.30pm) Contains displays on the geography, wildlife and history of the region. There's a short audio tour ($2) if you want to learn more. It also sells books and regional maps.

ℹ️ GETTING THERE & AWAY

AIR

Connellan airport is about 4km north from Yulara. **Qantas** (📞13 13 13; www.qantas.com.au) has direct flights from Alice Springs, Cairns, Sydney and Melbourne. **Virgin Australia** (📞13 67 89; www.virginaustralia.com) has flights from Sydney.

BUS

Daily shuttle transfers between Alice Springs and Yulara are run by AAT Kings (p221; adult/child one-way $159/80); Emu Run (p227; adult/child $135/80); and Gray Line (p229; adult/child $170/120).

CAR & MOTORCYCLE

One route from Alice to Yulara is sealed all the way, with regular food and petrol stops. It's 200km from Alice to Erldunda on the Stuart Hwy, where you turn west for the 245km journey along the Lasseter Hwy. The journey takes four to five hours.

 Alice Springs Desert Park

If you haven't managed to glimpse a spangled grunter or marbled velvet gecko on your travels, head to the **Desert Park** (📞08-8951 8788; www.alicespringsdesertpark.com.au; Larapinta Dr; adult/child $25/12.50; ⏰7.30am-6pm, last entry 4.30pm) where the creatures of central Australia are all on display in one place. The predominantly open-air exhibits faithfully re-create the animals' natural environments in a series of habitats: inland river, sand country and woodland.

It's an easy 2.5km cycle to the park. Alternatively, **Desert Park Transfers** (📞08-8952 1731; www.tailormadetours.com.au; adult/child $40/22) runs from Alice Springs five times daily. The cost includes park entry and pick-up/drop-off at your accommodation.

Try to time your visit with the terrific birds of prey show, featuring free-flying Australian kestrels, kites and awesome wedge-tailed eagles. To catch some of the park's rare and elusive animals, such as the bilby, visit the excellent nocturnal house. If you like what you see, come back at night and spotlight endangered species on the guided nocturnal tour (bookings essential).

To get the most out of the park pick up a free audioguide (available in various languages) or join one of the free ranger-led talks held throughout the day.

Above: Dingoes at Alice Springs Desert Park
GREG WOOD / GETTY IMAGES ©

Indigenous dot painting

❶ GETTING AROUND

A free shuttle bus meets all flights and drops off at all accommodation points around the resort; pick-up is 90 minutes before your flight.

Uluru Express (☏08-8956 2152; www.uluruexpress.com.au) falls somewhere between a shuttle-bus service and an organised tour. It provides return transport from the resort to Uluru and Kata Tjuta – see website for details.

Hiring a car will give you the flexibility to visit Uluru and Kata Tjuta whenever you want. Car rental offices are at the Tour & Information Centre and Connellan airport.

Alice Springs

This ruggedly beautiful town is shaped by its mythical landscapes, vibrant Aboriginal culture (where else can you hear six uniquely Australian languages in the main street?) and tough pioneering past. The town is a natural base for exploring central Australia, with Uluru-Kata Tjuta National Park a relatively close four-hour drive away.

❍ SIGHTS

Araluen Arts Centre   Gallery

For a small town, Alice Springs has a thriving arts scene, and the Araluen Arts Centre is at its heart. There is a 500-seat theatre, and four galleries with a focus on art from the central desert region.

The Albert Namatjira Gallery features works by the artist, who began painting watercolours in the 1930s at Hermannsburg. The exhibition draws comparisons between Namatjira and his initial mentor, Rex Battarbee, and other Hermannsburg School artists. It also features 14 early acrylic works from the Papunya Community School Collection. (☏08-8951 1122; www.artsandmuseums.nt.gov.au/araluen-cultural-precinct; cnr Larapinta Dr & Memorial Ave)

Museum of Central Australia   Museum

The natural history collection at this compact museum recalls the days of megafauna – when hippo-sized wombats and 3m-tall flightless birds roamed the

Goanna

Desert Wattle

Waterfall in Kings Canyon

land. Among the geological displays are meteorite fragments and fossils. The museum has a free audio tour, narrated by a palaeontologist, which helps bring the exhibition to life. (☏08-8951 1121; www.artsandmuseums.nt.gov.au/araluen-cultural-precinct/mca; cnr Larapinta Dr & Memorial Ave; ⏰10am-5pm Mon-Fri)

☞ TOURS

Dreamtime Tours　　Cultural Tour
This company runs the three-hour Dreamtime & Bushtucker Tour, where you meet Warlpiri Aboriginal people and learn a little about their traditions. As it caters for large bus groups it can be impersonal, but you can tag along with your own vehicle. (☏08-8953 3739; www.rstours.com.au; adult/child $85/42, self-drive $66/33; ⏰8.30-11.30am)

Foot Falcon　　Walking Tour
Local historian, author and teacher Linda Wells leads two-hour walks around town with insights into Alice's indigenous and

pioneering history. (☏0427 569 531; www.footfalcon.com; tours $30; ⏰4pm Mon-Fri, 3pm Sun)

Emu Run Experience　　Tour
Operates day tours to Uluru ($220) and two-day tours to Uluru and Kings Canyon ($520). Prices include park entry fees, meals and accommodation. There are also recommended small-group day tours through the West MacDonnell Ranges ($125), and an Aboriginal cultural day tour ($195). (☏1800 687 220 , 08-8953 7057; www.emurun.com.au; 72 Todd St)

🔒 SHOPPING

Talapi　　Arts
One of Alice Spring's newest galleries, Talapi is a beautiful space in the heart of town, exhibiting and promoting central desert indigenous art. It sources its artworks directly from Aboriginal-owned art centres and is a member of the Indigenous Art Code. Drop in to ask about upcoming exhibitions. (☏08-8953 6389; www.talapi.com.au; 45 Todd Mall)

Mural designed by Kaye Kessing, and painted by Bob Kessing, Kaye Kessing and Alice Springs Community members

Aboriginal Art World   Arts
Specialises in art from artists living in the central desert region around Alice Springs, particularly Pitjantjatjara lands. You can buy a completed work or commission your own piece. (📞08-8952 7788; www.aboriginal artworld.com.au; 89 Todd Mall)

✖ EATING

Piccolo's   Cafe $
This modern, stylish cafe is popular with locals for its excellent food and probably Alice's best coffee. It wouldn't be out of place in Melbourne except service is faster and friendlier. The BRAT is recommended. (📞08-8953 1936; Shop 1, Cinema Complex 11, Todd Mall; breakfast $10-18; ⏰7.30am-3pm Mon-Fri, to 2pm Sat, 8am-1.30pm Sun)

Epilogue Lounge   Tapas $$
This urban, retro delight is definitely the coolest place to hang in town. With a decent wine list, food served all day, and service with a smile, it is a real Alice Springs standout. It hadn't quite honed some of its

tapas dishes when we last visited – but a revamped menu was a work in progress. (📞08-8953 4206; 58 Todd Mall; tapas/mains $15/25; ⏰8am-11.30pm Wed-Mon)

Red Dog Cafe   Cafe $$
There is no better place to people-watch than here at one of the table and chairs strewn out over Todd Mall. Breakfasts are hearty; coffee is fresh and well brewed. Lunch is all about burgers, with a few veggie options thrown in. (📞08-8953 1353; 64 Todd Mall; breakfast $12.50, lunch $16.50)

Hanuman Restaurant   Thai $$
You won't believe you're in the outback when you try the incredible Thai- and Indian-influenced cuisine at this stylish restaurant. The delicate Thai entrees are a real triumph as are the seafood dishes, particularly the Hanuman prawns. Although the menu is ostensibly Thai, there are enough Indian dishes to satisfy a curry craving. There are several vegetarian offerings and a good wine list. (📞08-8953 7188; www.hanuman.com.au/alice-springs; 82 Barrett

PHILIP QUIRK / GETTY IMAGES ©

Dr, Doubletree by Hilton; mains $25-36; ⊙12.30-
2.30pm Mon-Fri, from 6.30pm daily;)

Overlanders
Steakhouse   Steak $$$
The place for steaks, big succulent cuts
of beef (and crocodile, camel, kangaroo
or emu). Amid the cattle station decor
(saddles, branding irons and the like) you
can try Stuart's Tucker Bag: a half sausage of croc, kangaroo, emu and camel.
(08-8952 2159; 72 Hartley St; mains $30-50;
⊙6pm-late)

INFORMATION

**Tourism Central Australia Visitor Information
Centre** (1800 645 199, 08-8952 5199; www.
discovercentralaustralia.com; cnr Todd Mall &
Parsons St; ⊙8.30am-5pm Mon-Fri, 9.30am-
4pm Sat & Sun;) This helpful centre can
load you up with stacks of brochures and the
free visitors guide. Weather forecasts and road
conditions are posted on the wall. National parks
information is also available.

GETTING THERE & AWAY

AIR
Alice Springs is well connected, with **Qantas**
(13 13 13, 08-8950 5211; www.qantas.com.
au) and **Virgin Australia** (13 67 89; www.
virginaustralia.com) operating daily flights to/
from major capital cities.

BUS
Greyhound Australia (1300 GREYHOUND/
1300 4739 46863; www.greyhound.com.au;
Shop 3, 113 Todd St) has regular services from
Alice Springs (check website for timetables and
discounted fares).

Emu Run (p227) runs the cheapest daily connections between Alice Springs and Yulara (one-
way adult/child $135/80). **Gray Line** (1300
858 687; www.grayline.com; Capricornia Centre
9, Gregory Tce) also runs between Alice Springs
and Yulara (one-way $170/120) .

Where to
Stay

The closest accommodation to Uluru
is at the Ayers Rock Resort in Yulara
village, 20km away. Expect premium
prices, reflecting the remote locale. Even
though there are almost 5000 beds, it's
wise to make a reservation, especially
during school holidays. Substantial
discounts are usually offered if you book
for more than two or three nights.

CAR & MOTORCYCLE
All the major companies have offices in Alice
Springs, and many have counters at the airport.
Talk to the **Tourism Central Australia Visitor
Information Centre** about its unlimited kilo-
metres deal before you book. A conventional
(2WD) vehicle will get you to most sights in the
MacDonnell Ranges and out to Uluru and Kings
Canyon via sealed roads.

TRAIN
A classic way to enter or leave the Territory is by
the Ghan, which can be booked through **Great
Southern Rail** (www.greatsouthernrail.com.au).

GETTING AROUND

TO/FROM THE AIRPORT
Alice Springs airport is 15km south of the town.
It's about $45 by taxi. The **airport shuttle**
(08-8952 2111; Gregory Tce; one way $16)
meets all flights and drops off passengers at city
accommodation.

BUS
The public bus service, **Asbus** (08-8944
2444), departs from outside the Yeperenye
Shopping Centre. The visitor information centre
has timetables.

TAXI
Taxis congregate near the visitor information
centre. To book one, call 13 10 08 or 08-
8952 1877.

AUSTRALIAN SCENICS / GETTY IMAGES ©

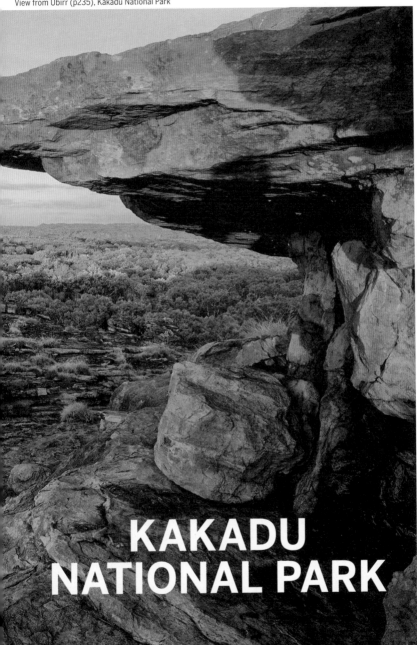
View from Ubirr (p235), Kakadu National Park

KAKADU
NATIONAL PARK

Kakadu National Park

Kakadu is a whole lot more than a national park. It's also a vibrant, living acknowledgment of the elemental link between the Aboriginal custodians and the country they have nurtured, endured and respected for thousands of generations. Encompassing almost 20,000 sq km (about 200km north–south and 100km east–west), it holds in its boundaries a spectacular ecosystem and a mind-blowing concentration of ancient rock art.

In just a few days you can cruise on billabongs bursting with wildlife, fly over the sprawling landscape in a helicopter or fixed-wing plane, examine 25,000-year-old rock paintings with the help of an Indigenous guide, swim in pools at the foot of tumbling waterfalls and hike through ancient sandstone escarpment country.

❶ In This Section

➡ Arriving in Kakadu

Many people choose to access Kakadu on a tour, which takes them around the major sights with the minimum of hassles, but it's just as easy with your own wheels, if you know what kinds of road conditions your vehicle can handle (Jim Jim Falls and Twin Falls, for example, are 4WD-access only).

Greyhound Australia (www.greyhound.com.au) runs a daily return coach service from Darwin to Jabiru ($66, 3½ hours).

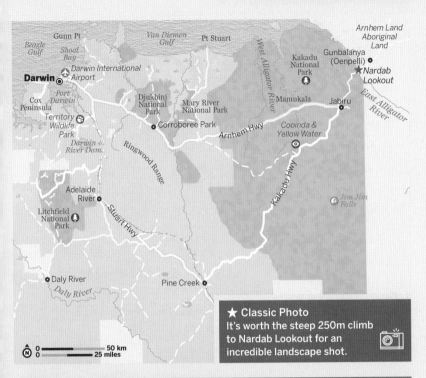

★ **Classic Photo**
It's worth the steep 250m climb to Nardab Lookout for an incredible landscape shot.

From left: Nightcliff Market food (p242); Viewing Yellow Water Billabong (p238); Nourlangie Billabong (p235)
JAMES BRAUND / GETTY IMAGES ©; DAVID WALL PHOTO / GETTY IMAGES ©; AUSTRALIAN SCENICS / GETTY IMAGES ©

Rock art, Ubirr

ANDREW WATSON / GETTY IMAGES ©

Indigenous Rock Art

Kakadu is one of Australia's richest, most accessible repositories of rock art. There are more than 5000 sites, which date from 20,000 years to 10 years ago.

Great For...

☑ Don't Miss

Maguk Gorge, once known as Barramundi Gorge, is an archetypal Top End waterhole, accessible to self-drivers.

History & Preservation

Rock paintings have been classified into three roughly defined periods: Pre-estuarine, which is from the earliest paintings up to around 6000 years ago; Estuarine, which covers the period from 6000 to around 2000 years ago, when rising sea levels brought the coast to its present level; and Freshwater, from 2000 years ago until the present day.

For local Aboriginal people, these rock-art sites are a major source of traditional knowledge and represent their archives. Aboriginal people rarely paint on rocks anymore, as they no longer live in rock shelters and there are fewer people with the requisite knowledge. Some older paintings are believed by many Aboriginal people to have been painted by mimi spirits, connect-

Anbangbang Shelter, Nourlangie

ANDREW BAIN / GETTY IMAGES ©

❶ Need to Know

Darwin or Katherine are the main access points for Kakadu; from either, you can take a tour bus, or drive yourself.

✕ Take a Break

Stop by Gagudju Lodge & Camping Cooinda (p238) and dine at **Mimi** (🕑dinner Apr-Sep) for great Australian bush tucker (including barramundi, crocodile and kangaroo).

various styles and from various centuries, command a mesmerising stillness.

The magnificent **Nardab Lookout** is a 250m scramble from the main gallery. Surveying the billiard-table-green floodplain and watching the sun set and the moon rise, like they're on an invisible set of scales, is glorious, to say the least. **Ubirr** (🕑8.30am-sunset Apr-Nov, from 2pm Dec-Mar) is 39km north of the Arnhem Hwy via a sealed road.

Nourlangie

The sight of this looming outlier of the Arnhem Land escarpment makes it easy to understand its ancient importance to Aboriginal people. Its long red-sandstone bulk, striped in places with orange, white and black, slopes up from surrounding woodland to fall away at one end in stepped cliffs. Below is Kakadu's best-known collection of **rock art**.

The 2km looped walking track (open 8am to sunset) takes you first to the **Anbangbang Shelter**, used for 20,000 years as a refuge and canvas. Next is the **Anbangbang Gallery**, featuring Dreaming characters repainted in the 1960s. Look for the virile Nabulwinjbulwinj, a dangerous spirit who likes to eat females after banging them on the head with a yam. From here it's a short walk to **Gunwarddehwarde Lookout**, with views of the Arnhem Land escarpment.

ing people with creation legends and the development of Aboriginal lore.

As the paintings are all rendered with natural, water-soluble ochres, they are very susceptible to water damage. Drip lines of clear silicon rubber have been laid on the rocks above the paintings to divert rain. As the most accessible sites receive up to 4000 visitors a week, boardwalks have been erected to keep the dust down and to keep people at a suitable distance from the paintings.

Where to See Rock Art

Ubirr & Around

It'll take a lot more than the busloads of visitors here to disturb Ubirr's inherent majesty and grace. Layers of rock-art paintings, in

Saltwater crocodile, Yellow Water Billabong (p238)

ANDREW WATSON / GETTY IMAGES ©

Native Wildlife

Kakadu has more than 60 species of mammals, more than 280 bird species, 120 recorded species of reptile, 25 species of frog, 55 freshwater fish species and at least 10,000 different kinds of insect.

Great For...

☑ **Don't Miss**

The alien 'cities' formed by the cathedral termite mounds that are found throughout Kakadu.

Birds

Abundant waterbirds and their beautiful wetland homes are a highlight of Kakadu. This is one of the chief refuges in Australia for several species, including the magpie goose, green pygmy goose and Budekin duck. Other fine waterbirds include pelicans, brolgas and the jabiru (or more correctly black-necked stork), Australia's only stork, with distinctive red legs and long beak. Herons, egrets, cormorants, wedge-tailed eagles, whistling kites and black kites are common.

The open woodlands harbor rainbow bee-eaters, kingfishers and the endangered bustard. Majestic white-breasted sea eagles are seen near inland waterways.

At night, you might hear barking owls calling – they sound just like dogs – or the

Rainbow bee-eaters

LOUISE DENTON PHOTOGRAPHY / GETTY IMAGES ©

ⓘ Need to Know

Most visitors see only a fraction of these creatures (except the insects), as many of them are shy, nocturnal or scarce.

ⓘ When to Go

Head out at dawn or dusk for your best chance of spotting wildlife, and keep your ears open.

★ Top Tip

Kakadu Animal Tracks (p240) runs tours with an Indigenous guide – you'll see thousands of birds.

to Kakadu and Arnhem Land – look for them at Nourlangie Rock, where individuals rest under rocky overhangs. At Ubirr, short-eared rock wallabies can be spotted in the early morning. You may see a sugar glider or a dingo in wooded areas in the daytime. Kakadu has 26 bat species, four of them endangered.

Reptiles

Twin Falls and Jim Jim Falls have resident freshwater crocodiles, which have narrow snouts and rarely exceed 3m, while the dangerous saltwater variety is found throughout the park.

Kakadu's other reptiles include the frilled lizard, 11 species of goanna, and five freshwater turtle species, of which the most common is the northern snake-necked turtle.

Kakadu has many snakes, though most are nocturnal and rarely encountered. The striking Oenpelli python was first recorded by non-Aboriginal people in 1976. The odd-looking file snake lives in billabongs and is much sought after as bush tucker. They have square heads, tiny eyes and saggy skin covered in tiny rough scales (hence 'file'). They move very slowly (and not at all on land), eating only once a month and breeding once every decade.

plaintive wail of the bush stone curlew. The raucous call of the spectacular red-tailed black cockatoo is often considered the signature sound of Kakadu.

At **Mamukala**, 8km east of the South Alligator River on the Arnhem Hwy, is a wonderful observation building, plus bird-watching hides and a 3km walking track.

Fish

You can't miss the silver barramundi, which creates a distinctive swirl near the water's surface. It can grow to more than 1m in length and changes sex from male to female at the age of five or six years.

Mammals

Several types of kangaroo and wallaby live in the park; the shy black wallaroo is unique

Jabiru

It may seem surprising to find a town of Jabiru's size and structure in the midst of a wilderness national park, but it exists solely because of the nearby Ranger uranium mine. It's Kakadu's major service centre, with a bank, newsagent, medical centre, supermarket, bakery and service station. You can even play a round of golf here.

Cooinda & Yellow Water

Cooinda is best known for the cruises on the wetland area known as Yellow Water, and has developed into a slick resort.

About 1km from the resort, the **Warradjan Aboriginal Cultural Centre** (www. gagudju-dreaming.com; ⊙9am-5pm) depicts Creation stories and has a great permanent exhibition that includes clap sticks, sugar-bag holders and rock-art samples. You'll be introduced to the moiety system (the law of interpersonal relationships), languages and skin names, and there's a minitheatre with a huge selection of films from which to choose. A mesmeric soundtrack of chants and didgeridoos plays in the background.

Gagudju Lodge & Camping Cooinda (☑1800 500 401; www.gagudju-dreaming.com; unpowered/powered sites $38/50, budget/lodge r from $75/310; ❄ @ ☎) is the most popular accommodation resort in the park. It's a modern oasis but, even with 380 camp sites, facilities can get very stretched. The budget air-con units share camping ground facilities and are compact and comfy enough. The lodge rooms are spacious and more comfortable, sleeping up to four people. There's also a grocery shop, tour desk, fuel pump and the excellent open-air **Barra Bar & Bistro** (mains $15-36; ⊙all day).

The turn-off to the Cooinda accommodation complex and Yellow Water wetlands is 47km down the Kakadu Hwy from the Arnhem Hwy intersection.

Just off the Kakadu Hwy, 2km south of the Cooinda turn-off, is the scrubby **Mardugal camping ground** (adult/child $10/free)– an excellent year-round camping area with shower and toilets.

Yellow Water Billabong

ANDREW WATSON / GETTY IMAGES ©

Darwin

Australia's only tropical capital, Darwin gazes out confidently across the Timor Sea. It's closer to Bali than Bondi, and many from the southern states still see it as a frontier outpost and a jumping-off point for Kakadu National Park.

But Darwin is a surprisingly affluent, cosmopolitan, youthful and multicultural city, thanks in part to an economic boom fuelled by the mining industry and tourism. It's a city on the move, but there's still a small-town feel and a laconic, relaxed vibe that fits easily with the tropical climate.

 SIGHTS

The bold redevelopment of the old Darwin **Waterfront Precinct** (www.waterfront. nt.gov.au) has transformed the city. The multimillion-dollar project features a cruise-ship terminal; luxury hotels; boutique restaurants and shopping; the Sky Bridge, an elevated walkway and elevator at the south end of Smith St; and a Wave Lagoon (p240).

The old Stokes Hill Wharf is well worth an afternoon promenade. At the end of the wharf an old warehouse is home to a food centre that's ideal for an alfresco lunch, a cool afternoon beer or a seafood dinner as the sun sets over the harbour.

Crocosaurus Cove   Zoo

If the tourists won't go out to see the crocs, then bring the crocs to the tourists. Right in the middle of Mitchell St, Crocosaurus Cove is as close as you'll ever want to get to these amazing creatures. Six of the largest crocs in captivity can be seen in state-of-the-art aquariums and pools. Other aquariums feature barramundi, turtles and stingrays, plus there's an enormous reptile house, allegedly displaying the greatest variety of reptiles in the country. (☑08-8981 7522; www.crocosaurus cove.com; 58 Mitchell St; adult/child $32/20; ☺9am-6pm, last admission 5pm)

 Visitor Resources

Admission to the park is via a 14-day Kakadu Park Pass: pick one up (along with the excellent *Visitor Guide* booklet) from the Bowali visitor information centre, Tourism Top End in Darwin, Gagudju Lodge Cooinda or the Katherine visitor centre. Carry it with you at all times, as rangers conduct spot checks (penalties apply for nonpayment).

The excellent **Bowali Visitor Information Centre** (☑08-8938 1121; www.kakadunationalparkaustralia.com/ bowali_visitors_center.htm; Kakadu Hwy, Jabiru; ☺8am-5pm) has walk-through displays that sweep you across the land, explaining Kakadu's ecology from Aboriginal and non-Aboriginal perspectives.

A great online site is Kakadu National Park (www.kakadu.com.au), which has a visitors guide, what's on listings and suggested itineraries to download.

Above: Black-necked stork
TONYFEDER / GETTY IMAGES ©

Museum & Art Gallery of the Northern Territory   Museum

This superb museum and gallery boasts beautifully presented galleries of Top End–centric exhibits. The Aboriginal art collection is a highlight, with carvings from the Tiwi Islands, bark paintings from Arnhem Land and dot paintings from the desert. An entire room is devoted to Cyclone Tracy, in a display that graphically illustrates life before and after the disaster. You can stand in a darkened room and

Tours of Kakadu

Kakadu Animal Tracks (0409 350 842; www.animaltracks.com.au) Based at Cooinda, this outfit runs seven-hour tours with an Indigenous guide combining a wildlife safari and Aboriginal cultural tour. You'll see thousands of birds, get to hunt, gather, prepare and consume bush tucker, and crunch on some green ants.

Top End Explorer Tours (08-8979 3615; www.kakadutours.net.au; adult/child $230/170) Small-group 4WD tours to Jim Jim and Twin Falls from Jabiru and Cooinda.

Ayal Aboriginal Tours (0429 470 384; www.ayalkakadu.com.au; adult/child $220/99) Full-day Indigenous-run tours around Kakadu, with former ranger and local, Victor Cooper, shining a light on art, culture and wildlife.

Kakadu Air (1800 089 113, 08-8941 9611; www.kakaduair.com.au) Offers 30-minute/one-hour fixed-wing flights for $150/250 per adult. Helicopter tours, though more expensive, give a more dynamic aerial perspective. They cost from $230 (20 minutes) to $650 (one hour) per person. Note flights are only available over Jim Jim Falls in the wet season – traditional owners request that the 'skies are rested' in the Dry.

Yellow Water Cruises (1800 500 401; www.gagudju-dreaming.com) Cruise the South Alligator River and Yellow Water Billabong spotting wildlife. Purchase tickets from Gagudju Lodge Cooinda (p238); a shuttle bus will take you from here to the tour's departure point. Two-hour cruises ($99/70 per adult/child) depart at 6.45am, 9am and 4.30pm; 1½-hour cruises ($72/50) leave at 11.30am, 1.15pm and 2.45pm.

listen to the whirring sound of Tracy at full throttle – a sound you won't forget in a hurry. (MAGNT; 08-8999 8264; www.magnt.net.au; 19 Conacher St, Fannie Bay; 9am-5pm Mon-Fri, 10am-5pm Sat & Sun) FREE

Territory Wildlife Park   Zoo
This excellent park showcases the best of Aussie wildlife. Pride of place must go to the aquarium, where a clear walk-through tunnel puts you among giant barramundi, stingrays, sawfish and saratogas, while a separate tank holds a 3.8m saltwater crocodile. To see everything you can either walk around the 4km perimeter road, or hop on and off the shuttle trains that run every 15 to 30 minutes and stop at all the exhibits. The turn-off to the park is 48km down the Stuart Hwy from Darwin; it's 12km further from the turn-off to the park. (08-8988 7200; www.territorywildlifepark.com.au; 960 Cox Peninsula Rd; adult/child/family $26/13/45.50; 8.30am-6pm, last admission 4pm)

ACTIVITIES

Wave & Recreation Lagoons   Water Park
The hugely popular Wave Lagoon is a hit with locals and travellers alike. There are 10 different wave patterns produced (20 minutes on with a 10-minute rest in between) and there are lifeguards, a kiosk and a strip of lawn to bask on. Adjacent is the Recreation Lagoon with a sandy beach, lifeguards and stinger-filtered seawater (although the nets and filters are not guaranteed to be 100% effective). (08-8985 6588; www.waterfront.nt.gov.au; Wave Lagoon adult/child $7/5; Wave Lagoon 10am-6pm)

TOURS

Batji Indigenous Waterfront Walking Tour   Cultural Tour
An excellent two-hour walking tour along the Esplanade run by the Larrakia people of Darwin. You will learn about the local wildlife, discover Lameroo beach and gain insight into places of cultural significance to the Larrakia people. (0416 731 353; www.

Wooden sculptures from the Tiwi Islands, Museum & Art Gallery of the Northern Territory (p239)

batjitours.com.au; adult/child $70/free; ⊘10am
Wed & Fri)

Darwin Explorer Bus Tour
Open-top bus tours that explore the major
sights of Darwin – you can hop on and
hop off buses with either a 24-hour or 48-
hour ticket. Tours depart every 30
minutes from the tourist information
centre. (🕿0416 140 903; www.theaustralianex-
plorer.com.au/darwin-explorer; 24hr ticket adult/
child $35/20)

Darwin Day Tours Tour
Runs an afternoon city tour that takes in
all the major attractions, including Stokes
Hill Wharf, the Museum & Art Gallery of the
Northern Territory and East Point Reserve.
Can be linked with a 'sunset fish 'n' chips
harbour cruise' ($55/40). (🕿1300 721 365;
www.darwindaytours.com.au; afternoon city tours
adult/child $75/38)

Anniki Pearl
Lugger Cruises Boat Tour
Three-hour sunset cruises on this historical
pearling lugger depart from Cullen Bay

Marina and include sparkling wine and
nibbles. You might recognise the ship from
the film *Australia*. (🕿0428 414 000; www.
australianharbourcruises.com.au; tours adult/
child $70/50)

Sunset Sail Boat Tour
This three-hour afternoon cruise aboard
the catamaran *Daymirri 2* departs from
Stokes Hill Wharf. Refreshments are
included but BYO alcohol. (🕿0408 795 567;
www.sailnt.com.au; tours adult/child $70/45)

Northern Territory
Indigenous Tours Cultural Tour
Upmarket Indigenous tours to Litchfield
National Park. (🕿1300 921 188; www.ntitours.
com.au; adult/child $249/124)

Sacred Earth
Safaris Adventure Tour
Multiday, small-group 4WD camping tours
around Kakadu, Katherine and the Kimberley. Two-day Kakadu tour starts at $850;
the five-day Top End National Parks Safari
is $2600. (🕿08-8555 3838; www.sacredearth
safaris.com.au)

 Mindil Beach Sunset Market

Food is the main attraction at this **market** (www.mindil.com.au; off Gilruth Ave; ⏰5-10pm Thu & 4-9pm Sun May-Oct) – from Thai, Sri Lankan, Indian, Chinese and Malaysian to Brazilian, Greek, Portuguese and more – all at around $6 to $12 a serve. But that's only half the fun – arts and crafts stalls bulge with handmade jewellery, fabulous rainbow tie-dyed clothes, Aboriginal artefacts, and wares from Indonesia and Thailand. Mindil Beach is about 2km from Darwin's city centre; an easy walk or hop on buses 4 or 6 which go past the market area.

As the sun heads towards the horizon, half of Darwin descends on the market, with tables, chairs, rugs, grog and kids in tow. Peruse and promenade, stop for a pummelling massage or to listen to rhythmic live music. Don't miss a flaming satay stick from Bobby's brazier. Top it off with fresh fruit salad, decadent cakes or luscious crepes.

Similar stalls (you'll recognise many of the stallholders) can be found at various suburban markets from Friday to Sunday.

Above: Mindil Beach Sunset Market
DANITA DELIMONT / GETTY IMAGES ©

 SHOPPING

Aboriginal Fine Arts Gallery   Arts
Displays and sells art from Arnhem Land and the central desert region. (www.aaia. com.au; 1st fl, cnr Mitchell & Knuckey Sts; ⏰9am-5pm)

Mbantua Fine Art Gallery   Arts
Vivid Utopian designs painted on everything from canvases to ceramics. (📞08-8941 6611; www.mbantua.com.au; 2/30 Smith St Mall; ⏰9am-5pm Mon-Sat)

Parap Village Market   Market
This compact, crowded food-focused market is a local favourite. There's the full gamut of Southeast Asian cuisine, as well as plenty of ingredients to cook up your own tropical storm. (www.parapvillage.com. au; Parap Shopping Village, Parap Rd, Parap; ⏰8am-2pm Sat)

Rapid Creek Market   Market
Darwin's oldest market is an Asian marketplace, with a tremendous range of tropical fruit and vegetables mingled with a heady mixture of spices and swirling satay smoke. (www.rapidcreekshoppingcentre. com.au; 48 Trower Rd, Rapid Creek; ⏰6.30am-1.30pm Sun)

Nightcliff Market   Market
A popular community market north of the city in the Nightcliff Shopping Centre. You'll will find lots of secondhand goods and designer clothing. (www.nightcliffmarkets.com. au; Pavonia Way, Nightcliff; ⏰6am-2pm Sun)

 EATING

Roma Bar   Cafe $
Roma is a local institution and the most reliable place for quality coffee in Darwin. It's a meeting place for lefties, literati and travellers. Well away from the craziness of Mitchell St, with free wi-fi and fresh juices, and you can get anything from muesli and eggs Benedict for breakfast to excellent toasted focaccia and even fish curry for lunch. (📞8981 6729; www.romabar.com.au; 9-11 Cavenagh St; mains $8-15; ⏰7am-4pm Mon-Fri, 8am-2pm Sat, 8am-1pm Sun; 📶)

Laneway Speciality Coffee   Cafe $
The pared back, industrial interior, corner location, and powerhouse coffee here have locals wondering if they could be in

Melbourne. Getting rave reviews, this place is fast becoming popular. Its well-prepared dishes use local and organic ingredients; the almost artistic bacon and egg roll is worth the trip here alone. For lunch the Wagyu beef burger beckons. (08-8941 4511; 4/1 Vickers St, Parap; mains $12-18; 8am-3pm Mon-Sat)

Stokes Hill Wharf
Seafood, Fast Food $$

Squatting on the end of Stokes Hill Wharf is a hectic food centre with a dozen food counters and plenty of outdoor tables lined up along the pier. This is a pumping place to head for some fish and chips, oysters, a stir-fry, a laksa or just a cold sunset beer. (Stokes Hill Wharf; mains $10-20; from 11am)

Exotic North Indian Cuisine
Indian $$

Offering outstanding value for quality Indian cuisine, this place has taken over the mantle of Darwin's best Indian restaurant. It's positioned right on the waterfront at Cullen Bay, making for extremely pleasant waterside dining in the evening. The service is attentive, there are high chairs for young 'uns and, unusually for Darwin, you can BYO wine. (08-8941 3396; www.exoticnorth indiancuisine.com.au; Cullen Bay Marina; mains $15-20; from 5pm)

Darwin Ski Club
Modern Australian $$

This place just keeps getting better. Already Darwin's finest location for a sunset beer, it now does seriously good tucker, too. The dishes are well prepared, and the menu is thoughtful and enticing. We had the pork belly and were astonished with the quality of the dish, while the chorizo and barramundi linguine also gets the thumbs up. Highly recommended by locals. (08-8981 6630; www.darwinskiclub. com.au; Conacher St, Fannie Bay; mains $18-24; 1-9pm)

there's a laconic, relaxed vibe that fits easily with the tropical climate

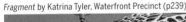
Fragment by Katrina Tyler, Waterfront Precinct (p239)

JOHN BORTHWICK / GETTY IMAGES ©

RICHARD I'ANSON / GETTY IMAGES ©

Wave Lagoon (p240), Darwin

Hanuman   Indian, Thai $$$

Ask most locals about fine dining in Darwin and they'll usually mention Hanuman. It's sophisticated but not stuffy. Enticing aromas of innovative Indian and Thai Nonya dishes waft from the kitchen to the stylish open dining room and deck. The menu is broad, with exotic vegetarian choices and banquets also available. (☎08-8941 3500; www.hanuman.com.au; 93 Mitchell St; mains $19-38; ☺noon-2.30pm & dinner from 6pm; 🔊)

Moorish Café   Middle Eastern $$$

Seductive aromas emanate from this divine terracotta-tiled cafe fusing North African, Mediterranean and Middle Eastern delights. The tapas can be a bit hit and miss but dishes such as the pork belly with chilli-chocolate sauce and Berber spiced kangaroo are tasty and reliable. It's a lovely dining experience, especially with a table overlooking the street. (☎08-8981 0010; www.moorishcafe.com.au; 37 Knuckey St; tapas $7-11, mains $33; ☺9am-2.30pm & 6-10pm Tue-Fri, 9am-10pm Sat)

🍷 DRINKING & NIGHTLIFE

Bogarts   Bar

Bogarts is one of Darwin's best bars and well worth the trek out into the suburbs. The decor is old movie posters, cane furniture and animal-print lounges in a mishmash that, strangely enough, works beautifully. It has a low-key ambience and is a local favourite for the over-30s crowd. (☎08-8981 3561; 52 Gregory St, Parap; ☺4pm-late Tue-Sat)

Tap on Mitchell   Bar

One of the busiest and best of the Mitchell St terrace bars, the Tap is always buzzing and there are inexpensive meals (nachos, burgers, calamari) to complement a great range of beer and wine. (www.thetap.com.au; 51 Mitchell St)

Deck Bar   Bar

At the nonpartying parliamentary end of Mitchell St, the Deck Bar still manages to get lively with happy hours, pub trivia and regular live music. Blurring the line between indoors and outdoors brilliantly, the namesake deck is perfect for people-watching. (www.thedeckbar.com.au; 22 Mitchell St)

Discovery & Lost Arc   Club
Discovery is Darwin's biggest nightclub and dance venue, with three levels featuring hip hop, techno and house, bars, private booths, karaoke, an elevated dance floor and plenty of partygoers. The Lost Arc is the classy chill-out bar opening on to Mitchell St, which starts to thaw after about 10pm. (www.discoverydarwin.com.au; 89 Mitchell St)

ENTERTAINMENT

Deckchair Cinema   Cinema
During the Dry, the Darwin Film Society runs this fabulous outdoor cinema below the southern end of the Esplanade. Watch a movie under the stars while reclining in a deckchair. There's a licensed bar serving food or you can bring a picnic (no BYO alcohol). There are usually double features on Friday and Saturday nights (adult/child $24/12). (☎08-8981 0700; www.deckchaircinema.com; Jervois Rd, Waterfront Precinct; adult/child $16/8; ☼box office from 6.30pm Apr-Nov)

Happy Yess   Live Music
This venue is Darwin's leading place for live music. A not-for-profit venue for musicians run by musicians, you won't hear cover bands in here. Original, sometimes weird, always fun. (www.happyyess.com; 12 Smith St, Browns Mart)

Darwin Entertainment Centre   Arts Centre
Darwin's main community arts venue houses the Playhouse and Studio Theatres, and hosts events from fashion-award nights to plays, rock operas, comedies and concerts. Check the website for upcoming shows. (☎08-8980 3333; www.darwinentertainment.com.au; 93 Mitchell St; ☼box office 10am-5.30pm Mon-Fri & 1hr prior to shows)

 Litchfield National Park

It may not be as well known as Kakadu, but many Territory locals rate Litchfield even higher, and it is certainly one of the best places in the Top End for bush-walking, camping and swimming. The 1500-sq-km national park encloses much of the spectacular Tabletop Range, a wide sandstone plateau; the **waterfalls** that pour off the edge of this plateau are a highlight of the park, feeding crystal-clear cascades and croc-free plunge pools.

The two routes to Litchfield (115km south of Darwin) from the Stuart Hwy join up and loop through the park.

About 17km after entering the park from Batchelor, you come to what looks like tombstones, but which are, in fact, **magnetic termite mounds**.

Another 6km further along is the turn-off to **Buley Rockhole** (2km), where water cascades through a series of rock pools. This turn-off also takes you to **Florence Falls** (5km), accessed by a 15-minute, 135-step descent to a deep pool surrounded by monsoon forest.

About 18km beyond the turn-off is a turn-off to the spectacular **Tolmer Falls**. A 1.6km loop track (45 minutes) offers beautiful views of the valley.

It's a further 7km along the main road to the turn-off for Litchfield's big-ticket **Wangi Falls** (pronounced 'wong-guy'; 1.6km). The falls flow year-round, spilling either side of a huge orange-rock outcrop and filling an enormous swimming hole bordered by rainforest.

Above: Florence Falls, Litchfield National Park
MANFRED GOTTSCHALK/GETTY IMAGES ©

ℹ INFORMATION

Tourism Top End (☎1300 138 886, 08-8980 6000; www.tourismtopend.com.au; cnr Smith & Bennett Sts; ⏱8.30am-5pm Mon-Fri, 9am-3pm Sat & Sun) Helpful office with hundreds of brochures; books tours and accommodation.

ℹ GETTING THERE & AWAY

AIR

Apart from the following major carriers arriving at Darwin International Airport, smaller routes are flown by local operators; ask a travel agent.

Jetstar (www.jetstar.com) Direct flights to the eastern coast capitals and major hubs.

Qantas (www.qantas.com.au) Direct flights to Perth, Adelaide, Canberra, Sydney, Brisbane, Alice Springs and Cairns.

Virgin Australia (www.virginaustralia.com) Direct flights between Darwin and Brisbane, Broome, Melbourne, Sydney and Perth.

BUS

Greyhound Australia (☎1300 GREYHOUND/ 1300 4739 46863; www.greyhound.com.au) operates long-distance bus services from the

Transit Centre (www.enjoy-darwin.com/transit -bus.html; 69 Mitchell St). There's at least one service per day up/down the Stuart Hwy, stopping at Pine Creek (three hours), Katherine (4½ hours), Mataranka (seven hours), Tennant Creek (14½ hours) and Alice Springs (22 hours).

For Kakadu, there's a daily return service from Darwin to Jabiru ($66, 3½ hours).

CAR & CAMPERVAN

For driving around Darwin, conventional vehicles are cheap enough, but most companies offer only 100km free, which won't get you very far. Rates start at around $40 per day for a small car with 100km per day.

There are also plenty of 4WD vehicles available in Darwin, but you usually have to book ahead and fees/deposits are higher than for 2WD vehicles.

JJ's Car Hire (www.jjscarhire.com.au; 7 Goyder Rd, Parap) is a good local operator.

TRAIN

The legendary Ghan train, operated by **Great Southern Rail** (www.gsr.com.au), runs weekly (twice weekly May to July) between Adelaide and Darwin via Alice Springs.

Tawny frogmouth

Termite mound, Litchfield National Park (p245)

ℹ GETTING AROUND

TO/FROM THE AIRPORT

Darwin International Airport (www.darwinairport.
com.au; Henry Wrigley Dr, Marrara) is 12km north
of the city centre, and handles both international
and domestic flights. **Darwin Airport Shuttle**
(☎08-8981 5066; www.darwinairportshuttle.
com.au) will pick up or drop off almost anywhere
in the centre for $16. When leaving Darwin book a
day before departure. A taxi fare into the centre is
about $35.

PUBLIC TRANSPORT

Darwinbus (www.nt.gov.au/transport) runs a
comprehensive bus network that departs from the
Darwin Bus Terminus (Harry Chan Ave), opposite
Brown's Mart.

A $3 adult ticket gives unlimited travel on the bus
network for three hours (validate your ticket when
you first get on). Daily ($7) and weekly ($20) travel
cards are also available from bus interchanges,
newsagencies and the visitor information centre.

Alternatively, the privately run **Tour Tub** (☎08-
8985 6322; www.tourtub.com.au; adult/child
$100/60) is a hop-on, hop-off minibus touring
Darwin's sights throughout the day.

🛏 Where to Stay

It's possible to stay in the national park
itself – there are a couple of cabin and
bungalow options in Jabiru, Kakadu's
major service centre. In Darwin,
backpackers are concentrated in a
small stretch of bar-heavy Mitchell St.
For a quieter stay, choose somewhere
outside the city centre like Cullen Bay or
Larrakeyah.

SCOOTER

Darwin Scooter Hire (☎08-8941 2434; www.
thescootershop.com.au; 9 Daly St) Rents out
mountain bikes/50cc scooters/motorbikes for
$20/60/180 per day.

TAXI

Call **Darwin Radio Taxis** (☎13 10 08;
www.131008.com).

Yellow Water Billabong (p238)

AUSTRALIAN SCENICS / GETTY IMAGES ©

AUSCAPE / UIG / GETTY IMAGES ©

FREMANTLE

Fremantle

Creative, relaxed, open-minded: Fremantle's spirit is entirely distinct from Perth's. Perhaps it has something to do with the port and the city's working-class roots. Or the hippies, who first set up home here a few decades ago and can still be seen casually bobbling down the street on old bicycles. Or perhaps it's just that a timely 20th-century economic slump meant that the city retained an almost complete set of formerly grand Victorian and Edwardian buildings, creating a heritage precinct that's unique among Australia's cities today.

Whatever the reason, today's clean and green Freo makes a cosy home for performers, professionals, artists and more than a few eccentrics. There's a lot to enjoy here – fantastic museums, edgy galleries, pubs thrumming with live music and a thriving coffee culture.

ℹ In This Section

➡ Arriving in Fremantle

Fremantle is in Zone 2 of the Perth public-transport system (Transperth); the journey takes 30 minutes and costs $4.50, and the station is right in the heart of things. Buses 103, 106, 107, 111 and 158 can also take you between Perth city centre and Fremantle.

From left: Stocks at the Round House (p253); Stalls at Fremantle Markets (p253); Fremantle Festival; Fremantle Prison (p252)

ANDREW WATSON / GETTY IMAGES ©; RICHARD I'ANSON / GETTY IMAGES ©; LYNN GAIL / GETTY IMAGES ©; ANDREW WATSON / GETTY IMAGES ©

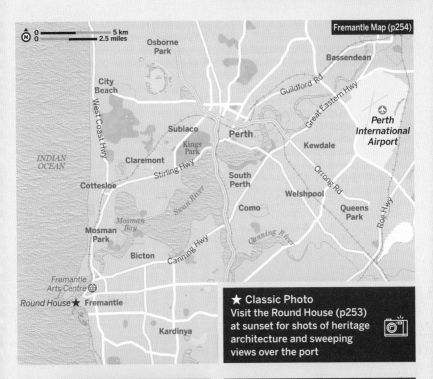

Fremantle Map (p254)

INDIAN OCEAN

Osborne Park

Bassendean

City Beach

Guildford Rd

Great Eastern Hwy

West Coast Hwy

Subiaco

Perth

Perth International Airport

Kings Park

Kewdale

Claremont

Stirling Hwy

Orrong Rd

Cottesloe

Swan River

South Perth

Welshpool

Roe Hwy

Como

Queens Park

Mosman Park

Mosman Bay

Canning River

Bicton

Canning Hwy

Fremantle Arts Centre

Round House ★ Fremantle

Kardinya

★ **Classic Photo**
Visit the Round House (p253) at sunset for shots of heritage architecture and sweeping views over the port

✿ What's On

Laneway (www.fremantle.lanewayfestival. com; ⏱early Feb) This hipster music festival is a lot of fun.

West Coast Blues 'n' Roots Festival (www.westcoastbluesnroots.com.au; ⏱late Mar-mid Apr) An eclectic music festival that manages to attract big names.

Fremantle Festival (www.fremantle.wa.gov. au/festivals; ⏱late Oct-early Nov) Now Australia's longest-running cultural festival, this event brings the town alive.

➜ Fremantle in Two Days

Spend your first morning at the **Fremantle Markets** (p253). After lunch there, head inland to the gothic thrills of **Fremantle Prison** (p252), then back towards the sea for dinner at **Bread in Common** (p256). Start the next morning whale-watching with **Oceanic Cruises** (p255), have lunch at **Canvas** (p257), then head to the **Maritime Museum** (p252). Finish up with a beer, meal and brewery tour at **Little Creatures** (p258).

◉ SIGHTS

Fremantle Prison   Historic Building

With its foreboding 5m-high walls, the old convict-era prison still dominates Fremantle. Daytime tour options include the Doing Time Tour taking in the kitchens, men's cells and solitary-confinement cells. The Great Escapes Tour recounts famous inmates and takes in the women's prison. Book ahead for the Torchlight Tour focusing on macabre aspects of the prison's history, and the 2½-hour Tunnels Tour (children must be over 12), which includes an underground boat ride and subterranean tunnels built by prisoners.

Entry to the gatehouse, including the Prison Gallery, gift shop and Convict Cafe is free. In 2010 its cultural status was recognised as part of the Australian Convict Sites entry on the Unesco World Heritage list.

The first convicts were made to build their own prison, constructing it from beautiful pale limestone dug out of the hill on which it was built. From 1855 to 1991, 350,000 people were incarcerated here, although the highest numbers held at any one time were 1200 men and 58 women. Of those, 43 men and one woman were executed on-site, the last of which was serial killer Eric Edgar Cooke in 1964. (📞08-9336 9200; www. fremantleprison.com.au; 1 The Terrace; adult/ child single day tour $20/11, combined day tours $28/19, Torchlight Tour $26/16, Tunnels Tour $60/40; ⊗9am-5.30pm)

Western Australian Museum – Maritime   Museum

Housed in an intriguing sail-shaped building on the harbour, just west of the city centre, the maritime museum is a fascinating exploration of WA's relationship with the ocean. Well-presented displays range from yacht racing to Aboriginal fish traps and the sandalwood trade. If you're not claustrophobic, take an hour-long tour of the submarine HMAS *Ovens*. The vessel was part of the Royal Australian Navy's fleet from 1969 to 1997. Tours leave every half-hour from 10am to 3.30pm.

Various boats are on display in the museum including *Australia II*, the famous winged-keel yacht that won the America's Cup in 1983 (ending 132 years of American

Fishing Boat Harbour

WALTER BIBIKOW / GETTY IMAGES ©

domination of the competition). Other boats include an Aboriginal bark canoe; an Indonesian outrigger canoe, introduced to the Kimberley and used by the Indigenous people; and a pearl lugger used in Broome. Even a classic 1970s panel van (complete with fur lining) makes the cut – because of its status as the surfer's vehicle of choice. (www.museum.wa.gov.au; Victoria Quay; adult/child museum $10/3, submarine $10/3, museum & submarine $16/5; ⊙9.30am-5pm)

Round House · Historic Building

Built from 1830 to 1831, this 12-sided stone prison is WA's oldest surviving building. It was the site of the colony's first hangings, and was later used for holding Aboriginal people before they were taken to Rottnest Island. On the hilltop outside is the Signal Station, where at 1pm daily a time ball and cannon blast were used to alert seamen to the correct time. The ceremony is re-enacted daily; book ahead if you want to fire the cannon.

To the Indigenous Noongar people, it's a sacred site because of the number of their people killed while incarcerated here. Freedom fighter Yagan was held here briefly in 1832. Beneath is an impressive 1837 Whalers' Tunnel carved through sandstone and used for accessing Bathers Beach, where whales were landed and processed. (☎08-9336 6897; www.fremantleroundhouse.com.au; Captains Lane; admission by donation; ⊙10.30am-3.30pm)

Fremantle Arts Centre · Gallery

An impressive neo-Gothic building surrounded by lovely elm-shaded gardens, the Fremantle Arts Centre was constructed by convict labourers as a lunatic asylum in the 1860s. Saved from demolition in the 1960s, it houses interesting exhibitions and the excellent Canvas (p257) cafe. During summer there are concerts, courses and workshops. (www.fac.org.au; 1 Finnerty St; ⊙10am-5pm)

Fremantle Markets · Market

Originally opened in 1897, these colourful markets were reopened in 1975 and today

 Public Sculptures

Enlivening Fremantle's streets are numerous bronze sculptures, many by local artist Greg James (www.gregjamessculpture.com).

In Fishing Boat Harbour is **To the Fishermen**, a cluster of bronze figures unloading and carrying their catch up from the wharf. There's a lively statue of former member for Fremantle and wartime Labor prime minister **John Curtin** (1885–1945) in Kings Sq, outside the Town Hall. Nearby is a Greg James sculpture of fellow sculptor **Pietro Porcelli** (1872–1943), in the act of making a bust.

Above: *To the Fishermen* by Greg James
AUSCAPE / UIG / GETTY IMAGES ©

draw slow-moving crowds, combing over souvenirs such as plastic boomerangs and swan-shaped magnets. The fresh-produce section is a good place to stock up on snacks. (www.fremantlemarkets.com.au; cnr South Tce & Henderson St; ⊙8am-8pm Fri, 8am-6pm Sat & Sun)

⊕ ACTIVITIES

Fremantle Trails · Walking

Pick up trailcards from the visitor centre for 11 self-guided walking tours: Art and Culture; Convict; CY O'Connor (a pioneering civil engineer); Discovery (a Fremantle once-over); Fishing Boat Harbour; Hotels and Breweries,;Maritime Heritage, Manjaree Heritage (Indigenous); Retail & Fashion; Waterfront; and Writers. (www.visitfremantle.com.au)

Fremantle

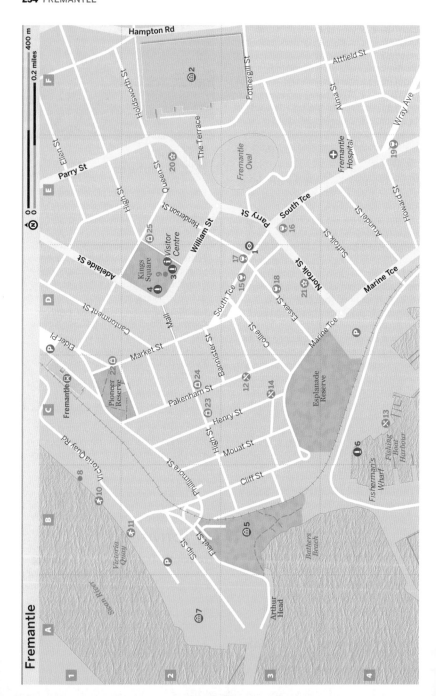

Fremantle

Oceanic Cruises Whale Watching
Departs B Shed, Victoria Quay, at 10.15am for a two-hour tour. Days of operation vary by month, so check the website. (☎08-9325 1191; www.oceaniccruises.com.au; adult/child $69/29; ☉mid-Sep–early Dec)

STS Leeuwin II Sailing
Take a three-hour trip on a 55m, three-masted tall ship; see the website for details of morning, afternoon or twilight sails. (☎08-9430 4105; www.sailleeuwin.com; Berth B; adult/child $99/69; ☉Fri-Sun Nov-mid Apr)

⊙ TOURS

Fremantle Tram Tours Bus Tour
Looking like a heritage tram, this bus departs from the Town Hall on an all-day hop-on, hop-off circuit around the city (adult/child $26/5).

The Ghostly Tour ($80/60) runs from 6.45pm to 10.30pm Friday and visits the prison, Round House and Fremantle Arts Centre (former asylum) by torchlight. Combos include Lunch & Tram (tram plus a lunch cruise on river; $89/54), Triple Tour (tram, river cruise and Perth sightseeing bus; $80/30), and Tram & Prison (incor-

porating the tram and Fremantle prison; $45/14). (☎08-9433 6674; www.fremantletrams.com.au)

Captain Cook Cruises Boat Tour
Cruises between Fremantle and Perth (adult/child $28/16) departing Fremantle at 11.05am, 12.45pm and 3.30pm (the last is one-way only). A three-hour lunch cruise departs at 12.45pm ($69/46). (☎08-9325 3341; www.captaincookcruises.com.au; C Shed)

Fremantle Indigenous Heritage Tours Walking Tour
Highly regarded tour covering the history of Fremantle and the Noongar and Wadjuk people. Book through the Fremantle visitor centre. (☎0405 630 606; www.indigenouswa.com; adult/child $50/15; ☉1.30pm Sat)

Two Feet & A Heartbeat Walking Tour
Operated by a younger, energetic crew, tours focus on Fremantle's often rambunctious history. 'Tight Arse Tuesdays' are good value. (☎1800 459 388; www.twofeet.com.au; per person $20-40; ☉10am daily)

★ **Top Five for Local History**
Fremantle Prison (p252)
Fremantle Trails (p253)
Fremantle Indigenous Heritage Tours
(p255)
WA Museum – Maritime (p252)
Round House (p253)

From left: Busker at Fremantle Markets (p253);
Fremantle breakfast; Little Creatures

🔒 SHOPPING

The bottom end of High St features interesting and quirky shopping. Fashion stores run along Market St, towards the train station. Queen Victoria St in North Fremantle is the place to go for antiques. Don't forget Fremantle Markets (p253) for clothes and souvenirs.

Japingka   Arts
Specialising in Aboriginal fine art from WA and beyond. Purchases come complete with extensive notes about the works and the artists that painted them. (www.japingka. com.au; 47 High St; ◷10am-5.30pm Mon-Fri, noon-5pm Sat & Sun)

Found   Arts, Crafts
The Fremantle Arts Centre shop stocks an inspiring range of WA art and craft. (www. fac.org.au; 1 Finnerty St; ◷10am-5pm)

Love in Tokyo   Clothing
Local designer turning out gorgeously fashioned fabrics for women. (www.loveintokyo. com.au; 61-63 High St; ◷10am-5pm Mon-Sat, noon-4pm Sun)

Didgeridoo Breath   Arts, Crafts
The planet's biggest selection of didgeridoos, Indigenous Australian books and CDs, and how-to-play lessons ranging from one hour to four weeks. You'll probably hear the shop before you see it. (www.didgeridoobreath. com; 6 Market St; ◷10.30am-5pm)

MANY6160   Arts, Crafts
A boho mash-up of local artists' studios and pop-up galleries and shops fills the spacious ground floor of the former Myer department store. (www.many6160.com; 2 Newman Ct; ◷10am-5pm Fri-Sun)

🍴 EATING

Flipside   Burgers $
Gourmet burgers with the option of dining in next door at Mrs Browns (p258). (www. flipsideburgers.com.au; 239 Queen Victoria St, North Fremantle; burgers $11.50-15.50; ◷5.30-9pm Mon-Wed, 11.30am-9pm Thu-Sun)

Bread in Common   Bistro, Bakery $$
Be initially lured by the comforting aroma of the inhouse bakery, before staying on for

ORIEN HARVEY / GETTY IMAGES ©

cheese and charcuterie platters, or larger dishes such as chargrilled chicken. There's a focus on comfort food and culinary flair, while big shared tables and a laid-back ambience encourage conversation over WA wines and Aussie craft beers and ciders. (www.breadincommon.com.au; 43 Pakenham St; shared platters $12-14, mains $21-26; ☻10am-10pm Mon-Fri, 9am-10pm Sat & Sun)

Moore & Moore
Cafe **$$**

An urban-chic cafe that spills into the adjoining art gallery and overflows into a flagstoned courtyard. With great coffee, good cooked breakfasts, pastries, wraps and free wi-fi, it's a great place to linger. (www.mooreandmoorecafe.com; 46 Henry St; mains $11-20; ☻7am-4pm; 📶)

Public & Co
Bistro, Tapas **$$**

Around 2.5km from central Fremantle, Public & Co is worth the journey for a relaxed meal in this spacious and airy corner bungalow. Shared plates, wood-fired pizza and top-notch burgers all reinforce a laid-back, WA-style approach to living. It also has one of the best craft beer selections in Perth. (www.publicandco.com.au; 25 Duoro St; shared plates $15-24, mains & pizza $15-28; ☻6pm-10pm Wed-Fri, 8am-4pm & 6-10pm Sat, 8am-3pm Sun)

Canvas
Cafe **$$**

Freo's best cafe is in the shaded courtyard of the Fremantle Arts Centre with a menu channelling Middle Eastern, Spanish and North African influences. Breakfast highlights include baked-egg dishes and lunch presents everything from jerk chicken wraps to bouillabaisse and Tasmanian salmon. (www.canvasatfremantleartscentre. com; Fremantle Arts Centre; mains $12-25; ☻8am-3pm Mon-Fri, 8am-4pm Sat & Sun; 📶)

Little Creatures
Pub Food **$$**

Little Creatures is classic Freo: harbour views, fantastic brews (made on the premises) and excellent food. It can get chaotic at times, but a signature Pale Ale with a wood-fired pizza will be worth the wait. More substantial shared plates include kangaroo with tomato chutney and grilled prawn skewers. No bookings. (www.littlecreatures. com.au; 40 Mews Rd, Fishing Boat Harbour; pizzas $19-24, shared plates $8-24; ☻10am-midnight Mon-Fri, from 9am Sat & Sun; 📶)

Live Music Venues

In creative and music-loving Freo, you won't be short on options to see a local band. Here are some of the best spots:

Fly by Night Musicians Club (www.flyby night.org; Parry St) Variety is the key at Fly by Night, a not-for-profit club that's been run by musos for musos for years. All kinds perform here, and many local bands made a start here. It's opposite the car park below the old Fremantle Prison.

X-Wray Cafe (www.facebook.com/xwray. fremantle; 3-13 Essex St; ⊘7am-midnight Mon-Sat, to 10pm Sun) There's something on every night (live jazz, rock, open piano) at this hipster hang-out, comprising a smallish indoor area and a large canvas-covered terrace. Light meals are available, kicking off with breakfasts.

Mojo's (www.mojosbar.com.au; 237 Queen Victoria St, North Fremantle; ⊘7pm-late) Local and national bands (mainly Aussie rock and indie) and DJs play at this small place, and there's a sociable beer garden out the back. First Friday of the month is reggae night; every Monday is open-mike night.

🅡 DRINKING & NIGHTLIFE

Sail & Anchor   Pub
Welcome to the best destination for the travelling beer geek in WA. Built in 1854, this Fremantle landmark has been impressively restored to recall much of its former glory. Downstairs is big and beer focused, with 27 taps delivering an ever-changing range of local and international craft beers. Occasional live music and decent bar food complete the picture. (www.sailandanchor. com.au; 64 South Tce; ⊘11am-midnight Mon-Sat, to 10pm Sun)

Little Creatures   Brewery
Try the Little Creatures Pale Ale and Pilsner, and other beers and ciders under the White Rabbit and Pipsqueak labels. Keep an eye out also for one-off Shift Brewers' Stash beers. Creatures NextDoor is an adjacent lounge bar with regular live entertainment and DJs. Live jazz kicks off at 4.30pm on Sundays, and there's comedy ($30) on Saturday nights from 8pm. (www.littlecreatures .com.au; 40 Mews Rd, Fishing Boat Harbour; ⊘10am-midnight Mon-Fri, from 9am Sat & Sun)

Who's Your Mumma   Bar
Industrial-chic lightbulbs and polished-concrete floors are softened by recycled timber at the laid-back Who's Your Mumma. An eclectic crew of South Freo locals crowd in for excellent cocktails, WA craft beer and moreish bar snacks including fluffy pork buns. Taco Thursdays are definitely good value with a Mexican accent. (www.facebook. com/whosyourmummabar; cnr Wray Ave & South Tce; ⊘4pm-midnight Mon-Sat, noon-10pm Sun)

Norfolk Hotel   Pub
Slow down to Freo pace at this 1887 pub. Interesting guest beers create havoc for the indecisive drinker, and the pub food and pizzas are very good. We love the heritage limestone courtyard, especially when sunlight peeks through the elms and eucalypts. Downstairs, the Odd Fellow channels a bohemian small bar vibe, and hosts regular live gigs from Tuesday to Saturday. (www.norfolkhotel.com.au; 47 South Tce; ⊘11am-midnight Mon-Sat, to 10pm Sun)

Monk   Microbrewery
Park yourself on the spacious front terrace or in the chic interior, partly fashioned from recycled railway sleepers, and enjoy the Monk's own brews (kolsch, mild, wheat, porter, rauch, pale ale). The bar snacks and pizzas are also good, and guest beers and regular seasonal brews always draw a knowledgeable crowd of local craft-beer nerds. (www.themonk.com.au; 33 South Tce; ⊘11.30am-late Mon-Fri, 8.30am-late Sat & Sun)

Mrs Browns   Bar
Exposed bricks and a copper bar combine with retro and antique furniture to create North Fremantle's most atmospheric bar. The music could include all those cult bands you thought were your personal

Heritage buildings on Phillimore St

secret, and an eclectic menu of beer, wine and tapas targets the more discerning, slightly older bar hound. And you can order in burgers from Flipside (p256) next door. (www.mrsbrownbar.com.au; 241 Queen Victoria St, North Fremantle; ⊙4.30pm-midnight Tue-Thu, noon-midnight Fri-Sun)

Whisper   Wine Bar

In a lovely heritage building, this classy French-themed wine bar also does shared plates of charcuterie and cheese. (www. whisperwinebar.com.au; 1/15 Essex St; ⊙noon-late Wed-Sun)

❶ INFORMATION

Fremantle Hospital At the edge of central Fremantle. (☎08-9431 3333; www.fhhs.health. wa.gov.au; Alma St)

Visitor Centre Bookings for accommodation, tours and hire cars. (☎08-9431 7878; www. visitfremantle.com.au; Kings Sq, Town Hall; ⊙9am-5pm Mon-Fri, 9am-4pm Sat, 10am-4pm Sun)

❶ GETTING THERE & AWAY

BOAT

A pleasant way to get here from Perth is by taking the 1¼-hour river cruise run by Captain Cook Cruises (p255).

TRAIN

Fremantle sits within Zone 2 of the Perth public-transport system (Transperth) and is only 30 minutes away by train. There are numerous buses between Perth's city centre and Fremantle, including routes 103, 106, 107, 111 and 158.

❶ GETTING AROUND

There are numerous one-way streets and parking meters in Freo. It's easy enough to travel by foot or on the free CAT bus service, which takes in all the major sights on a loop every 10 minutes from 7.30am to 6.30pm on weekdays, until 9pm on Friday and 10am to 6.30pm on the weekend.

Bicycles can be rented for free at the **visitor centre** (Kings Sq, Town Hall; ⊙9.30am-4.30pm Mon-Fri, to 3.30pm Sat, 10.30am-3.30pm Sun), an ideal way to get around Freo's storied streets. A refundable bond of $200 applies.

LUCINDA BLACK / GETTY IMAGES ©

MARGARET RIVER REGION

Margaret River Region

With vineyard restaurants, artisan food producers, and some of Australia's most spectacular surf beaches and rugged coastline, the Margaret River wine region packs attractions aplenty into a compact area.

Sleepy Yallingup conceals excellent beaches, restaurants and luxe accommodation; Margaret River township is the region's bustling foodie heart; and the best of the area's wineries are focused around Cowaramup and Wilyabrup. Throughout the region, an excellent craft-beer scene bubbles away.

Margaret River spills over with tourists every weekend and gets very, very busy at Easter and Christmas (when you should book weeks, if not months, ahead). Accommodation prices tend to be cheaper midweek.

❶ In This Section

➡ Arriving in Margaret River

Unusually for Western Australia, distances between the many attractions are short, and driving time is mercifully limited, making it a fantastic area to explore for a few days – you will get much more out of your stay here if you have your own wheels. Buses from Fremantle/Perth, run by TransWA and South West, serve Busselton and the larger centres in Margaret River.

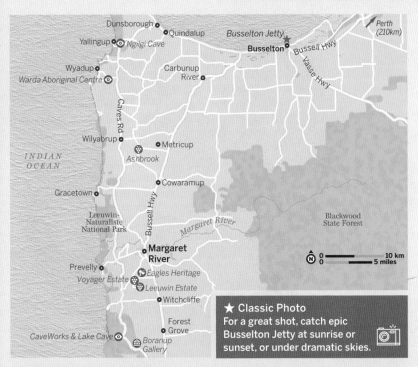

Dunsborough
Quindalup
Yallingup • Ngilgi Cave
Busselton Jetty
Busselton
Wyadup
Carbunup
River
Warda Aboriginal Centre

Bussell Hwy
Vasse Hwy
Perth (210km)

INDIAN OCEAN

Caves Rd

Wilyabrup
Metricup
Ashbrook
Cowaramup

Gracetown

Bussell Hwy

Margaret River

Leeuwin-
Naturaliste
National Park

Blackwood
State Forest

Margaret River

0 ___ 10 km
0 ___ 5 miles

Prevelly
Eagles Heritage
Voyager Estate
Leeuwin Estate
Witchcliffe

Forest
Grove

CaveWorks & Lake Cave
Boranup Gallery

★ **Classic Photo**
For a great shot, catch epic
Busselton Jetty at sunrise or
sunset, or under dramatic skies.

From left: Oak barrels at Brookland Valley Vineyard; Autumn grapevines; Smiths Beach
ANDREW WATSON / GETTY IMAGES ©; FRANCES ANDRIJICH / GETTY IMAGES ©; KEVEN OSBORNE/FOX FOTOS / GETTY IMAGES ©

KASZOJAD / GETTY IMAGES ©

Margaret River Wineries

Margaret River's climate and granite gravel loams make it ideal for growing chardonnay, sauvignon blanc and other grapes. Most of its wineries are boutique producers, well equipped for cellar-door sales and viticultural tourism.

Great For...

☑ **Don't Miss**

The art at Vasse Felix, including an outdoor sculpture trail and indoor art gallery,

Best Wineries & Restaurants

Vasse Felix (p269) Dating back to the 1960s, this is the oldest winery in the region. The setting is delightful, and it's home to one of Australia's best regional restaurants.

Leeuwin Estate (p272) Home to some of Australia's best chardonnay, Leeuwin Estate also stages open-air concerts and conducts tours of the wine-making operation.

Fraser Gallop (p268) A relative newcomer to the Margaret River scene, Fraser Gallop has quickly established itself as one of the region's leading producers.

Knee Deep in Margaret River (p269) Combining Australian familarity with Asian ingredients Knee Deep's restaurant is a lovely showcase for its wines.

JUPITERIMAGES / GETTY IMAGES ©

Flutes (p268) The in-house restaurant at Brookland Valley winery, Flutes is wonderfully situated overlooking a dam among the vines.

For details on wineries and restaurants in Margaret River, plus tours, maps, contacts and other information, see the excellent regional website www.margaretriver.com.

Tours

Margies Big Day Out   Winery Tour
Three wineries, two breweries, cheese, chocolate and lunch. (☎0416 180 493; www. margaretrivertourswa.com.au; tours $95)

Margaret River Tours   Winery Tour
Runs winery tours (half-/full day $80/140) and can arrange charters. (☎0419 917 166; www.margaretrivertours.com)

❶ Need to Know
Public transport in the area isn't extensive: consider taking a winery tour or bringing your own wheels.

✕ Take a Break
A few wineries in the region have picnic or barbeque areas so you can pack your own fare to accompany a bottle of something local.

★ Top Tip
Eat local: As well as wine, Margaret River also produces excellent dairy (especially cheese), olives, meat, seafood and other comestibles.

Wine for Dudes   Winery Tour
Includes a brewery, a chocolate factory, four wineries, a wine-blending experience and lunch. (☎0427 774 994; www.winefor dudes.com; tours $95)

Harvest Tours   Winery Tour
Food and wine tour with an emphasis on organic, sustainable and ethical producers. Lunch is included at Cullen Wines (p269). (☎0429 728 687; www.harvesttours.com.au; adult/child $155/55)

Taste the South   Winery Tour
Wine and craft-beer tours. The Hits with Kids tour combines kid-friendly vineyards with lamb feeding, sheep shearing and a chocolate factory. (☎0438 210 373; www. tastethesouth.com.au; per person from $95)

Bushtucker Tours   Guided Tour
Combines walking and canoeing up the Margaret River; plus aspects of Aboriginal culture, uses for flora, and a bush-tucker lunch. Also runs a Winery & Brewery Tour. (☎08-9757 9084; www.bushtuckertours.com; adult/child $95/40)

Yallingup & Around

Beachside Yallingup is a mecca for both surfers and wine aficionados. You're permitted to let a 'wow' escape when the surf-battered coastline first comes into view. For romantic travellers, Yallingup means 'place of love' in the Wardandi Noongar tongue.

Beautiful walking trails follow the coast between here and Smiths Beach. Canal Rocks, a series of rocky outcrops forming a natural canal, are just past Smiths Beach.

◎ SIGHTS & ACTIVITIES

Wardan
Aboriginal Centre   Cultural Experience

Offers a window into the lives of the local Wardandi people. There's a gallery (free admission), an interpretive display on the six seasons that govern the Wardandi calendar (adult/child $8/3), and the opportunity to take part in various experiences including stone tool making, and boomerang and spear throwing. A guided bushwalk explores Wardandi spirituality and the uses of various plants for food, medicine and shelter. (📞08-9756 6566; www.wardan.com.au; Injidup Springs Rd, Yallingup; experiences adult/child $20/10; ◷10am-4pm daily mid-Oct–mid-Mar, 10am-4pm Mon, Wed-Fri & Sun mid-Mar–mid-Jun & mid-Aug–mid-Oct, experiences Sun, Mon, Wed & Fri)

Ngilgi Cave   Cave
Between Dunsborough and Yallingup, this 500,000-year-old cave is associated in Wardandi spirituality with the victory of the good spirit Ngilgi over the evil spirit Wolgine. To the Wardandi people it became a kind of honeymoon location. A European man first stumbled upon it in 1899 while looking for his horse. Formations include the white Mother of Pearl Shawl and the equally beautiful Arab's Tent and Oriental Shawl. Tours depart every half-hour. Check online for other options.

More adventurous caving options include the two-hour Ancient Riverbed Tour (adult/child $60/39), the 45-minute Express Adventure Tour ($47/29), the 2½-hour Explorer Tour ($88/52), the three-hour Crystal Crawl Tour (adults only, $110) and

SHELDON LEVIS / GETTY IMAGES ©

the four-hour Ultimate Ngilgi Adventure (adults only, $158). The Above & Below ticket (adult/child $30/15) includes entry to the **Cape Naturaliste Lighthouse** (adult/child $14/7; ⏱tours every 30min 9.30am-4pm). Well-marked bushwalks start from here. (08-9755 2152; www.geographebay.com; Yallingup Caves Rd; adult/child $22/12; ⏱9am-5pm)

Yallingup Surf School   Surfing
Offers 90-minute lessons for beginners (one-hour lesson $50, three hours $125) and private coaching ($110). (📞08-9755 2755; www.yallingupsurfschool.com)

⊙ TOURS

Koomal Dreaming   Guided Tour
Yallingup local and Wardandi man Josh Whiteland runs tours showcasing Indigenous food, culture and music, usually also including bushwalking and exploration of the Ngilgi Cave. (📞0413 843 426; www.koomaldreaming.com.au; adult/child from $50/25)

⊗ EATING

Yallingup
Woodfired Bread   Bakery $
Look out for excellent sourdough, rye bread and fruit loaves at local shops and the Margaret River Farmers Market, or pick up some still-warm loaves at the bakery near Yallingup. (189 Biddle Rd; ⏱7am-6pm Mon-Sat)

Wills Domain   Winery $$$
Restaurant, gallery and wonderful hilltop views over vines. An innovative seven-course tasting menu (with/without wine match $139/99) is also available. (www.willsdomain.com.au; cnr Brash & Abbey Farm Rds; mains $29-40, charcuterie platters $38; ⏱tastings 10am-5pm, lunch noon-3pm)

Studio
Bistro   Modern Australian $$$
📝 Studio Bistro's gallery focuses on Australian artists, while the garden restaurant showcases subtle dishes such as pan-fried fish with cauliflower cream, radicchio,

★ **Top Five Indigenous Culture**

Wardan Aboriginal Centre (p266)

Tunbridge Gallery (p270)

Ngilgi Cave (p266)

Koomal Dreaming (p267)

Bushtucker Tours (p265)

From left: Ngilgi Cave; Splendid fairywrens; Dryandra

BEN CLARK / 500PX PRIME ©

PHOTO BY MARTIN COHEN / GETTY IMAGES ©

Coastal Detours

As enticing as the wine and food of inland Margaret River is, it would be criminal to neglect its lovely coastline. The area around Yallingup boasts a number of great swimming and surfing beaches (Bunker Bay, Eagle Bay and Smiths Beach, to name a few), while further south you'll find Cowaramup Bay, Gnarabup and Hamelin Bay.

There's also the famous 1.7km-long Busselton Jetty, lighthouses at Cape Leeuwin and Cape Naturaliste, and, from June to December, whale-watching.

Above: Moses Rock, south of Yallingup
CHERYL FORBES / GETTY IMAGES ©

peas and crab meat. Five-course degustation menus are offered on Friday and Saturday nights. Bookings recommended. (☎08-9756 6164; www.thestudiobistro.com.au; 7 Marrinup Dr; small plates $15-20, mains $28-39, degustation menu with/without wine matches $135/95; ⊙10am-5pm Thu-Mon, 6pm-late Fri & Sat; ☞)

Cowaramup & Wilyabrup

Cowaramup (Cow Town to some) is a couple of blocks of shops lining Bussell Hwy. Wilyabrup to the northwest is where the Margaret River wine industry began in the 1960s. This area has the highest concentration of wineries, and pioneers Cullen Wines and Vasse Felix are still leading the way.

◉ SIGHTS

Ashbrook   Winery
Ashbrook grows all of its grapes on-site. Its award-winning rieslings are rightly lauded. (www.ashbrookwines.com.au; 448 Tom Cullity Dr, Wilyabrup; ⊙10am-5pm)

Fraser Gallop   Winery
There's not a regular cellar door at present, but 'pop up' cellar doors and tasting appointments are offered. (☎08-9755 7553; www.frasergallopestate.com.au; 493 Metricup Rd, Wilyabrup)

Thompson Estate   Winery
A small-scale producer with an architectural-award-winning tastings and barrel room. (www.thompsonestate.com; 299 Tom Cullity Dr, Wilyabrup; ⊙11am-5pm Tue-Sun)

🔒 SHOPPING

**Margaret River
Regional Wine Centre**   Wine
A one-stop shop for Margaret River wine. (www.mrwines.com; 9 Bussell Hwy, Cowaramup; ⊙10am-7pm)

✖ EATING

Providore   Deli $
Voted one of Australia's Top 100 Gourmet Experiences by *Australian Traveller* magazine – given its amazing range of artisan produce, including organic olive oil, tapenades and preserved fruits, we can only agree. Look forward to loads of free samples. (www.providore.com.au; 448 Tom Cullity Dr, Wilyabrup; ⊙9am-5pm)

Flutes   Winery Restaurant $$$
Like many winery restaurants in the region, it's open for lunch, but not dinner. (☎08-9755 6250; www.flutes.com.au; Brookland Valley Vineyard, 4070 Caves Rd, Wilyabrup; mains $34-44; ⊙lunch Thu-Mon, daily summer)

Margaret Riviera   Deli $
Gourmet food store stocking local produce including olive oils, preserves and cheeses.

(www.margaretriviera.com.au; Bottrill St, Cowaramup; 🕙10am-5pm)

Margaret River Chocolate Company   Chocolates $

Watch truffles being made and sample chocolate buttons. (www.chocolatefactory.com.au; Harman's Mill Rd, Metricup; 🕙9am-5pm)

Margaret River Dairy Company   Cheese $

Cheese tastings north of Cowaramup. (www.mrdc.com.au; Bussell Hwy; 🕙9.30am-5pm)

Vasse Felix   Winery Restaurant $$$

Vasse Felix winery is considered by many to have the best fine-dining restaurant in the region, the big wooden dining room reminiscent of an extremely flash barn. The grounds are peppered with sculptures, while the gallery displaying works from the Holmes à Court collection is worth a trip in itself. (📞08-9756 5050; www.vassefelix.com.au; cnr Caves Rd & Harmans Rd S, Cowaramup; mains $32-39, 3-course menu $65; 🕙cellar door 10am-5pm, restaurant 10am-3pm)

Knee Deep in Margaret River   Restaurant $$$

📝 Small and focused could be the motto here. Only a handful of mains are offered – crafted with locally sourced, seasonal produce – and the open-sided pavilion provides a pleasantly intimate vineyard setting. (📞08-9755 6776; www.kneedeep-wines.com.au; 61 Johnson Rd, Wilyabrup; mains $28-38, 3-/5-course degustation $70/90; 🕙cellar door 10am-5pm, lunch noon-3pm)

Cullen Wines   Winery Restaurant $$$

📝 Grapes were first planted here in 1966 and Cullen has an ongoing commitment to organic and biodynamic principles in both food and wine. Celebrating a relaxed ambience, Cullen's food is excellent, with many of the fruits and vegetables sourced from its own gardens. (📞08-9755 5277; www.cullenwines.com.au; 4323 Caves Rd, Cowaramup; mains $25-38; 🕙10am-4pm)

METRIGNOME / GETTY IMAGES ©

From left: Canoeing on the Margaret River; Dessert at Voyager Estate (p272); Surfers at Gracetown Beach

Margaret River

Although tourists usually outnumber locals, Margaret River still feels like a country town. The advantage of basing yourself here is that after 5pm, once the wineries shut up shop, it's one of the few places with any vital signs. Plus it's close to the incredible surf of Margaret River Mouth and Southside, and the swimming beaches at Prevelly and Gracetown.

🔒 SHOPPING

Tunbridge Gallery   Arts
Excellent Aboriginal art gallery mainly featuring WA works. (www.tunbridgegallery.com.au; 101 Bussell Hwy; ⏰10am-5pm Mon-Sat, to 3pm Sun)

🍴 EATING

**Margaret River
Farmers Market**   Market $
 The region's organic and sustainable artisan producers come to town every Saturday. It's a top spot for breakfast. Check the website for your own foodie hit list. (www.margaretriverfarmersmarket.com.au; Lot 272, Bussell Hwy, Margaret River Education Campus; ⏰8am-noon Sat)

Margaret River Bakery   Cafe $
📷 Elvis on the stereo, retro furniture and kitsch needlework art – the MRB has a rustic, playful interior. It's the perfect backdrop to the bakery's honest home-style baking, often with a veg or gluten-free spin. Soak up the previous day's wine tasting with terrific burgers and pies. (89 Bussell Hwy; mains $10-18; ⏰7am-4pm Mon-Sat; 🍴)

Larder   Deli $$
Showcasing local Margaret River produce and gourmet foods, the Larder also sells take-away meals ($15 to $17) – a good option for dinner – and comprehensive breakfast packs, picnic hampers and barbecue fixings ($50 to $95). Occasional cooking classes complete the tasty menu. (www.thelarder.biz; 2/99 Bussell Hwy; ⏰9.30am-6pm Mon-Sat, 10.30am-4pm Sun)

LYNN GAIL / GETTY IMAGES ©

Settler's Tavern · Pub Food $$

There's live entertainment Thursday to Sunday at Settler's, so pop in for good pub grub and a beer, or choose a wine from the extensive list. Dinner options are limited in Margaret River, and Settler's is often wildly popular with locals and visitors. Try the mammoth Seafood Deluxe with a pint of the pub's own Great White Pale Ale. (www. settlerstavern.com; 114 Bussell Hwy; mains $16-36; ⏱11am-midnight Mon-Sat, to 10pm Sun)

Morries Anytime · Cafe $$

Settle into the clubby, cosmopolitan atmosphere of Morrie's for breakfast or lunch, or come back later for cocktails and tapas or dinner. Local beers from Colonial Brewing are on tap, and the menu smartly channels both Asian and European flavours. (www.morries.com.au; 2/149 Bussell Hwy; tapas $11-16, mains $15-34; ⏱7.30am-late)

Miki's Open Kitchen · Japanese $$$

Secure a spot around the open kitchen and enjoy the irresistible theatre of the

 Top Events

Drug Aware Pro (www.aspworldtour.com; ⏱Apr) Pro-surfing competition with concerts and fashion shows.

Margaret River Gourmet Escape (www.gourmetescape.com.au; ⏱late Nov) From Rick Stein and Heston Blumenthal to *MasterChef*'s George Calombaris, the Gourmet Escape food and wine festival attracts the big names in global and Australian cuisine.

Look forward to three days of food workshops, tastings, vineyard events and demonstrations. An inaugural added attraction in 2014 was a vineyard concert at Sandalford Estate featuring Kiwi music icon Neil Finn.

Miki's team creating innovative Japanese spins on the best of WA seafood and produce. Combine a Margaret River wine with the $55 multi-course tasting menu for the most diverse experience, and settle in to

Where to Stay

The Margaret River region seamlessly blends waves and wineries, so your accommodation options here range from beachside holiday parks to luxury cottages among the vines, in the towns of Yallingup, Cowaramup and Wilyabrup. If you're after something to do in the evenings once the wineries are closed, base yourself in Margaret River town itself.

Above: Old farmhouse, Cowaramup
ANDREW ROESLER / GETTY IMAGES ©

watch the laid-back Zen chefs work their tempura magic. Bookings recommended. (☑08-9758 7673; www.facebook.com/mikis openkitchen; 131 Bussell Hwy; small plates $12-16, large plates $28-37; ☺6pm-late Tue-Sat)

ⓘ INFORMATION

Visitor Centre (☑08-9780 5911; www. margaretriver.com; 100 Bussell Hwy; ☺9am-5pm) Bookings and information plus displays on local wineries.

ⓘ GETTING THERE & AROUND

Margaret River Beach Bus (☑08-9757 9532; www.margaretriverbackpackers.com.au) Minibus linking the township and the beaches around Prevelly ($10, three daily); summer only, bookings essential.

Transwa (☑1300 662 205; www.transwa.wa.gov. au) Coach SW1 (12 weekly) from Perth to Augusta

stops at Yallingup and Margaret River, with three coaches weekly continuing to Pemberton.
South West Coach Lines (☑08-9261 7600; www.transdevsw.com.au) Buses between Busselton and Augusta (12 weekly) stop at Cowaramup and Margaret River, linking with Perth on the weekends.

Around Margaret River

West of the Margaret River township, the coastline provides spectacular surfing and walks. Prevelly is the main settlement, with a few places to sleep and eat. Most of the sights are on Caves Rd or just off it.

ⓞ SIGHTS

Voyager Estate   Winery
The formal gardens and Cape Dutch–style buildings delight at Voyager Estate, the grandest of Margaret River's wineries. Tours of the estate are available ($25 to $75 including tastings and lunch). (☑08-9757 6354; www.voyagerestate.com.au; Stevens Rd; ☺10am-5pm, tours 11am Tue, Thu, Sat & Sun)

Leeuwin Estate   Winery
An impressive estate with tall trees and lawns gently rolling down to the bush, its Art Series chardonnay is one of the best in the country. Behind-the-scenes wine tours and tastings take place at 11am (adult/child $12.50/4). Big open-air concerts are regularly held here. (☑08-9759 0000; www. leeuwinestate.com.au; Stevens Rd; mains $31-39; ☺10am-5pm daily, dinner Sat)

CaveWorks & Lake Cave   Cave
The main ticket office for Lake, Mammoth and Jewel Caves, CaveWorks has excellent displays about caves, cave conservation and local fossil discoveries. There's also an authentic model cave and a 'cave crawl' experience. Behind the centre is Lake Cave, the prettiest of them all, where limestone formations are reflected in an underground stream. The vegetated

WAYNE WALTON / GETTY IMAGES ©

Lake Cave

entrance to this cave is spectacular and includes a karri tree with a girth of 7m.

Lake Cave is the deepest of all the caves open to the public. There are more than 300 steps down to the entrance (a 62m drop).

CaveWorks is 20km south of Margaret River, off Caves Rd. Single cave tickets include entry to CaveWorks. The Grand Tour Pass (adult/child $55/24), covering CaveWorks and all three caves, is valid for seven days, while the Ultimate Pass (adult/child $70/30) also includes Cape Leeuwin lighthouse. Fully-guided tours through Lake or Jewel Cave take one hour and run horly from 9.30am to 3.30pm. Self-guided tours through Mammoth Cave also take one hour; last entry 4pm. (08-9757 7411; www.

margaretriver.com; Conto Rd; single cave adult/child $22/10; 9am-5pm)

Eagles Heritage Wildlife Reserve
Housing Australia's largest collection of raptors, this centre, 5km south of Margaret River, rehabilitates many birds of prey each year. There are free-flight displays at 11am and 1.30pm. (08-9757 2960; www.eaglesheritage.com.au; 341 Boodjidup Rd; adult/child $17/10; 10am-4.15pm Sat-Thu)

Boranup Gallery Gallery
Local arts and crafts, 22km south of Margaret River, with a wide selection of jarrah furniture. (www.boranupgallery.com; 7981 Caves Rd; 10am-4pm)

Jim Jim Falls, Kakadu National Park (p232)

RICHARD I'ANSON / GETTY IMAGES ©

In Focus

Federation Square (p156), Melbourne

SCOTT E BARBOUR / GETTY IMAGES ©

Australia Today

*Australia's cultural and geographic identity has been
forged by 45 million years of isolation. Its harsh but
beautiful landscape continues to survive bushfires,
droughts and floods – a resilience that has rubbed off
on the Australian people. Hiding behind larrikin wit
and amicable informality, Australians have an innate
optimism that helped steer their economy through the
Global Financial Crisis. But can the good times last?*

Politics

Mimicking global warming, the Australian political climate has been overheated and
irritable of late. In 2013, the left-wing Labor Party was ousted from federal government by
the conservative Liberal-National Party Coalition. In the lead-up to the election, Labor was
destabilised by an extraordinary period of divisive infighting and factional power plays.
Australia's first female prime minister, Julia Gillard, lost the top job to Kevin Rudd in early
2013, whom she herself had ousted as PM in 2010.

Sitting back and rubbing their eyes in disbelief, the conservatives watched the
prime-ministerial circus play out. They then easily won the 2013 election, surfing into office

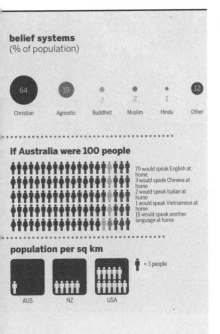

belief systems
(% of population)

64 Christian
19 Agnostic
2 Buddhist
2 Muslim
1 Hindu
12 Other

if Australia were 100 people

79 would speak English at home
3 would speak Chinese at home
2 would speak Italian at home
1 would speak Vietnamese at home
15 would speak another language at home

population per sq km

♦ ≈ 3 people

AUS   NZ   USA

on a wave of public dismay over Labor's leadership soap opera. New prime minister Tony Abbott had the look of a man standing on the threshold of a future he wasn't quite anticipating.

Then, in 2015, things started to go awry for Abbott. His popularity flagging, he made the bizarre choice of bestowing a knighthood on Prince Philip (husband of the British Queen) on Australia Day – a move lambasted by the media and hailed as 'un-Australian' by the public. Abbott survived a leadership challenge early in the year, only to be knocked out of the top job in September by Liberal Party leader Malcolm Turnbull.

But what with the rate of leadership change in recent years, by the time you read this there may be a different PM ruling the roost.

Real Estate Addiction

Australians love real estate. They love talking about it, building it, buying it, looking at it on TV and (most of all) making money selling it. When the GFC bit everybody in 2008, economists and bankers across the Western world very sensibly said, 'Whoops! We've been lending people money they can't afford to pay back, and they've been blowing it on home loans that are too expensive' – and real estate prices tumbled.

But not in Australia. Australians just kept on buying pricey houses, driving the market skywards. Now – having reached a tipping point where the median house price is more than five times the median annual household income – Australian real estate prices are among the least affordable on the planet.

City Scenes

Australian cities are in a constant state of growth, reinvention and flux, absorbing fresh influences from far corners of the globe. Multiculturalism prevails and cities here remain distinct: Sydney is a luscious tart, Melbourne an arty glamour puss, Brisbane a blithe playmate, Adelaide a gracious dame and Perth a free spirit. Not to mention bookish Hobart, hedonistic Darwin and museum-fixated Canberra. Aussie cities are charmers: spend some time getting to know one of them and it'll be hard for you to leave!

Cooks' Cottage (p167), Melbourne

TOM COCKREM / GETTY IMAGES ©

History

Australia is an ancient continent – rocks here have been dated back beyond the Archean aeon 3.8 billion years ago. Its Indigenous people have been here more than 50,000 years. Given this backdrop, 'history' as we describe it can seem somewhat fleeting...but it sure makes an interesting read!

Dr Michael Cathcart

80 million years ago

Continental Australia breaks free from the Antarctic land-mass and drifts north.

50,000 years ago

The first Australians arrive by sea to northern Australia.

1606

Dutch Navigator Willem Janszoon makes the first authenticated European landing on Australian soil.

Aboriginal rock art showing the arrival of European ships

DAVID KIRKLAND / DESIGN PICS / GETTY IMAGES ©

Europeans Arrive

By sunrise, the storm had passed. Zachary Hicks was keeping sleepy watch on the British ship *Endeavour* when suddenly he was wide awake. He summoned his commander, First Lieutenant James Cook. Ahead lay an uncharted country of wooded hills and gentle valleys. It was 19 April 1770. In the coming days Cook began to draw the first European map of Australia's eastern coast.

Two weeks later Cook led a party of men onto a narrow beach. The local Aboriginal people called the place Kurnell, but Cook gave it a foreign name: he called it Stingray Bay and later Botany Bay.

Cook's ship *Endeavour* was a floating annexe of London's leading scientific organisation, the Royal Society. The ship's gentlemen passengers included technical artists, scientists, an astronomer and a wealthy botanist named Joseph Banks. As Banks and his colleagues strode about the Aboriginal peoples' territory, they were delighted by the mass of new plants they collected.

1770	**1788**	**1835**
First Lieutenant James Cook claims the entire east coast of Australia for England.	Captain Arthur Phillip and the First Fleet – 11 ships and more than 1350 people – arrive at Botany Bay.	John Batman negotiates a land deal with the Kulin nation; Melbourne is settled that same year.

Fremantle Prison (p252)

WALTER BIBIKOW / GETTY IMAGES ©

When the Endeavour reached the northern tip of Cape York, Cook and his men could smell the sea-route home. And on a small, hilly island (Possession Island), Cook raised the Union Jack. Amid volleys of gunfire, he claimed the eastern half of the continent for King George III.

Cook's intention was not to steal land from the Aboriginal peoples. In fact he rather idealised them. 'They are far more happier than we Europeans', he wrote. 'They think themselves provided with all the necessaries of Life and that they have no superfluities.'

Convict Beginnings

Eighteen years after Cook's arrival, in 1788, the English were back to stay. They arrived in a fleet of 11 ships, packed with supplies including weapons, tools, building materials and livestock. The ships also contained 751 convicts and more than 250 soldiers, officials and their wives. This motley 'First Fleet' was under the command of a humane and diligent naval captain, Arthur Phillip. As his orders dictated, Phillip dropped anchor at Botany Bay. But the paradise that had so delighted Joseph Banks filled Phillip with dismay. So he left his floating prison and embarked in a small boat to search for a better location. Just a short way up the coast his heart leapt as he sailed into the finest harbour in the world. There, in a small cove, in the idyllic lands of the Eora people, he established a British penal settlement. He renamed the place after the British Home Secretary, Lord Sydney.

Phillip's official instructions urged him to colonise the land without doing violence to the local inhabitants. Among the Indigenous people he used as intermediaries was an Eora man named Bennelong, who adopted many of the white people's customs and manners. But Bennelong's people were shattered by the loss of their lands. Hundreds died of smallpox, and many of the survivors, including Bennelong himself, succumbed to alcoholism and despair.

In 1803, English officers established a second convict settlement in Van Diemen's Land (now Tasmania). Soon, reoffenders filled the grim prison at Port Arthur on the beautiful and wild coast near Hobart.

1851	1880	1901
A gold rush in central Victoria brings settlers from across the world. Democracy is introduced in the eastern colonies.	Bushranger Ned Kelly is hanged as a criminal – and remembered as a folk hero.	The Australian colonies form a federation of states. The federal parliament sits in Melbourne.

From Shackles to Freedom

At first, Sydney and the smaller colonies depended on supplies brought in by ship. Anxious to develop productive farms, the government granted land to soldiers, officers and settlers. After 30 years of trial and error, the farms began to flourish. The most irascible and ruthless of these new landholders was John Macarthur.

Macarthur was a leading member of the Rum Corps, a clique of powerful officers who bullied successive governors (including William Bligh of *Bounty* fame) and grew rich by controlling much of Sydney's trade, notably rum. But the Corps' racketeering was ended in 1810 by a tough new governor named Lachlan Macquarie. Macquarie laid out the major roads of modern-day Sydney, built some fine public buildings (many of which were designed by talented convict-architect Francis Greenway) and helped to lay the foundations for a more civil society. Macquarie also championed the rights of freed convicts, granting them land and appointing several to public office.

The Long Walk to Ballarat

During the 1850s gold rush in Victoria, the town of Robe in South Australia came into its own when the Victorian government whacked a $10-per-head tax on Chinese gold miners arriving to work the goldfields. Thousands of Chinese miners dodged the tax by landing at Robe instead, then walking the 400-odd kilometres to Bendigo and Ballarat: 10,000 arrived in 1857 alone. But the flood stalled as quickly as it started when the SA government instituted its own tax on the Chinese.

Southern Settlements

In the cooler grasslands of Van Diemen's Land, sheep farmers were thriving. In the 1820s they waged a bloody war against the island's Indigenous population, driving them to the brink of extinction. Now these settlers were hungry for more land.

In 1835 an ambitious young man named John Batman sailed to Port Phillip Bay on mainland Australia. On the banks of the Yarra River, he chose the location for Melbourne, famously announcing 'This is the place for a village'. Batman persuaded local Aboriginal peoples to 'sell' him their traditional lands (a whopping 250,000 hectares) for a crate of blankets, knives and knick-knacks. Back in Sydney, Governor Bourke declared the contract void, not because it was unfair, but because the land officially belonged to the British Crown.

At the same time, a private British company settled Adelaide in South Australia. Proud to have no links with convicts, these God-fearing folk instituted a scheme under which their company sold land to well-heeled settlers, and used the revenue to assist poor British labourers to emigrate. When these worthies earned enough to buy land from the company, that revenue would in turn pay the fare of another shipload of labourers.

1915	1939	1942
The Anzacs join a British invasion of Turkey: this military disaster spawns a nationalist legend.	Prime Minister Robert Menzies announces that Britain is at war; 'as a result, Australia is also at war'.	The Japanese bomb Darwin, the first of numerous air strikes on the northern capital.

Exterior of Melbourne Museum (p171)

WILL SALTER / GETTY IMAGES ©

Gold & Rebellion

Transportation of convicts to eastern Australia ceased in the 1840s. This was just as well: in 1851, prospectors discovered gold in New South Wales and central Victoria, including at Ballarat. The news hit the colonies with the force of a cyclone. Young men and some women from every social class headed for the diggings. Soon they were caught up in a great rush of prospectors, publicans and prostitutes. In Victoria the British governor was alarmed – both by the way the Victorian class system had been thrown into disarray, and by the need to finance the imposition of law and order on the goldfields. His solution was to compel all miners to buy an expensive monthly licence.

But the lure of gold was too great and in the reckless excitement of the goldfields, the miners initially endured the thuggish troopers who enforced the government licence. After three years, though, the easy gold at Ballarat was gone, and miners were toiling in deep, water-sodden shafts. They were now infuriated by a corrupt and brutal system of law which held them in contempt. Under the leadership of a charismatic Irishman named Peter Lalor, they raised their own flag, the Southern Cross, and swore to defend their rights and liberties. They armed themselves and gathered inside a rough stockade at Eureka, where they waited for the government to make its move.

In the predawn of Sunday 3 December 1854, a force of troopers attacked the stockade. It was all over in 15 terrifying minutes. The brutal and one-sided battle claimed the lives of 30 miners and five soldiers. But democracy was in the air and public opinion sided with the miners. The eastern colonies were already in the process of establishing democratic parliaments, with the full support of the British authorities.

Meanwhile, in the West...

Western Australia lagged behind the eastern colonies by about 50 years. Though Perth was settled by genteel colonists back in 1829, its material progress was handicapped by isolation, Aboriginal resistance and the arid climate. It was not until the 1880s that the discovery of remote goldfields promised to gild the fortunes of the isolated colony. At the

1945

Australia's motto: 'Populate or Perish!'. Over the next 30 years more than two million immigrants arrive.

1948

Cricketer Don Bradman retires with an unsurpassed test average of 99.94 runs.

1956

The Olympic Games are held in Melbourne: the flame is lit by running champion Ron Clarke.

time, the west was just entering its own period of self-government, and its first premier was a forceful, weather-beaten explorer named John Forrest. He saw that the mining industry would fail if the government did not provide a first-class harbour, efficient railways and reliable water supplies. Ignoring the threats of private contractors, he appointed the brilliant engineer CY O'Connor to design and build each of these as government projects.

Nationhood

On 1 January 1901, Australia became a federation. When the members of the new national parliament met in Melbourne, their first aim was to protect the identity and values of a European Australia from an influx of Asians and Pacific Islanders. The solution was a law which became known as the White Australia Policy. It became a racial tenet of faith in Australia for the next 70 years.

For whites who lived inside the charmed circle of citizenship, this was to be a model society, nestled in the skirts of the British Empire. Just one year later, white women won the right to vote in federal elections. In a series of radical innovations, the government introduced a broad social welfare scheme and it protected Australian wage levels with import tariffs.

Entering the World Stage

Living on the edge of a dry and forbidding land, isolated from the rest of the world, most Australians took comfort in the knowledge that they were a dominion of the British Empire. When war broke out in Europe in 1914, thousands of Australian men rallied to the Empire's call. They had their first taste of death on 25 April 1915, when the Australian and New Zealand Army Corps (the Anzacs) joined thousands of other British and French troops in an assault on the Gallipoli Peninsula in Turkey. It was eight months before the British commanders acknowledged that the tactic had failed. By then 8141 young Australians were dead. Before long the Australian Imperial Force was fighting in the killing fields of Europe. By the time the war ended, 60,000 Australians had died.

In the 1920s Australia embarked on a decade of chaotic change. The country careered wildly through the 1920s until it collapsed into the abyss of the Great Depression in 1929. World prices for wheat and wool plunged. Unemployment brought its shame and misery to one in three households.

Sticky Wicket

The year 1932 saw accusations of treachery on the cricket field. The English team, under captain Douglas Jardine, employed a violent new bowling tactic known as 'bodyline'. The aim was to unnerve Australia's star batsman, the devastatingly efficient Donald Bradman. The bitterness of the tour provoked a diplomatic crisis with Britain and became part of Australian legend. Bradman batted on. When he retired in 1948 he had a still-unsurpassed career average of 99.94 runs.

1965	1967	1975
Menzies commits Australian troops to the American war in Vietnam, and divides the nation.	In a national referendum, white Australians vote overwhelmingly to give citizenship to Indigenous people.	Against a background of reform and inflation, Governor General Sir John Kerr sacks the Whitlam government.

War with Japan

After 1933, the economy began to recover. Daily life was hardly dampened when Hitler hurled Europe into a new war in 1939. Though Australians had long feared Japan, they took it for granted that the British navy would keep them safe. In December 1941, Japan bombed the US Fleet at Pearl Harbor. Weeks later, the 'impregnable' British naval base in Singapore crumbled.

As the Japanese swept through Southeast Asia and into Papua New Guinea, the British announced that they could not spare any resources to defend Australia. But US commander General Douglas MacArthur saw that Australia was the perfect base for American operations in the Pacific. In fierce sea and land battles, Allied forces turned back the Japanese advance. Importantly, it was the USA, not the British Empire, who saved Australia. The days of alliance with Britain alone were numbered.

Visionary Peace

When WWII ended, a new slogan rang out: 'Populate or Perish!'. The Australian government embarked on a scheme to attract thousands of immigrants. People flocked from Britain and non-English-speaking countries. They included Greeks, Italians, Serbs, Croatians and Dutch, followed by Turks and many others.

In addition to growing world demand for Australia's primary products (wool, meat and wheat), there were jobs in manufacturing and on major public works, notably the mighty Snowy Mountains Hydro-Electric Scheme in the mountains near Canberra.

This era of growth and prosperity was dominated by Robert Menzies, the founder of the Liberal Party of Australia, and Australia's longest-serving prime minister. Menzies was steeped in British tradition, and was also a vigilant opponent of communism. As Asia succumbed to the chill of the Cold War, Australia and New Zealand entered a formal military alliance with the USA – the 1951 Anzus security pact. When the USA jumped into a civil war in Vietnam, Menzies committed Australian forces to battle. The following year Menzies retired, leaving his successors a bitter legacy.

In an atmosphere of youthful rebellion and new-found nationalism, the Labor Party was elected to power in 1972 under an idealistic lawyer named Gough Whitlam. In four short years his government transformed the country, ending conscription and abolishing university fees. He introduced a free universal health scheme, no-fault divorce, and the principles of Indigenous land rights and equal pay for women.

By 1975, the Whitlam government was rocked by inflation and scandal. At the end of 1975 his government was infamously dismissed from office by the governor general.

Australia Today

Today Australia faces new challenges. After two centuries of development, the strains on the environment are starting to show – on water supplies, forests, soil and the oceans.

1992	2000	2007
The High Court of Australia recognises the principle of native title in the Mabo decision.	The Sydney Olympic Games are a triumph of spectacle and goodwill.	Kevin Rudd is elected prime minister and says 'Sorry' to Australia's Indigenous peoples.

Aboriginal and Australian flags

Under John Howard, Australia's second-longest serving prime minister (1996–2007), the country grew closer to the USA, joining the Americans in their war in Iraq. The government's harsh treatment of asylum seekers, its refusal to acknowledge the reality of climate change, its anti-union reforms and the prime minister's lack of empathy with Indigenous peoples dismayed many liberal-minded Australians. But Howard presided over a period of economic growth and won continuing support in middle Australia.

In 2007, Howard was defeated by the Labor Party's Kevin Rudd, an ex-diplomat who immediately issued a formal apology to Indigenous Australians for the injustices they had suffered over the past two centuries. Though it promised sweeping reforms in environment and education, the Rudd government found itself faced with a crisis when the world economy crashed in 2008; by June 2010 it had cost Rudd his position. Incoming prime minister Julia Gillard, the first woman to hold the position, battled slow economic recovery and diminishing party support, eventually losing her job to a resurgent Rudd in June 2013. Rudd was then ousted again by his right-wing adversary Tony Abbott and the Liberal-National Party Coalition in the 2013 federal election. Then, in September 2015, Abbott was ousted in a leadership contest by Malcolm Turnbull, who became the fifth person to become Prime Minister in as many years.

2010

Rudd is ousted as prime minister by Julia Gillard, the first woman to hold the office.

2013

Gillard is deposed by Rudd, then Rudd is again ousted; this time by right-wing adversary Tony Abbott.

2015

Abbott is replaced by Malcolm Turnbull in a Liberal Party leadership spill. Touché!

Rock art, Ubirr (p234)

GRANT DIXON / GETTY IMAGES ©

Indigenous Australia

A visit to Australia would not be complete without experiencing the rich cultures of Aboriginal and Torres Strait Islander peoples. Visitors have an opportunity to learn and interact with the oldest continuous cultures in the world and share a way of life that has existed for over 50,000 years.
Cathy Craigie

Aboriginal Culture

Aboriginal cultures have evolved over thousands of years with strong links between the spiritual, economic and social lives of the people. This heritage has been kept alive from one generation to the next by the passing of knowledge through rituals, arts, cultural material and language.

Aboriginal culture has never been static, and continues to evolve with the changing times and environment. New technologies and mediums are now used to tell Aboriginal stories, and cultural tourism and hospitality ventures where visitors can experience an Aboriginal perspective have been established. You can learn about ancestral beings at particular natural landmarks, look at rock art that is thousands of years old, taste traditional foods or attend an Aboriginal festival or performance.

Land

Aboriginal land ethic is based on humans fitting into the ecology and not living outside of it. Everything is connected and not viewed as just soil and rocks but as a whole environment that sustains the spiritual, economic and cultural lives of the people. In turn, Aboriginal people have sustained the land by conducting ceremonies, rituals, songs and stories. For Aboriginal people land is intrinsically connected to identity and spirituality. Sacred sites can be parts of rocks, hills, trees or water and are associated with an ancestral being or an event that occurred. Often these sites are part of a Dreaming story and link people across areas.

Torres Strait Islanders

Aboriginal societies are diverse: not one homogenous group but several hundred different sovereign nations. Torres Strait Islanders are a Melanesian people with a separate culture to that of Aboriginal Australians but have a shared history with Aboriginal people, and together these two groups form Australia's Indigenous peoples.

The Arts

Aboriginal art has impacted the Australian landscape and is now showcased at national and international events and celebrated as a significant part of Australian culture. Exhibited in state institutions, independent theatres and galleries, Aboriginal art has slowly grown in its visibility. It still retains the role of passing on knowledge but today it is also important for economic, educational and political reasons.

Rock Art

Rock art is the oldest form of human art and Aboriginal rock art stretches back thousands of years. Rock art is found in every state of Australia and many sites are thousands of years old. There are a number of different styles of rock art across Australia. These include engravings in sandstone and stencils, prints and drawings in rock shelters.

Some of the oldest examples of engravings can be found in the Pilbara in Western Australia and in Olary in South Australia where there is an engraving of a crocodile. All national parks surrounding Sydney have rock engravings and can be easily accessed and viewed. At Gariwerd (the Grampians) in Victoria there are hand prints and hand stencils.

In the Northern Territory many of the rock-art sites have patterns and symbols that appear in paintings, carvings and other cultural material. Kakadu National Park has over 5000 recorded sites but many more are thought to exist.

Contemporary Art

The National Gallery of Australia in Canberra has a fantastic collection, but contemporary Aboriginal art can also be viewed at any public art gallery or in one of the many independent galleries dealing in Aboriginal work. The central desert area is still a hub for Aboriginal art and Alice Springs is one of the best places to see and buy art. Cairns is another hot spot for innovative Aboriginal art.

Music

Music has always been a vital part of Aboriginal culture. Songs were important for teaching and passing on knowledge; musical instruments were often used in healing, ceremonies

Indigenous artist

ANDREW WATSON / GETTY IMAGES ©

and rituals. The most well known instrument is the Yidaki or didgeridoo, which was traditionally only played by men in northern Australia.

This rich musical heritage continues today with a very strong contemporary music industry. Contemporary artists such as Dan Sultan and Jessica Mauboy have crossed over successfully into the mainstream, have won major music awards and can be seen regularly on popular programs and at major music festivals.

Performing Arts

Dance and theatre are a vital part of social and ceremonial life and important elements in Aboriginal culture. Historically, dances often told stories to pass on knowledge. Like other art forms, dance has adapted to the modern world and contemporary dance companies and groups have merged traditional forms into a modern interpretation. The most well-known dance company is the internationally acclaimed Bangarra Dance Theatre.

Theatre also draws on the storytelling tradition. Currently there are two major Aboriginal theatre companies, Ilbijerri in Melbourne and Yirra Yakin in Perth. Traditionally drama and dance came together in ceremonies or corroborees and this still occurs in many contemporary productions.

TV, Radio & Film

Aboriginal people have quickly adapted to electronic broadcasting and have developed an extensive media network of radio, print and television services. There are over 120 Aboriginal radio stations and programs operating across Australia in cities, rural areas and remote communities.

There is a thriving Aboriginal film industry and in recent years feature films including *The Sapphires*, *Bran Nue Day* and *Samson and Delilah* have had mainstream success. Since the first Aboriginal television channel, NITV, was launched in 2007, there has been a growth in the number of film-makers wanting to tell their stories.

Gurrumul

Described by *Rolling Stone* magazine as 'Australia's Most Important Voice', blind singer Geoffrey Gurrumul Yunupingu (www.gurrumul.com) sings in the Yolngu language from Arnhem Land. His angelic voice tells of identity, connecting with land and ancestral beings. Gurrumul has entranced Australian and overseas audiences and reached platinum with his two albums.

History of Indigenous Australia

First Australians

Many academics believe Aboriginal people came from somewhere else, and scientific evidence places Aboriginal people on the continent at least 40,000 to 50,000 years ago. However, Aboriginal people believe they have always inhabited the land.

At the time of European contact the Aboriginal population was grouped into 300 or more different nations with distinct languages and land boundaries. From the desert to the sea Aboriginal people shaped their lives according to their environments and developed different skills and a wide body of knowledge about their territory.

Colonised

The effects of colonisation started immediately after the Europeans arrived. Right from the start there was appropriation of land and water resources and an epidemic of diseases. Smallpox killed around 50% of Sydney Harbour's Indigenous population. A period of resistance occurred as Aboriginal people fought back to retain their land and way of life. As violence and massacres swept the country, many Aboriginal people were pushed further and further away from their traditional lands. In a period of just a hundred years, the Aboriginal population was decimated by 90%.

The Stolen Generations

When Australia became a Federation in 1901, a government policy known as the White Australia Policy was put in place. It was implemented to restrict nonwhite immigration to Australia but the policy also impacted on Indigenous Australia. Assimilation into the broader society was 'encouraged' by all sectors of government. An official policy of forcibly removing Aboriginal and Torres Strait Islander children from their families operated from 1909 to 1969. The generations of children who were taken from their families became known as the stolen generations. Today many still suffer from the trauma this policy inflicted.

On 13 February 2008 the then prime minister of Australia, Kevin Rudd, offered a national apology to the stolen generations.

Rights & Reconciliation

The relationship between Indigenous and 'white' Australia hasn't been an easy one. Aboriginal people had to adapt to the new culture but were treated like second-class citizens. Employment opportunities were scarce. This disadvantage has continued and even though successive government policies and programs have been implemented, there is still great disparity between Indigenous and other Australians, including lower standards of education, employment, health and living conditions, high incarceration and suicide rates, and a lower life expectancy.

Over the years several systematic policies have been put in place to aid reconciliation, but these have often had an underlying purpose including control over the land, decimating the population, protection, assimilation, self-determination and self-management. The history of forced resettlement, removal of children and the loss of land and culture cannot be erased even with governments addressing some of the issues. Current policies are focused on 'closing the gap' and centre on better delivery of essential services to improve lives.

Frilled-neck lizard

NATPHOTOS / GETTY IMAGES ©

Environment

Australia's plants and animals are just about the closest
things to alien life you are likely to encounter on earth.
That's because Australia has been isolated from the
other continents for a very long time – at least 45 million
years. Places like Sydney have preserved extraordinary
fragments of the original environment that are
relatively easy to access.
Dr Tim Flannery

Fundamentally Different

There are two really big factors that go a long way towards explaining nature in Australia: its soils and its climate. Both are unique.

On other continents in recent geological times, processes such as volcanism, mountain building and glacial activity have been busy creating new soil. All of these soil-forming processes have been almost absent from Australia. Under such conditions no new soil is created and the old soil is leached of all its goodness by the rain, and is blown and washed away. Australia is an old, infertile land, and life here has been adapting to these conditions for aeons.

Australia's misfortune in respect to soils is echoed in its climate. Most of Australia experiences seasons – sometimes very severe ones – yet life does not respond solely to them.

This can clearly be seen by the fact that although there's plenty of snow and cold country in Australia, there are almost no native trees that shed their leaves in winter, nor do many Australian animals hibernate. Instead there is a far more potent climatic force that Australian life must obey: El Niño.

El Niño is a complex climatic pattern that can cause major weather shifts around the South Pacific. The cycle of flood and drought that El Niño brings is profound. Australia's rivers – even the mighty Murray River, the nation's largest waterway – can be miles wide one year, yet you can literally step over its flow the next. This is the power of El Niño, and its effect, when combined with Australia's poor soils, manifests itself compellingly. As you might expect, relatively few of Australia's birds are seasonal breeders, and few migrate. Instead, they breed when the rain comes, and a large percentage are nomads, following the rain across the breadth of the continent.

Shark!

Despite media hype (and a particularly bad year in 2014, with five deaths), Australia has averaged just one shark-attack fatality per year since 1791 – a remarkably low number considering how many beaches there are around the coastline. Sydney in particular has a bad reputation. Attacks here peaked between 1920 and 1940, but since shark net installation began in 1937 there's only been one fatality (1963), and dorsal-fin sightings are rare enough to make the nightly news. Realistically, you're more likely to get hit by a bus – so look both ways before crossing the road on the way to the beach!

Fuel-Efficient Fauna

Australia is famous as the home of the kangaroo and other marsupials. Have you ever wondered why roos hop? It turns out that hopping is the most efficient way of getting about at medium speeds. This is because the energy of the bounce is stored in the tendons of the legs – much like in a pogo stick – while the intestines bounce up and down like a piston, emptying and filling the lungs without needing to activate the chest muscles.

Marsupials are so energy efficient that they need to eat one-fifth less food than equivalent-sized placental mammals (everything from bats to rats, whales and ourselves). But some have taken energy efficiency much further: if you visit a wildlife park or zoo you might notice that faraway look in a koala's eyes. Several years ago biologists announced that koalas are the only living creatures that have brains that don't fit their skulls. Instead they have a shrivelled walnut of a brain that rattles around in a fluid-filled cranium. There is no doubt that the koala is no Einstein of the animal world, and we now believe that it has sacrificed its brain to energy efficiency. Brains cost a lot to run – our brains typically weigh 2% of our body weight, but use 20% of the energy we consume. Koalas eat gum leaves, which are so toxic that koalas use 20% of their energy just detoxifying their food, leaving little energy for the brain.

The peculiar constraints of the Australian environment have not made everything dumb. The koala's nearest relative, the wombat (of which there are three species), has a large brain for a marsupial. These creatures live in complex burrows and can weigh up to 35kg, making them the largest herbivorous burrowers on earth.

Two unique monotremes (egg-laying mammals) live in Australia: the bumbling echidna, something akin to a hedgehog but bigger and spikier; and the platypus, a bit like an otter, with webbed feet and a duck-like bill. Echidnas are common along bushland trails, but platypuses are elusive, seen at dawn and dusk in quiet rivers and streams.

GREG ELMS / GETTY IMAGES ©

Food & Wine

Once upon a time in a decade not so far away, Australians proudly survived and thrived on a diet of 'meat and three veg'. Fine fare was a Sunday roast cooked to carcinogenic stages and lasagne was considered exotic. Fortunately, the country's culinary sophistication has evolved and, mirroring the population's cheeky and disobedient disposition, contemporary Australian cuisine now thrives on breaking rules and conventions.

Variety Is the Spice of Life

Visitors will find a huge range and wealth of food available in city restaurants, markets, delicatessens and cafes. Competition for the custom of savvy tastebud-owners is increasingly fierce, and standards are high. This is most evident in Sydney, Melbourne and Brisbane. In regional areas, variety diminishes along with the population.

Mod Oz?

The Australian propensity to absorb global influences is spurred by an inquisitive public willing to try new things. The result is dynamic and surprising cuisine, and what's hot this morning may be dated by tomorrow – or reinvented and improved.

MILTON WORDLEY / GETTY IMAGES ©

Immigration has been the key to Australia's culinary rise. A significant influx of migrants in the last 70 years, from Europe, Asia, the Middle East and Africa, has introduced new ingredients and new ways to use existing staples. Anything another country does, Australia does too: Vietnamese, Japanese, Fijian – no matter where it's from, there's an expat community here cooking and eating it. Dig deep enough and you'll find Jamaicans using scotch-bonnet peppers and Tunisians making tajine.

With this wealth of inspiration, urban Australians have become culinary snobs. In order to wow the socks off diners, restaurants must succeed in fusing contrasting ingredients and traditions into ever more innovative fare. The phrase Modern Australian (Mod Oz) has been coined to classify this unclassifiable technique: a melange of East and West, a swirl of Atlantic and Pacific Rim, and a dash of authentic French and Italian.

If this sounds overwhelming, fear not. Dishes are characterised by bold and interesting flavours, and fresh ingredients rather than fuss or clutter. Spicing ranges from gentle to extreme, seafood is plentiful and meats are tender and full flavoured. The range of food in Australia is its greatest culinary asset: all palates – timid or brave, shy or inquisitive – are well catered for.

Wine

Long recognised as some of the finest in the world, wine is now one of Australia's top exports. In fact, if you're in the country's cooler southern climes (or even in southeast Queensland), you're probably not far from a wine region. Some regions have been producing wines from the early days of settlement more than 220 years ago. Most wineries have small cellar door sales where you can taste for a nominal fee (or often free). Although

PHILIP GAME / GETTY IMAGES ©

★ **The Best Food Markets**

Queen Victoria Market (p158), Melbourne

Salamanca Market (p199), Hobart

Mindil Beach Sunset Market (p242), Darwin

Sydney Fish Market (p60)

Fremantle Markets (p253)

Queen Victoria Market (p158), Melbourne

plenty of good wine comes from big producers with economies of scale on their side, the most interesting wines are usually made by smaller, family-run wineries.

Beer

As the public develops a more demanding palate, Aussie beers are rising to the occasion, with a growing wealth of microbrewed flavours and varieties available. Have a look at www.findabrewery.com.au for brewery listings. Most beers have an alcohol content between 3.5% and 5.5% – less than many European beers but more than most in North America.

The terminology used when ordering beer varies state by state. In New South Wales you ask for a 'schooner' (425mL) if you're thirsty and a 'middy' (285mL) if you're not quite so dry. In Victoria a 285mL glass is a 'pot' and in Tasmania it's a '10 ounce' – but in most of the country you can just ask for a beer and wait to see what turns up. Pints (425mL or 568mL, depending on where you are) tend to warm quickly on a summer's day but are popular with the 'upsize' generation.

Spirits

In recent years, Tasmania – with its chilly Scotland-like highlands and clean water – has become a whisky producing hot spot. There are about a dozen distillers around the state now, bottling superb single malt for a growing international market. Keep an eye out for excellent drops from Sullivans Cove Whisky, Nant Distillery and Hellyers Road Distillery. Gins from Kangaroo Island Sprits in South Australia and Melbourne's Four Pillars are also impressive.

Coffee

Coffee has become a nationwide addiction: there are Italian-style espresso machines in virtually every cafe, boutique roasters are all the rage and, in urban areas, the qualified barista (coffee-maker) is the norm. Sydney, Melbourne and even subtropical Brisbane have borne generations of coffee snobs, but Melbourne takes top billing as Australia's caffeine capital. The cafe scene here rivals the most vibrant in the world: the best way to dunk yourself in it is by wandering the city centre's cafe-lined lanes.

Australian Rules football supporters

TOM COCKREM / GETTY IMAGES ©

Sport

Although Australia is relatively small population-wise (just over 23 million), its inhabitants constantly vie for kudos by challenging formidable sporting opponents around the globe in just about any event they can attempt. This has resulted in some extraordinary successes on the world stage. But it's the local football codes that really excite Aussies and tap into primal passions.

Australian Rules Football

Australia's number-one watched sport is Australian Rules football. Originally exclusive to Victoria, the Australian Football League (AFL; www.afl.com.au) has expanded into South Australia, Western Australia and even rugby-dominated New South Wales and Queensland. Long kicks, high marks and brutal collisions whip crowds into fevered frenzies: the roar of 50,000-plus fans yelling 'Carn the [insert team nickname]' and '*Baaalll!!!*' upsets dogs in suburban backyards for kilometres around.

★ **The Best Sporting Experiences**

Watching an AFL football game at the Melbourne Cricket Ground (p160)

Learning to surf at Byron Bay (p102)

Watching the Melbourne Cup (p28)

Watching the cricket in Melbourne (p160) or Sydney (p64)

MATT KING / STRINGER / GETTY IMAGES ©

Rugby

The National Rugby League (NRL; www.nrl.com.au) is the most popular football code north of the Murray River, with the season highlight the annual State of Origin series between New South Wales and Queensland. To witness an NRL game is to fully appreciate Newton's laws of motion – bone-crunching!

Meanwhile, the national rugby union team, the Wallabies, won the Rugby World Cup twice in the '90s and were runners-up in 2003, but couldn't make the semifinals in 2007. Third place in 2011 was some consolation, but coming second to New Zealand in 2015 was a bitter pill. In between World Cups, Bledisloe Cup games against New Zealand are hotly contested.

Soccer

Australia's star-studded national soccer team, the Socceroos, won the 2015 Asian Cup and qualified for the 2006, 2010 and 2014 World Cups, after a long history of almost-but-not-quite getting there. Results were mixed, but national pride in the team remains undiminished. The national A-League (www.a-league.com.au) has enjoyed increased popularity in recent years.

Cricket

The Aussies dominated international Test and one-day cricket for much of the naughties, but the retirements of once-in-a-lifetime players like Shane Warne and Ricky Ponting exposed a leaky pool of second-tier talent. A 'rebuilding phase' ensued, accompanied by several Test series losses to arch-rivals England. But things are looking up: Australia won the 2015 Cricket World Cup, and the one-day squad is again among the world's best.

Tennis

Every January, tennis shoes melt in the Melbourne heat at the Australian Open (www.ausopen.com), one of tennis' four Grand Slam tournaments. Tennis greats battle it out in the often searing heat, while spectators swelter courtside (or lounge at home in the air-con). Novak Djokovic currently holds the record for most titles.

Horse Racing

Australian's love to bet on the 'nags'. On the first Tuesday in November the nation stops for a world-famous horse race, the Melbourne Cup (www.melbournecup.com). In Victoria it's cause for a holiday. Australia's most famous cup winner was Phar Lap, who won in 1930, and later died of a mystery illness in the USA. Makybe Diva is a more recent star, winning three Melbourne Cups in a row before retiring in 2005.

The Twelve Apostles, Great Ocean Road (p190)

Australia Outdoors

Australia is a natural adventure playground and its sheer size means there is an incredible range of outdoor activities. The easy-on-the-eye landscape, so much of it still refreshingly free from the pressures of overpopulation, lends itself to any number of energetic pursuits and pure natural fun, whether you're on a wilderness trail or ski slope, under the sea beside a coral reef, or catching a wave.

Bushwalking

Bushwalking is supremely popular in Australia, with national parks and vast tracts of untouched scrub and forest providing ample opportunity. June to August are the best walking months up north; in the south, summer months are better.

Lonely Planet's *Walking in Australia* provides detailed information and trail notes for Australia's best bushwalks. Online, look at www.bushwalkingaustralia.org. The book *Sydney's Best Harbour & Coastal Walks* details the excellent 5.5km Bondi to Coogee Clifftop Walk and the 10km Manly Scenic Walkway, in addition to wilder walks.

Other good sources of bushwalking information and trail descriptions are outdoor stockists and the websites of the various state government national parks departments. Online, see www.lonelyplanet.com/australia/things-to-do/bushwalking-in-australia.

DOUGLAS PEARSON / GETTY IMAGES ©

Cycling

Avid cyclists have access to great routes and can tour the country for days, weekends or even on multiweek trips.

Victoria is a super state for on- and off-road cycling and mountain biking. Standout routes for longer rides in this state include the Murray to the Mountains Rail Trail and the East Gippsland Rail Trail. In Western Australia, the Munda Biddi Mountain Bike Trail offers 900km of pedal power; you can tackle the same distance on the Mawson Trail in South Australia. Down south, the Tasmania Trail is a 480km mountain-bike route across the island state. There's also a whole network of routes around the country that follow disused railway and tram lines: www.railtrails.org.au describes these and other routes.

Rates charged by most bike-hire companies for renting road or mountain bikes are usually around $20 per hour and $40 per day. Security deposits can range from $50 to $200, depending on the rental period.

Online, www.bicycles.net.au is a useful resource; in print, there's Lonely Planet's *Cycling Australia*.

Diving & Snorkelling

Professional Association of Diving Instructors (PADI) dive courses are offered throughout the country. Learning here is fairly inexpensive: PADI courses range from two to five days and cost anything between $350 and $850. Also, don't forget you can enjoy the marine life by snorkelling; hiring a mask, snorkel and fins is an affordable way to get underwater.

In Queensland, the Great Barrier Reef has more dazzling dive sites than you can poke a fin at. There are coral reefs off some mainland beaches and around several of the islands, and many day trips to the Great Barrier Reef provide snorkelling gear free.

North of Sydney in New South Wales, try Broughton Island near Port Stephens, and, further north, Fish Rock Cave off South West Rocks is renowned for its excellent diving, with shells, schools of clownfish and humpback whales. You can swim with grey nurse sharks at the Pinnacles near Forster, and leopard sharks at Julian Rocks Marine Reserve off Byron Bay. On the NSW south coast popular diving spots include Jervis Bay, Montague Island and Merimbula.

In WA, Ningaloo Reef is every bit as interesting as the east-coast coral reefs, without the tourist numbers.

Check out www.diveoz.com.au online for nationwide info.

Skiing & Snowboarding

Australia has a small but enthusiastic skiing industry, with snowfields straddling the NSW–Victoria border. The season is relatively short, however, running from about mid-June to early September, with unpredictable snowfalls. The top places to ski are in the Snowy Mountains in NSW (Perisher and Thredbo snowfields), and Mt Buller, Falls Creek and Mt Hotham in Victoria's High Country. Cross-country skiing is popular and most resorts offer lessons and equipment.

See www.ski.com.au for ski-cams, and www.ski-australia.com.au for info on the Perisher, Falls Creek, Mt Buller and Thredbo snowfields.

Surfing

World-class waves can be found all around Australia, from Queensland's subtropical Gold Coast, along the NSW coast and at beaches in Victoria, Tasmania, SA and WA. Visit surf shops for board hire and surf school info. If you've never surfed before, a lesson or two will get you started.

In NSW, Sydney is strewn with ocean beaches with decent breaks. Further north, Crescent Head is the longboard capital of Australia, and there are brilliant breaks at Lennox Head and Byron Bay. The NSW south coast also has great surf beaches – try Wollongong and Merimbula.

There are some magical breaks along Queensland's southeastern coast, most notably at Coolangatta, Burleigh Heads, Surfers Paradise, North Stradbroke Island and Noosa.

Victoria's Southern Ocean coastline has impressive surf. Local and international surfers head to Torquay, while Bells Beach hosts the annual Rip Curl Pro comp. For the less experienced, there are surf schools in Victoria at Anglesea, Lorne and Phillip Island. Elsewhere, southern WA is a surfing mecca (head for Margaret River), while Tasmania has some remote cold-water surf spots.

See www.coastalwatch.com for forecasts and surf-cams.

Wildlife Watching

Wildlife is one of Australia's top selling points. Most national parks are home to native fauna, although much of it is nocturnal so you may need good flashlight skills to spot it. Australia is also a twitcher's haven, with a wide variety of birdlife, particularly water birds.

In NSW there are platypuses and gliders in New England National Park, and 120 bird species in Dorrigo National Park. The Border Ranges National Park is home to a quarter of all of Australia's bird species. Willandra National Park is World Heritage–listed and has dense temperate wetlands and wildlife, and koalas are everywhere around Port Macquarie. In Victoria, Wilsons Promontory National Park teems with wildlife – in fact, wombats seem to have right of way.

In Queensland, head to Malanda for birdlife, turtles and pademelons (small wallabies); Cape Tribulation for even better birdlife; Magnetic Island for koala spotting; Fraser Island for dingoes; and the Daintree for cassowaries. In SA, make a beeline for Flinders Chase National Park on Kangaroo Island where you can see platypuses, kangaroos and New Zealand fur seals.

In Tasmania, Maria Island is another twitcher's paradise, while Mt William and Mt Field National Parks and Bruny Island teem with native fauna. In the Northern Territory, head for Kakadu National Park where birdlife is abundant and you can spot crocodiles. Western Australia also has ample birdwatching hot spots, while Canberra has the richest birdlife of any Australian capital city.

MATT MUNRO / GETTY IMAGES ©

Survival Guide

Directory A–Z

Accommodation

Australia offers everything from the tent-pegged confines of camp sites and the communal spaces of hostels to gourmet breakfasts in guesthouses, farmstays and indulgent resorts, plus the full gamut of hotel and motel lodgings.

During the summer high season (December to February) and at other peak times, particularly school holidays and Easter, prices are usually at their highest. Outside these times you'll find useful discounts and lower walk-in rates. Notable exceptions include central Australia, the Top End and Australia's ski resorts, where summer is the low season and prices drop substantially.

B&Bs

Australian bed-and-breakfast options include restored miners' cottages, converted barns, rambling old houses, upmarket country manors and beachside bungalows. Tariffs are typically in the midrange bracket, but can be higher. In areas that attract weekenders – historic towns, wine regions, accessible forest regions such as the Blue Mountains in New South Wales and the Dandenongs in Victoria – B&Bs are often upmarket, charging small fortunes for weekend stays in high season.

Some places advertised as B&Bs are actually self-contained cottages with breakfast provisions supplied. Only in the cheaper B&Bs will bathroom facilities be shared. Some B&B hosts may also cook dinner for guests (usually 24 hours' notice is required).

Online resources include:

Beautiful Accommodation (www.beautifulaccommodation. com) A select crop of luxury B&Bs and self-contained houses.

Hosted Accommodation Australia (www. australianbedandbreakfast.com. au) Listings for B&Bs, farmstays, cottages and homesteads.

OZ Bed and Breakfast (www. ozbedandbreakfast.com) Nationwide website.

Holiday Apartments

Costs For a two-bedroom flat, you're looking at anywhere from $140 to $200 per night, but you will pay much more in high season and for serviced apartments in major cities.

Facilities Self-contained holiday apartments range from simple, studio-like rooms with small kitchenettes, to two-bedroom apartments with full laundries and state-of-the-art entertainment systems: great value for multi-night stays. Sometimes they come in small, single-storey blocks, but in tourist hot spots such as the Gold Coast expect a sea of high-rises.

Hotels

Hotels in Australian cities or well-touristed places are generally of the business or luxury-chain variety (midrange to top end): comfortable, anonymous, mod-con-filled rooms in multi-storey blocks. For these hotels we quote 'rack rates' (official advertised

---

Book Your Stay Online

For more accommodation reviews by Lonely Planet authors, check out www. lonelyplanet.com/hotels. You'll find independent reviews, as well as recommendations on the best places to stay. Best of all, you can book online.

Practicalities

DVDs Australian DVDs are encoded for Region 4, which includes Mexico, South America, Central America, New Zealand, the Pacific and the Caribbean.

Newspapers Leaf through the daily *Sydney Morning Herald*, Melbourne's *Age* or the national *Australian* broadsheet newspaper.

Radio Tune in to ABC radio; check out www.abc.net.au/radio.

Smoking Banned on public transport, in pubs, bars and eateries, and in some public outdoor spaces.

TV The main free-to-air TV channels are the government-sponsored ABC, multicultural SBS and the three commercial networks – Seven, Nine and Ten. Numerous free spin-off and local channels enrich the viewing brew.

Weights & Measures Australia uses the metric system.

rates – usually upwards of $160 a night), though significant discounts can be offered when business is quiet.

Motels

Drive-up motels offer comfortable midrange accommodation and are found all over Australia, often on the edges of urban centres. They rarely offer a cheaper rate for singles, so are better value for couples or groups of three. You'll mostly pay between $120 and $160 for a simple room with a kettle, fridge, TV, air-con and bathroom.

Other Accommodation

There are lots of less-conventional and, in some cases, uniquely Australian accommodation possibilities scattered across the country.

Country farms sometimes offer a bed for a night, while some remote outback stations allow you to stay in homestead rooms or shearers' quarters and try activities such as horse riding. Check out **Hosted Accommodation**

Australia (www.australianbedandbreakfast.com.au) and **Farmstay Camping Australia** (www.farmstaycampingaustralia.com.au) for options. State tourist offices can also help.

Back within city limits, it's sometimes possible to stay in the hostels and halls of residence normally occupied by university students, though you'll need to time your stay to coincide with the longer university holiday periods.

Climate

Cairns

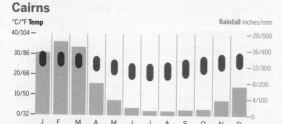

Sydney

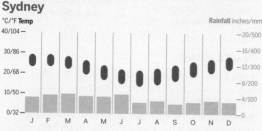

Melbourne

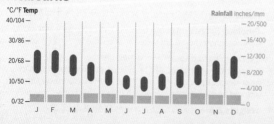

Customs Regulations

For detailed information on customs and quarantine regulations, contact the **Australian Customs & Border Protection Service** (☑1300 363 263, 02-6275 6666; www.customs.gov.au).

When entering Australia you can bring most articles in free of duty provided that customs is satisfied they are for personal use and that you'll be taking them with you when you leave. Duty-free quotas per person:

Alcohol 2.25L (over 18 years old)

Cigarettes 50 cigarettes (over 18 years old)

Dutiable goods Up to the value of $900 ($450 for under 18s)

Narcotics are illegal, and customs inspectors and their highly trained hounds are diligent in sniffing them out. Quarantine regulations are strict, so you *must* declare all goods of animal or vegetable origin – wooden spoons, straw hats, the lot. Fresh food (meat, cheese, fruit, vegetables etc) and flowers are prohibited.

Discount Cards

Travellers over 60 with some form of identification (eg a state-issued seniors card or overseas equivalent) are sometimes eligible for concession prices for public transport.

The internationally recognised International Student Identity Card (ISIC; www.isic.org) is available to full-time students aged 12 and over. The card gives the bearer discounts on accommodation, transport and admission to various attractions. The same organisation also produces the International Youth Travel Card (IYTC), issued to people under 26 years of age and not full-time students; also similar is the International Teacher Identity Card (ITIC), available to teaching professionals. All three cards are available online and from student travel companies ($30).

Electricity

220V/50Hz

Food

See the Food & Wine chapter (p292). Throughout this guide, the following price ranges refer to a standard main course:

$ less than $15
$$ $15 to $32
$$$ more than $32

Gay & Lesbian Travellers

Australia is a popular destination for gay and lesbian travellers, with the so-called 'pink tourism' appeal of Sydney especially big, thanks largely to the city's annual, high-profile and spectacular Sydney Gay & Lesbian Mardi Gras. In general, Australians are open-minded about homosexuality, but the further from the cities you get, the more likely you are to run into overt homophobia.

Throughout the country, but particularly on the east coast, there are tour operators, travel agents and accommodation places that make a point of welcoming gay men and lesbians.

Same-sex acts are legal in all states but the age of consent varies.

Major Gay & Lesbian Events

Midsumma Festival (www.midsumma.org.au) Melbourne's annual gay-and-lesbian arts festival features more than 100 events from mid-January to mid-February, with a Pride March finale.

Sydney Gay & Lesbian Mardi Gras (www.mardigras.org.au) A two-week festival culminating in the world-famous massive parade and party on the first Saturday in March.

Resources

Major cities have gay newspapers, available from clubs, cafes, venues and newsagents.

Gay & Lesbian Tourism Australia (Galta; www.galta.com.au) General info.

Same Same (www.samesame.com.au) News, events and lifestyle features.

Health

Healthwise, Australia is a remarkably safe country in which to travel, considering that such a large portion of it lies in the tropics. Few travellers to Australia will experience anything worse than an upset stomach or a bad hangover and, if you do fall ill, the standard of hospitals and health care is high.

Vaccinations

Visit a physician four to eight weeks before departure. Ask your doctor for an International Certificate of Vaccination (aka the 'yellow booklet'), which will list the vaccinations you've received.

Upon entering Australia, you'll be required to fill out a 'travel history card' detailing any visits to Ebola-affected regions within the last 21 days.

If entering Australia within six days of staying overnight or longer in a yellow-fever-infected country, you'll need proof of yellow-fever vaccination. For a full list of these countries visit

Where the Wild Things Are

Australia's profusion of dangerous creatures is legendary: snakes, spiders, sharks, crocodiles, jellyfish... Travellers needn't be alarmed, though – you're unlikely to see many of these creatures in the wild, much less be attacked by one.

Crocodiles Around the northern Australian coastline, saltwater crocodiles are a real danger. They also inhabit estuaries, creeks and rivers, sometimes a long way inland. Observe safety signs or ask locals whether that inviting-looking waterhole or river is croc-free before plunging in.

Jellyfish With venomous tentacles up to 3m long, box jellyfish (aka sea wasps or stingers) inhabit Australia's tropical waters. You can be stung during any month, but they're most common during the wet season (October to March) when you should stay out of the sea in many places. Stinger nets are in place at some beaches, but check before swimming. 'Stinger suits' (full-body swimsuits) and wetsuits prevent stinging. If you are stung, wash the skin with vinegar then go to a hospital.

Sharks Despite the media coverage, the risk of shark attack in Australia is no greater than in other countries with extensive coastlines. Check with surf life-saving groups about local risks.

Snakes There's no denying it: Australia has plenty of venomous snakes. Most common are brown and tiger snakes, but few species are aggressive. Unless you're messing around with or accidentally standing on one, it's extremely unlikely that you'll get bitten. The golden rule: if you see a snake, let it be. If you are bitten, prevent the spread of venom by applying pressure to the wound and immobilising the area with a splint or sling before seeking medical attention.

Spiders Australia has several poisonous spiders, bites from which are usually treatable with antivenins. The deadly funnel-web spider lives in New South Wales (including Sydney) – bites are treated as per snake bites (pressure and immobilisation before transferring to a hospital). Redback spiders live throughout Australia; bites cause pain, sweating and nausea. Apply ice or cold packs, then transfer to hospital. White-tailed spider bites may cause an ulcer that's slow and difficult to heal. Clean the wound and seek medical assistance. The disturbingly large huntsman spider is harmless, though seeing one can affect your blood pressure and/or underpants.

Internet Resources

There's a wealth of travel health advice on the internet:

Lonely Planet (www.lonely planet.com) A good place to start; check out the Thorntree forum.

World Health Organization (www.who.int/ith) Publishes *International Travel & Health*, revised annually, available free online.

MD Travel Health (www. mdtravelhealth.com) Complete travel health recommendations for every country, updated daily.

Government travel health websites include the following:

Australia (www.smartraveller. gov.au)

Canada (www.hc-sc.gc.ca)

UK (www.nhs.uk/livewell/ travelhealth)

USA (www.cdc.gov/travel)

Availability & Cost of Health Care

Facilities Australia has an excellent health-care system. It's a mixture of privately run medical clinics and hospitals alongside a system of public hospitals funded by the Australian government. There are also excellent specialised public-health facilities for women and children in major centres.

Medicare The Medicare system covers Australian residents for some health-care costs. Visitors from countries with which Australia has a reciprocal health-care agreement – New Zealand, the Republic of Ireland, Sweden, the Netherlands, Finland, Italy, Belgium, Malta, Slovenia, Norway and the UK – are eligible for benefits specified under the Medicare program.

Centers for Disease Control & Prevention (www.cdc.gov/travel).

The **World Health Organization** (www.who.int) recommends that all travellers should be covered for diphtheria, tetanus, measles, mumps, rubella, chicken pox and polio, as well as hepatitis B, regardless of their destination. While Australia has high levels of childhood vaccination coverage, outbreaks of these diseases do occur.

See www.humanservices.gov.au/customer/dhs/medicare.

Medications Painkillers, antihistamines for allergies, and skincare products are widely available at chemists throughout Australia. You may find that medications readily available over the counter in some countries are only available in Australia by prescription. These include the oral contraceptive pill, some medications for asthma and all antibiotics.

Insurance

Worldwide travel insurance is available at www.lonelyplanet.com. You can buy, extend and claim online anytime – even if you're already on the road.

Level of Cover A good travel insurance policy covering theft, loss and medical problems is essential. Some policies specifically exclude designated 'dangerous activities' such as scuba diving, skiing and even bushwalking. Make sure the policy you choose fully covers you for your activity of choice.

Car See p314 for information on vehicle insurance.

Health You may prefer a policy that pays doctors or hospitals directly rather than requiring you to pay on the spot and claim later. If you have to claim later make sure you keep all documentation. Check that the policy covers ambulances and emergency medical evacuations by air.

Internet Access

There are fewer internet cafes around these days than there were five years ago (thanks to

the advent of iPhones/iPads and wi-fi) but you'll still find them in most sizeable towns. Hourly costs range from $6 to $10. Most accommodation is phasing out internet terminals and kiosks in favour of wi-fi.

Most public libraries have internet access, but generally it's provided for research needs, not for travellers to check Facebook – so book ahead or find an internet cafe.

BYO

If you're bringing your palmtop or laptop, check with your Internet Service Provider (ISP) for access numbers you can dial into in Australia.

ISPs

Some major Australian ISPs:
Australia On Line (☏1300 650 661; www.ozonline.com.au)

Dodo (☏13 36 36; www.dodo.com)

iinet (☏13 19 17; www.iinet.net.au)

iPrimus (☏13 17 89; www.iprimus.com.au)

Optus (☏1800 780 219; www.optus.com.au)

Telstra (☏13 76 63; www.telstra.com.au)

Modem

Keep in mind that your PC-card modem may not work in Australia. The safest option is to buy a reputable 'global' modem before you leave home or buy a local PC-card modem once you get to Australia.

Wi-Fi

It's still rare in remote Australia, but wireless internet access is increasingly the norm in urban Australian accommodation. Cafes, bars and even

some public gardens and town squares also provide wi-fi access. For locations, visit www.freewifi.com.au.

Legal Matters

Most travellers will have no contact with Australia's police or legal system; if they do, it's most likely to be while driving.

Driving There's a significant police presence on central Australian roads, and police have the power to stop your car, see your licence (you're required to carry it), check your vehicle for roadworthiness, and insist that you take a breath test for alcohol (and sometimes illicit drugs).

Drugs First-time offenders caught with small amounts of illegal drugs are likely to receive a fine rather than go to jail, but the recording of a conviction against you may affect your visa status.

Visas If you remain in Australia beyond the life of your visa, you'll officially be an 'overstayer' and could face detention and then be prevented from returning to Australia for up to three years.

Arrested? It's your right to telephone a friend, lawyer or relative before questioning begins. Legal aid is available only in serious cases; for Legal Aid office info see www.nationallegalaid.org. However, many solicitors do not charge for an initial consultation.

Money

The Australian dollar comprises 100 cents. There are 5c, 10c, 20c, 50c, $1 and $2 coins,

Interstate Quarantine

When travelling within Australia, whether by land or air, you'll come across signs (mainly in airports and interstate train stations and at state borders) warning of the possible dangers of carrying fruit, vegetables and plants from one area to another. Certain pests and diseases (fruit fly, cucurbit thrips, grape phylloxera...) are prevalent in some areas but not in others: authorities would like to limit their spreading.

There are quarantine inspection posts on some state borders. Many posts are staffed and officers are entitled to search your car for undeclared items. Generally they will confiscate all fresh fruit and vegetables, so it's best to leave shopping for these items until the first town past the inspection point.

and $5, $10, $20, $50 and $100 notes. Prices in shops are often marked in single cents then rounded to the nearest 5c when you come to pay.

In this book, prices refer to the Australian dollar.

ATMs & Eftpos

ATMs Australia's 'big four' banks – ANZ, Commonwealth, National Australia Bank and Westpac – and affiliated banks have branches all over Australia, plus a slew of 24-hour automated teller machines (ATMs). But don't expect to find ATMs *everywhere,* certainly not off the beaten track or in small towns. Most ATMs accept cards issued by other banks (for a fee) and are linked to international networks.

Eftpos Most service stations, supermarkets, restaurants, cafes and shops have Electronic Funds Transfer at Point of Sale (Eftpos) facilities these days, allowing you to make purchases and even draw out cash with your credit or debit card.

Fees Bear in mind that withdrawing cash via ATMs or Eftpos may attract significant fees – check the associated costs with your bank first.

Credit Cards

Credit cards such as Visa and MasterCard are widely accepted for everything from a hostel bed or a restaurant meal to an adventure tour, and are pretty much essential (in lieu of a large deposit) for hiring a car. They can also be used to get cash advances over the counter at banks and from many ATMs, depending on the card, though these transactions incur immediate interest. Diners Club and American Express (Amex) are not as widely accepted.

Lost credit-card contact numbers:

American Express (☏1300 132 639; www.americanexpress.com.au)

Diners Club (☏1300 360 060; www.dinersclub.com.au)

MasterCard (☏1800 120 113; www.mastercard.com.au)

Visa (☏1800 450 346; www.visa.com.au)

Debit Cards

A debit card allows you to draw money directly from your home bank account using ATMs, banks or Eftpos machines. Any card connected to the international banking network – Cirrus, Maestro, Plus and Eurocard – should work with your PIN. Expect substantial fees.

Companies such as Travelex offer debit cards with set withdrawal fees and a balance you can top up from your personal bank account while on the road.

Exchanging Money

Changing foreign currency (or travellers cheques, if you're still using them) is usually no problem at banks throughout Australia, or at licensed money-changers such as Travelex or Amex in cities and major towns.

Taxes & Refunds

Goods & Services Tax (GST)
The GST is a flat 10% tax on all goods and services – accommodation, eating out, transport, electrical and other goods, books, furniture, clothing etc. There are exceptions, however, such as basic foods (milk, bread, fruit and vegetables etc). By law the tax is included in the quoted or shelf price, so all prices are GST-inclusive. International air and sea travel to/from Australia is GST-free, as is domestic air travel when purchased outside Australia by nonresidents.

Refund of GST If you purchase goods with a total minimum value of $300 from any one supplier no more than 30 days before you leave Australia, you are entitled under the Tourist Refund Scheme (TRS) to a refund of any GST paid. The scheme only applies to goods you take with you as hand luggage or wear onto the plane or ship. Also note that the refund is valid for goods bought from more than one supplier, but only if at least $300 is spent in each. For more info, see the website of the **Australian Customs & Border Protection Service** (1300 363 263, 02-6275 6666; www.customs.gov.au).

Income Tax Visitors pay tax on earnings made within Australia, and must lodge a tax return with the Australian Taxation Office (ATO). If too much tax was withheld from your pay, you will receive a refund. See the **Australian Taxation Office** (www.ato.gov.au) website for details.

Travellers Cheques

o The ubiquity and convenience of internationally linked credit and debit card facilities in Australia means that travellers cheques are virtually redundant.

o Amex and Travelex will exchange their associated travellers cheques, and major banks will change travellers cheques also.

o In all instances you'll need to present your passport for identification when cashing them.

Opening Hours

Business hours vary from state to state, but use the following as a guide. Note that nearly all attractions across Australia are closed on Christmas Day; many also close on New Years Day and Good Friday.

Banks 9.30am to 4pm Monday to Thursday; until 5pm on Friday. Some large city branches open 8am to 6pm weekdays; a few also till 9pm Friday.

Cafes All-day affairs opening from around 7am until around 5pm, or continuing their business into the night.

Petrol stations and roadhouses Usually open 8am to 10pm. Some urban service stations open 24 hours.

Post offices 9am to 5pm Monday to Friday; some from 9am to noon on Saturday. You can also buy stamps from newsagents and some delis.

Pubs Usually serve food from noon to 2pm and from 6pm to 8pm. Pubs and bars often open for drinking at lunchtime and continue well into the evening, particularly from Thursday to Saturday.

Restaurants Open around noon for lunch and from 6pm for dinner, typically serving until at least 2pm and 9pm respectively, often later. Big-city eateries keep longer hours.

Shops and businesses 9am to 5pm or 6pm Monday to Friday; until either noon or 5pm on Saturday. Sunday trading operates in major cities, urban areas and tourist towns. There is late-night shopping till 9pm in major towns (usually Thursday or Friday night).

Supermarkets Generally open from 7am until at least 8pm; some open 24 hours. Delis (general stores) also open late.

Public Holidays

Timing of public holidays can vary from state to state: check locally for precise dates. Some holidays are only observed locally within a state; where this is the case, the relevant town, city or region is also listed.

National

New Year's Day 1 January

Australia Day 26 January

Easter (Good Friday to Easter Monday inclusive) late March/ early April

Anzac Day 25 April

Queen's Birthday (except WA) Second Monday in June

Queen's Birthday (WA) Last Monday in September

Christmas Day 25 December

Boxing Day 26 December

Australian Capital Territory

Canberra Day Second Monday in March

Bank Holiday First Monday in August

Labour Day First Monday in October

New South Wales

Bank Holiday First Monday in August

Labour Day First Monday in October

Northern Territory

May Day First Monday in May

Show Day (Alice Springs) First Friday in July; (Darwin) fourth Friday in July

Picnic Day First Monday in August

Queensland

Labour Day First Monday in May

Tasmania

Regatta Day (Hobart) 14 February

Eight Hours Day First Monday in March

Bank Holiday Tuesday following Easter Monday

Hobart Show Day (Hobart) Thursday preceding fourth Saturday in October

Victoria

Labour Day Second Monday in March

Melbourne Cup Day First Tuesday in November

Western Australia

Labour Day First Monday in March

Foundation Day First Monday in June

School Holidays

o The Christmas/summer school holiday season runs from mid-December to late January.

o Three shorter school holiday periods occur during the year, varying by a week or two from state to state. They fall roughly from early to mid-April (usually including Easter), late June to mid-July, and late September to early October.

Safe Travel

Australia is a relatively safe place to travel by world standards – crime- and war-wise at any rate – but natural disasters regularly wreak havoc. Bushfires, floods and cyclones decimate parts of most states and territories, but if you pay attention to warnings from local authorities and don't venture into affected areas, you should be fine.

Telephone

Australia's main telecommunication companies:

Telstra (☎13 22 00; www.telstra.com.au)

Optus (☎1800 780 219; www.optus.com.au)

Vodafone (☎1300 650 410; www.vodafone.com.au)

Virgin (☎1300 555 100; www.virginmobile.com.au)

Toll-Free & Information Calls

o Many businesses have either a toll-free ☎1800 number, dialled from anywhere within Australia for free, or a ☎13 or ☎1300 number, charged at a local call rate. None of these numbers can be dialled from outside Australia (and often can't be dialled from mobile phones within Australia).

o To make a reverse-charge (collect) call from any public or private phone, dial ☎1800 738 3773 or ☎12 550.

o Numbers starting with ☎190 are usually recorded information services, charged at anything from 35c to $5 or more per minute (more from mobiles and payphones).

International Calls

When calling overseas you will need to dial the international access code from Australia (☎0011 or ☎0018), the country code and then the area code (without the initial ☎0). So for a London telephone number you'll need

to dial ☎0011-44-20, then the number. In addition, certain operators will have you dial a special code to access their service. If dialling Australia from overseas, the country code is ☎61 and you need to drop the ☎0 in state/territory area codes.

Local Calls

Local calls from private phones cost up to 30c, depending on the provider; local calls from public phones cost 50c. Calls to mobile phones attract higher rates and are timed.

Long-Distance Calls & Area Codes

Long-distance calls (over around 50km) are timed. Australia uses four Subscriber Trunk Dialling (STD) area codes. These STD calls can be made from any public phone and are cheaper during off-peak hours (generally between 7pm and 7am, and on weekends). Broadly, the main area codes are as follows.

State/ Territory	Area Code
ACT	☎02
NSW	☎02
NT	☎08
QLD	☎07
SA	☎08
TAS	☎03
VIC	☎03
WA	☎08

Area code boundaries don't necessarily coincide with state borders; for example some parts of NSW use the neighbouring states' codes.

Mobile (Cell) Phones

Numbers Numbers with the prefix 04xx belong to mobile phones.

Networks Australia's digital network is compatible with GSM 900 and 1800 (used in Europe), but generally not with the systems used in the USA or Japan.

Reception Australia's mobile networks service more than 90% of the population but leave vast tracts of the country uncovered.

Prioviders It's easy enough to get connected short-term: the main service providers (Telstra, Optus, Virgin and Vodafone) all have prepaid mobile systems. Buy a starter kit, which may include a phone or, if you have your own phone, a SIM card and a prepaid charge card. Shop around for the best offer.

Phonecards & Public Phones

Phonecards A variety of phonecards can be bought at newsagents, hostels and post offices for a fixed dollar value (usually $10, $20 etc) and can be used with any public or private phone by dialling a toll-free access number and then the PIN on the card. Shop around.

Public phones Most public phones use phonecards; some also accept credit cards. Old-fashioned coin-operated public phones are becoming increasingly rare (and if you do find one, chances are the coin slot will be gummed up or vandalised beyond function).

Time

Zones Australia is divided into three time zones: Western Standard Time (GMT/UTC plus eight hours), covering WA; Central Standard Time (plus 9½ hours), covering SA and the NT; and Eastern Standard Time (plus 10 hours), covering Tasmania, Victoria, NSW, the ACT and Queensland. There are minor exceptions – Broken Hill (NSW), for instance, is on Central Standard Time. For international times, see www.timeanddate.com/worldclock.

Daylight saving Clocks are put forward an hour. This system operates in some states during the warmer months (October to early April), but things can get pretty confusing. Queensland, WA and the NT stay on standard time, while in Tasmania daylight saving starts a month earlier than in SA, Victoria, ACT and NSW.

Tourist Information

The **Australian Tourist Commission** (www.australia.com) is the national government tourist body, and has a good website for pre-trip research. The website also lists reliable travel agents in countries around the world to help you plan your trip, plus visa, work and customs information.

Within Australia, tourist information is disseminated by various regional and local offices. Almost every major town in Australia has a tourist office of some type and they can be super helpful, with chatty staff (often retiree volunteers) providing local info not readily available from the state offices. If booking accommodation or tours from local offices, bear in mind that they often only promote businesses that are paying members of the local tourist association.

Travellers with Disabilities

o Disability awareness in Australia is high and getting higher.

o Legislation requires that new accommodation meets accessibility standards for mobility-impaired travellers, and discrimination by tourism operators is illegal.

o Many of Australia's key attractions, including many national parks, provide access for those with limited mobility and a number of sites also address the needs of visitors with visual or aural impairments. Contact attractions in advance to confirm the facilities.

o Tour operators with vehicles catering to mobility-impaired travellers operate from most capital cities.

o Facilities for wheelchairs are improving in accommodation, but there are still many older establishments where the necessary upgrades haven't been done.

Government Travel Advice

The following government websites offer travel advisories and information on current hot spots:

Australian Department of Foreign Affairs & Trade (www.smarttraveller.gov.au)

British Foreign & Commonwealth Office (www.gov.uk/fco)

Government of Canada (www.travel.gc.ca)

US State Department (www.travel.state.gov)

Resources

Deaf Australia (www.deafau.org.au)

e-Bility (www.ebility.com)

National Information Communication & Awareness Network (Nican; ☎02-6241 1220, TTY 1800 806 769; www.nican.com.au)

Spinal Cord Injuries Australia (SCIA; ☎1800 819 775; www.spinalcordinjuries.com.au)

Vision Australia (☎1300 847 466; www.visionaustralia.org)

Air Travel

Qantas (www.qantas.com.au) entitles a disabled person with high-support needs and the carer travelling with them to a discount on full economy fares; contact Nican for eligibility info and an application form. Guide dogs travel for free on Qantas, **Jetstar** (www.jetstar.com.au), **Virgin Australia** (www.virginaustralia.com.au) and their affiliated carriers. All of Australia's major airports have dedicated parking spaces, wheelchair access to terminals, accessible toilets, and skychairs to convey passengers onto planes via airbridges.

Train Travel

In NSW, CountryLink's XPT trains have at least one carriage (usually the buffet car) with a seat removed for a wheelchair, and an accessible toilet. Queensland Rail's Tilt Train from Brisbane to Cairns has a wheelchair-accessible carriage.

Melbourne's suburban rail network is accessible and guide dogs and hearing dogs are permitted on all public transport in Victoria. **Metlink** (☎1800 800 007; www.ptv.vic.gov.au) offers a free travel pass to visually impaired people and wheelchair users for transport around Melbourne.

Visas

All visitors to Australia need a visa (only New Zealand nationals are exempt, and even they receive a 'special category' visa on arrival). Application forms for the several types of visa are available from Australian diplomatic missions overseas, travel agents or the website of the **Department of Immigration & Citizenship** (www.immi.gov.au). Visa types are as follows.

eVisitor (651)

❍ Many European passport holders are eligible for a free eVisitor visa, allowing stays in Australia for up to three months within a 12-month period.

❍ eVisitor visas must be applied for online (www.immi.gov.au/e_visa/evisitor.htm). They are electronically stored and linked to individual passport numbers, so no stamp in your passport is required.

❍ It's advisable to apply at least 14 days prior to the proposed date of travel to Australia.

Electronic Travel Authority (ETA; 601)

❍ Passport holders from eight countries which aren't part of the eVisitor scheme – Brunei, Canada, Hong Kong, Japan, Malaysia, Singapore, South Korea and the USA – can apply for either a visitor or business ETA.

❍ ETAs are valid for 12 months, with stays of up to three months on each visit.

❍ You can apply for an ETA online (www.eta.immi.gov.au), which attracts a nonrefundable service charge of $20.

Visitor (600)

❍ Short-term Visitor visas have largely been replaced by the eVisitor and ETA. However, if you are from a country not covered by either, or you want to stay longer than three months, you'll need to apply for a Visitor visa.

❍ Standard Visitor visas allow one entry for a stay of up to three, six or 12 months, and are valid for use within 12 months of issue.

❍ Apply online at www.immi.gov.au; costs range from $130 to $335.

Volunteering

Lonely Planet's *Volunteer: A Traveller's Guide to Making a Difference Around the World* provides useful information about volunteering.

Women Travellers

Australia is generally a safe place for women travellers, although the usual sensible precautions apply:

Night-time Avoid walking alone late at night in any of the major cities and towns – keep enough money aside for a taxi back to your accommodation.

Pubs Be wary of staying in basic pub accommodation unless it looks safe and well managed.

Sexual harassment Rare, though some macho Aussie males still slip – particularly when they've been drinking.

Rural areas Stereotypically, the further you get from the big cities, the less enlightened your average Aussie male is likely to be about women's issues. Having said that, many women travellers say that they have met the friendliest, most down-to-earth blokes in outback pubs and remote roadhouse stops.

Hitchhiking Hitching is not recommended for anyone. Even when travelling in pairs, exercise caution at all times.

Drugged drinks Some pubs in Sydney and other big cities post warnings about drugged or 'spiked' drinks: probably not cause for paranoia, but play it safe if someone offers you a drink in a bar.

Transport

Getting There & Away

Australia is a long way from just about everywhere – getting there usually means a long-haul flight. If you're short on time on the ground, consider internal flights – they're affordable (compared with petrol and car-hire costs), can usually be carbon offset, and will save you some *looong* days in the saddle. Flights, cars and tours can be booked online at www.lonelyplanet.com/bookings.

Entering the Country

Arrival in Australia is usually straightforward and efficient, with the usual customs declarations. There are no restrictions for citizens of any particular foreign countries entering Australia – if you have a current passport and visa, you should be fine.

Air

High season (with the highest prices) for flights into Australia is roughly over the country's summer (December to February); low season generally tallies with the winter months (June to August), though this is actually peak season in central Australia and the Top End. Australia's international carrier is **Qantas** (www.qantas.com.au), which has an outstanding safety record (...as Dustin

Hoffman said in *Rainman*, 'Qantas never crashed').

International Airports

Australia has numerous international gateways, with Sydney and Melbourne being the busiest.

Sydney Airport (02-9667 9111; www.sydneyairport.com.au; Airport Dr, Mascot) Sydney's Kingsford Smith Airport, 10km south of the city centre, is Australia's busiest airport, handling flights from all over the country and the world. The international (T1) and domestic (T2 and T3) terminals are 4km apart on either side of the runway.

Melbourne Airport (www.melbourneairport.com.au; Centre Rd, Tullamarine) Most major airlines have direct domestic and international flights to Melbourne Airport in Tullamarine, 22km northwest of the city centre. Domestic and international flights are offered by, among others, Qantas, Jetstar, Virgin Australia and Tiger Airways.

Other international gateways include the following:

Cairns Airport (www.cairnsairport.com; Airport Ave)

Darwin International Airport (www.darwinairport.com.au; Henry Wrigley Dr, Marrara) Located 12km north of the city centre, Darwin airport handles both international and domestic flights.

Gold Coast Airport (www.goldcoastairport.com.au; Longa Ave, Bilinga)

Perth Airport (www.perthairport.com; George Wiencke Dr)

Climate Change & Travel

Every form of transport that relies on carbon-based fuel generates CO_2, the main cause of human-induced climate change. Modern travel is dependent on aeroplanes, which might use less fuel per kilometre per person than most cars but travel much greater distances. The altitude at which aircraft emit gases (including CO_2) and particles also contributes to their climate change impact. Many websites offer 'carbon calculators' that allow people to estimate the carbon emissions generated by their journey and, for those who wish to do so, to offset the impact of the greenhouse gases emitted with contributions to portfolios of climate-friendly initiatives throughout the world. Lonely Planet offsets the carbon footprint of all staff and author travel.

Getting Around

Air

Australia's main (and highly safe and professional) domestic airlines are **Qantas** (www. qantas.com.au) and **Virgin Australia** (www.virginaustralia.com.au), servicing all the main centres with regular flights. **Jetstar** (www.jetstar.com.au), a subsidiary of Qantas, and **Tiger Airways** (www.tigerair.com), a subsidiary of Singapore Airlines, are generally a bit cheaper and fly between most Australian capital cities.

Air Passes

Qantas offers a discount-fare Walkabout Air Pass for passengers flying into Australia across the Pacific with Qantas or American Airlines. The pass allows you to link up around 60 domestic Australian destinations for less than you'd pay booking flights individually. See www.qantas.com.au/travel/airlines/air-pass/us/en for details.

Bicycle

Australia has much to offer cyclists, from bike paths winding through most major cities to thousands of kilometres of good country roads. There's lots of flat countryside and gently rolling hills to explore and, although Australia is not as mountainous as, say, Switzerland or France, mountain bikers can find plenty of forest trails and high country.

Hire Bike hire in cities is easy, but if you're riding for more than a few hours or even a day, it's more economical to invest in your own wheels.

Legalities Bike helmets are compulsory in all states and territories, as are white front-lights and red rear-lights for riding at night.

Maps You can get by with standard road maps, but to avoid low-grade unsealed roads, the government series is best. The 1:250,000 scale is suitable, though you'll need lots of maps if you're going far. The next scale up is 1:1,000,000 – widely available in map shops.

Weather In summer carry plenty of water. Wear a helmet with a peak (or a cap under your helmet), use sunscreen and avoid cycling in the middle of the day. Beware summer northerly winds that can make a north-bound cyclist's life hell. Southeasterly trade winds blow in April, when you can have (theoretically) tail winds all the way to Darwin. It can get very cold in Victoria, Tasmania, southern South Australia and the New South Wales mountains, so pack appropriate clothing.

Transport If you're bringing in your own bike, check with your airline for costs and the degree of dismantling or packing required. Within Australia, bus companies require you to dismantle your bike and some don't guarantee that it will travel on the same bus as you.

Information

The national cycling body is the **Bicycle Federation of Australia** (www.bfa.asn.au). Each state and territory has a touring organisation that can also help with cycling information and put you in touch with touring clubs. **Bicycles Network Australia** (www.bicycles.net.au) offers information, news and links.

Bicycle NSW (www.bicyclensw.org.au)

Bicycle Network Tasmania (www.biketas.org.au)

Bicycle Network Victoria (www.bicyclenetwork.com.au)

Bicycle Queensland (www.bq.org.au)

Bike SA (www.bikesa.asn.au)

Bicycle Transportation Alliance (www.btawa.org.au) In WA.

Cycling Northern Territory (www.nt.cycling.org.au)

Pedal Power ACT (www.pedalpower.org.au)

Bus

Australia's extensive bus network is a reliable way to get around, though bus travel isn't always cheaper than flying and it can be tedious over huge distances. Most buses are equipped with air-con, toilets and videos; all are smoke-free. There are no class divisions on Australian buses (very democratic), and the vehicles of the different companies all look pretty similar.

Small towns eschew formal bus terminals for a single drop-off/pick-up point (post office, newsagent, corner shop etc).

Greyhound Australia (www.greyhound.com.au) Runs a national network (notably not across the Nullarbor Plain between Adelaide and Perth, nor Perth to Broome). Book online for the cheapest fares.

Firefly Express (www.fireflyexpress.com.au) Runs between Sydney, Canberra, Melbourne and Adelaide.

Premier Motor Service (www.premierms.com.au) Greyhound's main competitor along the east coast.

V/Line (www.vline.com.au) Connects Victoria with NSW, South Australia and the ACT.

Greyhound Bus Passes

Greyhound offers a slew of passes geared towards various types and routes of travel: see www.greyhound.com.au/passes for details. Greyhound also offers a discount of up to 10% for members of YHA, VIP, ISIC and other approved organisations.

Kilometre Pass

These are the simplest passes, giving you specified amounts of travel starting at 1000km ($189), ascending in logical increments (2500km, 5000km, 7500km, 10,000km, 15,000km, 20,000km) to a maximum of 25,000km ($2675). A 5000km pass costs $785; 10,000km is $1435. Passes are valid for 12 months, and you can travel where and in whatever direction you please, stopping as many times as you like. Use the online kilometre calculator to figure out which pass suits you. Book at least a day ahead to secure your seat.

Hop-on, Hop-off & Short Hop Passes

These passes allow you to traverse popular routes, mostly along the east coast but also between Cairns and Alice Springs and Adelaide and Darwin via Alice Springs. Travel is in one direction, and you can jump on and off buses as many times as you like. Passes are valid for three months once travel begins, with six months in which to get started.

See also **Oz Experience** (🕿1300 300 028; www.ozexperience.com) a backpacker travel option utilising Greyhound services.

Costs

Following are the average one-way bus fares along some well-travelled routes, booked online:

Route	Adult/Child
Adelaide–Melbourne	$105/85
Brisbane–Cairns	$310/270
Cairns–Sydney	$500/430
Sydney–Brisbane	$190/160
Sydney–Melbourne	$135/115

Car & Motorcycle

Driving Licence

To drive in Australia you'll need to hold a current driving licence issued in English from your home country. If the licence isn't in English, you'll also need to carry an International Driving Permit, issued in your home country.

Choosing a Vehicle

2WD Depending on where you want to travel, a regulation 2WD vehicle might suffice. They're cheaper to hire, buy and run than 4WDs and are more readily available. Most are fuel efficient, and easy to repair and sell. Downsides: no off-road capability and no room to sleep!

4WD Four-wheel drives are good for outback travel as they can access almost any track you get a hankering for. And there might even be space to sleep in the back. Downsides: poor fuel economy, awkward to park and more expensive to hire/buy.

Campervan Creature comforts at your fingertips: sink, fridge, cupboards, beds, kitchen and space to relax. Downsides: slow and often not fuel-efficient, not great on dirt roads and too big for nipping around the city.

Motorcycle The Australian climate is great for riding, and bikes are handy in city traffic. Downsides: Australia isn't particularly bike-friendly in terms of driver awareness, there's limited luggage capacity, and exposure to the elements.

Renting a Vehicle

Larger car-rental companies have drop-offs in major cities and towns. Most companies require drivers to be over the age of 21, though in some cases it's 18 and in others 25.

Suggestions to assist in the process:

● Read the contract cover to cover.

● Bond: some companies may require a signed credit-card slip, others may actually charge your credit card; if this is the case, find out when you'll get a refund.

● Ask if unlimited kilometres are included and, if not, what the extra charge per kilometre is.

● Find out what excess you'll have to pay if you have a prang, and if it can be lowered by an extra charge per day (this option will usually be offered to you whether you ask or not). Check if your personal travel insurance covers you for vehicle accidents and excess.

● Check for exclusions (hitting a kangaroo, damage on unsealed roads etc) and whether you're covered on unavoidable unsealed roads (eg accessing camp sites). Some companies also exclude parts of the car from cover, such as the underbelly, tyres and windscreen.

● At pick-up inspect the vehicle for any damage. Make a note of anything on the contract before you sign.

● Ask about breakdown and accident procedures.

● If you can, return the vehicle during business hours and insist on an inspection in your presence.

The usual big international companies all operate in Australia (Avis, Budget, Europcar, Hertz, Thrifty). The following websites offer last-minute discounts and the opportunity to compare rates between the big operators:

● www.carhire.com.au

● www.drivenow.com.au

● www.webjet.com.au

4WDs

Having a 4WD is essential for off-the-beaten-track driving into the outback. The major car-hire companies have 4WDs.

Renting a 4WD is affordable if a few people get together: something like a Nissan X-Trail (which can get you through most, but not all, tracks) costs around $100 to $150 per day; for a Toyota Landcruiser you're looking at around $150 up to $200, which should include unlimited kilometres.

Check the insurance conditions, especially the excess (which can be up to $5000), as they can be onerous and policies might not cover damage caused when travelling off-road. A refundable bond is also often required – this can be as much as $7500.

Campervans

Companies for campervan hire – with rates from around $90 (two-berth) or $150 (four-berth) per day, usually with minimum five-day hire and unlimited kilometres – include the following:

Apollo (📞1800 777 779; www. apollocamper.com) Also has a backpacker-focused brand called Hippie Camper.

Britz (📞1300 738 087; www. britz.com.au)

Jucy Rentals (📞1800 150 850; www.jucy.com.au)

Maui (📞1300 363 800; www. maui.com.au)

Mighty Cars & Campers (📞1800 670 232; www. mightycampers.com.au)

Spaceships Campervans (📞1300 132 469; www. spaceshipsrentals.com.au)

Travelwheels (📞1800 289 222; www.travelwheels.com.au)

One-Way Relocations

Relocations are usually cheap deals, although they don't allow much time flexibility. Most of the large hire companies offer deals, or try the following operators. See also www. hippiecamper.com and www. drivenow.com.au.

imoova (📞1300 789 059; www. imoova.com)

Relocations2Go (📞1800 735 627; www.relocations2go.com)

Transfercar (📞02-8011 1870; www.transfercar.com.au)

Insurance

Third-party insurance With the exception of NSW and Queensland, third-party personal-injury insurance is included in the vehicle registration cost, ensuring that every registered vehicle carries at least minimum insurance (if registering in NSW or Queensland you'll need to arrange this privately). We recommend extending that minimum to at least third-party property insurance – minor collisions can be amazingly expensive.

Rental vehicles When it comes to hire cars, understand your liability in the event of an accident. Rather than risk paying out thousands of dollars, consider taking out comprehensive car insurance or paying an additional daily amount to the rental company for excess reduction (this reduces the excess payable in the event of an accident from between $2000 and $5000 to a few hundred dollars).

Exclusions Be aware that if travelling on dirt roads you usually will not be covered by insurance unless you have a 4WD (read the fine print). Also, many companies' insurance won't cover the cost of damage to glass (including the windscreen) or tyres.

Auto Clubs

Under the auspices of the **Australian Automobile Association** (02-6247 7311; www.aaa.asn.au) are automobile clubs in each state, handy when it comes to insurance, regulations, maps and roadside assistance. Club membership (around $100 to $150) can save you a lot of trouble if things go wrong mechanically. If you're a member of an auto club in your home country, check if reciprocal rights are offered in Australia. The major Australian auto clubs generally offer reciprocal rights in other states and territories.

AANT (Automobile Association of the Northern Territory; 13 11 11; www.aant.com.au) NT.

NRMA (National Roads & Motorists' Association; 13 11 22; www.mynrma.com.au) NSW and the ACT.

RAC (Royal Automobile Club of Western Australia; 13 17 03; www.rac.com.au) WA.

RACQ (Royal Automobile Club of Queensland; 13 19 05; www.racq.com.au) Queensland.

RACT (Royal Automobile Club of Tasmania; 13 27 22; www.ract.com.au) Tasmania.

RACV (Royal Automobile Club of Victoria; 13 72 28; www.racv.com.au) Victoria.

Road Rules

Australians drive on the left-hand side of the road and all cars are right-hand drive.

Give way An important road rule is 'give way to the right' – if an intersection is unmarked (unusual) and at roundabouts, you must give way to vehicles entering the intersection from your right.

Speed limits The general speed limit in built-up and residential areas is 50km/h. Near schools, the limit is usually 25km/h (sometimes 40km/h) in the morning and afternoon. On the highway it's usually 100km/h or 110km/h; in the NT it's either 110km/h or 130km/h. Police have speed radar guns and cameras and are fond of using them in strategic locations.

Seatbelts and car seats It's the law to wear seatbelts in the front and back seats; you're likely to get a fine if you don't. Small children must be belted into an approved safety seat.

Drink-driving Random breath-tests are common. If you're caught with a blood-alcohol level of more than 0.05% expect a fine and the loss of your licence. Police can randomly pull any driver over for a breathalyser or drug test.

Mobile phones Using a mobile phone while driving is illegal in Australia (excluding hands-free technology).

Hazards & Precautions

Behind the Wheel

Fatigue Be wary of driver fatigue; driving long distances (particularly in hot weather) can be utterly exhausting. Falling asleep at the wheel is not uncommon. On a long haul, stop and rest every two hours or so – do some exercise, change drivers or have a coffee.

Road trains Be careful overtaking road trains (trucks with two or three trailers stretching for as long as 50m); you'll need distance and plenty of speed. On single-lane roads get right off the road when one approaches.

Unsealed roads Unsealed road conditions vary wildly and cars perform differently when braking and turning on dirt. Don't exceed 80km/h on dirt roads; if you go faster you won't have time to respond to a sharp turn, stock on the road or an unmarked gate or cattle grid.

Animal Hazards

o Roadkill is a huge problem in Australia, particularly in the NT, Queensland, NSW, SA and Tasmania. Many Australians avoid travelling once the sun drops because of the risks posed by nocturnal animals on the roads.

o Kangaroos are common on country roads, as are cows and sheep in the unfenced outback. Kangaroos are most active around dawn and dusk and often travel in groups: if you see one hopping across the road, slow right down, as its friends may be just behind it.

o If you hit and kill an animal while driving, pull it off the road, preventing the next car from having a potential accident. If the animal is only injured and is small, perhaps an orphaned joey (baby kangaroo), wrap it in a towel or blanket and call the relevant wildlife rescue line:

Department of Parks & Wildlife (Wildcare Helpline ☑08-9474 9055; www.parks. dpaw.wa.gov.au) WA.

Department of Environment & Heritage Protection (☑1300 264 625; www.ehp.qld.gov.au) Queensland.

NSW Wildlife Information, Rescue & Education Service (WIRES; ☑1300 094 737; www. wires.org.au)

Wildcare Inc NT (☑0408 885 341, 08-8988 6121; www. wildcarent.org.au)

Parks & Wildlife Service (☑ after hours 03-6165 4305, 1300 827 727; www.parks.tas. gov.au) Tasmania.

Wildlife Victoria (☑1300 094 535; www.wildlifevictoria.org.au)

Fuel

Fuel types Unleaded and diesel fuel is available from service stations sporting well-known international brand names. LPG (liquefied petroleum gas) is not always stocked at more remote roadhouses; if you're on gas it's safer to have dual-fuel capacity.

Costs Prices vary from place to place, but at the time of writing unleaded was hovering between $1.20 and $1.50 in the cities. Out in the country, prices soar – in outback NT, SA, WA and Queensland you can pay as much as $2.20 per litre.

Availability In cities and towns petrol stations proliferate, but

distances between fill-ups can be long in the outback. That said, there are only a handful of tracks where you'll require a long-range fuel tank. On main roads there'll be a small town or roadhouse roughly every 150km to 200km. Many petrol stations, but not all, are open 24 hours.

Local Transport

See regional chapters for detailed info.

Tours

Backpacker-style and more formal bus tours offer a convenient way to get from A to B and see the sights on the way. Following are some multi-state operators; see regional chapters for smaller companies operating within individual states and territories.

AAT Kings (☑1300 228 546; www.aatkings.com) Big coach company (popular with the older set) with myriad tours all around Australia.

Adventure Tours Australia (☑1300 654 604; www. adventuretours.com.au) Affordable, young-at-heart tours in all states.

Autopia Tours (☑03-9397 7758; www.autopiatours.com. au) One- to three-day trips from Melbourne, Adelaide and Sydney.

Groovy Grape Tours (☑1800 661 177; www.groovygrape. com.au) Small-group, SA-based operator running one-day to one-week tours ex-Adelaide, Melbourne and Alice Springs.

Nullarbor Traveller (☑1800 816 858; www.thetraveller.net. au) Small company running relaxed minibus trips across the Nullarbor Plain between SA and WA.

Oz Experience (☑1300 300 028; www.ozexperience.com) Backpacker tour covering central, northern and eastern Australia in a U-shaped route – Cairns, Brisbane, Sydney, Melbourne, Adelaide, Alice Springs and Darwin – utilising Greyhound bus services.

Train

Long-distance rail travel in Australia is something you do because you really want to – not because it's cheap, convenient or fast. That said, trains are more comfortable than buses, and there's a certain long-distance 'romance of the rails' that's alive and kicking. Shorter-distance rail services within most states are run by state rail bodies, either government or private.

The three major interstate services in Australia are operated by **Great Southern Rail** (☑13 21 47; www. greatsouthernrail.com.au) namely the Indian Pacific between Sydney and Perth, the Overland between Melbourne and Adelaide, and the Ghan between Adelaide and Darwin via Alice Springs. There's also the new high-speed Spirit of Queensland service between Brisbane and Cairns, operated by **Queensland Rail** (☑13 16 17; www.queenslandrail. com.au). Trains from Sydney to Brisbane, Melbourne and Canberra are operated by **NSW TrainLink** (☑13 22 32; www.nswtrainlink.info). Within Victoria, **V/Line** (www.vline. com.au) runs trains, linking up with buses for connections into NSW, South Australia and the ACT.

Behind the Scenes

Acknowledgments

Climate map data adapted from Peel MC, Finlayson BL & McMahon TA (2007) 'Updated World Map of the Köppen-Geiger Climate Classification', *Hydrology and Earth System Sciences*, 11, 163344.
Illustration p44-5 by Javier Zarracina.

This Book

This book was curated by Hugh McNaughtan and researched and written by Kate Armstrong, Brett Atkinson, Carolyn Bain, Celeste Brash, Peter Dragicevich, Anthony Ham, Paul Harding, Alan Murphy, Miriam Raphael, Charles Rawlings-Way, Benedict Walker, Steve Waters and Meg Worby, with contributions from Michael Cathcart, Cathy Craigie, Tim Flannery and Tracy Whitmey.

This guidebook was commissioned in Lonely Planet's Melbourne office, and produced by the following:

Destination Editor Tasmin Waby
Series Designer Campbell McKenzie
Cartographic Series Designer Wayne Murphy
Product Editor Kate Mathews
Senior Cartographers Corey Hutchison, Anthony Phelan
Book Designer Jessica Rose
Assisting Editors Gabrielle Stefanos, Saralinda Turner
Cover Researchers Campbell McKenzie, Naomi Parker
Associate Product Directors Sasha Baskett, Liz Heynes
Thanks to Andrew Bigger, Jennifer Carey, Katie Coffee, Daniel Corbett, Ruth Cosgrove, Laura Crawford, Brendan Dempsey-Spencer, James Hardy, Anna Harris, Victoria Harrison, Kerrianne Jenkins, Indra Kilfoyle, Georgina Leslie, Dan Moore, Darren O'Connell, Katie O'Connell, Kirsten Rawlings, Diana Saengkham, Dianne Schallmeiner, Julie Sheridan, Ellie Simpson, Lyahna Spencer, John Taufa, Ross Taylor, Angela Tinson, Lauren Wellicome, Dora Whitaker, Juan Winata

---

Send Us Your Feedback

We love to hear from travellers – your comments keep us on our toes and help make our books better. Our well-travelled team reads every word on what you loved or loathed about this book. Although we cannot reply individually to postal submissions, we always guarantee that your feedback goes straight to the appropriate authors, in time for the next edition. Each person who sends us information is thanked in the next edition, the most useful submissions are rewarded with a selection of digital PDF chapters.

Visit lonelyplanet.com/contact to submit your updates and suggestions or to ask for help. Our award-winning website also features inspirational travel stories, news and discussions.

Note: We may edit, reproduce and incorporate your comments in Lonely Planet products such as guidebooks, websites and digital products, so let us know if you don't want your comments reproduced or your name acknowledged. For a copy of our privacy policy visit lonelyplanet.com/privacy.

Index

Symbols & Map Key

Look for these symbols to quickly identify listings:

- ◎ Sights
- ✪ Activities
- ⊕ Courses
- ⊙ Tours
- ✪ Festivals & Events
- ✪ Eating
- ⊖ Drinking
- ✪ Entertainment
- ⊕ Shopping
- ⓘ Information & Transport

Find your best experiences with these Great For... icons.

 Budget

 Food & Drink

 Drinking

 Cycling

 Shopping

Sport

Art & Culture

Events

Photo Op

Scenery

Family Travel

 Short Trip

 Detour

 Walking

 Local Life

 History

 Entertainment

 Beaches

 Winter Travel

 Cafe/Coffee

Nature & Wildlife

These symbols and abbreviations give vital information for each listing:

- ✔ Sustainable or green recommendation
- **FREE** No payment required

- ☎ Telephone number
- ⊙ Opening hours
- Ⓟ Parking
- ⊖ Nonsmoking
- ✳ Air-conditioning
- @ Internet access
- �� Wi-fi access
- ⊠ Swimming pool
- ⊞ Bus
- ⊟ Ferry
- ⊟ Tram
- ⊟ Train
- ⊡ English-language menu
- ✐ Vegetarian selection
- ⬥ Family-friendly
- ⬥ Pet-friendly

Sights

- ⓐ Beach
- ⓑ Bird Sanctuary
- ⓒ Buddhist
- ⓓ Castle/Palace
- ⓔ Christian
- ⓕ Confucian
- ⓖ Hindu
- ⓗ Islamic
- ⓘ Jain
- ⓙ Jewish
- ⓚ Monument
- ⓛ Museum/Gallery/ Historic Building
- ⓜ Ruin
- ⓝ Shinto
- ⓞ Sikh
- ⓟ Taoist
- ⓠ Winery/Vineyard
- ⓡ Zoo/Wildlife Sanctuary
- ⓢ Other Sight

Points of Interest

- ⓐ Bodysurfing
- ⓑ Camping
- ⓒ Cafe
- ⓓ Canoeing/Kayaking
- ● Course/Tour
- ⓔ Diving
- ⓕ Drinking & Nightlife
- ⓖ Eating
- ⓗ Entertainment
- ⓘ Sento Hot Baths/ Onsen
- ⓙ Shopping
- ⓚ Skiing
- ⓛ Sleeping
- ⓜ Snorkelling
- ⓝ Surfing
- ⓞ Swimming/Pool
- ⓟ Walking
- ⓠ Windsurfing
- ⓡ Other Activity

Information

- ⓢ Bank
- ⓣ Embassy/Consulate
- ⓤ Hospital/Medical
- @ Internet
- ⓥ Police
- ⓦ Post Office
- ⓧ Telephone
- ⓨ Toilet
- ⓩ Tourist Information
- ● Other Information

Geographic

- ⓐ Beach
- ⋈ Gate
- ⓑ Hut/Shelter
- ⓒ Lighthouse
- ⓓ Lookout
- ▲ Mountain/Volcano
- ⓔ Oasis
- ⓕ Park
-)(Pass
- ⓖ Picnic Area
- ⓗ Waterfall

Transport

- ⓐ Airport
- ⓑ BART station
- ⓒ Border crossing
- ⓣ Boston T station
- ⓤ Bus
- ⧈ Cable car/Funicular
- ⓥ Cycling
- ⓦ Ferry
- Ⓜ Metro/MRT station
- ⧈ Monorail
- Ⓟ Parking
- ⓧ Petrol station
- ⓢ Subway/S-Bahn/ Skytrain station
- ⓨ Taxi
- ⧈ Train station/Railway
- ⋊⋊ Tram
- ⓩ Tube Station
- Ⓤ Underground/ U-Bahn station
- ● Other Transport

Our Story

A beat-up old car, a few dollars in the pocket and a sense of adventure. In 1972 that's all Tony and Maureen Wheeler needed for the trip of a lifetime – across Europe and Asia overland to Australia. It took several months, and at the end – broke but inspired – they sat at their kitchen table writing and stapling together their first travel guide, *Across Asia on the Cheap*. Within a week they'd sold 1500 copies. Lonely Planet was born.

Today, Lonely Planet has offices in Melbourne, London, Oakland, Franklin, Delhi and Beijing, with more than 600 staff and writers. We share Tony's belief that 'a great guidebook should do three things: inform, educate and amuse'.

Our Writers

Hugh McNaughtan

A former English lecturer and food writer, Hugh moved to the UK with his young family in 2013, and took up travel writing full time. He's written (and eaten) his way through Maluku, Lithuania, Bulgaria and Britain, but still has a soft spot for the fabulous food of his home town, Melbourne.

Kate Armstrong

Kate is a Victorian, but for years has enjoyed migrating northwards for the warmth and laid-back attitudes of sunny Queensland. With more than 30 overseas LP titles to her name, Kate also finally enjoyed getting her car dirty in her own backyard. See more adventures at www.katearmstrong.com.au and @nomaditis.

Carolyn Bain

On a recent Lonely Planet research trip Carolyn covered 6500km of glorious NSW scenery under big blue skies, from the scorching sands of Mungo to the vineyards of Mudgee. The outback's 40°C temps made a change from her usual travel-writing stomping grounds of Iceland and Denmark. Read more at carolynbain.com.au.

Brett Atkinson

Brett is based in Auckland, New Zealand and has covered around 50 countries as a guidebook author and travel and food writer. See www.brett-atkinson.net for his most recent work and upcoming travels.

Celeste Brash

Celeste has contributed to around 50 Lonely Planet guidebooks and her award-winning writing has appeared in publications from *BBC Travel* to National Geographic's *Intelligent Traveller*. After 15 years in the South Pacific she now lives with her husband and two children in Portland, Oregon.

More Writers

STAY IN TOUCH
lonelyplanet.com/contact

AUSTRALIA Levels 2 & 3, 551 Swanston St, Carlton, Victoria 3053
☏ 03 8379 8000, fax 03 8379 8111

USA 150 Linden Street, Oakland, CA 94607
☏ 510 250 6400, toll free ☏ 800 275 8555, fax 510 893 8572

UK 240 Blackfriars Road, London SE1 8NW
☏ 020 3771 5100, fax 020 3771 5101

Although the authors and Lonely Planet have taken all reasonable care in preparing this book, we make no warranty about the accuracy or completeness of its content and, to the maximum extent permitted, disclaim all liability arising from its use.

All rights reserved. No part of this publication may be copied, stored in a retrieval system, or transmitted in any form by any means, electronic, mechanical, recording or otherwise, except brief extracts for the purpose of review, and no part of this publication may be sold or hired, without the written permission of the publisher. Lonely Planet and the Lonely Planet logo are trademarks of Lonely Planet and are registered in the US Patent and Trademark Office and in other countries. Lonely Planet does not allow its name or logo to be appropriated by commercial establishments, such as retailers, restaurants or hotels. Please let us know of any misuses: lonelyplanet.com/ip.

ROFESSION

Peter Dragicevich

After a decade of frequent flights between his native New Zealand and Sydney, the lure of the bright lights and endless beach days drew Peter across the Tasman on a more permanent basis. For the best part of the next decade he would call Sydney's inner suburbs home, while serving as general manager for various newspaper and magazine titles. More recently he's co-authored dozens of titles for Lonely Planet, including the *East Coast Australia* and *Sydney* guidebooks.

Anthony Ham

Anthony (anthonyham.com) was born in Melbourne, grew up in Sydney and spent much of his adult life travelling the world. He recently returned to Australia after 10 years living in Madrid and brings to this guide more than 15 years' experience as a travel writer. As a recently returned expat, Anthony is loving the opportunity to rediscover his country and indulge his passion for wilderness.

Paul Harding

Though born and raised down south in Victoria, Paul has an enduring passion for the great Australian outback – and for a great road trip. A travel writer and photographer, and backpacker at heart, Paul has contributed to almost 40 Lonely Planet guides, including numerous Australia titles. He still lives in Melbourne.

Alan Murphy

Alan has travelled extensively across Australia and worked on several Australian guidebook titles for Lonely Planet. The Northern Territory, with its ancient landscapes, outback characters and Indigenous culture holds a special place in his heart. He recently criss-crossed the enormous expanse of the Territory and loved discovering new places.

Miriam Raphael

Miriam has authored more than a dozen books for Lonely Planet. She regularly enthuses on all things travel for a range of Australian and international publications, while blogging about intrepid journeys with kids at SevenSuitcases.com. After many years living in Australia's extraordinary Northern Territory she has recently returned to her hometown of Sydney.

Charles Rawlings-Way

As a likely lad, Charles suffered in shorts through Tasmanian winters, and in summer counted the days till he visited his grandparents in Adelaide. Little did he know that southeast Queensland was just as alluring – a fact confirmed by more recent encounters with Brisbane's bookshops, bars and band rooms. An underrated rock guitarist and proud father of daughters, Charles has penned 20-something guidebooks for Lonely Planet.

Benedict Walker

Currently hanging by the beach near his Mum, in hometown Newcastle, Ben's plan of 'livin' the dream' – spending his days between his three great loves, Australia, North America and Japan – seems to be coming to fruition. Ben has also co-written LP's *Japan, Canada* and *Florida* guidebooks, written and directed a play, toured Australia managing travel for rockstars and is an avid photographer toying with his original craft of film-making. See www.wordsandjourneys.com for more.

Steve Waters

Steve was recently in the north of WA for the sixth time, and while some things hadn't changed (huge distances, heat, blowing a tyre on the Kalumburu Rd), others were totally different (Cape Range NP after the floods, volunteering for the Mornington Bird Census, trying to find the same restaurant in Exmouth). Steve's written online articles on WA and co-authored previous editions of *Australia, Indonesia, Great Adventures* and *Best in Travel*.

Meg Worby

This was Meg's fourth trip to ever-beautiful Tasmania, her seventh trip to temperate Queensland and her 780th re-entry into her most habitable home state of South Australia. She is a former member of Lonely Planet's languages, editorial, web and publishing teams in Melbourne and London.

CONTRIBUTING AUTHORS

Michael Cathcart Michael teaches history at the Australian Centre, University of Melbourne, broadcasts on ABC Radio National and has presented history programs on ABC TV. Michael wrote the History section.

Cathy Craigie Cathy is a freelance writer and cultural consultant and has extensive experience in Indigenous affairs. Cathy wrote the Indigenous Australia section.

Tim Flannery Tim is a scientist, explorer and writer. He lives in Sydney where he is a professor in the faculty of science at Macquarie University. Tim wrote the Environment section.

Tracy Whitmey Though UK born and Kiwi by choice, Tracy knows Victoria well, having lived and explored there for almost 10 years. Tracy wrote the Great Ocean Road box in the Melbourne chapter.